Studies on the History of Society and Culture
Victoria E. Bonnell and Lynn Hunt, Editors

PONT-ST-PIERRE
1398 –1789

PONT-ST-PIERRE
1398 – 1789

Lordship, Community,
and Capitalism in
Early Modern France

JONATHAN DEWALD

UNIVERSITY OF CALIFORNIA PRESS
BERKELEY   LOS ANGELES   LONDON

University of California Press
Berkeley and Los Angeles, California

University of California Press, Ltd.
London, England

© 1987 by
The Regents of the University of California

Library of Congress Cataloging-in-Publication Data

Dewald, Jonathan.
  Pont-St-Pierre, 1398–1789.

  (Studies on the history of society and culture)
  Bibliography: p.
  Includes index.
  1. Pont-Saint-Pierre (France)—History.
2. Roncherolles family. 3. France—Nobility—
Case studies. 4. Pont-Saint-Pierre (France)—Economic
conditions. I. Title. II. Series.
DC801.P8365D48 1987 944'.24 86-7057
ISBN 0-520-05673-6 (alk. paper)

Printed in the United States of America

1 2 3 4 5 6 7 8 9

*For Elsie Wurzburger Dewald
and Emma Fredericka Dewald*

Contents

Illustrations

Tables

Preface

I began this study in 1976, intending something less complicated than has now emerged. At that time I was completing a book on the new nobility, the *noblesse de robe*, in sixteenth- and early seventeenth-century Normandy. Comparison with the military nobility seemed appropriate to that investigation, and for that purpose I undertook a brief analysis of the accounts of the barony of Pont-St-Pierre, one of the handful of upper Norman lordships about which extensive documentation survives. Like other historians, I had been impressed by evidence that the old nobility successfully adapted to the difficult conditions of the sixteenth century; I expected to find in the documents concerning Pont-St-Pierre further evidence of the nobles' success, and that indeed proved to be the case. My study of Pont-St-Pierre was to be a brief demonstration of how one noble family surmounted the economic troubles of the sixteenth century.

Closer acquaintance with these documents, however, forced me to change my interpretations and enlarge my questions. Pont-St-Pierre's archives allowed me to extend my inquiry beyond the confines of the sixteenth century. As I moved back to the fourteenth century and forward to the eighteenth, the magnitude of the changes that the lordship underwent became more apparent. So also did its failures of adaptation, its ambiguous responses to economic change. Pont-St-Pierre's documents also permitted an approach to the village communities over which the lordship had control, and here too there were surprises. Through much of the early modern period, the lordship's influence over local life was far stronger than I had expected, but paternalism and deference coexisted with economic attitudes that surprised me by their aggressiveness and their orientation to the marketplace.

Rather than a history of the nobility's successes, the study has become a history of how nobles and villagers affected one another during the Old Regime and a history of what this relationship meant for the evolution of the French countryside. I have tried to present as fully as possible the lived reality, the daily texture of this relationship, but this is not an effort at total history. The sources preclude access to some questions, and others cannot be followed evenly over the period: information about ordinary villagers is far more extensive in the eighteenth century than in earlier years, whereas manorial accounts are numerous in the fifteenth century, scarce in the seventeenth and eighteenth. My treatment of other subjects—for instance, village demography—has been deliberately limited. I have tried to retain my focus on analytical history. Although I hope to have recreated something of the experience of village life, my main concern has been to answer a series of questions about how the Old Regime functioned, how power was exercised within it, what effects these arrangements had on the people who lived under them.

I have accumulated large obligations in the course of this study. A Summer Stipend and a Fellowship from the National Endowment for the Humanities made possible early stages of research; other valuable support has come from the Regents' Fellowship program, the Committee on Research, and the School of Humanities of the University of California, Irvine. I have benefited again and again from the courtesy and competence of the staffs at the Archives Départementales of the Eure and of the Seine-Maritime; I wish particularly to thank Catherine Blondel and Alain Roquelet for the help they have given me. Archivists and librarians at a long series of other institutions have likewise helped at every turn in this project. The comte de Caumont, M. Robert Chapuis, and the marquis A. J. de Nicolay graciously allowed me to consult their families' private papers.

Several colleagues read earlier versions of this book and offered valuable suggestions, corrections, and encouragement. It is a great pleasure to thank Joyce Appleby, Gene Brucker, Sam Clark, James Given, Philip Hoffman, Lynn Hunt, Michael Johnson, Jobey Margadant, Ted Margadant, David Rankin, Orest Ranum, Jeffrey Sawyer, and Donald Sutherland for their thoughtful readings. Carolyn Dewald has read numerous versions and has constantly offered support and suggestions. I first encountered many of the problems taken up here in a series of conversations with the late Andrew Appleby and owe much to his learning and insights. Both early and late in this project, I discussed my ideas with gatherings of historians at Irvine and Berkeley; their comments have influenced the book in important ways. Finally, this book like my previous work owes much to the insights, support, and friendship that I have received from Brigitte Lainé, Georges Mouradian, Anne Palier, Denis Palier, Elisabeth Smadja, and Gérard Smadja.

Whatever errors remain in this work are of course my responsibility alone.

Abbreviations

AD Eure	Archives Départementales de l'Eure
AD S-M	Archives Départementales de la Seine-Maritime
AN	Archives Nationales, Paris
BM	Bibliothèque Municipale, Rouen
BN	Bibliothèque Nationale, Paris
Caillot	AD S-M, E, Fonds Caillot de Coquéraumont
Pont-St-Pierre	AD S-M, E, Fonds de la baronnie de Pont-St-Pierre
Comptes	AD S-M, E, Fonds de la baronnie de Pont-St-Pierre, Comptes
Tabel. Pont-St-Pierre	Tabellionage de Pont-St-Pierre (NOTE: The four series above have not been inventoried. Throughout, I refer to specific registers and *liasses* in them by dates or by provisional numbers or by specific titles on them.)
l.	*livre tournois*
s.	*sol*
d.	*denier*

Unless otherwise noted, measurements throughout are those of the Old Regime. In the eighteenth century, the acre (divided into four *vergées* and 160 *perches*) equaled .6866 hectares in St-Nicolas de Pont-St-Pierre and Romilly; it equaled .5675 hectares in St-Pierre de Pont-St-Pierre, Pîtres, and la Neuville-Chant-d'Oisel (see Comte d'Arundel de Condé, "Les anciennes mesures agraires de Haute Normandie," *Annales de Normandie* 18, no. 1 [March 1968]: 3–60).

Introduction

Early modern France was an aristocratic society, a society in which feudal authority and fine distinctions of birth formed the patterned backdrop of daily life. Every voice from the period tells us these facts, but their meaning remains surprisingly unclear. We rarely know how the nobility's presence shaped local societies or how the nobility's values and economic practices influenced rural economic development. We know little of the hatreds or loyalties that the nobility inspired among ordinary people and little of what these emotions meant for local politics.

This book studies the nobility's impact on early modern French society. It examines, first, the economic and political resources that the nobles controlled. I have sought to determine how much money the nobles had, the sources from which they acquired it, what they did with it; and I have sought to evaluate their influence over local affairs and their dealings with the royal bureaucracies set above them. But I have attempted also to measure the effects of the nobles' wealth and power on local life. As a result, this is as much a book about farmers, village merchants, and urban landowners as it is about the nobility itself.

Ultimately such questions demand statistical answers, answers that would establish typical patterns among the wide variations of early modern society. A central premise of this study, however, is that these questions need first to be studied in the workings of a single local society. Only thus, I believe, can the interconnected effects of the nobility's presence be properly seen; only thus can relationships among different kinds of change emerge. Further, it is only by focusing on a small geographical area that the nobility's

1

history can be seen in a chronological perspective sufficiently broad to show the principal changes that the nobles underwent. Hence this is a case study. Here I examine the history of a single large lordship, the barony of Pont-St-Pierre, an estate that dominated five parishes near Rouen. This book follows the barony's history from the late fourteenth century to the Revolution. For 360 of these years, Pont-St-Pierre belonged to a single family, the Roncherolles; the family's changing fortunes, values, and behavior supply the second theme of this history. Finally, I have attempted to situate these histories of property and family within the history of village social and economic relations—to explore the ways in which nobles and village society determined one another's fate.

Even a case study, of course, demands a context. I have sought throughout to supply quantitative and comparative evidence, so as to place the examples of Pont-St-Pierre and the Roncherolles within a setting of provincial norms. In many ways, we can determine the degree to which Pont-St-Pierre and the Roncherolles were typical of Norman lordships and noble families. But Normandy itself was an exceptional province in early modern France. Its agricultural wealth exceeded that of most provinces, and it had a more active commerce and industry than most. Because of its wealth and proximity to Paris, it felt more than most other regions the hand of royal government. Pont-St-Pierre presents the problem of the French nobility in a particular form. Here we encounter the nobility in a commercially active, wealthy, closely governed province.

The two parts into which the study is divided reflect my concern to understand rural history in terms of the dialogue between villagers and the Old Regime's ruling groups. The first part focuses on the communities within the barony of Pont-St-Pierre. It considers their geography and economic development, and it examines the changing wealth and power of the merchants, farmers, and petty nobles who lived in them. Part Two considers the lordship and its owners, the Roncherolles. Such an organization means that the most vivid actors in the story appear only late in the exposition. But this organization also permits the reader to view the lordship and its owners with a clear understanding of the social forces that they confronted. Reconstructing their confrontation is the central task of this study.

Inevitably the historian's approach to the problem of the French nobility is tinged by the long tradition of aristocratic complaint. Sensi-

tive nobles throughout the Old Regime believed that their order had
been pushed to the margins of contemporary life. "I wish to God,"
wrote Blaise de Monluc in the late sixteenth century, "that as in Spain
we [nobles] had always resided in the cities! We would be richer, and
we would have more authority. We hold the countryside, and they
the cities, and so we have to pass through their hands, and for the
smallest business we have with great effort to trot through the city."[1]
"On my return from Brest," remembered Chateaubriand, 250 years
later, "four masters (my father, my mother, my sister, and I) inhabited the château of Combourg. A cook, a cleaning woman, two
lackeys, and a coachman were all the servants. A hunting dog and
two old horses were hidden away in a corner of the stable. These
twelve beings disappeared in a manor house where one would hardly
have noticed one hundred knights, their ladies and servants, the
horses and hounds of the good king Dagobert. No outsider presented
himself at the château during the whole year, except for a few gentlemen . . . who requested hospitality on their way to plead their cases
at the Parlement."[2] Chateaubriand here offers large interpretation in
the guise of concrete recollection. Like Monluc, he believed that the
nobility of the Old Regime had lost its central role in society. His
recollections contrast the isolation and meager scale of the eighteenth-century noble household with the crowded sociability of its
medieval predecessor, a contrast symbolic of larger changes in the
nobility's position.[3]

Much of the best recent literature on the nobility has sought to
revise this tradition of complaint, to show the ease with which the
nobles adapted to political and economic change over the Old Regime. Recent studies have shown the nobles' close connections with
the absolutist state and the degree to which the state served aristocratic interests.[4] Historians have traced the nobles' successes in dealing with a developing capitalist economy and have argued that the

1. Blaise de Monluc, *Commentaires, 1521–1576,* ed. Paul Courteault (Paris, 1964),
685.
2. Pierre Clarac, ed., *Chateaubriand, Mémoires d'outre-tombe,* 3 vols. (Paris, 1973),
1:119–20.
3. See ibid., 1:173.
4. Guy Bois, *Crise du féodalisme: Economie rurale et démographie en Normandie orientale du début du XIVe siècle au milieu du XVIe siècle* (Paris, 1976), 364; Robert Brenner,
"Agrarian Class Structure and Economic Development in Pre-Industrial Europe," *Past
and Present* 70 (February 1976): 30–75, and "The Agrarian Roots of European Capitalism," *Past and Present* 97 (November 1982): 16–113; Daniel Dessert, *Argent, pouvoir, et
société au Grand Siècle* (Paris, 1984); William Beik, *Absolutism and Society in Seventeenth-
Century France: State Power and Provincial Aristocracy in Languedoc* (Cambridge, 1985).

nobility took the lead in introducing modern business practices and farming techniques to the countryside.[5] "It is obvious," Emmanuel Le Roy Ladurie has written, "that the 'seigneury,' or what is commonly called by that name, was one of the essential frameworks of agrarian capitalism."[6] François Furet has taken much the same view: far from impeding the development of rural capitalism, he writes, "the *seigneurie*, with its stewards . . . and bourgeois middlemen, was the vehicle of that development."[7] In a summary of recent research on the eighteenth century, William Doyle has taken the argument for the nobility's modernity still farther: "Far from a caste of feudal remnants, the nobility was an order that was constantly absorbing the richest and most enterprising members of the third estate, renewing in the process its wealth, its energies, and its genetic stock."[8]

A great deal in the history of the Roncherolles and their estates supports historians' recent emphasis on the aristocracy's successes during the Old Regime. The Roncherolles survived four centuries of tumultuous historical change. They preserved their leading position in society despite warfare and depopulation, inflation, the rise of the bureaucratic state, even the French Revolution. Over most of the period, their wealth increased rapidly. They reasoned carefully about their economic interests and pursued them tenaciously. In important respects, the history of Pont-St-Pierre and its owners is a history of continuity and adaptation.

But at a more fundamental level, I argue here, Monluc and Chateaubriand were correct in their complaints. In the region of Pont-St-Pierre, the nobles underwent a series of difficult changes during the early modern period, changes forced upon them by the development of a commercial economy, a bureaucratic state, and a richer and better educated peasantry. The nobles adapted to many of the developments in the society around them, but their capacity to adapt was

5. Jean-Marie Constant, "Nobles et paysans en Beauce aux XVIe et XVIIe siècles" (Thèse d'Etat, University of Paris IV, 1978); James Wood, *The Nobility of the* Election *of Bayeux, 1463–1666: Continuity Through Change* (Princeton, 1980); J. Russell Major, "Noble Income, Inflation, and the Wars of Religion in France," *The American Historical Review* 86, no. 1 (February 1981): 21–48; Jean Meyer, *La vie quotidienne en France au temps de la Régence* (Paris, 1979), 135.

6. Emmanuel Le Roy Ladurie, "De la crise ultime à la vraie croissance, 1660–1789," in Le Roy Ladurie, Hugues Neveux, and Jean Jacquart, *Histoire de la France rurale* (Paris, 1975), 2:431.

7. François Furet, *Interpreting the French Revolution*, trans. Elborg Forster (Cambridge, 1981), 95.

8. William Doyle, *Origins of the French Revolution* (New York, 1980), 120.

ultimately inadequate to the tasks that they faced. Thus a principal theme in this study is the nobles' loss of control over rural society and their inability to profit fully from its economic development.

A complementary theme concerns the role of the village in economic development. Recent historiography has in general emphasized opposition between modernizing large landowners and villagers wedded to precapitalist, traditional economic practices. Marxist and liberal historians alike have seen peasant property and peasant values as the principal obstacles to the modernization of the countryside. Since Marc Bloch, they have seen large landowners at odds with a peasantry that was deeply conservative, its efforts stunted (in the words of Jean Meyer) by "a certain refusal to enrich oneself at any price, a rhythm of work traced on the feeling of needs reduced to a minimum."[9] I argue here for a different assessment of the peasantry's role. In Pont-St-Pierre and the surrounding villages, peasant property had virtually disappeared by about 1620. Communal restrictions on individual economic initiative were weak, and the market shaped most economic choices. In this region, rural capitalism manifested itself chiefly among a village elite of farmers and merchants. It was they who were best able to profit from the economic opportunities that the Old Regime offered. In Pont-St-Pierre, I argue, the large estate rather than the peasant community posed the main limits on rural economic development. Enthusiasm for an unregulated economy and pressure for technological change came from the village.

Pont-St-Pierre cannot tell us what was typical in French society during the Old Regime. Close examination of its experiences, however, can tell us important things about that society: about the ways in which power was exercised, about the nature of economic change and the forces that limited change, about the interplay of values and actions. It offers us, in other words, one version of how the Old Regime functioned and how it eventually fell apart.

9. Meyer, *La vie quotidienne*, 317. See also Hugues Neveux, *Vie et déclin d'une structure économique: Les grains du Cambrésis (fin du XIVe–début du XVIIe siècle)* (Paris, The Hague, and New York, 1980), 284–336, for explanation of agricultural stagnation in terms of farmers' indifference to profit. For a characteristic recent interpretation of peasant concerns in terms of anticapitalistic, communal ideals, see Florence Gauthier and Guy-Robert Ikni, "Le mouvement paysan en Picardie: Meneurs, pratiques, maturation et signification historique d'un programme (1775–1794)," in Jean Nicolas, ed., *Mouvements populaires et conscience sociale, XVIe–XIXe siècles* (Paris, 1985), 435–448.

I

LAND AND COMMUNITY

I

BOURG AND VILLAGE

L ike most large lordships during the Old Regime, the barony
of Pont-St-Pierre was a sprawling affair. At the end of the
fourteenth century, the barony's owners collected seigneurial rents
from eight communities, and their judicial powers extended more
widely still.[1] Four communities, however, comprised the core of the
lordship. At the barony's center stood the bourg of Pont-St-Pierre
itself, divided (despite its diminutive size) into the two parishes of
St-Pierre and St-Nicolas. Most residents of the adjoining villages of
Romilly-sur-Andelle and Pîtres, just to the west of Pont-St Pierre,
held their properties from the barony. To the north the barony en-
compassed most of the large village of la Neuville-Chant-d'Oisel,
separated from Pont-St-Pierre by the large forest of Longbouel.
These communities differed sharply from one another in geography,
economic orientation, and even in culture. The differences among
them—and especially the differences between Pont-St-Pierre, at the
lordship's center, and la Neuville, at its periphery—determined
much of the barony's functioning.

Pont-St-Pierre lies in the valley of the Andelle River, about 4.5
kilometers from its juncture with the Seine.[2] At Pont-St-Pierre the

1. Comptes, 1398–99.
2. On the geography of the region, the best treatment remains Jules Sion, *Les
paysans de la Normandie orientale: Pays de Caux, Bray, Vexin Normand, Vallée de la Seine*
(Paris, 1909; repr. Brionne, 1981); see also Jean-Pierre Fruit, *Vexin normand ou vexin
parisien? Contribution à l'étude géographique de l'espace rural* (Paris, 1974).

9

river valley is narrow, well under one kilometer in width. On either side, the terrain rises sharply to broad plateaus that stand about 90 meters above the valley floor. Vineyards grew on these slopes in the sixteenth century, and even in the late eighteenth century there remained vineyards downstream from Pont-St-Pierre, at Amfreville-sous-les-Monts.[3] The river itself, wrote a seventeenth-century traveler, "carries fine trout, is clear, limpid, and very strong."[4] In the seventeenth century it passed through Pont-St-Pierre in three channels, and its presence dominated the bourg's character, creating marshes, meadows and gardens, mill emplacements, and every year a major event in the community's life, as timber from the enormous forest of Lyons upstream was shipped to the juncture with the Seine.[5]

The Andelle was not entirely inaccessible to navigation, and in the seventeenth century small boats, about one-twentieth the size of those that plied the Seine, used its channels to bring wine upstream from the juncture with the Seine.[6] In the late seventeenth century there were thoughts of enlarging the river and making it navigable to larger boats, in hopes of easing the shipment of timber from the forests upstream.[7] But the idea was never pursued, and the Andelle continued in the eighteenth century to flow in several narrow channels. Timber continued to be floated down the river, "not in rafts, like the Burgundian timber floated down the Seine to Paris, but separately, log by log." At the juncture with the Seine the wood was retrieved from the water, allowed to dry, then shipped by boat to Rouen or Paris. Inhabitants and seigneur alike had rights over any of this wood that caught in the river grasses, and thus (it was reported in the mid–seventeenth century) had a positive incentive to leave the river "deliberately badly cleaned and full of tall grasses."[8] A century later the *procureur fiscal* of Pont-St-Pierre's High Justice had the same complaint: one stream of the river, he reported, "is so full of mud, silt, and grasses that the water cannot flow freely."[9]

3. Comptes, 1515–16; for *vignerons* at Amfreville in the eighteenth century, AD S-M, Tabel. Pont-St-Pierre, 3, 10 May 1772, 14 March 1773.

4. Chanoine Porée, ed., *Du Buisson-Aubenay, Itinéraire de Normandie* (Rouen and Paris, 1911), 54.

5. Ibid.

6. AD S-M, Tabel. Pont-St-Pierre, 1642–47, 7 October 1646: the sale of "un bateau d'Andelle flottant sur lad riviere & portant viron vingt muids de vin," for 140 l. Cf. ibid., 1651–54, 31 October 1652, for the sale of a wine boat on the Seine, which carried 500 muids of wine and cost 3,900 l.

7. BM, MS Martainville Y 40: "Mémoire concernant la Généralité de Rouen. Dressé par M. de Vaubourg, Me des Requêtes Intendant en lad. Gnalité 1698," fol. 3r.

8. Porée, *Du Buisson-Aubenay, Itinéraire*, 53–55.

9. AD Eure, 86 B 49, 16 July 1740.

Pont-St-Pierre was a very old settlement. There had been a Caro-lingian palace at Pîtres, just downstream, and it had been the site of three major church councils in the 860s.[10] In the tenth century both Pont-St-Pierre and Pîtres had mills, and Pont-St-Pierre was already described as a bourg—that is, as something more significant than a mere village.[11] As such, its inhabitants enjoyed a special place within the seigneurial system, privileges that by the end of the Old Regime defined the difference between a bourg and a village. Residents of the bourg held their houses and lands without paying seigneurial rents or mutation taxes; they were, as an eighteenth-century lawyer described their status, "freed from the yoke of feudalism."[12]

The bourg's early development resulted partly from the strategic position that it occupied. Pont-St-Pierre offered control of the junc-ture of the Andelle and Seine valleys, and this fact assured it a considerable role in the political struggles of the early Middle Ages. In addition, from the 1130s on Pont-St-Pierre became part of a larger system of fortifications established by the dukes of Normandy: a line of châteaus along the Andelle that paralleled those on the border between Normandy and France and formed part of the outer de-fenses of Rouen.[13] Pont-St-Pierre's importance in this system of de-fenses was reinforced by its position at the intersection of two im-portant lines of communication. The road from Rouen to Château Gaillard, the greatest fortress of medieval Normandy and the center-piece of Rouen's defenses, crossed the Andelle at Pont-St-Pierre; and movement up the Andelle Valley from Pont-de-l'Arche, another important fortress, had to pass through Pont-St-Pierre as well.[14]

Pont-St-Pierre's military significance diminished after 1204, when the French monarchy conquered Normandy; the boundary between Normandy and the Ile de France abruptly lost its status as one of Europe's most embattled military frontiers. But the bourg's military role did not entirely disappear before the mid-seventeenth century. The Norman Estates complained in the late sixteenth century that

10. Abbé Cochet, "Note sur les restes d'un palais de Charles-le-Chauve (861–69), retrouvés à Pîtres," *Mémoires de la Société des Antiquaires de Normandie*, 24:156–65. 1859.

11. Marie Fauroux, *Recueil des actes des ducs de Normandie (911–1066)*, Mémoires de la Société des Antiquaires de Normandie, vol. 36, no. 120, pp. 284–85. Caen, 1961.

12. David Houard, *Dictionnaire analytique, historique, étymologique, critique, et inter-prétatif de la coutume de Normandie*, 4 vols. (Rouen, 1782), 1:197–99, s.v. "Bourgage."

13. Jean Yver, "Les châteaux forts en Normandie jusqu'au milieu du XIIe siècle: Contribution à l'étude du pouvoir ducal," *Bulletin, Société des Antiquaires de Normandie* 53 (1955–56): 90, 97, 103.

14. F. M. Powicke, *The Loss of Normandy*, 2d. ed. (Manchester, 1960), 178–202.

owners of such strategic points throughout the province were forti-
fying them; these "maisons fortes" were constructed "at the expense and ruin of the people, . . . [and] are simply hideouts for
thieves and brigands."[15] The château of Pont-St-Pierre had a small
military role during the Hundred Years' War, after which it had to
be rebuilt.[16] Thereafter its military importance continued to reflect its
proximity to the fortresses of Pont-de-l'Arche and Château Gaillard,
which between them still controlled a large share of the Seine Valley
above Rouen. Philip Augustus had conquered Château Gaillard in
1204, but four centuries later the deputies to the Estates of Normandy remained uneasy about the threat that the great fortress
posed, and control of Pont-de-l'Arche became one of the critical
strategic issues of the Fronde in Normandy.[17] Pont-St-Pierre's military importance through the early modern period was magnified by
the fact that its owners, the Roncherolles, also owned two other
châteaus along the road from Rouen to les Andelys, at Heuqueville
and Roncherolles (see map 1). The bourg had ceased in 1204 to form
part of the ducal system of fortifications, but the sixteenth and seventeenth centuries replaced this function with a familial military
complex, in which the strategic importance of each element was
enhanced by its relation to the others.[18] Pont-St-Pierre retained its
potential military significance until the late seventeenth century.

The second of Pont-St-Pierre's obvious geographical advantages,
its water power, remained important into the nineteenth century. In
the mid–eighteenth century there were at least fourteen mills in Pont-
St-Pierre and in Romilly, just downstream. Two of them were the
seigneurial grain mills of the barons of Pont-St-Pierre; the rest were
fulling mills.[19] Their presence reflected not only the suitability of the
fast-flowing river itself but also Pont-St-Pierre's proximity to the Seine
and the major weaving centers along it, notably Elbeuf. The "manufacture d'Elbeuf" only received its royal charter and regulations in

15. Charles de Robillard de Beaurepaire, ed., *Cahiers des Etats de Normandie sous le règne de Henri IV* . . . , 2 vols. (Rouen, 1880–82), 1:85 (cahier of 1595).
16. AD Eure, E 2392, Chartrier de Pont-St-Pierre, 1.
17. Robillard de Beaurepaire, *Cahiers . . . règne de Henri IV*, 1:141; for the role of Pont-de-l'Arche during the Fronde, Paul Logié, *La Fronde en Normandie*, 3 vols. (Amiens, 1951), 2:200–204.
18. See below, Chapter 5.
19. Caillot, liasse "Paroisse de Pont-St-Pierre, . . . moulins," inquest 14 May 1749. In the seventeenth century, there had also been paper making at Romilly: AD S-M, Tabel. Pont-St-Pierre, 1660–66, 26 July 1664: "honnorable hoe Michel deschamps me pappetier demeurant en la parroisse de st georges de Romilly au hameau de haulterive."

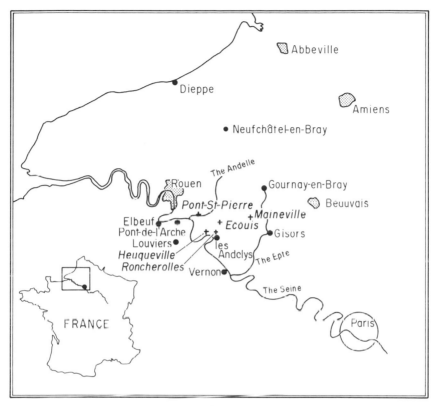

Map 1. Politics and geography: Upper Normandy and the Roncherolles' estates

1667, but by the 1690s its weavers produced every year nine to ten thousand "pieces of cloth . . . in the style of Holland and England."[20] Seventy years later Elbeuf remained a center of activity. A traveler described it as "the most populous, most animated of any of the towns we've seen since Versailles" and concluded that "a swarm of bees is not busier than the inhabitants of this bourg"; and by 1751 annual production reached 16,500 pieces of cloth.[21] Cloth woven at Elbeuf was shipped by boat to Pîtres, then by cart to Romilly and Pont-St-Pierre for fulling. In the early eighteenth century, some

20. Jeffry Kaplow, *Elbeuf During the Revolutionary Period: History and Social Structure* (Baltimore, 1964), 22–25; BM, MS Martainville Y 40, fol. 22r.
21. P. Bernier, ed., "Voyage de Antoine-Nicolas Duchesne au Havre et en Haute Normandie, 1762," *Mélanges, Société de l'Histoire de Normandie*, 4th series (1898): 210; Kaplow, *Elbeuf*, 41.

manufacturers of Elbeuf strengthened this economic relationship by acquiring financial interests in the mills on the Andelle.[22] The mills further shaped the valley's geography, bringing canalization of the Andelle's water and occasional flooding; and they created a fruitful source of litigation, as mill owners competed among themselves for water and with others over such matters as the passage of timber down the river.[23]

The narrow valley, with its damp and occasionally flooded soil, was best suited for pasture rather than arable farming. Its land was not infertile, in contrast to the land immediately downstream in the villages of Romilly and Pîtres, which an intendant in the 1670s dismissed as "land for onions."[24] But in fact little of Pont-St-Pierre's land was devoted to grains: about 16 percent of the bourg's area in the mid–eighteenth century, allowing an average of about two-thirds of an acre for each of the bourg's households.[25] Indeed, few residents of Pont-St-Pierre owned much land of any kind: in 1605 the median holding of the barony's sixty-eight seigneurial tenants there was .24 hectares, far below even the most optimistic estimates of the land needed for self-sufficiency in the seventeenth century.[26]

Partly as a result of these geographical possibilities and limits, Pont-St-Pierre's population was strikingly diverse from an early period. Witnesses from Pont-St-Pierre who appeared before the barony's High Justice in the 1680s—a period when the bourg had about eighty households[27]—included three surgeons, four cabaretiers-hoteliers, four merchants, eleven artisans of various kinds, and three seigneurial or royal officials.[28] This collection of artisans, merchants, officials, and other professionals made up nearly one-third of the bourg's households. Three generations later, in 1756, the subdelegate

22. Caillot, liasse "Paroisse de Romilly, Matières diverses," 6 April 1717; AD S-M, Tabel. Pont-St-Pierre, 12 September 1741; AD Eure, 86 B 102, Haute Justice, Pont-St-Pierre, "Police 1702–1789," 2 July 1713, complaint against the Lancelevée family.

23. Caillot, liasse "Paroisse de Romilly, Matières diverses," 6 April 1717.

24. BN, Cinq Cents Colbert, 274: Voysin de la Noiraye, "Estat et description de la generalité de Rouen," fol. 189r. Voysin described Pont-St-Pierre itself as divided among "labeur prez et bois."

25. Calculated from Pierre Duchemin, *La baronnie de Pont-St-Pierre* (Gisors, 1894), 187.

26. Pont-St-Pierre, unclassified terrier; Pierre Goubert, "The French Peasantry in the Seventeenth Century: A Regional Example," *Past and Present* 10 (November 1956): 66–67, for the problem of peasant self-sufficiency.

27. Population statistics are presented below, pp. 37–38.

28. AD Eure, 86 B 105–6, Haute Justice, Pont-St-Pierre.

who drew up Pont-St-Pierre's *vingtième* roll likewise emphasized the diversity of crafts carried on in the village: locksmiths, blacksmiths, tailors, and bakers all seemed to him worthy of note.[29]

This kind of economic activity had characterized Pont-St-Pierre from the high Middle Ages. By 1284 the bourg's seigneurial market had been joined by a specialized market for cloth and tanners' shops (yet another craft that relied heavily on abundant water supplies), and seigneurial levies on market transactions in the bourg amounted to one-fifth of the lordship's total income. In the fifteenth century twice-yearly fairs were established, and by the early fifteenth century there was already at least one tavern. Such commercial development on the site of feudal political power was typical of medieval Normandy. Throughout the province manorial lords sought to stimulate commercial development by establishing markets and fairs, as a means of improving their own incomes. At the same time, a center of manorial administration offered a market that attracted sellers of a wide range of goods.[30] A further stimulus to commercial development came in the 1620s, when groups of Rouennais cloth manufacturers began to establish themselves in the bourg; like merchants throughout northern Europe, they were seeking the cheaper and more docile labor of the countryside. They were allowed to establish themselves only with the promise that they would contribute to the bourg's taxes and "soubz le bon plaisir aucthoritté et consentem de madame la baronne de pont st pierre."[31] Even in the seventeenth century, commercial development remained closely tied to the barony's influence.

Despite its tiny population, Pont-St-Pierre thus had a long history of urban functions. It had also one of the marks of urban geography (see map 2). Although it apparently had no walls, its residents could

29. AD Eure, C 318, "Minute du Rôle [des vingtièmes] de la Paroisse de St-Nicolas du Pont-St-Pierre . . . , Observations génrralles."

30. Léopold Delisle, *Cartulaire normand de Philippe-Auguste, Louis VIII, Saint Louis, et Philippe-le-Hardi* (Caen, 1882; repr. Geneva, 1978), no. 976, p. 249; analyzed in Robert Carabie, *La propriété foncière dans le très ancien droit normand (XIe–XIIIe siècles): 1. La propriété domaniale* (Caen, 1943), 199–203. For Pont-St-Pierre's fairs, AD Eure, E 2392, 41–49; for its tavern, Paul Le Cacheux, *Actes de la chancellerie d'Henri VI concernant la Normandie sous la domination anglaise (1422–1435)*, 2 vols. (Rouen and Paris, 1908), 2:351. For seigneurial encouragement of markets and fairs, L. Musset, "Une transformation du régime seigneurial: L'essor des bourgs ruraux normands (XIe–XIIe siècles)," *Revue historique de droit français et étranger* 26 (1948): 169–70; and "La mise en valeur de la forêt de Gouffern au moyen âge et le bourg rural de Saint-Nicolas de Vignats," *Bulletin, Société des Antiquaires de Normandie* 52 (1952–54): 223–48. See also André Plaisse, *La baronnie du Neubourg: Essai d'histoire agraire, économique, et sociale* (Paris, 1961), 393–455.

31. AD S-M, Tabel. Pont-St-Pierre, 1625–32, 10 September 1628, 26 May 1629.

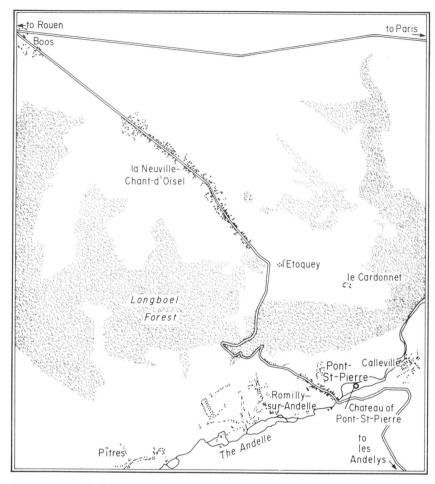

Map 2. The Andelle Valley today: La Neuville-Chant-d'Oisel, Pîtres, Pont-St-Pierre, and Romilly

prevent unwanted outsiders from entering by blocking the bridges over the Andelle; in 1581 guards were posted at each end of the bourg to turn back travelers from nearby villages where the plague had been reported.[32] By the seventeenth century residents had acquired the titles and some of the institutions of contemporary urban economic life as well. The bourg's notaries occasionally used the phrase "bour-

32. AD Eure, 86 B 4, Plumitifs, Haute Justice de Pont-St-Pierre, 2 September 1581.

geois de Pont-St-Pierre" to describe their clients;[33] the expression reflected their sense of the community's fundamental urbanity, its functions as a center of commerce, administration, and services. In this sense the "rural bourgeoisie" was a local reality in the seventeenth and eighteenth centuries.[34] Pont-St-Pierre also had some of the corporate institutions that the Old Regime thought important for the organization of mercantile and artisanal activities. Throughout the seventeenth century apprenticeship contracts bound boys from the area around the bourg to its artisans, in a wide range of crafts: "the craft of butcher," "the trade of shopkeeper and waxmaker," "the craft of shoemaker," "the craft of candle- and waxmaker," "the craft of barrel- and caskmaker." These contracts usually established three years of apprenticeship, during which the masters normally were required to lodge and feed their apprentices. Substantial expense was required to obtain this training; masters received about 40 l. each year from the boys' families.[35]

Guild members enjoyed a close relationship with the barony of Pont-St-Pierre. Representatives of the guilds were to be present at the opening sessions of the baronial court, and new masters had their right to practice their crafts registered there.[36] There was also a more fundamental convergence of economic assumptions and interests between the guilds and the lordship, for both sought the restriction of economic activity to officially sanctioned institutional settings. In 1700 the butchers of Pont-St-Pierre demanded that the High Justice confirm their seizure of several pieces of pork offered for sale by three men "who have displayed and retailed outside the markets of this bourg without any right, without having been received in this bourg or having ever been called to the High Justice (*aux assizes*) or having taken any oaths."[37] Pont-St-Pierre's merchants and baronial

---

33. E.g. AD Eure, E 1221, Tabel. Pont-St-Pierre, 16 December 1541: "honn hoe Guille de Laestre bourg dem aud Pont St Pierre"; 4 July 1543: "Anth Grimouyn bourg marchant dem aud Pont St Pierre"; AD S-M, Tabel. Pont-St-Pierre, 29 January 1603: "hon hoe Je Leber bourgeois demeur aud pont st. pierre"; 13 June 1619: "feu hon homme charles le hec vivant bourgeois demeur au bourg du pont st pierre"; 13 February 1761: "le sieur Pierre Antoine Le Vavasseur bourgeois du pont saint pierre."

34. For debate about the concept of a rural bourgeoisie, see Alfred Cobban, *The Social Interpretation of the French Revolution* (Cambridge, 1968), 107–10.

35. For examples of apprenticeship contracts, AD S-M, Tabel. Pont-St-Pierre, 7 May 1600, 10 October 1605, 18 April 1650, 13 December 1654, 15 March 1659, 6 July 1659.

36. See, for example, AD Eure, 86 B 102, 1702 (no month given), for the guild representatives present at the High Justice's assizes of that year.

37. AD Eure, 86 B 22, 11 December 1700.

officials had a natural affinity of economic interests. The barons and their agents sought to limit commerce to the barony's own markets, where they levied a form of sales tax—the *coutumes*—on all transactions; they also (I shall argue below, in Chapter 6) had a genuine commitment to the close regulation of economic life. Guildsmen like the butchers turned readily to them for protection against competition from people outside the corporate economic structure.

Guildsmen were not alone in their appreciation of the outlook that the lordship embodied. In various ways, a substantial share of Pont-St-Pierre's population depended directly on its role as a local political center. This was of course the case for the seigneurial and royal officials; it was true as well of the hotel and cabaret keepers, who profited from the visits of litigants and rent payers, of the millers who held the barony's grain mills, and of everyone who leased the lesser rights that the barony exercised. A complex occupational structure resulted directly from the presence of seigneurial power. The lordship offered benefits to Pont-St-Pierre's residents, and it exacted from them few of the seigneurial levies that it imposed on most of its subjects.

It is only in the late seventeenth and eighteenth centuries that a clear view of Pont-St-Pierre's bourgeoisie becomes possible. At that time, as probate inventories suggest,[38] it was a group whose separation from agricultural life was in some ways very striking. None of Pont-St-Pierre's residents owned more than scraps of land. The inventories show that the bourg's wealthiest residents also owned little livestock. The nineteen inventories from 1687 through 1775 include in all only twenty-one horses, eight cows, and no sheep; and the amount of livestock that these "bourgeois" owned declined over the eighteenth century. These were not farmers who sought to improve their social standing by adding mercantile or official titles;[39] their lack of livestock shows their detachment from farming. By the mid–eighteenth century, a surprising number also looked the part of the bourgeois: five of the thirteen inventories from between 1750 and 1775 included wigs.

Pont-St-Pierre's bourgeoisie fell into three groups. There were, first, a few bourgeois in the Old Regime's sense of the term: men and women living from their rents and bonds without working.[40]

---

38. The probate inventories on which this discussion is based are discussed below, Appendix A.

39. On this tendency, see Goubert, "The French Peasantry."

40. See, for instance, Pierre Goubert, *The Ancien Régime: French Society 1600–1750,* trans. Steve Cox (New York, 1974), 236–39; and Michel Vovelle, *Ville et campagne au XVIIIe siècle (Chartres et la Beauce)* (Paris, 1980), 135–66.

One of the nineteen inventories concerns such a figure, from 1761, and his lot was an unenviable one. His possessions included signs of respectability and a certain culture; he owned two wigs and "several old books by different authors." But his only other possessions were some old bedding and clothing, and his goods in all were evaluated at the pitiful sum of 45 l.

A second group consisted of professionals—notaries and surgeons—and officials of the barony or the state. For this group as well, the inventories suggest strained circumstances. Six inventories of the possessions of such bourgeois survive, all from the period 1752–75. Four of the six included books in substantial numbers: the average size of these four libraries was over twenty books, an investment in culture that probably equaled that of the local nobility.[41] But culture did not always translate into economic success. Pont-St-Pierre's professional bourgeois, despite their reading and their connections to local political and administrative power, enjoyed only mediocre fortunes. Four inventories include evaluations of the cash, bonds, and movable goods catalogued; two of them showed very small fortunes, of under 500 l. Their widows' complaints, however self-interested, similarly testify to the difficult position that these men occupied. When the the widow of a notary was asked whether her husband had left any cash, she replied that "on the contrary, since her husband's death she had been obliged to borrow money, and even before her said husband's death." Likewise, the widow of a surgeon of la Neuville, having shown the notaries "such few movables as her late husband has left," complained of her heavy debts and of the fact that she had been "abandoned by her parents, those of her husband residing some sixty leagues from the region."[42] Even Nicolas Nollent, the very competent business agent of the marquis de Pont-St-Pierre during the 1730s and 1740s, left movables that amounted to only 100 l. in value—this despite his ownership of two swords, a wig, two silver snuff boxes, and fifteen books. Nollent's debts at his death amounted to well over 800 l. and were paid by the marquis himself.[43] Only one of the professional men among the six whose inventories survive was clearly prosperous—and he was a cloth merchant as well as a surgeon.

For it was the merchants—the third group within Pont-St-Pierre's bourgeoisie—who were the bourg's economically dominant group. Their houses were substantial: of twelve examples, seven included

41. See below, Chapter 3, for nobles' libraries.
42. AD S-M, Tabel. Pont-St-Pierre, 30 June 1765.
43. AD S-M, Tabel. Pont-St-Pierre, 22 August 1756.

at least a kitchen, two bedrooms, and a shop. Most had a significant amount of cash at the time of their deaths: on average, 319 l. for the inventories from 1687 to 1750, 252 l. from 1752 to 1775. And the total value of their movables was impressive. The median value for the years 1687–1750 was 4,508 l.; for the years 1752–75 it was 1,500 l.[44] The merchants were less involved with written culture than the other bourgeois of Pont-St-Pierre. Only three of the twelve merchants owned books, only one of them more than five. But they controlled resources that were far superior to those of other groups in the bourg.

Their prosperity rested on several foundations. Tavernkeepers, of course, profited from the bourg's situation at the juncture of two lines of transport, and through the mid–eighteenth century they were probably the bourg's wealthiest residents.[45] Jacques Bouffard, an innkeeper who died in 1729, illustrates the wealth that these men might attain and the range of their economic activities. Bouffard's liquid assets were estimated at 6,000 l., and he left at his death 1,379 l. in cash. Innkeeping provided the capital for Bouffard's other pursuits, including leases of tithes and seigneurial rents and the wood trade.[46] Such diversity of interests was characteristic of Pont-St-Pierre's mercantile bourgeoisie. Other innkeepers took leases of seigneurial revenues; butchers invested in fulling mills.[47]

Bouffard was typical also in the scale of his interests, for Pont-St-Pierre's modest commercial activity required large investments and significant risks. In 1746, following the death of the merchant Noel Du Ponché, his widow found herself faced with about 10,000 l. in debts; 8,360 l. of this was for a cutting of wood that Du Ponché had undertaken in a nearby lordship.[48] In 1741 the merchant Pierre de

---

44. Conversion of nominal values into some measure of real wealth, of course, would make the decline that these figures suggest still more striking: from a median total value of 237 *setiers* of wheat at Paris to 61 *setiers* (calculated from M. Baulant, "Le prix des grains à Paris de 1431 à 1788," *Annales ESC* 23, no. 3 (May–June 1968): 520–40). Such a result strengthens an argument made here that the bourg's prosperity was declining in the later eighteenth century. However, the very small number of cases involved here makes such arguments highly speculative.

45. Cf. the similar emphasis on the role of innkeepers in Jean Nicolas, *La Savoie au XVIIIe siècle: Noblesse et bourgeoisie*, 2 vols. (Paris, 1978), 2:862–65.

46. AD S-M, Tabel. Pont-St-Pierre, 28 February 1729.

47. AD S-M, Tabel. Pont-St-Pierre, 6 November 1614, 3 September 1620, 1 June 1636, 5 November 1649, 22 March 1656, for the example of the Chenevièvres, receivers of the lordship of Deux Amants, hotel keepers, with one son apprenticed as a candlemaker at Pont-St-Pierre; AD S-M, Tabel. Pont-St-Pierre, 23 April 1639, for the example of Robert Leber, butcher and fulling mill owner.

48. AD S-M, Tabel. Pont-St-Pierre, 13 June 1746.

Lessard owed 1,800 l. to merchants at le Neubourg, the center of the livestock trade in Normandy, "for merchandise of oxen, cows, and sheep."[49] The wine trade demanded comparable expenditures. The hotel keeper Marin Le Duc owed about 1,500 l. "to several merchants" at his death in 1616, and deliveries of wine in this period to Pont-St-Pierre's tavernkeepers regularly amounted to hundreds of livres.[50]

By the mid–eighteenth century, a large share of such merchants' capital was going to stocks of consumer luxury goods. In the two generations before the Revolution, there took place at Pont-St-Pierre what may be called the rise of the shopkeeper.[51] Probate inventories supply a striking picture of the varied goods that were available in the bourg's shops. This included an extraordinary range of cloth: at the shop of Charles Boromée Le Clerc, whose possessions were inventoried in 1771, customers could find dozens of stockings of both cotton and wool; yards of cotton cloth (blue, white and blue, scarlet, pink); *siamoise* in various colors; a carton of bands of muslin; damask silk handkerchiefs; yards of lace, in a number of styles and qualities; boxes of ribbon; and box after box of buttons. This stock was expensive; at his death Le Clerc was in debt for 3,200 l., most of it owed to Rouennais cloth and lace merchants, and other examples suggest that this was typical of the stocks that the bourg's shopkeepers held in these years.[52] By the mid–eighteenth century even books could be bought in Pont-St-Pierre's shops. At the shop of Antoine Le Grain in 1752, there were "three *imitation de jésucrit*," along with "eight quires of paper and seven quires of paper for envelopes." Pont-St-Pierre's shops appealed to fashion and to the needs of written culture.

With investments and debts of this order, Pont-St-Pierre's merchants occupied an uncertain position: they were highly vulnerable to commercial failure, but they also had the hope of impressive social advancement. The Lancelevée family, millers and merchants who

49. AD S-M, Tabel. Pont-St-Pierre, 10 June 1741. On le Neubourg, see Plaisse, *La baronnie de Neubourg*, and Hugues Neveux and Bernard Garnier, "Valeur de la terre, production agricole, et marché urbain au milieu du XVIIIe siècle," *Problèmes agraires et société rurale: Normandie et Europe du nord-ouest (XIVe–XIXe siècles)*, Cahier des Annales de Normandie (Caen, 1979), 11:44–99.

50. AD S-M, Tabel. Pont-St-Pierre, 11 February 1616, 9 June 1602, 3 September 1620.

51. See Fernand Braudel, *Civilisation matérielle, économie, et capitalisme, XVe–XVIIIe siècle*, 3 vols. (Paris, 1979), 2:44–57.

52. See AD Eure, 86 B 110, 18 March 1784, for a merchant's claim that his stock of 2,000 l. had been stolen from his shop.

resided in Romilly, illustrate both possibilities. The family had included fullers and farmers in Romilly since at least the early seventeenth century, and from an early date they had been a violent presence along the river. In 1654 the tenants who had leased rights to the barony's fishing monopoly complained of Romain Lancelevée's repeated infractions, to the point that the tenants "have not been able to make any profit, because of the threats of the said Lancelevée, who swears that he will throw them over the wheel of his mill."[53] By the early eighteenth century, the two branches of the family owned eight fulling mills and several houses and plots of land in Romilly.[54] But in the next generation the family's fortunes diverged. In 1730 Claude Lancelevée sold a fulling mill to his more prosperous cousin, Nicolas. The mill itself, the act of sale noted, "is in complete ruin and no longer capable of working." Most of the purchase price (1,700 l.) went directly to Claude's creditors. In 1731 Claude sold another mill under identical circumstances: the mill itself was "in decay and total ruin," and most of the purchase price went to pay his debts.[55]

As Claude's fortunes collapsed, however, his cousin Nicolas was thriving. As a sign of his success, he and his son (at this point "merchant in Romilly") in 1754 rented an imposing house in Romilly, belonging to the widow of a Rouennais magistrate. The house included a formal courtyard, vestibule, large kitchen, salon, and "grande salle" on the first floor; a large bedroom and three smaller rooms on the second floor; and three small bedrooms "à la mansarde" on the third floor. This was an aristocratic house, and it included such marks of status as a pigeon house and asparagus and artichoke gardens. Its rent was suitably high: 180 l. yearly.[56] A generation later, the family had completed its social ascent. "Mr louis Baptiste lancelevée" was now "procureur du Roy en la maitrise des Eaux et forêts du pont de larche." He remained the owner of a large fulling mill in Romilly, but he now rented it out to a tenant.[57] It was possible—so the example of the Lancelevées demonstrated—for local merchants to take over the marks of urban and aristocratic status and to rise into a modestly imposing officialdom. But there was nothing inevitable about such success, and the risks of collapse were greater than the likelihood of ascent.

53. AD S-M, Tabel. Pont-St-Pierre, 2 June 1654.
54. Ibid., 23 May 1710; 29 April 1716.
55. Ibid., 28 December 1730, 12 March 1731.
56. Ibid., 1758, act inserted after 27 October 1758, dated 28 July 1754.
57. Ibid., 1764–73, 21 September 1771.

Farther from the center of the lordship, geography, occupations, and forms of economic activity all were very different; and so, consequently, were ties between communities and lordship. On both sides of the Andelle the land rises sharply from Pont-St-Pierre, on the south to the immense plain of the Vexin normand, on the north to the plaine de Boos (see map 2).[58] The barony of Pont-St-Pierre extended only to the north. It took in a large share of the forest of Longbouel, which occupied the slope from the river valley to the plain and a substantial part of the plain as well. In the seventeenth century the forest of Longbouel was one of the smaller forests in the province; its 3,500 arpents made it about one-sixth the size of the nearby forest of Lyons. By that time the forest had suffered extensive depredations; about half of it consisted of trees less than ten years old, and its oldest trees were only fifteen to twenty years.[59] The barons of Pont-St-Pierre held a little less than half of the forest. The rest belonged to the Crown.

Today the forest ends with the plaine de Boos itself. The needs of agriculture have led to the clearance of nearly all of the flat land suitable for plowing and have left to the forest only the steep slopes that separate plain from river valley. In the Old Regime the forest extended much further along the plain. It formed a boundary between the villages of the plain and the river valley that was sharper than what the traveler experiences today, and it formed a nearer and more vivid backdrop to life in the village. Sixteenth-century maps (see fig. 2) of the area convey a sense of the forest's presence; they show, for instance, that two of la Neuville's largest farms were entirely surrounded by forest.

Yet the forest seems not to have been a menacing presence, for villagers were in it a great deal. Work in the forest was a principal resource for the residents of the village of la Neuville, especially in the winter, when agricultural employment was lacking.[60] The forest was an important resource in other ways, and both prosperous and poor villagers regularly visited it to collect firewood and to pasture livestock, despite the barons' efforts to preserve a monopoly on the forest.[61] Villagers also entered the forest to hunt. In principle royal

---

58. This discussion of the region's geography and its effects rests heavily on Sion, *Les paysans de la Normandie orientale.*

59. Edmond Esmonin, ed., *Voysin de la Noiraye: Mémoire sur la généralité de Rouen* (1665) (Paris, 1913), 116–17. On the exploitation and progressive deterioration of the forest of Longbouel, see below, Chapter 6.

60. AD S-M, C 2212, dossier 7: "État des pauvres et des secours. . . , la Neuville."

61. See below, Chapter 6.

Figure 1. Forest and villages: The sixteenth century (AN, KK 948)

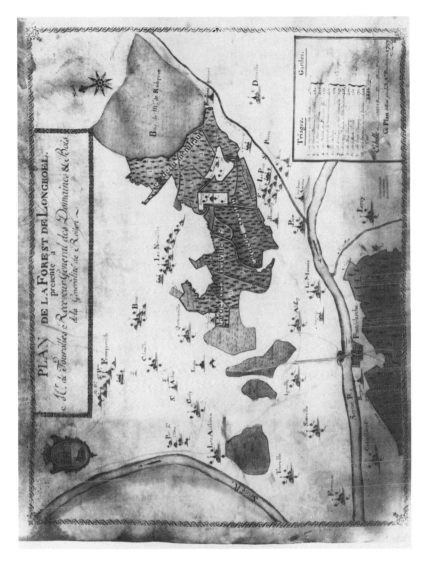

Figure 2. Forest and villages: The eighteenth century (AD S-M, Plan 322: C 2948)

legislation forbade villagers (and anyone else who did not own a fief) to hunt wildlife even on their own properties, let alone in seigneurial forests,[62] but this legislation had little effect on the villages around Pont-St-Pierre. Villagers of any substance at all owned at least one hunting gun, and they used them. The shops of Pont-St-Pierre's merchants offered "poudre à gibier" and "plomb à gibier" for customers to purchase, in substantial quantities.[63]

Insofar as the forest was a threat, it was because of the danger that its wildlife posed to villagers' crops and because of more fundamental, political controversies. In their list of grievances drawn up in 1789, the inhabitants of la Neuville included a complaint about the damage that wildlife did to the harvests.[64] However ineffectual, royal and seigneurial efforts to restrict hunting created their share of antagonisms and material losses. Rights to the forests' other resources created equal antagonisms, which were played out in a series of lawsuits that lasted through the sixteenth and seventeenth centuries.[65] These too remained vivid in 1789. In 1789 the residents of la Neuville demanded that the Crown restore villagers' pasturage rights in the forest, a right that "would be of great use for those who have children, who could have a cow in order to have milk to raise their children."[66]

Beyond the forest was the plaine de Boos, extending nearly to Rouen itself and occupied by a series of substantial villages. By the seventeenth century about half of the barony of Pont-St-Pierre's subjects resided in one of these villages, la Neuville-Chant-d'Oisel.[67] The contrast between its setting and that of the bourg of Pont-St-Pierre is striking today and must have been even more so in the Old Regime. In contrast to Pont-St-Pierre's closely grouped houses, the houses of la Neuville are scattered—with no apparent connection

62. François Isambert et al., *Recueil général des anciennes lois françaises depuis l'an 420, jusqu'à la Révolution de 1789*, 29 vols. (Paris, 1821–33), 18 (August 1661–December 1671): 299 (Forest Code of 1669, title 30, art. 28).
63. See the probate inventories listed below, Appendix A, for the frequency of guns; for the availability of powder and shot, AD S-M, Tabel. Pont-St-Pierre, 7 January 1687, 12 July 1701, 11 October 1752. Cf. Pierre Goubert, *La vie quotidienne des paysans français au XVIIe siècle* (Paris, 1982), 64–65, and Nicole Castan, *Justice et répression en Languedoc à l'époque des lumières* (Paris, 1980), 92–93, for the frequency of guns elsewhere and for the dangers that they were seen to pose.
64. AD S-M, 4 BP 6012: Cahiers de doléances, Sergenterie de Pont-St-Pierre, 3.
65. Discussed in detail below, pp. 147–49.
66. AD S-M, 4 BP 6012, 3.
67. For la Neuville's history, Jules Lamy, *Histoire de la Neuville-Champ-d'Oisel* (Rouen, 1950).

with one another—for more than 3 kilometers along the road to les Andelys, in the classic configuration of a *village-rue* (see fig. 3);[68] the village included three isolated hamlets as well. In contrast to the humidity of the Andelle Valley, the plain is dry; the porous chalk substratum of the soil rapidly absorbs the frequent rains. This contrast had direct economic effects. Villages of the plain had none of the industrial opportunities that the Andelle Valley derived from its readily available water power, and there were none of the meadows that dominated Pont-St-Pierre.[69] Instead, the plain allowed arable farming. Even today it presents enormous vistas of grain fields; in the Old Regime, when its acreage was more exclusively devoted to grain and enclosures less often broke up the landscape, the effect must have been stronger still. As figure 4 shows, la Neuville-Chant-d'Oisel in the later eighteenth century presented the typical features of the openfield village, with hundreds of narrow strips of land interspersed with occasional larger fields and enclosed farms.

Set on the dry plain, with neither the water resources nor the obvious military importance of the river valley, la Neuville and the villages near it were much later settlements than Pont-St-Pierre, despite their superior aptitude for arable farming. An important Roman road cut across a corner of la Neuville, but (as its name suggests) most of the village was cleared only in the thirteenth century, in the great high-medieval wave of land clearance. In the early thirteenth century the king founded the Cistercian convent of Fontaine Guérard, and in 1209 he gave the nuns 70 acres cleared in the forest of Longbouel; in 1256 there was a royal gift of another 50 acres, to compensate the nuns for a transfer of lands to the monastery of Royaumont. Characteristically, although an important share of the nuns' lands was to be cleared from the plain, the convent itself was established next to the Andelle. It was also characteristic of the halting progress of the plain's development that an abbess was first named at Fontaine Guérard only in 1253.[70]

Other parts of la Neuville's territory had developed somewhat earlier. The monastery of Lyre, which continued throughout the Old Regime to own the principal tithes in la Neuville, apparently held a

---

68. See the brief summary in Armand Frémont, *Atlas géographique de la Normandie* (Paris, 1977), 135.

69. See the excellent discussion in Sion, *Les paysans de la Normandie orientale*, 67ff.

70. Delisle, *Cartulaire normand*, no. 1098, p. 296; no. 561, p. 104; Sydney M. Brown and Jeremiah F. O'Sullivan, eds., *The Register of Eudes of Rouen* (New York, 1964), 178: "we consecrated the new abbess of Fontaine-Guérard, where there had never yet been an abbess."

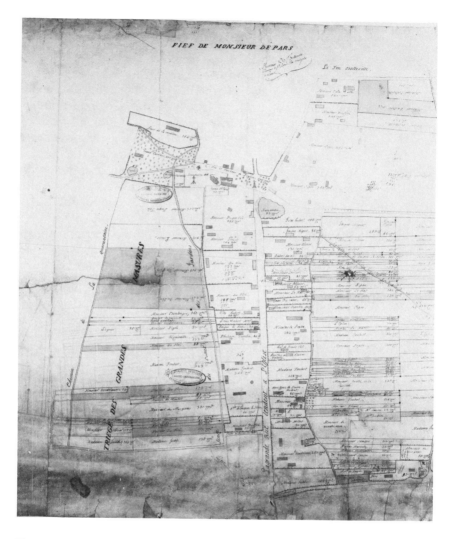

Figure 3. La Neuville: Public space and the village-rue *(AD S-M, Plan 178)*

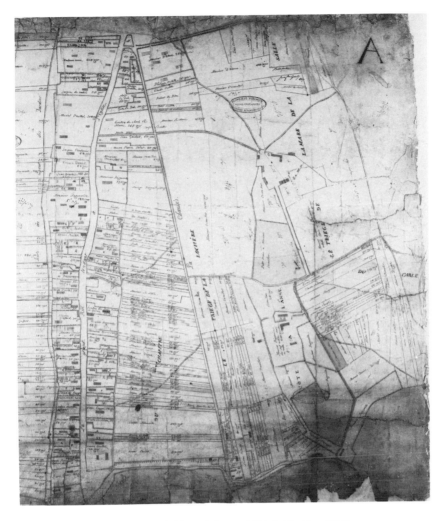

Figure 4. La Neuville: Open fields and farms (AD S-M, Plan 178)

TABLE 1. Laboureurs' *Dowries, la Neuville-Chant-d'Oisel*

	1603–1650	*1657–1686*	*1701–1750*	*1752–1761*	*1765–1782*
Mean dowry	271 l. (21 s.f.)	400 l. (26 s.f.)	1,220 l. (67 s.f.)	945 l. (49 s.f.)	2,576 l. (102 s.f.)
Median dowry	300 l. (23 s.f.)	400 l. (26 s.f.)	600 l. (33 s.f.)	550 l. (29 s.f.)	2,808 l. (112 s.f.)
Highest dowry	600 l. (46 s.f.)	400 l. (26 s.f.)	5,000 l. (276 s.f.)	3,924 l. (205 s.f.)	4,500 l. (179 s.f.)
N	9	2	10	6	7

SOURCE: Appendix B; grain prices from Micheline Baulant, "Les prix des grains à Paris de 1431 à 1788," *Annales ESC* 23, no. 3 (May–June 1968): 520–40.
NOTE: s.f. = setiers froment, Paris.

chapel in la Neuville from the mid–eleventh century, and in the early thirteenth century there began a succession of vicars at the church of St. Mary of Chant-d'Oisel, at the end of the village nearest Rouen.[71]

La Neuville's population by the eighteenth century included a few innkeepers, at least one surgeon, and a sprinkling of merchants. But the village's farmers—its *laboureurs*—dominated its economic life. La Neuville numbered fifteen *laboureurs* in the mid–eighteenth century. They constituted only about 5 percent of the village's total population, but they controlled the village's principal resources in much the same way that the merchants dominated the resources of Pont-St-Pierre: when in 1768 there was insufficient grain at the market of Pont-St-Pierre, the barony's officials turned immediately to the *laboureurs* as the group that would be expected to control whatever marketable surpluses might be found in the region.[72] They also dominated local employment. Virtually all of la Neuville's *laboureurs* employed two servants, and during the harvest they employed substantial groups of casual laborers as well.[73]

Few of the *laboureurs* owned more than scraps of land in the seventeenth and eighteenth centuries,[74] but their marriage contracts show the group's increasing liquid wealth over these years. *Laboureurs'* dowries (as table 1 shows) increased slowly in the seventeenth century and in the first half of the eighteenth; in the 1750s there was even a slight decline. But already during the early eighteenth century there were a few very large dowries, far larger than the highest

71. Jules Lamy, *La Neuville-Chant-d'Oisel* (Darnétal, 1981), 10–11.
72. Caillot, liasse 237, 31 March 1768.
73. See below, Chapter 2.
74. See below, Chapter 2.

TABLE 2. *Village Endogamy*, Laboureurs, *la Neuville-Chant-d'Oisel*

	1603–1650	1657–1686	1701–1750	1752–1782
Bride and groom from la Neuville	5	2	7	11
Groom from elsewhere	4	2	2	0
Bride from elsewhere	2	1	2	3
Total	11	5	11	14

SOURCE: Appendix B.

dowries of the seventeenth century. After 1765, so the dowries suggest, there was an explosion of *laboureur* prosperity. The typical dowry in this period was nearly five times that of the first half of the century and more than seven times the typical dowries of the seventeenth century.[75]

As they grew richer, it appears, the *laboureurs* of la Neuville also grew to be a more tightly knit group. Increasingly, as table 2 shows, marriages consolidated alliances within the village rather than uniting the *laboureurs* with groups from elsewhere. In the seventeenth century, marriages typically united la Neuville's *laboureurs* with families from outside the parish. During the first half of the eighteenth century, on the other hand, only one-third of the marriages involved a bride or groom from outside the village; and between 1752 and 1782 this was true of only about one-fifth of the marriages. As the economic stakes of the *laboureurs'* marriages became larger, marriage increasingly became a mechanism uniting families within a local ruling group—a group that was increasingly cohesive. This consolidation was especially important because the *laboureurs'* marriages contrasted sharply in this respect with those of la Neuville's population at large; marriage with a bride or groom from outside the village was increasingly frequent within la Neuville as a whole as the eighteenth century advanced. An increasingly cohesive and closely united group of *laboureurs* thus stood apart from a village population that (as we shall see) was becoming increasingly mobile in the eighteenth century.

75. Cf. the emphasis on farmers' eighteenth-century prosperity in Emmanuel Le Roy Ladurie, "De la crise ultime à la vraie croissance," in Le Roy Ladurie, Hugues Neveux, and Jean Jacquart, *Histoire de la France rurale* (Paris, 1975), 2:440–41.

Relations between village and bourg were complex and changed dramatically over the course of the Old Regime. Distance was a primary element in the relationship. Pont-St-Pierre and la Neuville were bound together in the same lordship from the thirteenth century through 1789, but it is well over an hour's walk from the center of la Neuville to Pont-St-Pierre, even more from outlying parts of the village. To go from one to the other requires not only traversing the forest but also dealing with the very sharp gradient by which the road descends from plain to river valley. Charles Estienne in the sixteenth century described the ascent from the Andelle Valley to the plain further upstream at Fleury-sur-Andelle as "la montaigne,"[76] and the effect at Pont-St-Pierre is similar. Indeed, the inconvenience of the journey probably grew in the eighteenth century, as heavy carts increasingly replaced beasts of burden in local transport.

Distance allied with more fundamental differences to produce at least among residents of the plain a sense of the foreignness of the river valley; as Jules Sion reported in the early twentieth century, "the valleys live a sufficiently different kind of life that the inhabitants of the plains do not consider them as real parts of the Caux or the Vexin."[77] With its economic variety, limited arable farming, artisanal organization, and long-standing seigneurial presence, Pont-St-Pierre was a very different kind of community from la Neuville.

In the sixteenth and seventeenth centuries, such perceptions of difference did not necessarily interfere with the workings of the lordship as a unified entity, for difference created complementarities between plain and river valley. This was true at the level of basic production: the plain supplied grain, the valley livestock, leather goods, and artisanal products. A survey of grain stocks within the barony in 1768 made clear the valley's dependence on the plain. The barony's officials listed the twenty-two *laboureurs* within the borders of the barony who were expected to supply grain to the market of Pont-St-Pierre. Three were to be found in the parish of Romilly, four in Pîtres, none in Pont-St-Pierre itself, and fifteen in la Neuville.[78] For its basic food supply, the valley depended heavily on the plain.

In turn, residents of the plain depended on the bourg for a wide range of services. This included milling, which required the valley's

76. Charles Estienne, *La guide des chemins de France,* ed. Jean Bonnerot, 3d ed. (Paris, 1553), facsim. repr. Bibliothèque de l'Ecole des Hautes Etudes, fasc. 267 (Paris, 1936), 123–24.

77. Sion, *Les paysans de la Normandie orientale,* 91.

78. Caillot, liasse 237, "Droits en général," 31 March 1768.

water power, save for a brief interval in the late sixteenth century, when a windmill functioned at la Neuville. There were also the legal services that Pont-St-Pierre offered as the center of a High Justice: notaries and practitioners, as well as the High Justice itself. Villagers in la Neuville likewise sought medical care in the bourg, apparently on a regular basis: for bleedings, bandagings, and medicines.[79] And villagers needed the markets and fairs of the bourg. La Neuville and Pont-St-Pierre displayed the interchanges that were to be found between market towns and agricultural villages throughout preindustrial Europe.[80]

By the eighteenth century, however, these complementary relations were under strain. The residents of Pont-St-Pierre expressed their sense of change in their *cahier* of grievances in 1789. "We request," they wrote, "that His Majesty be so good as to take note of the damage and considerable loss that are caused by the markets held on Sundays and holidays in the villages that surround the towns and bourgs of the entire kingdom; these markets are supplied with merchandise of every kind. Let them be altogether suppressed; or rather, let the laws that have pronounced their suppression be properly enforced. It should be noted that the bourgs of the kingdom have been established in imitation of the cities; the territory of all the cities contains a very small area; the reason for this is that they have been given as their role (*pour partage*) commerce; the bourgs have been up to now and ought to be considered from the same viewpoint."[81] The residents of the bourg were complaining of a loss of economic centrality. Economic functions that once had been their monopoly were now being performed in even modest agricultural villages, and they asked that the state intervene to suppress this free development of local markets.

The residents' demand echoed complaints by eighteenth-century seigneurial officials and prefigured struggles between bourg and village after 1789. Throughout the eighteenth century seigneurial officials had sought to enforce the bourg's market monopoly on such

---

79. AD Eure, 86 B 105–10, Haute Justice de Pont-St-Pierre, Procédures criminelles, passim.

80. On the role of market towns, with their fairs and taverns, as "central places" for rural cultural as well as economic life, see, for instance, R. H. Hilton, *The English Peasantry in the Later Middle Ages* (Oxford, 1975), 76–94; Peter Burke, *Popular Culture in Early Modern Europe* (London, 1978), 109–12; Eugen Weber, *Peasants into Frenchmen: The Modernization of Rural France, 1870–1914* (Stanford, 1976), 232–40, 407–12. Cf. G. William Skinner, "Marketing and Social Structure in Rural China (Part 1)," repr. in George M. Foster et al., eds., *Peasant Society: A Reader* (Boston, 1967), 63–98.

81. AD S-M, 4 BP 6012, art. 8.

basic products as grain and cotton against the efforts of both merchants and producers to sell their goods privately and thus evade seigneurial market rights.[82] Seigneurial authorities sought to suppress local markets on moral grounds as well. The barony's attorney, the *procureur fiscal,* complained in 1747 "that there is held every Sunday and holiday a market in the parish of la Neuville-Chant-d'Oisel." He sought its suppression as a violation of the Sabbath, but with little effect. Twenty years later his successor reported that "every Sunday and holiday in the villages under this jurisdiction shops are kept open and every sort of merchandise is sold publicly, in this bourg and in the parishes of la Neuville-Chant-d'Oisel, Pître, and Romilly."[83] The revolutionaries of the Year IV faced the more fundamental problem of assuring food supplies, but their program was essentially the same. It involved defending Pont-St-Pierre's position as the "market of the canton" and severely correcting "the indifference (*l'insouciance*) and disobedience of the farmers and millers" in the surrounding villages. Pont-St-Pierre demanded that the nine "communes that previously supplied the market of Pont-St-Pierre" continue to do so, and in response the cantonal administration voted that one-fifth "of the available stock of every farmer be taken for the supply of the market."[84]

In part these complaints reflected the spread of market relations throughout the upper Norman countryside, a development that brought profits as well as competition to the bourg. One indication of their spread is the frequency with which John Law's bank notes were to be found in the villages around Pont-St-Pierre. Like Amiens and other cities, la Neuville experienced a wave of debt repayments with devalued bank notes in 1720. Bank notes were the objects of theft as well as of more normal use in the village.[85]

82. See below, Chapter 6.

83. Caillot, liasse 237: "Droits en général," printed "Ordonnance de police. . . ," 15 July 1747; "Ordonnance de police," 28 June 1766.

84. AD Eure, 220 L 1: "Registre des délibérations et arrêtés de l'Administration Municipale du Canton de Pont-Saint-Pierre. . . ," fol. 9r, 20 Nivose An IV.

85. AD Eure, E 1263, Tabel. Pont-St-Pierre, 26, 28, 29 October 1720; 86 B 107, Haute Justice de Pont-St-Pierre, Procédures criminelles, 1712–23, 9 June 1720. Cf. the similar conclusions of Pierre Dardel, "Influence du système de Law sur la situation économique de la Haute Normandie (Rouen-Bolbec-Cany)," *Actes du 81e Congrès National des Sociétés Savantes, Rouen-Caen, 1956: Section d'histoire moderne et contemporaine,* 121–41; for questions about the degree to which the bank notes penetrated local societies, see Pierre Deyon, *Amiens, capitale provinciale: Etude sur la société urbaine au XVIIe siècle* (Paris and The Hague, 1967), 318–21, and Jean Meyer, *La vie quotidienne en France au temps de la Régence* (Paris, 1979), 229–35.

TABLE 3. *Market Tolls (Coutumes),* *Pont-St-Pierre*

Years	Rental of Coutumes	Years	Rental of Coutumes
1454–1455	7.50 l.	1558–1559	50.00 l. and 50 lbs. flax
1455–1456	16.25 l.	1560–1561	50.00 l. and 50 lbs. flax
1458–1459	13.00 l.	1570–1571	52.00 l. and 52 lbs. flax
1459–1460	13.00 l.	1571–1572	52.00 l. and 52 lbs. flax
1460–1461	15.50 l.	1572–1573	52.00 l. and 52 lbs. flax
1461–1462	18.00 l.	1573–1574	80.00 l. and 80 lbs. flax
1465–1466	15.00 l.	1581–1585	81.00 l. and 81 lbs. flax
1466–1467	15.00 l.	1624–1630	160.00 l. and 160 lbs. flax
1477–1478	12.00 l.	1632–1638	180.00 l.
1479–1480	12.00 l.	1638–1644	200.00 l.
1480–1481	12.00 l.	1649–1659	300.00 l. and 25 boisseaux oats
1481–1482	12.00 l.	1656–	310.00 l. and 25 boisseaux oats
1482–1483	12.00 l.	1684–1693	600.00 l. and 120 boisseaux oats
1506–1507	40.00 l.	1701–	600.00 l.
1513–1514	29.60 l.	1704–1710	600.00 l.
1515–1516	45.00 l.	1717–	500.00 l.
1521–1522	40.00 l.	1740–	900.00 l.
		1773–1782	1,300.00 l.

SOURCES: Comptes; Caillot, liasses 237, "Droits en général"; 241, "Matières diverses."

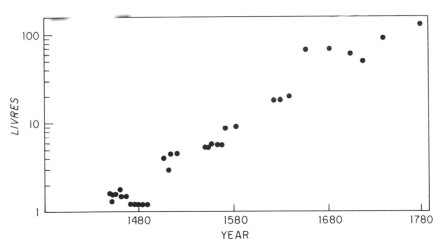

Figure 5. Market tolls in Pont-St-Pierre

TABLE 4. *Movable Wealth, Merchants and* Laboureurs

	1687–1751	1752–1775
Merchants' mean value (Pont-St-Pierre)	4,207 l.	2,011 l.
N	5	4
Laboureurs' mean value (la Neuville)	2,389 l.	3,276 l.
N	14	13

SOURCE: Appendix A.

A more direct indication of the market economy's growing impact on the region is provided by the evolution of market tolls in Pont-St-Pierre (see table 3 and fig. 5). The barons collected set amounts for the various goods that changed hands in their market, regardless of their prices; the sums for which they leased these rights thus reflect real changes in the volume of commerce in the baronial market rather than fluctuations in prices. The *coutumes'* value rose relatively slowly before the seventeenth century; in the 1580s they were worth only about twice what they had been worth in 1515–16. A century later their value had increased sevenfold; after a period of stagnation in the early eighteenth century, increases resumed from about 1740 on. In Pont-St-Pierre the agrarian crises of the late seventeenth century did not prevent a striking increase in the volume of monetary exchanges. The growing number of such exchanges gave increased importance to the seigneurial market—as it had encouraged the spread of shops in the villages around the market.

The bourg's decline as a local center was thus relative rather than absolute, but it was nonetheless clear. One index of change is provided by the changing relative wealth of the leading groups within the two communities: Pont-St-Pierre's merchants and la Neuville's *laboureurs*. Table 4 compares the two groups' total movable wealth, as it is shown in the notaries' estimates included in inventories after death. Such a comparison can be only approximate; there are only a small number of examples, and the notaries may have based their estimates on changing criteria. Nonetheless, the comparison demonstrates the economic equality that the most prosperous villagers enjoyed with the merchants of the bourg by the mid–eighteenth century; and it suggests that the *laboureurs* were on average wealthier than the merchants of the bourg. Certainly this was the case with

TABLE 5. *Populations of Pont-St-Pierre and la Neuville*

Year	Pont-St-Pierre			la Neuville	Pont-St-Pierre as % of la Neuville
	St-Pierre	St-Nicolas	Total		
1452–1453[a]	8	71	79	74	106.8
1488–1503[a]	27	122	149	151	98.7
1664[b]	16	62	78	221	35.3
1713[c]	31	61	92	255	36.1
1722[d]	30	64	94	304	30.9
1787[d]	30	67	97	331	29.0
1800[e]	114	359	473	1,422	33.3
1806[e]	139	358	497	1,470	33.8

SOURCES: For 1452, BN MS Fr. 25911, nos. 809, 810. For 1453, BN MS Fr. 25902, no. 6. For 1488, BN MS Fr. 25921, nos. 380, 350. For 1503, BN MS Fr. 25926, no. 390. For 1664, Jacques Dupâquier, *Statistiques démographiques du bassin parisien* (Paris, 1977), 553–54, 552. For 1713, ibid. For 1722, le sr. de Masseville, *Etat géographique de la province de Normandie*, 2 vols. (Rouen, 1722), 2:637, 634. For 1787 (7 October), AD S-M, C 1112, "Subdélégation de Rouen . . . Assemblées municipales." For 1800 (20 Messidor, Year VIII), AD Eure, 6 M 35, "Tableaux du dénombrement de la population . . ."; AD S-M, 6 M 1-1, "Dénombrement de la population. . . ." For 1806 (1 January), AD Eure, 6 M 35; AD S-M, 6 M 1-2, "Tableaux de la population: Arrondissement de Rouen, 1806."

[a] *Feux de monnéage.* [b] *Feux utiles, inutiles.* [c] *Feux taillables.*
[d] *Feux.* [e] Population.

regard to the most prosperous in each group. Among the merchants whose effects were inventoried after 1751, the most prosperous had an estate estimated at 4,500 l.; the goods of the most prosperous of la Neuville's *laboureurs* in these years were evaluated at 15,000 l.—and two of the village's other *laboureurs* had goods estimated at more than 4,500 l. On the eve of the Revolution, la Neuville's wealth was still more evident. The nine villagers elected to la Neuville's municipal assembly in 1787 paid an average of 289 l. in *tailles;* the eight members of Pont-St-Pierre's two assemblies paid an average of 43 l.[86]

Population changes were a second indication of the bourg's declining role. Table 5 and figure 6 present the population of Pont-St-Pierre and la Neuville over the early modern period. Again, their statistics are only approximations, for they are based on the notoriously fluid unit of the household, the *feu.* But they demonstrate the extent to which relations between bourg and village changed over the 350 years from the Hundred Years' War to the First Empire. In

86. AD S-M, C 1112, "Subdélégation de Rouen, . . . Assemblées municipales. . . ," 7 October 1787.

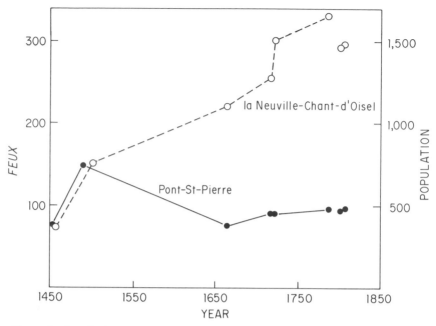

Figure 6. Population: Pont-St-Pierre and la Neuville

the late Middle Ages, Pont-St-Pierre had been slightly more populous than la Neuville. By the mid–seventeenth century, its population was only one-third that of la Neuville.

In their *cahier* of 1789, the residents of Pont-St-Pierre blamed
some of their troubles on changing patterns of communication. They
complained that they paid taxes for improvement of the roads
"without in any way benefiting from the use of the major roads
(*grandes routes*)"; and they asked the Crown "to order the reestab-
lishment of the *grande route des Andelys,* which passes through Pont-
St-Pierre and joins the route from Rouen to Paris" at the village of
Boos.[87] What the residents put down to royal neglect in fact reflected
a more fundamental change: a position of strategic importance had
become an economic liability in the later seventeenth and eighteenth
centuries, as Château Gaillard became a picturesque ruin and as the
main road from Rouen to Paris became one of the kingdom's most
important lines of transportation.[88] The road to Paris bypassed Pont-

87. AD S-M, 4 BP 6012, art. 2.
88. On the importance of this road, see C. E. Labrousse and Fernand Braudel,
eds., *Histoire économique et sociale de la France* (Paris, 1970), 2:166–86.

St-Pierre, but it did cut through la Neuville-Chant-d'Oisel, allowing the villagers direct and easy access to the larger economic world. Pont-St-Pierre's situation in its river valley had conferred safety in the Middle Ages; in the internal peace that followed the Fronde, the bourg's location simply made it difficult to reach and supply.

Another basic economic change had a similar effect. This was the spread of cotton spinning as a principal economic resource in the eighteenth-century Norman countryside.[89] On the eve of the Revolution spinning rather than agriculture was believed to be the principal occupation in both Pont-St-Pierre and la Neuville, to the point that widespread suffering followed the collapse of cotton prices in 1788.[90] The development of cotton spinning posed another threat to the geographical advantages of the river valley, for the eighteenth-century cotton industry offered industrial and mercantile possibilities that the plain's lack of water power had previously denied—and would again deny in the nineteenth century, with the development of water-driven spinning mills.

Cotton spinning not only gave employment to a large share of la Neuville's population. It also offered new mercantile possibilities to the village's wealthier residents. *Laboureurs* were well placed to profit from the development of cotton spinning. They had the funds to invest in the raw materials that the trade required, and they also controlled the means of transportation that the entrepreneur needed. When two cotton merchants in Romilly broke up their partnership in 1770, they made clear the degree to which farming had been fundamental to their enterprise: they agreed that one of them could carry his cotton "to Rouen and les Andelys by the horses and carts of the farm" that they held jointly and that he could "make use of the servants of the said farm to undertake the said transports," provided that he "promises to carry and bring back by the said carts, horses, and workmen of the said farm . . . all of the merchandise of spun and raw cotton that will come from the commerce" of the other.[91] The

89. On the importance of the "proto-industrialization" of the upper Norman countryside, see Marc Bouloiseau, "Aspects sociaux de la crise cotonnière dans les campagnes rouennaises en 1788–1789," *Actes du 81e Congrès National des Sociétés Savantes, Rouen-Caen, 1956: Section d'histoire moderne et contemporaine*, 403–28; Pierre Dardel, *Commerce, industrie, et navigation à Rouen et au Havre au XVIIIe siècle: Rivalité croissante entre ces deux portes—La Conjoncture* (Rouen, 1966), 108–23; Jean-Pierre Bardet, *Rouen aux XVIIe et XVIIIe siècles: Les mutations d'un espace social*, 2 vols. (Paris, 1983); and William M. Reddy, *The Rise of Market Culture: The Textile Trade and French Society, 1750–1900* (Cambridge, 1984), 24–47.
90. AD S-M, C 2212, dossier 7: "Etat des pauvres. . . ."
91. AD S-M, Tabel. Pont-St-Pierre, 25 April 1770.

TABLE 6. *Residence of People in Debt to Michel Bultel, 1769*

	Number	Total Value of Debts	
Rouen	10 (47.6%)	3,610 l.	(58.6%)
Paris	4 (19.0%)	787	(12.8%)
Subtotal	14 (66.7%)	4,397	(71.4%)
Other			
Verdun	1	51	
Angers	1	240	
Versailles	1	211	
Saumur	1	250	
Orléans	1	300	
Grandville	1	461	
St-Quentin	1	250	
Subtotal	7 (33.3%)	1,763	(28.6%)
Total	21	6,160	

SOURCE: AD S-M, Tabel. Pont-St-Pierre, 14 September 1769.

cotton trade required control of transportation—and in this the *laboureurs* were uniquely advantaged.

As a result, la Neuville's residents in the eighteenth century might move in economic networks that had little to do with Pont-St-Pierre. The business dealings of individual villagers make clear the large economic world that they inhabited in the eighteenth century. "Michel Bultel vivant lab.," for instance, left behind "a bundle of notes and letters of exchange" at his death in 1769, and these offer one view of the economic world of an eighteenth-century farmer (see table 6). Like several other substantial farmers in eighteenth-century la Neuville, Bultel was heavily involved in the cotton trade. As the list of his debtors suggests, the trade involved him in economic relations throughout northern France. The largest share of his activity was apparently with Rouennais businessmen: they made up just under half of the people from whom he held obligations and letters of exchange, and their debts counted for just over half of the total value that was owed him. But the remainder of this commercial paper involved Bultel in relations outside the province, with Paris and seven provincial towns. None of his bills was on residents of

Pont-St-Pierre. Bultel's economic network apparently had little to do with the bourg; instead, it involved the major commercial centers of northern France.

At the very end of the Old Regime, another economic change further strengthened the region's growing cosmopolitanism. This was the establishment in 1782 in Romilly of a copper foundry on the site of what had been four fulling mills. In 1788 the foundry expanded, taking up two more fulling mills, and in 1792 it expanded again, replacing three more mills. Romilly's foundry represented a new kind of industry in the Andelle Valley, and its effects on local perceptions must have been striking. The foundry's scale was immense; in 1789 it employed 250 workers. It visibly bound the region to international trade networks; its copper ore came from Sweden, its coal from England.[92] And it brought to the region a large group of foreigners, for along with English coal the foundry relied on English technology and English skilled workers. Their presence was highly visible. Thus in 1785 two English workers—"natives of England, and they do not at all understand the French language"—agreed before Pont-St-Pierre's notary on compensation following a noisy dispute in which one had insulted the other's wife.[93]

Nearby, in the town of Louviers, another major industrial center was created in these years, the cotton mill of M. Decretot. Arthur Young visited the mill in the late 1780s and described the several levels of innovation that it brought to the region. Like Romilly's copper mills, it was an enormous enterprise for the age, "the most considerable to be found in France," according to Young, and it too relied on English skills: "It is conducted," reported Young, "by 4 Englishman, from some of Mr. Arkwright's mills." Its machinery was novel and laborsaving. But above all the factory brought forth a steady flow of innovative products: "The beauty and the great variety of his inventions remind me more of the fertility of Mr. Wedgwood's inventions, than of any other fabric I have seen in France.

92. See the excellent series of articles by Guy Richard: "Les fonderies de Romilly-sur-Seine et les débuts de la metallurgie non ferreuse en Haute Normandie," *Actes du 88e Congrès National des Sociétés Savantes: Section d'histoire moderne et contemporaine, 1963*, 451–67; "Les nobles metallurgistes dans le département de l'Eure de 1789 à 1850," *Actes du 87e Congrès National des Sociétés Savantes: Section d'histoire moderne et contemporaine, 1962*, 741–52; "La metallurgie normande en 1845," *Revue d'histoire de la sidérurgie* 5, no. 1 (January–March 1964): 4. See also Louis Bergeron, *France under Napoleon*, trans. R. R. Palmer (Princeton, 1981), 184, 189.
93. AD Eure, E 1268, Tabel. Pont-St-Pierre, 28 December 1785.

TABLE 7. *The Ability to Sign, la Neuville-Chant-d'Oisel*

	Sign	Mark	Unknown	Total
Men				
1685–1694[a]	34 (33.0%)	68 (66.0%)	1 (1.0%)	103
1680–1710[b]	26 (39.4%)	40 (60.6%)	0	66
1780–1789[c]	68 (68.7%)	31 (31.3%)	0	99
Women				
1685–1694[a]	3 (2.9%)	98 (95.1%)	2 (2.0%)	103
1680–1710[b]	2 (8.3%)	22 (91.7%)	0	24
1780–1789[c]	45 (45.5%)	54 (54.5%)	0	99

SOURCE: AD S-M, 4 E 1900, 1904; AD Eure, 86 B 105–10.

[a] All first marriages.
[b] Residents testifying before Haute Justice de Pont-St-Pierre.
[c] All first marriages.

M. Decretot brings out something new for every year, and even for every season."[94] For the villagers of the region, commercial innovation had taken concrete local form, both in new kinds of industrial organization and in new products.

New relations between villagers, the bourg, and the wider world were not a matter of economic change alone. There were cultural changes as well. The eighteenth century brought a dramatic increase in village literacy—and with it still wider exchanges between the village and the world beyond the bourg (see table 7). At the end of the seventeenth century, two-thirds of the men and nine-tenths of the women in la Neuville had been unable to sign their names, well or badly. A century later the situation had been completely transformed. On the eve of the Revolution, 70 percent of the men and nearly half of the women were able to sign their names.[95]

For la Neuville's *laboureurs*, this cultural change came earlier, and

94. Arthur Young, *Travels in France During the Years 1787, 1788, and 1789*, ed. Constantia Maxwell (Cambridge, 1950), 309–10.

95. Because the Old Regime's schools taught reading before writing, historians have taken the ability to sign to indicate competence in dealing with written materials; methodological questions surrounding the use of signatures to estimate literacy are discussed by François Furet and Jacques Ozouf, *Lire et écrire: L'alphabétisation des Français de Calvin à Jules Ferry*, 2 vols. (Paris, 1977), 1:20–27, and Jean Quéniart, *Culture et société urbaine dans la France de l'Ouest au XVIIIe siècle* (Paris, 1978). For recent emphasis on the critical role of literacy in producing modern modes of thought, see Jack Goody, *The Domestication of the Savage Mind* (Cambridge, 1977), and Walter J. Ong, *Interfaces of the Word: Studies in the Evolution of Consciousness and Culture* (Ithaca, 1977).

TABLE 8. Laboureurs' *Ability to Sign, la Neuville-Chant-d'Oisel*

	Sign	Mark	Unknown	Total
Men				
1603–1650	7	3	4	14
1657–1686	3	3	0	6
1701–1750	10	2	0	12
1752–1782	16	0	0	16
Women				
1603–1650	0	1	13	14
1657–1686	0	5	1	6
1701–1750	1	11	0	12
1752–1761	3	5	0	8
1765–1782	6	1	1	8

SOURCE: Appendix B.

its effects were deeper. Table 8 sets out the frequency with which marriage contracts of the village's *laboureurs* and their children included signatures of the bride and groom. At the end of the seventeenth century, *laboureurs'* wives were typically illiterate, but at least half of the men in the early seventeenth century were literate, and in the eighteenth century virtually all of them were. The women of these families acquired literacy in the later eighteenth century; and by the 1780s nearly all of them were literate as well—at a time when just under half of the village's total female population was literate.

This cultural revolution in the village affected relations with the bourg, for a wide divergence in degrees of literacy had characterized these relations in the late seventeenth century. In the bourg as well as in the village, literacy spread in the eighteenth century; for women the effect was as dramatic as it was in la Neuville (see table 9). The bourg thus retained its cultural lead in the late eighteenth century. But that lead was very different from what it had been a century earlier. In the late seventeenth century, a substantial majority of the men in Pont-St-Pierre had been able to sign their names; at most 40 percent of the men in la Neuville had been able to. At the end of the Old Regime, the large majority of men in each community could sign: two-thirds of the men in la Neuville, 90 percent of those in Pont-St-Pierre. The bourg was no longer a necessary point of mediation between the written culture of the city and the village.

La Neuville's eighteenth-century cultural transformation showed

TABLE 9. *The Ability to Sign, Pont-St-Pierre*

	Sign	*Mark*	*Total*
Men			
1680–1710[a]	26 (60.5%)	17 (39.5%)	43
1780–1789[b]	28 (84.8%)	5 (15.2%)	33
Women			
1680–1710[a]	2 (6.1%)	31 (93.9%)	33
1780–1789[b]	20 (60.6%)	13 (39.4%)	33

SOURCE: AD Eure, 86 B 105–6; Archives Communales, Pont-St-Pierre, parish registers.
[a] Witnesses before the Haute Justice (too few marriages were recorded in late seventeenth-century Pont-St-Pierre to permit meaningful conclusions from this source).
[b] All first marriages.

itself in other ways. With the rise of literacy came the acquisition of books by the village's prosperous minority of *laboureurs*. Of twenty-eight inventories compiled after the deaths of *laboureurs* between 1689 and 1766, only two included books; of seven such inventories from 1768 to 1771, four included books. In this respect the *laboureurs* were catching up, with about one generation of delay, with the bourgeois elite of Pont-St-Pierre.[96] The same years saw the *laboureurs* acquire clocks and mirrors, small and inexpensive objects that might have as large an effect as books on these villagers' thinking. Among the twenty-eight examples from before 1768, there were three *laboureurs* who owned mirrors and one who owned a watch; among the seven from 1768 to 1771, four owned mirrors and five owned clocks or watches. In this the village was decidedly ahead of the bourg by the 1770s. Not one of the twelve merchants' inventories from late seventeenth- and eighteenth-century Pont-St-Pierre included a watch, and only three included mirrors.[97]

In fact the arrival of books in *laboureurs'* houses was only the last phase in the process by which writing became a part of daily life in the eighteenth-century village. By mid-century most of the village's

96. For emphasis on the development of literacy in eighteenth-century Normandy, see Furet and Ozouf, *Lire et écrire*, 1:177–79, 220–27, 2:101–51; Quéniart, *Culture et société*, 519–20. On mass publishing within the province, Jean Quéniart, *L'imprimerie et la librairie à Rouen au XVIIIe siècle* (Paris, 1969), 135–38.
97. Appendix A lists the inventories on which these conclusions are based. For the implications of timepieces in European society, David Landes, *Revolution in Time: Clocks and the Making of the Modern World* (Cambridge, Mass., 1983), 1–4, 7; on the development of the French clock-making industry, 257–73.

laboureurs owned silver cups engraved with names and humorous, sentimental, or proverbial mottoes: "jaime la douceur," "rien ne resiste a lamour," "sa douceur menchante," "l'occasion fait le larron," "le renard est pris," and, with an image of Bacchus, "je les amuse."[98] Of the eighteen *laboureurs'* inventories drawn up between 1742 and 1771, only four lacked these inscribed cups.[99] Writing had become a part of villagers' festive and sentimental life.[100] Earlier still, writing had been a part of most *laboureurs'* business practices. The inventories from the late seventeenth century show the care with which leases, accounts, and family papers were preserved.

A final sign of change was the growing comfort of *laboureurs'* houses. Of ten *laboureurs'* inventories from 1689 to 1716, two described one-room houses and six described houses of only two rooms, a kitchen and a bedroom. Construction contracts suggest the crowded dimensions of such buildings: about 25 feet long and 15 feet wide, divided across the middle into two rooms, with two doors and apparently only one window.[101] In contrast, among seventeen inventories from between 1742 and 1771, nine *laboureurs'* houses had at least three rooms, a kitchen and at least two bedrooms; none had only one room.[102] Two houses from the late eighteenth century survive today in la Neuville, and (although they have been substantially rebuilt since the eighteenth century) both testify to prosperous villagers' concern with domestic comfort. One has two stories, the other three; both include a substantial amount of brick, in place of the plaster and half-timber construction traditional in the area; and both have markers indicating their owners' pleasure in the construction—one indicating simply the date, "1789," the other announcing "Jai été placé par François Lefevre en L'année 1797." Concern for interior comfort was also evident in the development of more substantial furniture in the eighteenth century.[103]

Our series of inventories breaks off after 1771, and thus it is not possible to follow the progress of village luxury in the generation

98. Examples taken from AD S-M, Tabel. Pont-St-Pierre, 27 July, 14 September 1769.

99. Appendix A.

100. Cf. Maurice Agulhon, *The Republic in the Village: The People of the Var from the French Revolution to the Second Republic,* trans. Janet Lloyd (Cambridge, 1982), 121–22, for the significance of similar artifacts in southern France.

101. AD S-M, Tabel. Pont-St-Pierre, 18 April 1612; ibid., 11 May 1776.

102. Appendix A.

103. See Goubert, *La vie quotidienne,* 56–66, for the lack of comforts in seventeenth-century peasant homes.

TABLE 10. *Origins of Newlyweds,*
la Neuville-Chant-d'Oisel (first marriages only)

	1685–1694	1780–1789
Both from la Neuville	75 (72.8%)	49 (49.5%)
Groom from another parish	15 (14.6%)	38 (38.4%)
Bride from another parish	4 (3.9%)	6 (6.1%)
Bride or groom (not known) from another parish	8 (7.8%)	0
Both from another parish	0	6 (6.1%)
Unknown	1 (1.0%)	0
Total	103	99

SOURCE: AD S-M, 4 E 1900, 1904.

before the Revolution. Only one inventory survives, that of Jean Baptiste Gaudoit, a farmer and timber merchant whose business affairs became so entangled that just after his death in 1786 the Bailliage of Rouen supervised the sale of his effects. Despite his financial troubles, Gaudoit owned a gold pocket watch, an umbrella, "a large mirror with a gilded frame," a smaller mirror, a clock, a cask of Burgundy wine, and a cask and a dozen bottles of wine of unspecified origins; even this last was a sign of change in the cider-drinking upper Norman countryside. Gaudoit employed three servants and dealt in large sums of money: over fifteen months between late 1785 and early 1787, he and his heirs sold over 5,000 l. of wood, mostly to Rouennais customers.[104]

By the late eighteenth century la Neuville's residents moved in a wide economic world, and their culture had been decisively enlarged. Their relationship to the village itself was also new in these years, for by the 1780s a large percentage were newcomers to la Neuville. Table 10 describes what is known of the origins of the young men and women marrying in la Neuville in the 1680s and the 1780s. At the end of the seventeenth century, three-fourths of the marriages in la Neuville united men and women who had both been born in the village. A century later this was true of only one-half of the village's marriages. Mobility had become a typical experience for couples setting up households in la Neuville; 44.5 percent of the grooms were new to the village. The exception, as seen above, was the village elite of

104. AD S-M, 4 BP 5569.

laboureurs, who became more firmly rooted in the village as the century progressed. Doubtless their power within the village was all the greater as they came to embody continuity within local affairs.

Change in eighteenth-century la Neuville was rapid and pervasive, touching diverse levels of village experience. When villagers bought mirrors, they acquired a new sense of themselves and of their society; mirrors implied a new awareness of individuality, a new concern for clothing and changing fashions, new assumptions about the purposes of buying and about the rewards of economic activity. Clocks implied an abstract understanding of work discipline, a detachment from the natural and traditional rhythms of agrarian life. Reading and writing brought an intensified awareness of the world beyond the village and an enhanced ability to deal effectively with that world. Economic development pushed the village in the same directions. Farmers were richer in the eighteenth century, and they involved themselves in a wider range of economic activities. Other villagers were more often literate, more mobile, less dependent on agricultural employment.

These changes had important political implications, for they placed new strains on the relationship between la Neuville and the bourg of Pont-St-Pierre, between the periphery of the lordship and its center. Some degree of strain had probably always existed between the two communities, for Pont-St-Pierre had always enjoyed far more of the profits of seigneurial administration than the villages around it had. But well into the eighteenth century potential conflict was muted by the fact of complementarity. La Neuville depended on Pont-St-Pierre because the bourg was in important respects an urban community in the early modern period, despite its tiny population. Set in a narrow river valley, it had little arable land for its residents to cultivate. Instead, it offered legal, medical, and administrative services; its merchants offered substantial stocks of a wide variety of goods; it controlled significant lines of transportation, and its innkeepers profited from the stream of travelers along them; and it benefited from its position as a center of seigneurial administration. Because of the functions that it performed, the bourg was also a center of literacy. Pont-St-Pierre formed a center to which residents of mainly agricultural villages like la Neuville naturally turned to meet a variety of needs.

As la Neuville's connections with the urban economy and culture of northern France became closer, Pont-St-Pierre's centrality became

more artificial, and increasingly required seigneurial police intervention for its maintenance. By the late eighteenth century, Pont-St-
Pierre was less populous and farther from important lines of transport than la Neuville; its merchants were probably less wealthy and
less cultivated than la Neuville's farmers. "Urbanization" of the
eighteenth-century countryside had undercut the bourg's claims to
special status and posed new problems for seigneurial authority.[105]

105. Charles Tilly, *The Vendée* (Cambridge, Mass., 1964), 10–13 and passim; Jan
De Vries, *European Urbanization, 1500–1800* (Cambridge, Mass., 1984), 8–13, 240–49.

II
PROPERTY AND PRODUCTION

T hose who succeed me will take great care to conserve the property of le Fossé, first because it has been acquired very advantageously . . . and second, because it is a very fine property, well assembled, with a commodious house, a pigeon house, water, meadows, oaks, well planted, the whole contiguous, its revenue very certain. And it is worth now more than 24,000 livres, which will increase in the future with God's aid, as its value improves with the growth of what has been newly planted, and I would not accept 30,000 livres for it. It must be kept."[1]

These are the words of the Rouennais magistrate Gentien Thomas, confiding to his account book in about 1600. His comments suggest the complex ways in which figures such as Thomas thought about land. A first concern that emerges from his comments is for the estate's self-sufficiency. Le Fossé was valuable to Thomas partly because of the range of goods that it could supply, because of the degree that it would free him from dependence on the open market. Equally important, though, were the attitudes that he expressed toward the free market in land. Gentien Thomas was aware of the land market and of his own success in dealing with it. He had bought le Fossé under advantageous conditions, and he knew its value to be rising. But his dynastic concerns shaped his view of the

---

1. AD S-M, 10 J 13, Chartrier de Bosmelet, Accounts of Gentien Thomas, fol. 75r–v.

property as much as his economic calculations. Le Fossé's value lay partly in Thomas's hope that it would be a support for his family's continuity over the generations, an assurance of its place within the social order.

This chapter examines landownership and land management within the barony of Pont-St-Pierre from the perspective that Thomas's comments suggest: that is, with the understanding that land was both an economic resource and something more, a foundation for families' development and an indicator of how the social order functioned. In the first part of the chapter, I will consider how land was distributed and how its distribution changed over the early modern period; in the second part, I will consider some of the ways in which it was managed and attempt to understand how fully its productive capacities were used. A larger question necessarily underlies these inquiries, the question of French agricultural underdevelopment. At the end of the Old Regime as in previous centuries, French agriculture was unable to supply the society's basic needs. Pont-St-Pierre occupied a favored position in a wealthy province, but there too the threat of hunger remained a reality in 1789—150 years after the last great subsistence crises in England. Close study of the region can tell us a good deal about the sources of this underdevelopment.

Gentien Thomas spoke of landowning in terms of his sense of his family's continuity and self-sufficiency—but this sense coexisted with his understanding of land as a commodity to be bought and sold. Alertness to the connections between land and the market—both the market for land itself and the market for produce—was an early fact in the villages around Pont-St-Pierre. Pierre de Roncherolles, the baron of Pont-St-Pierre and a military nobleman, in 1590 arranged the receivership of the barony of Maineville, which belonged to his nephew and ward; among the provisions of the contract was the requirement that the receiver for all products of the farm "await the season to sell it at the highest price of the year" and that he auction leases of the estate's subsidiary elements in public "to the highest bidder for the profit and increase of the said receipts as has been done in the past."[2] Gentien II Thomas, like his father a magistrate in Rouen's Chambre des Comptes, expressed a similar view in his account book, about a property in Romilly that he had

2. AD Eure, E 1250, Tabel. Pont-St-Pierre, 23 August 1590.

TABLE 11. *Frequency of Land Sales, Pont-St-Pierre and Heuqueville*

Years	Sales	Inheritances	Total
1398–1399	8	5	13
1414–1415	4	2	6
1515–1516	14	1	15

SOURCE: Comptes, 1398–99, 1414–15, 1515–16.

purchased in 1625. He was particularly pleased with the quality of hay that two of his meadows there produced, "which should be sold yearly during Lent, which is the most suitable season because there is to be found very little in the area that is of high quality, such as this is."[3]

Such comments reflected the fact that from an early date land around Pont-St-Pierre had in some ways been treated as a commodity that could readily be bought and sold. Elements of a land market had existed there since at least the late fourteenth century. Analysis of the mutation fees —*treizièmes*—that the barons of Pont-St-Pierre received from their two principal estates, Pont-St-Pierre and Heuqueville, shows the importance of the region's land market in the late fourteenth, early fifteenth, and early sixteenth centuries (see table 11). There are numerous reasons to mistrust such statistics: the barons and their agents were not so careful in collecting the *treizièmes* in the late Middle Ages as at the end of the Old Regime; possibly they were more easily defrauded in cases of inheritance than in sales, which normally gave rise to notarized documents and public announcements; possibly local notables received exemptions from the *treizièmes* as marks of baronial favor. Despite such considerations, however, the statistics make it clear that land sales were commonplace occurrences in Pont-St-Pierre and in the villages around it during the late fourteenth and early fifteenth centuries: more common, indeed, than transfer by inheritance.[4] In this area, the pace of land sales during the late Middle Ages seems not to have been qualitatively different from

3. Caillot, liasse 253, "Paroisse de Romilly, Ferme," register entitled "Nottes des contrats contenant les heritages qui composoient la ferme du manoir segouin." For similar comments by Charles Maignart, another Rouennais magistrate who owned land at this time at Pont-St-Pierre, see Jonathan Dewald, *The Formation of a Provincial Nobility: The Magistrates of the Parlement of Rouen, 1499–1610* (Princeton, 1980), 184–85.

4. Cf. the importance that has recently been attributed to land sales in medieval England: Alan MacFarlane, *The Origins of English Individualism: The Family, Property, and Social Transition* (London, 1978), 118–30, passim.

TABLE 12.   *Turnover of Estates Within the Barony of Pont-St-Pierre*

Estate	Number of Sales	Dates Sold
Le Veneur (la Neuville)	2	1601, 1742
Boscleborgne (Romilly)	3	1564, ?, 1739
Les Maisons (Pont-St-Pierre)	5	1506, 1670, ca. 1710, 1765,[a] 1768[a]
Chantdoisel (la Neuville)	2	1581, 1751
Manoir Segouin (Romilly)	6	15??, 1625, 1638, 1657, 1679, 1710

SOURCES: For le Veneur, AD S-M, 2 B 441, no. 236; Leger, notaire à Rouen, 22 May 1742. For Boscleborgne, communications from M. Robert Chapuis. For les Maisons, Caillot, 241, 255; AD Eure, E 2396, 2, 27 January 1715; AD S-M, Tabel. Pont-St-Pierre, 1764–73, 12 March 1765. For Chantdoisel, Archives of the marquis de Caumont, Versailles; AD S-M, Le Coq, notaire à Rouen, 3 December 1751. For Manoir Segouin, Caillot, 253, "Paroisse de Romilly, Ferme."

[a] Sold with barony of Pont-St-Pierre.

that in the late eighteenth century. Between 1768 and the Revolution, there were typically about a dozen sales of land yearly in the villages that made up the barony of Pont-St-Pierre.[5]

It was not only small plots of land that thus changed hands on the open market; as table 12 shows, the larger domains around Pont-St-Pierre were bought and sold as well. In this they were very different from the barony of Pont-St-Pierre itself, which the Roncherolles family inherited in the early fifteenth century and sold only in 1765. A record for instability was established by the estate of Manoir Segouin, in Romilly; this estate was sold at least once in the sixteenth century, then again in 1625, 1638, 1657, 1679, and 1710. But the other estates within the barony also changed hands during these years.

Between the early fifteenth and the late eighteenth centuries, changes in landownership had a profound effect on rural society in the villages around Pont-St-Pierre. It is possible to trace this process from a relatively early date because of the survival of manorial surveys (*terriers*) and related documents listing the land that the barony's seigneurial tenants held. Such an inquiry necessarily focuses on the village of la Neuville-Chant-d'Oisel, in which nearly all the arable land within the barony was to be found. There are prob-

5. Pont-St-Pierre, "Recettes des treizièmes, 1769–93," discussed below, pp. 66–72.

TABLE 13. *Distribution of Land, la Neuville-Chant-d'Oisel, 1413–1776*
(percentage of total land)

Year	Landowners					
	Top 5%	Top 10%	Top 25%	2d 25%	3d 25%	Lowest 25%
1413	17.2	29.4	58.2	26.1	10.9	4.8
1423–1425[a]	15.0	26.2	53.0	27.0	14.4	5.5
1487	23.1	37.0	62.5	22.1	11.7	3.8
1524[a]	30.3	45.9	69.4	18.5	8.2	4.0
1544[a]	34.8	49.0	72.5	16.1	8.3	3.1
1587[a]	33.3	48.4	72.4	15.8	8.0	3.8
1600–1604[a]	—	66.7	85.0	9.7	4.0	1.3
1635	56.5	73.6	86.8	8.3	3.7	1.3
1736	44.7[b]	61.4[b]	83.4[b]	10.6	4.3	1.7
1776	54.0	72.9	88.3	8.0	2.7	1.0

SOURCE: Appendix C.
Throughout, values refer to area of arable land; *masures* have been excluded from these calculations.
[a] Refers to Fief du Chapitre in la Neuville only
[b] This is a minimum value.

lems in using manorial surveys, some of which are considered in Appendix C. Nonetheless, they provide a reasonably accurate picture of how land was distributed and how its distribution changed.[6]

Tables 13 and 14 and figures 7 and 8 present the evolution of property in la Neuville. The story that they recount is one of an increasing concentration of landownership. From the late Middle Ages to the mid–seventeenth century, the principal landowners in la Neuville took a steadily larger share of the village's arable land. Their progress was halted during the later seventeenth and early eighteenth centuries, but it resumed between 1736 and 1776. Over the full 350 years, the change was dramatic. The wealthiest 5 percent of la Neuville's landowners had held just over one-sixth of the village's land in 1413; in 1776 they held just over one-half. The wealthiest 10 percent increased their share by 148 percent, from

6. Among the studies that employ these documents and discuss their limitations are Jean Jacquart, *La crise rurale en Ile de France, 1550–1670* (Paris, 1974), 101–64, 248–53, 723–31; and Albert Soboul, "Sur l'étude des documents fonciers: Terriers, cadastres, et compoix," repr. in *Problèmes paysans de la Révolution, 1789–1848* (Paris, 1983), 63–86.

TABLE 14. *Percentage of Change in Land Distribution,*
la Neuville-Chant-d'Oisel, 1413–1776

Year	Landowners					
	Top 5%	Top 10%	Top 25%	2d 25%	3d 25%	Lowest 25%
1413–1487	+34.3	+25.9	+7.4	−15.3	+7.3	−20.8
1487–1587	+44.2	+30.8	+15.8	−28.5	−31.6	0
1587–1635	+69.7	+52.1	+17.4	−47.5	−53.8	−65.8
1635–1736	−20.9	−16.6	−3.9	+26.7	+16.2	+30.8
1736–1776	+20.8	+18.7	+5.9	−24.5	−37.2	−41.1
Total	+214.0	+148.0	+51.7	−69.3	−75.2	−79.2

SOURCE: Appendix C.

nearly one-third to nearly three-fourths. The shares held by less prosperous groups declined in similar measure. In the late Middle Ages petty landowners had held a substantial share of la Neuville's arable: the second quartile of landowners held just over one-fourth (26.1 percent), the third quartile just over one-tenth (10.9 percent). In 1776 these two groups together held only 10.7 percent of the total. The middling group of landowners had effectively disappeared from la Neuville.[7]

As important as the decline of middling landowners was the fact that an increasing share of la Neuville's population owned either tiny scraps of arable land or none at all. The poorest one-fourth of the village's landowners had held less than 5 percent of its arable in 1413; by 1776 this share had fallen to just 1 percent. But even these figures conceal the extent of the decline, for they concern only arable land and thus say nothing of the increasing numbers who owned only a house and a garden, known in Normandy as a *masure*. In 1413 only a tiny number of property owners in la Neuville held just a house or garden, and through the mid–sixteenth century this group amounted to fewer than 4 percent of the village's landowners (see table 15). Fiscal rolls from the fifteenth and early sixteenth centuries confirm the rarity of such circumstances and indicate the specific causes that gave rise to them: a listing of seventy-four residents of la Neuville in 1453 included as poor only four "poor widows,

7. For summary of other studies showing the process of concentration of landowning in the sixteenth and seventeenth centuries, see Emmanuel Le Roy Ladurie, Hugues Neveux, and Jean Jacquart, *Histoire de la France rurale* (Paris, 1975), esp. 2:265–75.

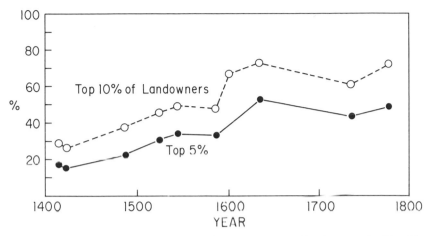

Figure 7. Land held by top 5 percent and top 10 percent of landowners: La Neuville

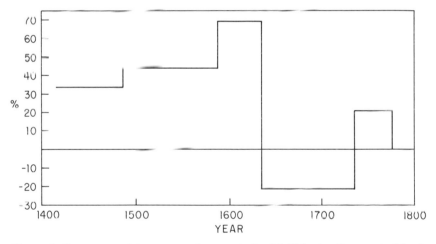

Figure 8. Percentage of increase or decrease in land held by top 5 percent of land-owners: La Neuville

beggars who have nothing . . . and who have fallen into decrepitude because of old age" and a fifth who declared himself illegitimate; a listing of 151 residents in 1503 included only four "poor and beggars."[8] But by 1635 those who owned only a house and garden made up 16.4 percent of the property-owners of la Neuville, and in

8. BN, MS Français 25902, no. 6; 25926, no. 390.

TABLE 15. *Ownership of* Masures *Only*

Year	Total Landowners	N Owning Masure Only	% of Total
1413	105	1	1.0
1423–1425[a]	67	2	3.0
1487	28	0	0.0
1544[a]	191	7	3.7
1635	292	48	16.4
1736	271	36	13.3
1776	278	63	22.7

SOURCE: Appendix C.

[a] Refers to Fief du Chapitre only.

the last decades of the Old Regime they made up well over one-fifth of the total. A new social group had been created in la Neuville, a group of people who owned a house and garden in the village but had no share in its arable land.[9] By the end of the Old Regime, the village possessed a proletariat of a sort that it had not had 350 years earlier.

The evolution toward greater concentration of landowning in la Neuville was a nearly continuous process between the early fifteenth and the late eighteenth centuries. It continued through the population decline and economic stagnation of the Hundred Years' War and through the population growth and buoyant economic development of the sixteenth century. But the critical moment in the process came in the late sixteenth and early seventeenth centuries— the period that also saw an explosion in the numbers who owned no arable land in the village. In this half century, from the Catholic League to the French entry in the Thirty Years' War, the leading 5 percent of the village's landowners increased their share of its land by nearly 70 percent; conversely, the share of the middle half of the village's landowners fell by nearly 50 percent, from nearly one-fourth of the village's arable to only 12 percent. The fifteenth and sixteenth centuries had brought steady but gradual erosion of the small landowners' situation. Between 1587 and 1635 the process accelerated dramatically. The pattern that these years established remained essentially unchanged for the remainder of the Old Regime.

9. Cf. W. G. Hoskins, *The Midland Peasant: The Economic and Social History of a Leicester Village* (London, 1957), 143–47, 185–90, 216–17, for the similar and contemporaneous development of a rural proletariat in England.

The later seventeenth and early eighteenth centuries brought a retreat of the large landowners, the mid–eighteenth century their reassertion. But change in both periods brought only oscillations around the central patterns that had been established by 1635. In 1776 as in 1635, the leading 5 percent of la Neuville's landowners held about half of the arable land, the leading 10 percent held about three-fourths, and the leading 25 percent held about four-fifths.

Change in the distribution of land in la Neuville was linked to a series of changes in the character of the village's leading landowners and in the ways that land was held. By the late eighteenth century, in the first place, the largest share of land in the village was held for cash rents. Table 16 presents for the year 1776 the distribution of land between *fermage* and direct management, divided by categories of annual worth. By the late eighteenth century, most land in la Neuville was held by tenant farmers: 64 percent as measured by annual value. Tenant farming was most prevalent, of course, in the case of the village's largest properties. Twenty-one of the thirty properties worth at least 300 l. annually were held by *fermage*, as six of the seven worth at least 1,000 l. were. But equally striking is the fact that so many of the village's very small properties were involved in the system of leases: 13 percent of all holdings worth less than 300 l. were leased out, and even the very smallest properties were leased out with about this frequency.

The prevalence of tenant farming was a natural corollary to the growing concentration of the village's property in a few hands, for by the late eighteenth century few of the village's small landowners could hope to survive as self-sufficient farmers. It was precisely the middling landowners, those who most closely approximated a self-sufficient peasantry, who were the principal victims of changing patterns of ownership in la Neuville. For the vast majority of the village's landowners in the late eighteenth century—probably for all of the 241 (89 percent of the total) whose properties were worth less than 300 l. yearly—there could be no hope of subsisting on only what their land produced. They needed instead to work for others and to treat their land as a supplementary resource, in many instances more efficiently leased out than worked directly.[10]

Leaseholding testifies to a pervasive monetarization of the rural economy by the later eighteenth century. In la Neuville both rich

10. Cf. Pierre Goubert's classic description of this situation, in *Beauvais et le Beauvaisis de 1600 à 1730: Contribution à l'histoire économique et sociale de la France au XVIIe siècle*, 2 vols. (Paris, 1960).

TABLE 16. *The Importance of Tenant Farming, 1776 (values in l.)*

Yearly Value of Individual's Property (l.)	Fermage		Direct Management		Unknown		Total	
	N	Value	N	Value	N	Value	N	Value
4–49	66 (43%)	1,549 (42%)	74 (48%)	1,821 (50%)	13 (9%)	303 (8%)	153	3,673
50–99	20 (42%)	1,296 (42%)	28 (58%)	1,761 (58%)	0	0	48	3,057
100–299	18 (45%)	2,967 (47%)	22 (55%)	3,294 (53%)	0	0	40	6,261
Subtotal	104 (43%)	5,812 (45%)	124 (52%)	6,876 (53%)	13 (5%)	303 (2%)	241	12,991
300–999	15 (65%)	7,914 (66%)	8 (35%)	4,039 (34%)	0	0	23	11,953
1,000 +	6 (86%)	13,733 (77%)	1 (14%)	4,000 (23%)	0	0	7	17,733
Subtotal	21 (70%)	21,647 (73%)	9 (30%)	8,039 (27%)	0	0	30	29,686
Total	125 (46%)	27,459 (64%)	133 (49%)	14,915 (35%)	13 (5%)	303 (1%)	271	42,677

SOURCE: AD S-M, C 582, no. 114: Imposition territoriale, 1776.

NOTE: Because not all entries specify the extent of *fermage*, if any part of an individual's property was managed directly his total holding is included under the heading Direct Management; thus these figures slightly understate the importance of *fermage* in la Neuville.

and poor were required to treat their land as a source of cash rents rather than as a source of subsistence. And cash rents meant production for the market as a means of meeting the need for cash. The involvement of very small farmers in the market was one of the differences between France and England that surprised and vexed Arthur Young as he traveled through northern France in the 1780s: "AUG. 9th. Market Day. Coming out of the town I met at least an hundred asses, some loaded with a bag, others [with] a sack, but all apparently with a trifling burden, and swarms of men and women. This is called a market, being plentifully supplied; but a great proportion of all the labour of a country is idle in the midst of harvest, to supply a town which in England would be fed by one-fortieth of the people. Whenever this swarm of triflers buzz in a market, I take a minute and vicious division of the soil for granted."[11] For Young, widespread involvement in the market did not mean that agriculture was stimulated by commercial pressures, quite the contrary; but he was struck by the extent to which French small holders were drawn to the market and its cash transactions.

The development of leaseholds and of the market relations that they implied was closely linked to a second aspect of the process of concentration of landowning, the growing prominence of city dwellers among the leading landowners in the village and the sharp decline of peasant property (see table 17). At the start of the sixteenth century, residents of la Neuville had formed a narrow majority of the village's principal landowners. Among the nonresidents, the principal group had been the clergy; there were no royal officials and only one bourgeois of Rouen among the twelve most prosperous landowners in the village. In this instance, it appears that the chief vehicle by which urban money flowed into rural property was the clergy, especially the prosperous cathedral canons of Rouen.[12]

Over the sixteenth century, however, the character of urban investment changed radically. Urban investment was secularized; first bourgeois of Rouen, then royal officials and lawyers, fully displaced the clergy and took over much of the share that had

11. Arthur Young, *Travels in France During the Years 1787, 1788, and 1789*, ed. Constantia Maxwell (Cambridge, 1950), 97.
12. Guy Bois, *Crise du féodalisme: Economie rurale et démographie en Normandie orientale du début du XIVe siècle au milieu du XVIe siècle* (Paris, 1976), 142–43, 156–57, likewise emphasizes the limited scope of urban investments in the land before the sixteenth century.

TABLE 17. *Leading Landowners, la Neuville-Chant-d'Oisel*

	1524[a]	1544[a]	1587[a]	1635	1736	1776
Priests	4	2	0	0	0	0
Seigneurial officials	2	0	0	0	0	0
Bourgeois of Rouen	1	5	3	1	1	1
Lawyers and officials	0	2	4	7	8	4
Ecuyers, nobles hommes, sieurs	0	0	0	6	1	4
Laboureurs	0	0	2	0	0	3
Other local landowners	5	3	3	0	2	0
Unspecified	0	0	0	1	0	0
Total	12	12	12	15	12	12

SOURCE: Appendix C.

[a] Refers to Fief du Chapitre only.

belonged to local landowners as well.[13] By 1736 eight of the village's twelve principal landowners were Rouennais judges and lawyers. Most of the same families dominated village landowning in 1776, although fewer of them were actively engaged in legal careers: four of the twelve principal landowners in that year were lawyers or judges, four others were simply gentlemen, without further professional designation.

The increasing importance of such figures among la Neuville's landowners brought a fundamental transformation in the character of landowning, for such landowners created a series of substantial domains within la Neuville and the villages nearby. The most successful of these landowners were the Busquet family, Rouennais *parlementaires* who acquired the vavasory of Chant-d'Oisel in 1581. At that time the property included about 56 acres of domain lands and 44 acres of dependent tenures; in 1751, when the family sold the property, its domain had expanded to 141 acres: partly by new additions to the estate, partly by the recovery of its dependent tenures, which

13. For summary of other analyses of this process, see Le Roy Ladurie, Neveux, and Jacquart, *Histoire de la France rurale*, 2:261–75.

had shrunk to a mere 15.7 acres.[14] Not all estate owners were so successful as the Busquets, but expansion was typical of those domains within the barony of Pont-St-Pierre whose histories can be followed. In la Neuville, the estate of le Veneur expanded its domain by 24 percent between 1601 and 1746;[15] in Romilly, the estate of Manoir Segouin grew by about 162 percent between 1537 and 1710[16] and that of Boscleborgne grew by 31 percent between 1737 and 1762;[17] in Pont-St-Pierre itself, the estate of les Maisons grew by 27 percent between 1522 and 1529, and it continued to expand thereafter.[18] Apparently the main exceptions to this pattern of expansion were the region's monastic properties. The property of Cardonnay, belonging to the nuns of Fontaine Guérard, amounted to 70 acres in 1214 and 68 acres in 1620; but even this domain expanded in the following years, reaching 89 acres in 1778.[19]

Such landowners as the Busquets enjoyed a number of advantages in their efforts to enlarge their properties. Doubtless the most important were the insecurity and indebtedness that most small property-owners labored under during the sixteenth and seventeenth centuries. Pont-St-Pierre's notarial records show the steady accumulation of small properties by urban landowners, who could dispose of the ready capital that allowed them to take advantage of others' financial difficulties.[20] But the political dimensions of the process were also important. In the middle years of the sixteenth century, the Crown began auctioning off marginal lands, notably near the royal forests, and landowners around Pont-St-Pierre took advantage of the opportunity that the sales offered. In 1563 Jean Maignart, a councillor in Rouen's Cour des Aides, petitioned the Crown "in order to obtain as a *fieffe* a certain part of the forest of Longbouel,

14. Archives of the Busquet de Caumont family, Versailles. On the family, see Dewald, *The Formation*, 88–89, 93, 178–79; and Robert Busquet de Caumont, *Histoire économique et sociale d'une lignée de huit conseillers au parlement de Normandie: Les Busquet de Chandoisel et de Caumont* (Mémoire D.E.S., Paris, Faculté de Droit, 1961).

15. AD S-M, 2 B 441, no. 235; 2 B 447, no. 73; Chambre des Comptes de Rouen, Aveux.

16. Caillot, liasse 253, "Paroisse de Romilly, Ferme."

17. Summaries of documents generously supplied me by the property's current owner, M. Robert Chapuis; also AD Eure, E 2397, "Chartrier de Pont-St-Pierre, Aveu de la vavassorie du Bosc le Borgne à Romilly, 1778."

18. Discussed in Dewald, *The Formation*, 175–78.

19. AD S-M, 80 H 8, Abbaye de Fontaine Guérard, Ferme de Cardonnay.

20. For the role of debt in the consolidation of the Maignarts' properties, see Dewald, *The Formation*, 204–5. For analyses of the role of debt in the consolidation of landed estates elsewhere, Le Roy Ladurie, Neveux, and Jacquart, *Histoire de la France rurale*, 2:259–61.

completely useless, consisting of wasteland and brush." Over the next two years royal commissioners evaluated Maignart's request, and in 1565 he was granted 25 acres of land next to the forest, which he added to his estate les Maisons in Pont-St-Pierre; in exchange, he had only to pay a modest ground rent of 4 l. per acre.[21] Financial pressure on the monarchy also led in the sixteenth century to sales of church lands, and Jean Maignart took advantage of these as well. In 1563 he bought the tiny seigneury of Bec, the lordship from which he held the estate of les Maisons.[22]

Maignart was apparently typical of Norman landowners. Throughout the province, landowners were taking advantage of the Crown's financial troubles and solidifying their estates by the purchase of marginal lands taken from the royal domains. In 1571 the Norman Estates expressed their concern about the sales, because these lands had in fact been used as village commons. They protested "that it has pleased Your Majesty to establish a commission to sell for your profit . . . several common lands and pastures, along the forests and other empty and waste lands of this province, something that does great injury to the poor inhabitants of the province . . . the said poor inhabitants have used and possessed them since time immemorial to feed their livestock." The Estates worried about the effects of the sales on the nobility as well; numerous "gentlemen by the rights of their fiefs possess a great part [of the commons] both for their own use and for that of their subjects."[23]

But by the early seventeenth century the Estates' anxieties had changed; they now worried about efforts by crown and church to reclaim these alienated properties. Their anxieties suggest the importance of the property transfer that had taken place. "There are five hundred gentlemen," they complained in 1609, "who, having expended their blood and the larger part of their property in the service of the Crown . . . , will now see themselves deprived of whatever small property remains to them, constrained to abandon the land of their birth and to go off with a white cane in hand to

21. AD Eure, E 2392, "Chartrier de Pont-St-Pierre, Inventaire des titres," 139–41. See also Michel Devèze, *La vie de la forêt française au XVIe siècle*, 2 vols. (Paris, 1961), 2:264–74.

22. Dewald, *The Formation*, 177–78; because the monks of Bec Hellouin were able to repurchase the fief in 1565, the Maignart family only secured full ownership of Bec in 1627.

23. Charles de Robillard de Beaurepaire, ed., *Cahiers des Etats de Normandie sous le règne de Charles IX* (Rouen, 1891), 78–79.

beg for their livelihood." A year later they complained about the uncertainties that the Crown had created by allowing the Church to repurchase lands alienated during the Wars of Religion: "This disturbance brings great disorder to family affairs because of the inheritance divisions, sales, exchanges of lands that they have acquired." In 1629 there were more complaints about the Crown's attempt to recover alienated domain lands: numerous nobles, so the Estates argued, "used what remained of their property to improve and maintain (*approffiter et maintenir*) these lands, to clear them, plant them, and make them productive, having built there houses and other needed buildings"; and a year later there was the further claim that the formerly unproductive domain lands "at present are the major part of the properties of both the nobility and the Third Estate."[24] These were implausible claims, but they nonetheless point to the Crown's role in the development of such estates as the Maignarts' les Maisons.

Wealthy aristocrats, such as the barons of Pont-St-Pierre themselves, also had a role in this process. Well into the seventeenth century the barons of Pont-St-Pierre continued to make substantial grants of land to estate officials and lesser nobles. Like the Crown, the barons usually made these grants in exchange for small, permanently fixed ground rents, but their main purpose seems to have been to secure the loyalty and service of local notables. In 1527, for instance, Louis de Roncherolles, the baron of Pont-St-Pierre, made over to "Jehan de Rondes his receiver, son of Master Girard de Rondes," 27.5 acres of land in Pîtres and a mill in the adjoining village of Romilly; in the next two years he granted de Rondes an additional 14 acres of land in Pont-St-Pierre.[25] Girard de Rondes had been a lawyer in Pont-St-Pierre in the early sixteenth century and had served the Roncherolles as a business agent on at least one occasion; Jehan de Rondes, after his service as the Roncherolles' receiver, became the vicomte in Pont-St-Pierre's High Justice. The de Rondes did not claim nobility, but they were connected with the petty nobles of the region: Girard de Rondes's nephew was "Jacques de Bornez escu[ier]" in Pont-St-Pierre.[26] The de Rondes had acquired

24. Robillard de Beaurepaire, *Cahiers des Etats de Normandie sous le règne de Henri IV. . .* , 2 vols. (Rouen, 1880–82), 2:164; *Cahiers des Etats de Normandie sous les règnes de Louis XIII et de Louis XIV*, 3 vols. (Rouen, 1871–78), 1:14–15, 2:164, 180.

25. AD Eure, E 2392, 8–9.

26. AD Eure, E 1216, Tabel. Pont-St-Pierre, 15 October 1506, 3 March, 20 November 1507; E 1217, 27 June 1512, act dated 1533 (*sic*).

from the baron of Pont-St-Pierre a substantial estate in exchange for only a small fixed rent.

A century later the economic and political assumptions that had made the de Rondes' fortune still prevailed: despite the experience of a century of inflation and booming markets for agricultural commodities, the barons of Pont-St-Pierre were still granting substantial properties to their local dependents. In 1625 Pierre de Roncherolles granted 25 acres to one petty nobleman in his service, 24 acres to another, again in exchange for small fixed rents: 2 s. per acre in one case, 1 s. per acre in the other.[27] Like the Crown itself, the barons of Pont-St-Pierre played a significant role in the growth of substantial domains and in the larger process by which rural property became increasingly concentrated; the creation of large properties reflected political as well as economic circumstances in the sixteenth and seventeenth centuries. The people best able to create substantial domains were those who enjoyed direct connections with political power: officials and lesser nobles who were dependent on the barons of Pont-St-Pierre; or those who, like the magistrate Jean Maignart, could secure a favorable hearing for their requests to purchase crown lands.

Both the Crown and the barons of Pont-St-Pierre were also ready to confer on these new estates the symbols of seigneurial standing: to assist, in other words, the process by which estates that had only ambiguous claims to seigneurial authority acquired it. Such complaisance toward lesser landowners persisted into the mid–seventeenth century. Thus in the 1650s the baron granted to three large landowners within the barony the right to construct dovecotes on their properties, again in exchange for modest ground rents. Such grants had little economic importance, but they were rich in symbolic meanings. For dovecotes were among the most visible manifestations of seigneurial status, and (so the *cahiers* of 1789 make clear) they were among the aspects of lordship that villagers most resented: the pigeons took a substantial toll in grain. Because of this cost, the Norman custom limited the construction of dovecotes, permitting only one in each *fief de haubert*—a limitation that the baron's grants seem to have violated. What the barons gained from these transactions, beyond a small supply of pigeons and wine, was above all loyalty from local landowners; one of the three who received this right was already the barony's farmer general, another was a bourgeois of Rouen, the third was a

27. AD S-M, Tabel. Pont-St-Pierre, 7, 21 January 1625.

Rouennais fiscal official. Landowners gained the honor that seigneurial property brought with it.[28]

The Crown too was ready to meet landowners' demands for the
trappings of seigneurial authority. The Estates of Normandy asked
in 1593 "that the creations of fiefs not take place, because of the
rights to have dovecotes and others attributed to them, because of
the damage that the neighbors of these newly erected fiefs receive
from them." Three years later they complained about "all the High
Justices that have been erected and reestablished during the last
twenty years" and asked that all be revoked. In 1629 they expressed
concern about yet another mark of seigneurial authority, the right to
hold markets: "Many have obtained from Your Majesty letters au-
thorizing the establishment in their villages of new markets; this has
ruined the commerce of the cities."[29] The church land sales of the
later sixteenth century had some of the same effects, although they
were less clearly directed to meeting demands for social status. In
Pont-St-Pierre and elsewhere in upper Normandy, a central theme
in the history of landed property over the early modern period was
the spread of the emblems of seigneurial power to estates that had
no traditional claim to them. Both the Crown and the barons of
Pont-St-Pierre contributed to the process and profited from it.

In view of these advantages and possibilities, it is not surprising
that large property expanded throughout upper Normandy; changes
within the barony of Pont-St-Pierre were typical of the region as a
whole. The evolution of twenty-six upper Norman estates can be
followed over the early seventeenth century, as seen in table 18;
these are estates for which there survive at least two feudal ac-
knowledgements (*aveux*) between 1600 and 1650, setting out their
area and character. Most of these estates belonged to the traditional
nobility. Only one was owned by a bourgeois of Rouen, only six by
royal officials. The domains of twelve of these estates remained unchanged over the seventeenth century; and one estate's domain
shrank. But the remaining thirteen estates were growing, in some
cases dramatically; in eight instances, domain areas increased by
more than 50 percent. The mean area of all estates, declining, stag-

28. AD S-M, Tabel. Pont-St-Pierre, 1652–54, 17 June 1651; 1655–59, 4 May 1657,
31 December 1658. On the significance of dovecotes, see, for instance, Jerome Blum,
The End of the Old Order in Rural Europe (Princeton, 1978), 83; Dewald, *The Formation*,
166.

29. Robillard de Beaurepaire, *Cahiers . . . règne de Henri IV*, 1:46, 118; *Cahiers . . .
règnes de Louis XIII et de Louis XIV*, 2:159–60.

TABLE 18. *The Expansion of the Estate, 1600–ca. 1650*

Type of Change	Number of Fiefs
Decline	1
No change	12
Moderate growth[a]	6
Extensive growth[b]	5
Growth from nonexistent domain	2
Total	26

SOURCE: AD S-M, 2 B 440–47, Aveux, Chambre des Comptes, Rouen.
[a] Increase of 50 percent or less in area.
[b] Increase of more than 50 percent in area.

nant, or growing, increased by just one-third between about 1600 and about 1650.

By the accession of Louis XVI, land in la Neuville was heavily concentrated in the hands of a few families, most of them Rouennais magistrates and gentlemen. During the last fifteen years of the Old Regime, however, there was a striking reversal in the evolution of property ownership. The principal landowning families divested themselves of many of their holdings, and the principal beneficiaries of their sales were local figures, in particular local *laboureurs*.

This process can be followed in detail from the register of *treizièmes*—seigneurial taxes on property transfers—that the barony's officials kept between 1768 and 1793.[30] Over the twenty years before the Revolution, there were 183 sales of land in la Neuville-Chant-d'Oisel, involving the transfer of 406,413 l. of property: at a rough estimate, about one-third of the property within the village changed hands in these years, far more than was sold during the Revolution. The pace of sales accelerated slightly over these years: there were an average of 8.1 sales each year between 1770 and 1776, 9.2 sales each year between 1777 and 1782, and 10.1 sales each year between 1783 and 1789. The price of land also increased during these years (as seen in fig. 9). The average price of arable land increased by 57 percent between 1770–76 and 1777–81; prices fell slightly in the 1780s, but overall there was a 39 percent increase between 1770–76 and 1783–89.[31] This was not a feverish land mar-

30. Pont-St-Pierre, "Recettes des treizièmes, 1769–93".
31. In calculating prices of land, I have excluded sales of land encumbered by *rentes* or rights to repurchase, and I have excluded land that was sold with houses. I have included the *vin de marché* as part of the purchase price.

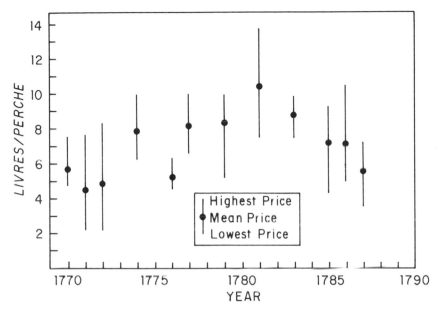

Figure 9. The price of land at la Neuville (years with at least four examples)

ket, but it was active, and over the generation between 1770 and the Revolution its impact was substantial indeed.

Land was expensive in late eighteenth century la Neuville. Plots of arable land cost on an average 942 l. per acre in the early 1770s, 1,312 l. per acre during the six years before the Revolution. This was the yearly income of many local nobles, and for rural laborers it represented several years' income. Gardens and farms might be more expensive still. These facts make the social dimensions of the late eighteenth-century land market especially striking—for despite the expense that land represented, local figures managed to buy up a large share of the property that changed hands. This was true both of land sold in substantial blocks, described in the *treizièmes* as "fermes" and analyzed in table 19, and for the mass of smaller transactions, analyzed in tables 20 and 21.

During the last generation of the Old Regime, there took place a reversal of what had been the central theme in la Neuville's early modern economic history. For 350 years, with only brief interruption, urban and aristocratic elites had taken a steadily larger share of the village's land. During the twenty years before the Revolution, this process reversed. Nobles, magistrates, and Rouennais merchants all sold large quantities of land; those who profited from

TABLE 19. *Sellers and Buyers of* Fermes, *la Neuville-Chant-d'Oisel*

Sellers' Status	Number of Sales	Value of Sales
Military nobles	5	30,288 l. (− 13.4%)
Nobles de robe	3	121,312 (= 53.5%)
Bourgeois or merchants of Rouen	3	51,600 (= 22.8%)
Unknown	3	23,600 (= 10.4%)
Total	14	226,800

Buyers' Status	Number of Purchases	Value of Purchases
Nobles de robe	1	24,000 l. (= 10.6%)
Bourgeois or merchants of Rouen	2	101,312 (= 44.7%)
Merchants of la Neuville	5	47,488 (= 20.9%)
Laboureurs	4	32,200 (= 14.2%)
Unknown residents of la Neuville	2	21,800 (= 9.6%)
Total	14	226,800

SOURCE: Pont-St-Pierre, "Recettes des treizièmes, 1769–93."

the situation were above all village merchants and farmers. These groups' success is most sharply visible in the sales of isolated plots of arable land and *masures,* the small sales that made up the vast majority of transactions (169 of 183). Members of the Old Regime's ruling groups, the military and official nobilities, sold 42 percent of this land and bought only 1 percent; Rouennais bourgeois and businessmen sold 12 percent of the total and bought 1 percent. Residents of la Neuville, in contrast, bought more than half of the land that was sold in these years and sold only 9 percent of the total. La Neuville's merchants bought 21,259 l. worth of these properties, its *laboureurs* 40,371 l.; together the two groups sold two plots of land worth in all 540 l.

Only fourteen farms were sold during the twenty years before the Revolution, but these sales accounted for 55.8 percent of the total value of what was sold; the average value of these properties was 16,200 l. These transactions are of particular importance because of the quantities of capital that they required. They are important for another reason: these concentrated properties (as will be seen in

TABLE 20. *Sellers of Other Property, la Neuville-Chant-d'Oisel*

Sellers' Status	Number of Sales	Value of Sales
Nobles	5	3,622 l.
Nobles de robe	30	72,526
Bourgeois or merchants of Rouen	23	22,200
Subtotal	58	98,348
Merchant, la Neuville	1	400
Artisans, la Neuville	6	3,822
Journaliers, la Neuville	16	6,066
Laboureurs, la Neuville	1	140
Unknown, la Neuville	10	5,636
Subtotal	34	16,064
Merchant, nearby village	1	1,050
Artisans, nearby village	2	972
Journaliers, nearby village	2	1,006
Laboureurs, nearby village	4	1,838
Unknown, nearby villages	9	14,978
Subtotal	18	19,844
Sieurs, otherwise unspecified	7	5,704
Unknown	52	39,653
Subtotal	59	45,357
Total	169	179,613

SOURCE: Pont-St-Pierre, "Recettes des treizièmes, 1769–93."

more detail below) dominated the village's agriculture and supplied much of the grain that was put on the market. Eight of these fourteen farms were sold by nobles, whether of the robe or the sword; three others were sold by Rouennais bourgeois or businessmen. Nobles purchased only one of the fourteen farms, Rouennais bourgeois two others. Eleven of the fourteen purchases went to rural merchants and *laboureurs*, most of them from la Neuville itself. These groups were not able to compete for the very largest properties that came on the market; the two farms purchased by bour-

TABLE 21. *Buyers of Other Property, la Neuville-Chant-d'Oisel*

Buyers' Status	Number of Purchases	Value of Purchases
Military nobles	1	800 l.
Nobles de robe	1	1,200
Bourgeois or merchants of Rouen	2	2,548
Subtotal	4	4,548
Merchants, la Neuville	17	21,259
Artisans, la Neuville	18	11,980
Journaliers, la Neuville	2	1,226
Jardinier, la Neuville	3	5,136
Piqueur des chemins, la Neuville	2	800
Forest guard, la Neuville	1	190
Laboureurs, la Neuville	20	40,371
Unspecified, la Neuville	21	17,077
Subtotal	84	98,039
Laboureurs, nearby villages	5	9,324
Seigneurial official, nearby village	1	212
Unspecified, nearby villages	2	4,274
Subtotal	8	13,810
Facteur des bois, prob. la Neuville	1	375
Sieurs, otherwise specified (most prob. la Neuville)	15	18,248
Unknown	57	44,593
Subtotal	73	63,216
Total	169	179,613

SOURCE: Pont-St-Pierre, "Recettes des treizièmes, 1769–93."

geois of Rouen were together worth 101,312 l., only slightly less than the total value of the eleven farms purchased by residents of la Neuville and nearby villages. Nonetheless, rural success in purchasing substantial properties is striking. It indicates an impressive accu-

TABLE 22. *Property of Ten Leading Landowners in la Neuville, 1774–1789*

Landowner	Property in 1774 (In Annual Revenue)	Purchases 1774–1789 (In Capital)	Sales 1774–1789 (In Capital)
Le S. Marquis de Vintimille	3,870 l.	0	0
La dame du Perré	3,620 l.	0	22,170 l. (887 l. revenue)[a]
Le S. des Parts	3,280 l.	0	0
Le S. Pigou, conseiller au Parlement	2,344 l.	0	80,672 l. (3,227 l. revenue)[a]
Le S. de Repainville	1,990 l.	0	20,590 l. (824 l. revenue)[a]
Madame Judde	1,560 l.	0	0
Les héritiers du S. de Noyon	1,314 l.	0	0
Le S. Beaufort, écuyer	1,118 l.	0	32,078 l. (1,283 l. revenue)[a]
Le S. Marquis de Rozey	900 l.	0	0
Le S. Etienne de Veillant, laboureur	801 l.	440 l. (17.6 l. revenue)[a]	0

SOURCE: AD S-M, C 555, Vingtièmes, la Neuville, compared with Pont-St-Pierre, "Recettes des treizièmes, 1769–93."

[a] Revenues are estimated at 4 percent of purchase price.

mulation of wealth in the late eighteenth-century countryside, and it meant a decisive shift in the balance of economic power within the village. Increasingly, the village's principal resource was under the control of a local ruling group.

Just how impressive this change was can be seen from table 22, which lists the leading landowners of la Neuville in 1774, their status, and the balance of their purchases and sales between 1774 and 1789. In the years between 1774—the date at which the *vingtièmes* provide exact estimates of landed incomes in la Neuville—and the Revolution, four of the village's ten leading landowners sold large quantities of land. Equally striking, only one of the ten bought any land at all—and he was a *laboureur*. These years witnessed a transformation of the elite that dominated property ownership within the village. This transformation, like the changes traced in Chapter 1, testifies to the growing importance of the village's merchants and large farmers in the later eighteenth century; the growing comfort of their lives coincided with their growing command of the village's land.

Like the spread of small luxuries in the countryside, the development of local property-ownership was an essentially new phenomenon in the late eighteenth century. Relatively few records survive for the inheritance divisions of la Neuville's *laboureurs,* but these (when taken together with the *terriers*) make it clear how little arable land even the village's leading farmers controlled before the late eighteenth century. Only one of the fourteen *laboureurs* whose properties table 23 summarizes could have hoped for economic independence. The rest owned only small parcels of arable land—and considerably less in the mid–eighteenth century than their predecessors of the early seventeenth century. These *laboureurs'* economic power had little to do with the control of land; it rested instead on their ownership of livestock and farm equipment and on the capital that allowed them to face the expenses—for seed, rents, and subsistence—that taking a substantial lease required. The control of land that the village merchants and *laboureurs* gained at the end of the Old Regime placed this group in full control of the means of production for the first time since the late Middle Ages.

In part this transformation must be understood in terms of changes in the French aristocracy's economic values; as Robert Forster has pointed out, at the end of the Old Regime, even prosperous aristocratic families ceased to view land as an attractive investment and preferred instead to place their funds in government bonds and other speculations.[32] For some families (as we shall see in detail in Chapter 3) choice was less important than necessity; the Beaufort family, thus, was one of several families of the *noblesse d'épée* whose debts forced them to withdraw from la Neuville after the mid–eighteenth century. But clearly the main explanation for the ability of *laboureurs* and village merchants to dominate the late eighteenth-century land market was the prosperity that these groups enjoyed, the prosperity that showed itself in the growing elegance of their lives: the larger houses, books, mirrors, and clocks that the village elite purchased after about 1750.

---

32. Robert Forster, "The Survival of the Nobility during the French Revolution," *Past and Present* 37 (July 1967): 71–86.

TABLE 23. Laboureurs' *Property*

Date Recorded	Arable Owned (acres)
1604	.78
1606	2.23
1606	17.46
1621	1.25
1625	2.00
1628	2.88
Mean holding, 1604–28 ($N = 6$)	4.43
1700	5.08
1731	4.61
1732	3.00
Mean holding, 1700–32 ($N = 3$)	4.23
1745	.31 (+"piece" of unknown area)
1746	0
1757	.25
1760	.38
1774	0
Mean holding, 1745–74 ($N = 5$)	.19 (+ "piece")

SOURCES: AD S-M, E, Tabel. Pont-St-Pierre, 1600–1607, 1 May 1604, 14 June 1606, 16 November 1606; Ibid., 1619–24, 23 May 1621; Ibid., 1625–32, 30 December 1625, 15 November 1628, 2 October 1700; AD Eure, E 1264, Tabel. Pont-St-Pierre, 23 June 1731; AD S-M, Tabel. Pont-St-Pierre, 9 December 1732; Ibid., 1745–46, 3 January 1745, 11 November 1746; Ibid., 1757, 29 July 1757; Ibid., 1760, 16 August 1760; AD Eure, E 1267, Tabel. Pont-St-Pierre, 17 April 1774.

NOTE: *Masures* have not been included in these summaries because their area usually is not specified in the inheritance divisions.

Their wealth came from several sources. Most important were opportunities that farmers and village merchants enjoyed outside agriculture because of the development of rural industry and commerce in these years. La Neuville's more prosperous residents managed from the early eighteenth century on to derive large profits from the trade in spun cotton. They served as the intermediaries between urban merchants and the poor villagers who spun the raw cotton into thread, and this was a profitable situation. There were other nonagricultural possibilities that the later eighteenth century offered to such well-off villagers. The market for wood was booming, and villagers who could mobilize the capital and horses that were needed to lease substantial sections of forest could profit from it. Tavernkeepers profited from the increasing pace of commerce and travel and perhaps also from the general buoyancy of the economy, which allowed villagers to spend more time and money in the taverns.

Such sources of prosperity were external to the agricultural economy. They reflected the ways in which the development of the eighteenth-century economy as a whole offered especially profitable opportunities for rich villagers. Villagers' prosperity probably also indirectly reflected a cultural change, the rise of literacy and of record keeping. As their probate inventories show, the region's farmers increasingly kept detailed written records; as a result they must have had a better sense than their predecessors of their economic situation—and of their rights against the landowners from whom they rented farms.

The contributions of agriculture itself to villagers' prosperity are less clear. The fundamental questions about the *laboureurs'* position in these years concern the interplay of prices and rural rents. The *laboureurs'* situation in this respect was not an easy one. They enjoyed nothing comparable to the secure tenure and stable rents of their fellows to the north in the Cambrésis.[33] In Normandy, leases were almost invariably arranged for nine years; and after a prolonged slump in rents between about 1660 and the early eighteenth century, rents began to rise. Rents can be followed on five of the principal properties of la Neuville and Pont-St-Pierre (table 24). *Laboureurs* might encounter widely differing conditions when they rented substantial properties, so these examples suggest, but all benefited from the long stagnation of rents between about 1660 and the mid–eighteenth century. In most cases, rents only began to increase significantly after 1770 or 1780, in some cases doubling by the time of the Revolution.[34] The mid–eighteenth century was a golden age for farmers in other respects. While the rents that they paid re-

---

33. Hugues Neveux, *Vie et déclin d'une structure économique: Les grains du Cambrésis (fin du XIVe–début du XVIIe siècle)* (Paris, The Hague, and New York, 1980), 329–36.

34. Rents apparently collapsed throughout France in the later seventeenth and early eighteenth centuries. See, for instance, Emmanuel Le Roy Ladurie, *Les paysans de Languedoc*, 2 vols. (Paris, 1966), 1:594–95; Pierre Goubert, *Clio parmi les hommes* (Paris, 1976), 54–62.

TABLE 24. *The Evolution of Rents, la Neuville and Pont-St-Pierre*

Property and Date of Lease	Annual Rent (l.)
Letocqué	
1651–60	750 (44 s.f.)
1661–70	600 (35 s.f.)
1683–89	600 (48 s.f.)
1685–94	600 (40 s.f.)
1762–71	850 (36 s.f.)
1768–81	900 (34 s.f.)
1771–80	900 (34 s.f.)
Cardonnay	
1521–30	*métayage*
1606–15	*métayage*
1761–70	1,000 (46 s.f.)
1770–79	1,500 (56 s.f.)
1779–88	2,500 (114 s.f.)
Le Veneur	
1719–28	800 (38 s.f.)
1742–51	900 (55 s.f.)
Bernières-Les Maisons	
1691–1700	800 (40 s.f.)
1761–70	850 (39 s.f.)
1767–79	885 (32 s.f.)
Douville-Calleville	
1730–39	709 (45 s.f.)
1739–48	650 (34 s.f.)
1748–57	650 (34 s.f.)
1761–70	850 (39 s.f.)
1772–81	1,000 (41 s.f.)
1781	1,278 (62 s.f.)
1782–90	1,350 (60 s.f.)

SOURCES: For Letocqué, AD S-M, Tabel. Pont-St-Pierre, 20 March 1651; AD Eure, H 1266, 8 July 1661; AD S-M, Tabel. Pont-St-Pierre, 22 May 1683, 29 July 1685; AD Eure, H 1266, 20 November 1760; AD S-M, Tabel. Pont-St-Pierre, 30 January 1768, 18 May 1771. For Cardonnay, AD S-M, 80 H 10. For le Veneur, AD S-M, Tabel. Pont-St-Pierre, 24 February 1720; AD S-M, Leger, notaire à Rouen, 22 May 1742. For Bernières-Les Maisons, AD S-M, Tabel. Pont-St-Pierre, 12 March 1692; Caillot, 241; AD S-M, Tabel. Pont-St-Pierre, 12 February 1767. For Douville-Calleville, Comptes, 1740ff.; Caillot, 241, 218.

NOTE: s.f. = *setiers froment*, Paris.

mained constant, toward the middle of the century grain prices entered a period of dramatic instability, rising every few years to the point of provoking popular unrest. From the mid–eighteenth century, each decade brought grain rioting to the region: in 1752 in Rouen; in 1757 in Louviers, Forges, and les Andelys; in 1768 in Rouen, Boos, Darnétal, and Gournay; in 1775 in Vernon, les Andelys, Gournay, and Gisors.[35] For the *laboureurs* and merchants who controlled the region's food supply, these years of difficulty offered windfall profits. Their situation was further helped by the development of transportation in these years, which allowed them access to a larger range of markets, and by the Crown's efforts to end restrictions on the grain trade. For five years in the mid-1760s, farmers and merchants could trade in foodstuffs as they wished, free of the careful controls that governments had previously exercised.[36] The experiment probably brought a permanent change in attitudes along with short-term profits. For several years, villagers were required to think in terms of national markets and to use the commercial techniques that such markets demanded.

After 1768, however, the *laboureurs'* situation was less favorable. Rising rents after 1770 took most of the gains that higher grain prices brought, and the Norman authorities after 1768 successfully resisted new efforts at free trade: the Parlement of Rouen refused to register Turgot's declaration of 1774 reintroducing freedom to the grain trade.[37] The profits from agriculture itself formed an insufficient basis for the *laboureurs'* successful entry in the land market during the last twenty years of the Old Regime. Cottage industry and village commerce rather than agriculture were the principal means by which leading villagers could get rich.

Examination of agricultural methods in the region of Pont-St-Pierre suggests a similar conclusion. By the mid–eighteenth century, land in the region had been concentrated in large units; leasing arrangements required that nearly all villagers produce for the market; and farmers had become prosperous. All of the conditions had been assembled, it would seem, that the Physiocrats thought necessary for agricultural progress. But in fact little progress took place.

35. Charles Desmarest, *Le commerce des grains dans la généralité de Rouen à la fin de l'ancien régime* (Paris, 1926), 86, 97, 144–47, 199–202.
36. Ibid., passim; Steven L. Kaplan, *Bread, Politics, and Political Economy in the Reign of Louis XV*, 2 vols. (The Hague, 1976), 1:90ff., 2:407–90.
37. Desmarest, *Le commerce des grains*, 197.

Assuring the area's supply of basic foodstuffs remained a preoccupation for seigneurial officials throughout the eighteenth century and for their successors during the Revolution. In 1699 there was a riot in Pont-St-Pierre when two *laboureurs* from la Neuville attempted to ship their grain "somewhere other than the ordinary market."[38] In 1768 the barony's *procureur fiscal* complained that Pont-St-Pierre's market "found itself without sufficient grain" and expressed his fear that a comparable shortage at the next week's market "might cause disturbances." The barony's sergeants were instructed to visit all of the *laboureurs* within its boundaries and order them to bring grain to the next week's market.[39] In February 1789 there were new shortages and a threat of rioting, and there were similar scenes in July of that year;[40] throughout the Revolution the food supply remained a source of anxiety.[41] The threat of hunger—ultimately, of agricultural failure—remained a reality in Pont-St-Pierre as in less advanced regions of France.

Contemporary officials, anxiously watching over the harvest and fearful of hunger's political impact, had an overwhelming sense of the complex range of factors that governed the food supply. In 1722 the subdelegate of Rouen reported to his superior about the state of the harvest: "The product of this harvest is about the same as last year's. The *laboureurs* and tithe collectors of the various cantons that I have consulted are in agreement that there are about one-fifth more sheaves than last year and that the product in grain will be about the same because it requires about one-fifth more sheaves for a bushel. . . . The grain . . . produces much more flour than last year, and in consequence more bread . . . this year's grain is very sought after in the markets, it is selling for a higher price than last year's."[42] A harvest that yielded about 20 percent more sheaves than that of the year before produced about the same amount of grain; but the grain was of higher quality than the previous year's and would produce more bread—and hence sold for higher prices. Problems of grain storage yielded equally intricate calculations. In 1771 the subdelegate of Rouen reported that the wheat "has partly

38. AD Eure, 86 B 105, Haute Justice de Pont-St-Pierre, Procédures criminelles, 22 September 1699.
39. Caillot, liasse 237, "Droits en général," 31 March 1768.
40. AD Eure, 86 B 110, 28 February, 25 July 1789.
41. See below, Chapter 7.
42. AD S-M, C 112, reports by subdelegates on harvest, art. 126, 15 September 1773. For careful analysis of this perspective on the problems of eighteenth-century agriculture, see Kaplan, *Bread, Politics, and Political Economy*, 1:1–90, passim.

sprouted, without color, and cannot be stored, which gives hope that after the seeding it may fall from the excessive price to which it has currently climbed."[43] On the eve of the following harvest, he wrote to confirm his prediction but also to point out a new problem that the situation entailed: "Although the previous year was good in grains, they have been harvested in such bad weather that it was impossible to store them, and there remains only one-tenth of a year's worth."[44] The poor conditions of the previous harvest had driven down prices in the short term, because the damp grain could not be stored for the usual length of time; but this meant that by the following June stocks had begun to run low, about two months before the next harvest. To these officials, shortage in the marketplace came at the end of complex and unpredictable chains of circumstances.[45]

Reformers, of course, viewed the matter in larger and simpler terms. For Vauban in the late seventeenth century the problem was that the land was carelessly farmed, this the result primarily of fiscal pressures on the peasantry; and he reported the view that lands in Normandy produced about one-fourth less than they might, "because of the bad cultivation of most of them."[46] A century later, Arthur Young adopted a similar viewpoint, with emphasis on the problem of fallow lands. Upper Normandy evoked his particular scorn: "Considering the fertility of the soil, which is great, Picardy and Normandy are amongst the worst cultivated countries I have seen. . . . Go from Elbeuf to Rouen, if you would view a desert."[47]

In the region around Pont-St-Pierre, crop rotations were more complicated than Young believed. But even in the mid–eighteenth century, fallows continued to occupy about one-third of the arable land. This was the conclusion of the Enquête agricole of the Year VI,[48] and it is confirmed by the example of the largest—hence presumably most efficient and heavily capitalized—farms in the region of Pont-St-Pierre. These were the farms that dominated such villages as la Neuville and to which government officials looked to assure the country's food supply. But on only one of the eight farms analyzed

43. AD S-M, C 112, art. 6, 15 September 1771.

44. Ibid., art. 47, 15 June 1772.

45. Such comments make clear the tenuous relationship between the course of agricultural prices and the history of agricultural production; prices in the market reflected a very wide range of circumstances, not simply the quantities harvested.

46. E. Coornaert, ed. *Vauban, Projet d'une dixme royale* (Paris, 1933), 40–41.

47. Arthur Young, *Travels in France*, 280, 312.

48. AD S-M, L 475: "Enquête agricole, An VI."

TABLE 25. *Fallows on Eight Farms*

Year	Tenant	Village	Total Acreage	Fallow Acreage
1746	J. Le Boucher	la Neuville	34.0	12.0 (35.2%)
1747	J.-G. Mignot	la Neuville	40.0	16.0 (40.0%)
1747	C. Boullenger	la Huguere	146.4	52.0 (35.5%)
1747	A. Poitevin	Gouy	24.9	7.6 (30.5%)
1754	J. Ravette	la Huguere	90.4	27.0 (29.9%)
1760	N. Duval	Ménil Raoult	26.0	8.0 (30.8%)
1765	P. de Pitre	Pîtres	30.3	11.0 (36.3%)
1772	G. Jamelin	Ménil Raoult	45.6	16.3 (35.7%)
Total			437.6	149.9 (34.3%)

SOURCE: AD S-M, Tabel. Pont-St-Pierre, 4 May 1746; 14 April, 18, 25 May 1747; 2 July 1754; 28 May 1760; 30 April, 6 July 1765; 1 July 1772.

in table 25 did the fallow occupy less than 30 percent of the total arable; on five more than 35 percent of the land was in fallow, and overall 34 percent of the land was in fallow.

To be sure, some elements of progress can be seen, and during the Old Regime's last twenty years these acquired considerable importance. Farmers gave their fallow land more care as the early modern period advanced. In the early seventeenth century, the nuns of Fontaine Guérard required that the tenant of their farm of Cardonnay, in la Neuville, give the fallow one plowing at the end of his lease; in a lease arranged in 1776 they required that the fallow receive two plowings.[49] By the mid–eighteenth century this was the typical but not yet universal practice on the region's large farms.[50]

There was also during these years a continuing pressure to reduce the fallows, which led to frequent infringements and occasional larger changes. Leases throughout the area typically included formulaic clauses requiring (as the nuns of Fontaine Guérard put it) that tenants cultivate "by fields and seasons (*par soldes et saisons*)," "like the neighbors who are good cultivators, without taking [the fields] out of rotation."[51] But the nuns' leases of Cardonnay show their hesitantly developing willingness to allow tenants to make use

49. AD S-M, 80 H 10: "Abbaye de Fontaine Guérard, Baux," 26 May 1606, 10 December 1776.
50. AD S-M, Tabel. Pont-St-Pierre, 2 July 1754, 30 April 1765.
51. AD S-M, Tabel. Pont-St-Pierre, 1679–89, 22 May 1683; 1761, 16 May 1761.

of the fallow. In 1521 they agreed that their tenant "may grow every year 1 acre of forage on the land that will be composted for growing wheat"; in 1587 they allowed their tenants "to plow and sow 2 acres of land at the time and season of the fallows in peas, vetch or other forage, or linen, for their sole profit, with the condition that they will restore the field to a state for growing wheat"; and in 1778 there was a provision that the tenant "may grow clover for the feeding of his livestock every year on the lands that are to be fallow, of which he nonetheless cannot plant more than 4 acres."[52] These were significant advances. The peas and vetch that were planted on the fallow in the sixteenth century and the clover introduced in the eighteenth were all nitrogen-fixing crops, which offered the possibility of improving the soil without leaving it fallow. But even in the late eighteenth century the nuns sought to limit such use of the fallow to a mere 4 acres, roughly 13 percent of the area that the fallow normally covered.[53]

What landowners feared was the spoliation of their properties by tenants whose short leases—almost invariably set for nine years—gave them little incentive to treat their farms carefully; and there were realistic grounds for fear. In 1771 a noble landowner in Romilly described a tenant's abuse of his farm. The tenant had planted the entire fallow in oats and barley; he had also failed to fertilize before planting his wheat and had turned his livestock onto the farm's meadow before the second cutting, destroying the new growth and several young trees as well.[54] In this situation, landowners saw resistance to innovation as a defense of their long-term interests. But even in this case, the outraged landowner acknowledged that "suivant l'usage du pays" some encroachment on the fallow was appropriate. He would not have objected, so he claimed, had the tenant cultivated about half of the farm's fallow: about 1 acre of oats, "some peas and vetch . . . and 3 acres of fallow" were what he viewed as a normal use of the 5.75 acres that were the farm's *solle de jachère.*[55]

Similar arguments were occurring elsewhere in the Andelle Valley in 1770s, and in some of these the tenant's position was considerably stronger. In 1771 the new owner of the barony of Pont-St-Pierre, the

52. AD S-M, 80 H 10, leases of 4 November 1521, 9 February 1587, 5 February 1778.
53. AD S-M, 80 H 8, Arpentage, ferme de Cardonnay.
54. Caillot, liasse 253, "Paroisse de Romilly, Ferme," 13 November 1771.
55. Ibid.

Rouennais magistrate Caillot de Coquéraumont, brought suit against one of his farmers; the farmer, so Caillot argued, had violated his lease by cultivating a part of the fallow. The tenant's lawyer argued that such encroachments on the fallow had become widespread in the region—that his client, in effect, had acted "suivant l'usage du pays." "In the valley of the Andelle," the lawyer claimed, "the larger part of the land is cultivated, so to speak, in two fields; that is, one plants part of the land in wheat, another part in oats, and another in peas, vetch, and fallows. It is to be observed that the part planted in peas and vetch is normally fertilized to prepare it to receive wheat the following season." Here were suggestions of the possibility of continuous cultivation, with forage crops taking the place of outright fallow. Two months after the lawyer presented these arguments, Caillot and his tenant reached a settlement that went still further toward eliminating the fallow. It was agreed that the tenant would seed one-third of the farm in wheat and one-third in oats; on the remaining third, which the tenant "was to leave fallow," Caillot "consented" that he plant 3 acres of peas, provided that he could adequately fertilize them, "and that the remainder of the said fallow the said Duval [the tenant] promises to plow twice, harrow, and plant two and one-half acres in oats, . . . and the remainder of the said fallow the said Duval can plant for his profit in oats alone, the said Duval promising to sow the clover seeds that will be given him by the said lord president de Coqueromont on the whole [field of] oats of the said farm, as also on the spring wheat that the said Duval may plant. These seeds will be sown before planting the said oats."[56] Caillot was here attempting to bring to his farm methods of continuous cultivation that had recently been publicized by Rouen's Royal Society of Agriculture,[57] but pressure to end the fallows had in fact first come from his tenant.

This agreement was not the solution that the two parties hoped for. Within two years, the tenant Duval had left the farm and Caillot had leased its main buildings to another farmer;[58] in the short term, innovation was not necessarily profitable. Nonetheless, the effort is significant for several reasons. It is one among several examples of

56. Caillot, liasse 241, "Matières diverses," 10 January 1771, factum for Pierre Duval; 17 March 1771, agreement Caillot-Duval.

57. *Délibérations et mémoires de la Société Royale d'Agriculture de la Généralité de Rouen*, 2 vols. (Rouen, 1763–67), 1:135–36.

58. Caillot, liasse 241, 1 April 1773, lease to Jean Massé.

the spread of clover in the area around Pont-St-Pierre, starting in the 1720s.[59] Clover was increasingly being planted in the area to create pasturage and as part of a system of continuous cultivation, which would eliminate fallows altogether; contemporaries entertained high hopes for the new crop.[60]

If Caillot's agreement with his tenant typified the optimism of the late eighteenth century, however, it also displayed the fundamental divergence of interests between tenant and landowner—the one seeking to maximize the profits that he could draw from the property during the nine years of his lease, the other defending his property's long-term productivity. Aristocratic landowners with an interest in improvement might supply clover seeds to their tenants in the hope of resolving the conflict between long- and short-term interests; but the initiative in this bargaining about the reduction of the fallows clearly came from the tenants.

A second divergence between owners and tenants, a divergence over investment, also affected agricultural development. Contemporaries reasoned with harsh clarity about the limited interest that either owners or tenants had in making substantial capital investments.[61] For tenants, of course, there was little interest in improving barns, mills, apple presses, or the like, since other tenants might well profit from their efforts. Especially from the seventeenth century on, landowners sought to deal with this problem by requiring of their tenants specified amounts of labor and materials to maintain their farms.[62] But this was not a complete solution, especially since buildings deteriorated rapidly in the early modern period. For mills, wrote Vauban in the late seventeenth century, "I assume that one should leave one-fourth [of yearly income] for repairs."[63] A half century later, those who supervised the collection of the *vingtièmes* at Pont-St-Pierre assumed that one-fifth of a mill's yearly revenue had to be spent to

59. AD S-M, Tabel. Pont-St-Pierre, 10 February 1724; AD Eure, 86 B 110, 26 February 1774.

60. For emphasis on progress in Norman agriculture during the eighteenth century, André Bourde, "L'agriculture à l'anglaise en Normandie au XVIIIe siècle," *Annales de Normandie* 8, no. 2 (May 1958): 215–33.

61. For the problem of investment in French agriculture, see Robert Forster, "Obstacles to Agricultural Growth in Eighteenth-Century France," *American Historical Review* 75, no. 6 (October 1970): 1600–1615. I will consider in detail the problem of investment with regard to the barony of Pont-St-Pierre below, in Chapter 6.

62. For instance, AD S-M, Tabel. Pont-St-Pierre, 21 July 1737, a lease at la Neuville requiring that the tenant use a set amount of thatch in repairing "the walls and buildings."

63. Coornaert, *Vauban, Projet,* 62.

maintain it in proper operation.[64] Tenants could not be expected to make investments of this magnitude in properties they leased for limited periods.

More surprising is the reluctance of landowners themselves to spend the money that would be needed to maintain and improve their properties. Their reluctance derived in part from an unwillingness to make an investment whose profits would have to be shared with the tenant, at least until new leases could be arranged. Gentien II Thomas worried about this problem with regard to his farm in Romilly, which he had purchased in 1625: he described in his account book his "plan to have a gate constructed at my said mills to have the livestock pass through that come to carry off the wood loaded at my said island [after the wood had floated down the Andelle]. From the said livestock I might draw a great profit (*grand proffit*) yearly. But my miller wanting to share in the booty (*buttin*) because of the interruption of his mills, I have put off making the said gate up to now."[65] Thomas's scheme would have allowed him to take full advantage of his farm's position near the Andelle by charging tolls on the transport of lumber that had been floated down the river. But his hopes of "un grand proffit" conflicted with his unwillingness to share the "buttin" with his tenant. Thomas's intensely rational calculation of his interests in the short term stood in the way of eventual long-term profits.

The colliding interests of landowners and tenants thus reduced the range of investments that either might find attractive and left as the only unambiguous opportunity for investment movable goods that the tenant might take with him at the end of his nine-year lease: livestock and farm tools. The eighteenth century brought changes in patterns of livestock ownership in the region of Pont-St-Pierre, but these (as seen in table 26) were ambiguous in their impact on agricultural production. On the one hand, the *laboureurs* of la Neuville owned more horses in the 1760s than three generations earlier. On the average each *laboureur* had four, and one-fourth of them had five or six. At the start of the eighteenth century, the average had been 3.5, and none of the *laboureurs* owned more than four. In addition, five of the twelve late eighteenth-century *laboureurs* owned donkeys. These were characteristic signs of change in the eighteenth-century

64. AD Eure, C 318, "Minute du Rôle [des vingtièmes] . . . pont st. pierre."

65. Caillot, liasse 253, "Paroisse de Romilly, Ferme," register of "Nottes des contrats. . . ." Cf. Robert Forster, *The House of Saulx-Tavanes: Versailles and Burgundy, 1700–1830* (Baltimore, 1971), 90–91.

TABLE 26. *Mean Number of* Laboureurs' *Livestock,
la Neuville-Chant-d'Oisel*

Year	N	Horses	Asses	Cows	Heifers and Calves	Sheep	Pigs	Poultry
1713–1716	6	3.5	0	4.3	2.7	88.7	4.7	3.5
1742–1751	7	3.9	0.3	3.4	1.0	59.0	6.6	19.5
1760–1771	12	4.1	0.4	4.0	0.9	37.3	3.3	30.9

SOURCE: Appendix B.

economy: the development of roads and of needs for transport, the growing care and more frequent plowings used in preparing land for cultivation. There was a second improvement from the early eighteenth century, likewise a reflection of larger changes: the development of poultry raising. Only one of the six early eighteenth-century *laboureurs* held any poultry at all, but by the mid–eighteenth century the large majority owned poultry (five of the seven *laboureurs* from the 1742–51 period, nine of the twelve from 1760 to 1771), and the size of flocks continued to grow: at least half of the *laboureurs* whose inventories were drawn up between 1760 and 1771 had more than forty birds. Presumably these flocks were raised for a growing market for inexpensive meat and eggs—a market for which the nearby pays de Bray had begun producing some years earlier.

But equally dramatic was the decline over the same years in the number of sheep that the *laboureurs* owned. There was a decline in the size of the average flock, from nearly ninety between 1713 and 1716 to fewer than forty between 1760 and 1771; and a growing number of *laboureurs* kept no sheep at all. All of the early eighteenth-century *laboureurs* had sheep, but eight of the nineteen from after 1742 had none. Their choice is especially striking because la Neuville's farmers enjoyed easy access to two of France's most active centers of woolen cloth production, Elbeuf and Louviers. Their failure to profit from this situation stemmed in fact from a larger problem. Elbeuf's woolen industry used only Spanish wools. The uneven wool of local sheep was suited only "to make mattresses," the result as much of the carelessness with which they were raised as of the breeds from which they were drawn.[66] For this reason, sheep raising

66. Jeffry Kaplow, *Elbeuf During the Revolutionary Period: History and Social Structure* (Baltimore, 1964), 25; Jean Vidalenc, "L'agriculture dans les départements de Normandie à la fin du Premier Empire," *Annales de Normandie* 7, no. 2 (May 1957): 191.

was simply not profitable. "A good farmer, who keeps track of his profits," a contemporary Norman expert reported, "expects no revenue from his flock beyond the fertilizer that he can get from it"; the cost of maintaining a flock nearly matched the income that it would bring.[67] Sheep ceased to be profitable, it seems, because the increasing efficiency of the international economy made local products uncompetitive. Woolen cloth could be made from imported wool; for less solid fabrics, there was the booming cotton cloth industry.

Farmers responded to these changes by reducing the scale of their flocks, and their response had important consequences for the rural economy. Flocks of sheep had been the principal source of fertilizer for the wheat-growing regions throughout the Parisian basin.[68] Their declining numbers posed a fundamental obstacle to efforts to reduce the fallow and replace it with forage crops. The loss was especially serious because other forms of livestock ownership did not develop to compensate for the loss of sheep raising. Particularly striking is the stagnation of the farmers' dairy herds: herds typically numbered about four cows both in the early eighteenth century and in the 1760s. This too appears to have been an essentially economic choice, a reflection of the complex development of markets for dairy products. Owning dairy cattle reached its high point of profitability in the seventeenth century, when the animals' annual worth amounted to about one-fifth of their total value. In the first sixty years of the eighteenth century, the cost of dairy cattle nearly doubled, while the rent that they could produce remained unchanged (table 27). It is thus not surprising that farmers failed to expand their herds in these years. Simply to maintain their herds required a much larger investment than had earlier been necessary.

But more than rising costs were involved. The workings of the eighteenth-century market economy also increased the difficulty of dairy farming, just as it did in the case of sheep raising. Again, it was the increasing availability of specialized products of higher quality that made success more difficult. "Every inhabitant of Normandy," began a report to Rouen's Royal Society of Agriculture, "knows the defects in the butter produced there; but few know that these defects reside far less in the quality of the milk than in the

67. *Délibérations et mémoires de la Société Royale d'Agriculture de la Généralité de Rouen*, 1:176–77.
68. Ibid., 1:177; Jean Meuvret, *Le problème des subsistances à l'époque Louis XIV: La production des céréales dans la France du XVIIe et du XVIIIe siècle*, 2 vols. (Paris and The Hague, 1977), 1:121–36.

TABLE 27. *Value and Returns of Dairy Cattle*

Year	N	Number with Value Known	Mean Value (l.)	Mean Rent (l.)	Mean Rate of Return (%)
1553	2	2	8.5	1.2	14.1
1600–1619	25	11	18.4	4.9	26.6
1620–1649	29	14	26.4	5.2	19.7
1650–1679	29	10	25.8	5.3	20.5
1689–1729	3	1	27.0	5.0	18.5
1760–1773	6	6	50.2	5.5	9.1

SOURCE: Tabel. Pont-St-Pierre.

manner of running the dairy. One district alone has this talent, and no other has been able to profit from [dairy production] in the years since it has enjoyed it." The report referred to the pays de Bray, and it described in detail the extraordinary care that farmers there took in producing their butter: their use of vaulted cellars, much like wine cellars, where the cream could be kept at even temperatures; the repeated scourings of utensils; the cleanliness of everyone who came near the cream. Without these measures, the butter would acquire a sour taste—the taste, in fact, of most butter produced elsewhere in the province.[69] These were the standards that eighteenth-century dairy production had to meet. As it had in the case of wool, the increasing efficiency of the market required farmers to produce goods of higher quality, goods that would match what was produced in such specialized centers as the pays de Bray. To do so would have required a complex range of investments: in fixed capital such as buildings but also in training workers and in the firewood and soap that constant cleaning demanded. Acquiring dairy cattle and planting meadows represented only the first steps in a much larger process.

In comparison with the obstacles to investment—deriving from the strained relations between landlords and tenants and from larger currents in the economy—the effect of communal pressures on agricultural progress was slight. Some communal practices existed in the Andelle region and occasionally vexed prosperous farmers. Within the barony of Pont-St-Pierre, the judges called together the leading *laboureurs* every July, on the eve of the harvest; with their advice a

69. *Délibérations et mémoires de la Société Royale d'Agriculture de la Généralité de Rouen*, 1:207ff.

closing date for the harvest was set, after which gleaning and pasturage on the stubble might begin.[70] Through much of the eighteenth century, substantial numbers of women from a variety of social classes took part in gleaning: there were forty in a recently harvested field in la Neuville in 1761, *fileuses de coton* and the wives and widows of both day laborers and village merchants, coming directly behind the farmer's own wagons and that of the tithe collector.[71] Farmers occasionally sought to drive out the gleaners and occasionally expressed their indignation at this limitation on their property rights. In 1761 a *laboureur* in la Neuville chased away a group of gleaners and beat one of them with a stick, shouting "that he would not accept her gleaning on a field that belonged to him" and that his livestock were about to enter the field to graze on the stubble.[72] The authorities had another objection to gleaning, that it offered the poor an alternative to working on the harvest; and thus in 1789 the barony's judges forbade "all able-bodied persons who are fit to work on the harvest to glean."[73] Farmers and seigneurial judges viewed gleaning as an irritating infringement of property rights and as a cause of labor problems, but the practice did not significantly restrict individualistic economic choices.

Nor did other common rights. Communal crop rotations had apparently not prevailed in Normandy even during the Middle Ages.[74] There did exist the right to pasture animals on the newly harvested stubble, the right of *vaine pâture*. But this right had never been so important in Normandy as in other provinces, and by the mid–eighteenth century it had lost most of its force. Norman jurists believed by the later seventeenth century that "whoever wishes to forbid access to (*défendre*) his land may enclose it," and by the mid–eighteenth century even enclosure was unnecessary to keep out others' animals. In 1766, in the midst of the Crown's effort to put into practice physiocratic principles of free trade and individualistic property rights, the *procureur général* of the Parlement of Rouen wrote to the *contrôleur général*: "I believe that the government can do nothing more suited to its views . . . than to establish throughout the kingdom the usage established in Normandy. . . . It suffices for

70. For instance, AD Eure, 86 B 67, Haute Justice de Pont-St-Pierre, Plumitifs, 23 July 1785, 25 July 1789.
71. AD Eure, 86 B 109, Haute Justice de Pont-St-Pierre, Procédures criminelles, 19 August 1761; for a similar example, ibid., 2 April 1740.
72. Ibid., 19 August 1761.
73. AD Eure, 86 B 67, Haute Justice de Pont-St-Pierre, Plumitifs, 25 July 1789.
74. Bois, *Crise du féodalisme*, 144–45.

the proprietor or tenant of a property to plant in one or two places only a few branches with strings of straw to indicate his intention of forbidding access."[75] Such individualism was obviously in the interests of most farmers and landowners, but it aroused little opposition within the larger communities—probably because the Normans had traditionally enjoyed extensive rights to graze their animals in the nearby forests.[76] The community offered scant resistance to agricultural progress.[77]

Landowning around Pont-St-Pierre underwent a twofold revolution in the early modern period. From about 1400 to about 1770, property came to be increasingly concentrated, to the benefit chiefly of a small group of urban magistrates and nobles. The land market itself worked in this direction, and so did the state and the seigneurial system. The result was the creation of a series of estates[78] within the villages near Pont-St-Pierre and the virtual elimination of significant peasant property: among the three hundred or so nonnoble households that made up mid-eighteenth-century la Neuville, probably only one owned sufficient land to feed its members. The result of this long revolution was a pervasive monetarization of the village economy: most land in la Neuville was rented out for cash rents, and virtually everyone in the village had either to farm land on this basis or to work as a wage laborer.

This was the organization of rural life on which physiocratic theorists placed their hopes for agricultural improvement. Here agriculture bore few marks of a peasant community; market stimuli touched the rural economy with full force. But by 1789 there had been only halting changes in the region's agriculture, the result not of an eighteenth-century agricultural revolution but of incremental changes since at least the sixteenth century. By 1789 some inroads had been made on the fallow, forage crops were widely planted,

75. Quoted Odile de Colombel, "La vaine pâture en Normandie," *Normannia* 11, nos. 2–3 (April–September 1938): 101, 92–93.
76. Ibid., passim. Cf. the stress on the role of *vaine pâture* in inhibiting agricultural progress in André Plaisse, *L'évolution de la structure agraire dans la campagne du Neubourg*, Cahiers des études rurales (Paris and The Hague, 1964), 2:60.
77. For further discussion of the rural community, see below, Chapter 4.
78. Cf. Jean Gallet, *La seigneurie bretonne (1450–1680): L'exemple du Vannetais* (Paris, 1983), for emphasis on the significance of this process in lower Brittany. It is important to recognize that the concentration of property in early modern Normandy still lagged far behind that in contemporary England: see Hoskins, *The Midland Peasant*, 216–17, and Margaret Spufford, *Contrasting Communities: English Villagers in the Sixteenth and Seventeenth Centuries* (Cambridge, 1974), 46–159.

and plowing had probably improved. But hunger remained a threat throughout the eighteenth century, and herds of livestock were if anything smaller at the end of the century than at the beginning.

In the Andelle Valley, it appears, the failure of the market economy to produce material progress reflected the uncertainties that surrounded investment in agriculture throughout the Old Regime. Landowners and tenant farmers had divergent interests with regard to investment; and the conflict between them meant that neither spent money on improvements in the land or the buildings on it. Tenants might still spend money on livestock, whose profits went entirely to them, but here other economic changes restricted investment. The hoped-for suppression of the fallows had to await the fertilizer that larger herds could supply.

In these circumstances, the most profitable investments for *laboureurs* and other wealthy villagers were outside agriculture altogether: they were in the cotton industry, in taking over leases of woodlands, or in other rural businesses. These ventures allowed farmers to use the resources that they controlled—especially their horses and carts—to take advantage of the most buoyant areas of the eighteenth-century economy. With agricultural production essentially stagnant, it was in these areas that possibilities for new wealth lay.

New wealth there was. Between 1770 and the Revolution, local figures—above all village merchants and *laboureurs*—dominated the land market, at the expense of those urban notables who had accumulated so much property during the previous 350 years. Doubtless they were encouraged in their purchases by the intense pressure on rents that characterized the last twenty years of the Old Regime. But they were enabled to make these investments—often involving large sums of money—by the new economic possibilities that the later eighteenth century brought to the village. The ability of village merchants and *laboureurs* to control land in the late eighteenth century formed part of the village's new relationship to the larger world.

III

THE LOCAL NOBILITY

D uring much of the Old Regime, a small community of petty nobles resided within the barony of Pont-St-Pierre. Their status and economic resources gave them a large role in local life, and their presence helped to shape both the village community and the seigneurial system. This chapter attempts to understand the conditions of their lives from two perspectives: a close examination of the histories of the families that resided within the barony itself and a broader, more statistical consideration of the upper Norman nobility as a whole.

At the start of the eighteenth century, there were four households of lesser nobles residing within the barony's limits, all of them in la Neuville-Chant-d'Oisel, in addition to the household of the baron of Pont-St-Pierre, in Pont-St-Pierre itself. Resident nobles thus made up just over 1 percent of the 347 households in the two communities. This situation was typical of the upper Norman countryside. Table 28 summarizes the relations between total population and numbers of nobles in two elections, those of Rouen and Gisors.

Rural nobles at the start of the eighteenth century were sufficiently numerous to be a real presence in the countryside around Rouen. Nearly half of the parishes in these two elections (44 percent in the election of Rouen, 51 percent in the election of Gisors) had resident nobles, and a majority of these rural nobles lived in parishes with at least two noble households. Nobles were not only a common presence in the countryside; many were also in a position to enjoy the

TABLE 28. *The Rural Nobility in 1703*

	Election of Rouen[a]	Election of Gisors
Parishes		
Total number	214	86
Number with noble households	95 (44%)	44 (51%)
1 noble household	60	25
2 noble household	23	12
3 or more noble households	12	7
Households		
Total number	17,514	7,500
Number of noble households	154 (.88%)	74 (.99%)

SOURCES: AD S-M, C 311, Capitation de la noblesse, élection de Rouen, élection de Gisors, 1703; Jacques Dupâquier, *Statistiques démographiques du bassin parisien, 1636–1720* (Paris, 1977), 515–17, 556–57.

[a] Including the banlieue but not the city or faubourgs of Rouen.

support within their communities of other members of their order. Even in the early eighteenth century, a majority of the region's noble households were to be found in its principal city, Rouen; there were 272 noble households in the regional capital in addition to about 160 families of high royal officials. Nonetheless, the rural nobility in 1703 remained a large and broadly distributed group.

The Roncherolles, the owners of the barony of Pont-St-Pierre until the later eighteenth century, were a family that had been notable in the region since about 1400. An eighteenth-century genealogist traced their descent from Frederick Barbarossa and described them as "incontestably" an important family since 800.[1] But the other noble families that resided within the barony were of recent origins, and their attachments to the area around Pont-St-Pierre were more recent still. The Landault family traced its nobility to 1582, but even in the early eighteenth century its claim to noble status was uncertain; in 1715 it had to defend its status against an attempt to make it pay the *franc-fief*, the tax imposed on commoners who acquired feudal properties. The Landaults only appeared in la Neuville in 1676, when a marriage with a Rouennaise brought the family a farm there; before then they had resided in Poitou. Their

1. François-Alexandre Aubert de la Chesnaye-Desbois, *Dictionnaire de la noblesse . . .* , 15 vols. (Paris, 1770–86), 12:288.

move to Normandy coincided with a dramatic improvement in the family's fortunes. In 1635 Charles Landault had complained to the seneschal of Poitiers "that his small revenue prevents him from being able to serve the king in the feudal host (*ban et arrière ban*) as he would wish, since he does not possess any fief or noble domain but only a small farm (*métairie roturière*) . . . whose revenue is about 15 or 20 l."[2] The Rassent family likewise traced its nobility to the late sixteenth century. Nicolas I Rassent had been doyen of the Parlement of Rouen in 1594, and his son became a president in the city's Chambre des Comptes. Nicolas I acquired the family's estate in la Neuville, but the family's regular residence there apparently began in the later seventeenth century.[3]

A third family, the Cottons, was likewise an urban family that had been ennobled in the late sixteenth century, when its members held the office of *secrétaire du roi;* but its status was cast into doubt a century later, when the intendant argued that it had lost its nobility because of the family's participation in Rouen's Protestant uprising of 1562. The family's status was only confirmed in 1669. Like the Rassents, the Cottons had acquired their property in la Neuville in the late sixteenth century. As late as 1634, however, the Cottons were members of Rouen's city council; their residence in the countryside only began in the later seventeenth century.[4] Finally, the Bigot family was probably attached to a notable Rouennais family of magistrates and bourgeois, although the connection is unclear. It had held property in la Neuville since at least the 1630s.[5]

These four families did not enjoy the advantages of either long presence in the region or immemorial noble status. All based their claims to noble status on late sixteenth-century titles; probably all were of urban origins; three of the four began their residence in the countryside sometime after 1650. Such families occupied a much more tenuous place in local society than the Roncherolles, who by the early eighteenth century had held Pont-St-Pierre for nearly three hundred years.

2. BN, Carrés d'Hozier, 369, fols. 164, 171, 172, 174, 183; Pièces Originales, 1634. On the *franc-fief* as a critical mark of noble status, J.-R. Bloch, *L'anoblissement en France au temps de François Ier* (Paris, 1934), 214.

3. BN, Carrés d'Hozier, 527, passim; Henri de Frondeville, *Les conseillers du Parlement de Normandie au seizième siècle (1499–1594)* (Paris and Rouen, 1960), 402–9.

4. BN, Pièces Originales, 874, fols. 26v–27r; AD S-M, Tabel. Pont-St-Pierre, 25 June 1655; Charles Robillard de Beaurepaire, *Cahiers des Etats de Normandie sous le règne de Henri IV . . .* , 2 vols. (Rouen, 1880–82), 2:316–19.

5. Caillot, Terrier, la Neuville-Chant-d'Oisel, ca. 1635.

But despite their recent ennoblements and their urban origins, most of these families shared membership in the *noblesse d'épée* with the barons of Pont-St-Pierre. All four of the noble families in la Neuville had served in the military, in a few cases with notable success. In 1693, for instance, Alexandre César de Rassent held the position of governor of the château of Arques, an important fortress near Dieppe; he owed the position to a cousin, who held the position of *lieutenant général des armées du roi*.[6] Such familial involvement was characteristic. The Landault family had two sons in the same regiment in the Italian campaigns of the early 1700s; one of them was killed, the other seriously wounded. Earlier their father had served "as a volunteer in the service of . . . his uncle, a captain" in another regiment, and he too had been wounded.[7] The Cottons had supplied two soldiers in the mid–seventeenth century, a *capitaine de milice* in the early eighteenth century, an infantry captain during the Seven Years' War, and another soldier who was killed "in the king's service" during the same war.[8] The Bigots were the least military of these families, but in 1721 Jean-Baptiste Bigot was *lieutenant de grenadiers*.[9]

Yet these same families were also closely bound to the world of judges and lawyers, both in Rouen and in the smaller towns of the province. All had ancestors from this milieu, and most consolidated their connections to it by marriages and by the more personal connections of friendship. The Cotton family displayed the modest level at which such ties might function. François Cotton in 1701 married the daughter of a *procureur* in the Parlement of Rouen; in the next generation, the widow of a *procureur* in the election of Pontaudemer—apparently a relative—made over all of her property to François Cotton's granddaughters, "because of the strong affection" that she held for the family; and in turn one of these granddaughters married a *procureur* in the Chambre des Comptes of Rouen.[10] The *procureurs* stood at the margins of honor-

6. BN, Carrés d'Hozier, 527, fols. 34, 36.

7. Ibid., 369, fols. 181–82. On the importance of such connections, André Corvisier, *L'armée française de la fin du XVIIe siècle au ministère de Choiseul: Le soldat*, 2 vols. (Paris, 1964), 2:750.

8. BN, Pièces Originales, 874, fols. 26–27, 19.

9. AD S-M, 2 B 443: Chambre des Comptes, Aveux: no. 35, *aveu* of 18 March 1721.

10. BN, Pièces originales, 874, fols. 26–27, 24; AD S-M, Tabel. Pont-St-Pierre, 1732, 24 March 1732. Cf. James B. Wood, *The Nobility of the Election of Bayeux, 1463–1666: Continuity through Change* (Princeton, 1980), 99–119, for emphasis on intermarriage between nobles and local officials.

able society in early modern France, and in the early sixteenth century their profession was thought to be incompatible with noble status.[11] Both the Bigots and the Landaults were allied with families of *avocats* in the Parlement of Rouen,[12] a substantially more respectable form of alliance but nonetheless distant from ideals of intermarriage within the military nobility. The mixing of military nobles with lawyers and judges, of the *noblesse d'épée* with the world of the robe, was a fundamental fact for these noble families. All of them traced their backgrounds to the city, and all had close connections to lawyers and judges—but all were military families.[13]

The early eighteenth-century fiscal rolls that list the resident nobles within these villages[14] also provide indications of their wealth and place within local society. In 1703 the Roncherolles stood at the top of a complex hierarchy of provincial nobles. The baron of Pont-St-Pierre was one of the three most heavily taxed nobles living in the election of Rouen outside the city itself; and his was one of the two noble households in the countryside around Rouen that employed as many as six servants (he employed ten). The three other noble households listed within the barony (the fourth of la Neuville's families, the Cottons, were not included in this roll) held a very different position. Each employed only one servant, this at a time when most substantial farmers in the region employed at least two. Two of the three were taxed at 20.67 l., exactly the median for the rural election of Rouen and one-nineteenth the tax levied on the baron of Pont-St-Pierre; the third was taxed at slightly below the median rate, at 18.6 l. The capitation took approximately 1 percent of nobles' in-

11. On the *procureurs'* status, see Roland Mousnier, *La vénalité des offices sous Henri IV et Louis XIII*, 2d ed. (Paris, 1971), 549–50; Bernard Guenée, *Tribunaux et gens de justice dans le bailliage de Senlis à la fin du moyen âge (vers 1380–vers 1550)* (Paris, 1963), 212, 437; Lennard Berlanstein, *The Barristers of Toulouse in the Eighteenth Century (1740–1793)* (Baltimore, 1975), 6–8, 34–39.
12. AD S-M, Tabel. Pont-St-Pierre, 1767, 28 April 1767.
13. For discussion of relations between military nobles and royal officials, see Jonathan Dewald, *The Formation of a Provincial Nobility: The Magistrates of the Parlement of Rouen, 1499–1610* (Princeton, 1980), 101–9; for the eighteenth century, Emile G. Léonard, *L'armée et ses problèmes au XVIIIe siècle* (Paris, 1958), 163–71, and David Bien, "La réaction aristocratique avant 1789: L'exemple de l'armée," *Annales ESC* 29, no. 1 (January–February 1974): 23–48, no. 2 (March–April 1974): 505–34, and "The Army in the French Enlightenment: Reform, Reaction, and Revolution," *Past and Present* 85 (November 1979): 68–98.
14. AD S-M, C 311, "Etat de repartition faitte pour la capitation de la noblesse de la ville faubourgs et élection de rouen pour lannée 1703."

Figure 10. The local nobles: A manor at la Neuville-Chant-d'Oisel (Cliché COU-CHAUX © 1981 Inventaire général/SPADEM)

comes;[15] thus the three noble households of la Neuville had incomes that hovered around 2,000 l.

What style of life could such an income support? Inventories after death suggest the modest superiority that the local nobles enjoyed over the more prosperous farmers around them. Jean-Baptiste Bigot, *écuyer*, sieur de Bolleville, was one of the three gentlemen listed as residing in la Neuville in 1703. Following his death twelve years later his house and papers were inventoried.[16] The inventory displays an impressive house, far larger than those of any of Bigot's *roturier* neighbors. (Figure 10 illustrates a similar house at la Neuville.) There were eight bedrooms, a "grande salle," and two kitchens, and there were four fireplaces, luxury indeed in la Neuville.

15. For discussions of this use of the capitation, see Jean Meyer, *La noblesse bretonne au XVIIIe siècle*, abr. ed. (Paris, 1972), 31–40, 359–60; Guy Chaussinand-Nogaret, *La noblesse au XVIIIe siècle: De la féodalité aux lumières* (Paris, 1976), 65–92. Cf. the skeptical comments of Georges Frêche, *Toulouse et la région Midi-Pyrénées au siècle des lumières (vers 1670–1789)* (Paris, 1974), 382.

16. AD S-M, Tabel. Pont-St-Pierre, 14 March 1715.

The house was clearly a center of social life, again in contrast to the situation of most residents of la Neuville: there were thirty-six chairs, and such marks of elegance as mirrors, three "paintings of various personages," and some worn wall hangings. Although he regularly resided in the countryside, Bigot also rented a room in Rouen and thus had contact with the life of the provincial capital.

Bigot's house set him sharply apart from even the most prosperous of his nonnoble neighbors, whose houses in the early eighteenth century rarely included more than three rooms.[17] But in other respects his situation was less distinctive. In his own room there were to be found only four "large books by various authors," along with a few more in the room apparently occupied by his son. His kitchen lacked culinary stylishness: there were no implements for making coffee or chocolate, and his numerous plates and cutlery— another sign of sociability—were of pewter; Bigot owned less silver than several farmers in la Neuville, only one silver cup and a silver candlestick. He had only 46 l. 10 s. in cash, and no watch or clock. Like his neighbors, Bigot used homemade linen thread; his kitchen held a spinning wheel and a comb for linen and several loops of spun thread. The notary estimated that Bigot's movables were worth in all 980 l., including livestock (he owned three horses, five cows, and two calves): this at a time when a single plow horse might cost about 200 l., a nobleman's riding horse about 800 l.[18]

Bigot's relatively modest mode of life was apparently typical of the lesser nobles in the region of the Andelle Valley. Probate inventories summarize the contents of seven other nobles' houses from the surrounding region in about 1700.[19] Only one of these households was more elaborate than Bigot's. It alone had a substantial library; the other nobles apparently had as little involvement with written culture as Bigot. Most of the nobles, like Bigot, made use of homespun cloth; indeed, Bigot's neighbor François Cotton had three spinning wheels and eighty pounds of linen and hemp waiting to be spun. Few of the nobles had elaborate tableware; only one had silverware—the rest used pewter. None had clocks or watches.

Three of these seven nobles were genuinely poverty-stricken. Anne

17. See above, Chapter 1.
18. Appendix B; Caillot, liasse 1, Registre de recette et dépense.
19. AD S-M, Tabel. Pont-St-Pierre, 22 April 1692 (Adrian Caruel); 9 April 1696 (Anne de Byard); 5 October 1696 (Alexandre de Bailleur); 3 February 1698 (Charles de Gangny); 19 November 1710 (Dominique de Gallentine); 27 April 1712 (Jean de Gonnelieu); 4 July 1737 (François de Cotton).

de Byard, who died at St-Aubin-la-Campagne in 1696, lived with his wife in two rooms; his only luxuries were a book—*The Imitation of Jesus Christ*—and a bird cage; the inventory listed a suit and a pair of leather breeches as his only clothing, and six pewter spoons and a pewter cup as his only tableware. A year later Pierre de Byard, also of St-Aubin-la-Campagne and apparently Anne's relative, complained to the lieutenant general of the bailliage that he and his family were "in a state of extreme need, unable to subsist or support their children, having no possessions."[20] Adrian Caruel of la Neuville (d. 1692) and Alexandre de Bailleur of St-Crespin-du-Bequet (d. 1696) lived in comparable circumstances: de Bailleur, despite his titles "chevallier seigneur du Mesnil Tournant" and despite his ownership of two wigs, had ony two suits, a pair of breeches, and four shirts for clothing; he owned no books, pictures, or mirrors, and his only luxuries were arms—a sword, a pair of pistols, and a broken hunting gun; his only furniture was a "little bed." Caruel likewise owned neither books nor pictures, and his clothing was limited to two suits, a coat, a hat, and "an old pair of slippers"; his only luxury was "an old broken sword." Like Pierre de Byard, Caruel's wife had vividly described her family's circumstances in a complaint to the lieutenant general, in 1683: "Because the harsh ness of the times (*la disette du temps*) has reduced her to great need, having insufficient revenue to maintain herself, the said Sr. Caruel her husband, and her whole family, the said petitioner must sell a part of her property to supply their food and maintenance, . . . to prevent their dying of hunger."[21] The miserable state of Caruel's possessions at his death nine years later indicates that this dramatic language was appropriate to the family's situation.

Such figures confronted the real possibility that their descendants would slip into the peasantry or the middle classes of the small market towns. In 1766 Martin Ricoeur, an illiterate *laboureur* at Amfreville-sous-les-Monts, described his descent from the family of "Martin Landigeoir escer"; the farmer Ricoeur's grandmother had been Landigeoir's sister and thus had been an aunt of François Cotton, one of the military nobles who resided in la Neuville-Chant-

20. AD S-M, Tabel. Pont-St-Pierre, 31 March 1697.
21. AD S-M, Tabel. Pont-St-Pierre, 1695–96, 5 November 1696, 9 April 1696; 1692, 22 April 1692; 1679–89, 17 September 1683. For debate about the reality of noble poverty, see Jean-Marie Constant, "Nobles et paysans en Beauce aux XVIe et XVIIe siècles" (Thèse d'Etat, University of Paris IV, 1978), 128–30; Wood, *The Nobility of the Election of Bayeux*, 120–55; and Jean Meyer, "Un problème mal posé: La noblesse pauvre—L'exemple breton au XVIIIe siècle," *Revue d'histoire moderne et contemporaine* 18 (April–June 1971): 161–88.

d'Oisel.[22] In 1760 there resided in Pont-St-Pierre "demoiselle Marie Catherine Le Long . . . daughter of Claude Le Long *escuyer* lord of Longpré, who was son of Samuel Le Long, *écuyer*, and of damoiselle Madeleine de Boullainvilliers, coheiress . . . of the late messire Claude de Boullainvilliers, chevalier, lord of Feugerolles, her second cousin." Marie Catherine Le Long's first cousin was married to another *écuyer*, in the nearby parish of Cormeilles. But her own husband had been the "sieur Antoine le Vavasseur, in his lifetime merchant in the bourg of Pont-St-Pierre," and her daughter was married to a "merchant and money changer residing at Pont-de-l'Arche."[23] In the countryside, the local nobility blended easily into the Third Estate of merchants and farmers.

The impoverished nobleman, whose only marks of status were the weapons symbolic of military activity and the titles "écuyer" or "chevalier," was a reality in upper Normandy at the turn of the eighteenth century. How common a reality? Not surprisingly, nobles' requests to the intendant for tax reductions suggest the frequency of such situations in the early eighteenth century. René Amand D'Avane, *écuyer*, described himself as "in great need, in no condition to pay [the capitation tax], having no servants and great difficulty to survive." Pierre Marc Le Boucher, *écuyer*, complained that he was "in no condition to pay because of the situation of his affairs, having less than 400 l. revenue yearly." The dame Duquesne described herself as "having the misfortune to be among those nobles who have no property."[24]

The capitation rolls provide a quantitative view of noble poverty in upper Normandy. In the early eighteenth century, they suggest, between one-third and one-half of the rural nobles in the region were at least close to poverty. Of 135 noble households in the rural election of Rouen, 41 percent were taxed at 9 l. or less; of seventy-four noble households in the nearby election of Gisors, 45 percent were taxed at this level.[25] This represented an income of about 800–900 l., an income that sufficed for a certain level of respectability but which for François de la Noue in the sixteenth century already de-

22. AD S-M, Tabel. Pont-St-Pierre, 20 December 1766.
23. AD S-M, Tabel. Pont-St-Pierre, 15 September 1760; 20 May, 3 June 1756; 25 May 1757.
24. AD S-M, C 410, "Capitation. Requêtes de contribuables," 2 April, 3 March, 29 November 1729.
25. AD S-M, C 311.

fined noble poverty.[26] Below even this level was a fringe of the genuinely impoverished: 8 percent of the noble households in the election of Rouen and 14 percent in the election of Gisors were assessed at less than 9 l. Such assessments represented incomes of only a few hundred livres and denoted households that were at the level of bare subsistence. Numbers of servants were a more public indication of reduced circumstances. About half of all nobles in each election employed only one servant, and many had no servants at all: 16 percent of the total in the election of Rouen, 15 percent in the election of Gisors.[27] Genuine poverty, of the kind that de Byard, Caruel, and de Bailleur represented, was exceptional among the rural nobles in the region near Rouen. But about one-tenth of the rural nobles were poor in this way, and about 40 percent had incomes that set them just above the level of poverty.

Such poverty was not new in the eighteenth century. Three generations earlier, in 1635, the feudal call-up for the bailliage of Rouen illustrated a similar degree of noble poverty within the region. Of the 113 nobles who presented themselves in response to the lieutenant general's call for service, nineteen (17 percent) were unable to supply a horse and arms for military service.[28]

Contemporaries believed that the fiscal system encouraged nobles to involve themselves in estate management. They could claim tax exemptions for farms that they cultivated themselves, whereas their tenant farmers had to pay taxes and accordingly paid lower rents.[29] Partly for this reason, nobles in the area around Pont-St-Pierre were closely involved in the daily activities of farming. The inventories after death of Jean-Baptiste Bigot and his neighbors include the full range of farm implements: Bigot owned two harrows, two plows, pitchforks, sickles, horse collars, in addition to his plow horses and dairy cows. More surprising is the fact that urban landowners such as the Gallentyne family, Rouennais magistrates who owned an estate in Romilly, seem likewise to have owned the imple-

26. François de la Noue, *Discours politiques et militaires*, ed. F. E. Sutcliffe (Geneva, 1967), 150. See also Roland Mousnier, *Les institutions de la France sous la monarchie absolue, 1598–1789*, 2 vols. (Paris, 1974–80), 1:134–35.

27. Calculated from AD S-M, C 311.

28. AD S-M, 4 BPxxx, 2, "Rôle du ban et arrière ban, bailliage de Rouen, 1635." (Note: this roll is severely damaged, and its first several pages are illegible.)

29. Edmond Esmonin, *La taille en Normandie au temps de Colbert (1661–1683)* (Paris, 1913), 225–28. Philip Hoffman is currently investigating the impact of fiscal policy on early modern French agriculture.

ments and livestock necessary for direct management of their property.[30] The sources show the Bigots in the fields directing day laborers during the harvest and even collecting manure along the road to fertilize their fruit trees.[31] When Pierre Cotton arranged with his widowed stepmother for her residence in his house in 1660, the details of farm management formed part of their agreement: the stepmother was allowed, "if I wish, to raise some cows, pigs, and poultry . . . with the provision that the manure will belong to the said lord Cotton."[32]

Nobles' requests for tax relief tell a similar story of close involvement with estate management and with the details of agricultural life. Simon Le Maistre, *écuyer*, sieur d'Ectot, complained that "he runs a farm of forty-five acres of land, which is practically all the property that he owns, and he owns no fief at all"; Adrian de Bailleul, chevalier, that "to complete his misfortunes, it has fallen to him to manage a considerable farm, . . . not having been able to find tenants because of the miseries of the times"; Jean-Baptiste Fittere du Verpray, that he had "only one farm, which he manages"; Joseph de Marolles, *escuier ordinaire du Roy*, that he was "obliged to manage his property of Ambleville, the tenant to whom he had leased it having abandoned it because he could not pay its rent." Even when they did not directly manage their properties, these complaints indicate, nobles regarded close supervision of their properties as essential to maintaining their revenues. Thus Antoine de la Motte, *écuyer*, explained to the intendant that he was "burdened with family and kept in by his gout, which absolutely prevents him from acting in his business affairs, causing him substantial losses and leaving him unable to pay his capitation tax."[33] Like all complaints about the weight of taxation, such statements need not be taken at face value. They are important not for the accuracy of the details that they present but for the assumptions that they embody and that were assumed to be legitimate and persuasive to the intendant; close involvement in the estate was one of these assumptions. Further, it was an assumption that prosperous nobles advanced as readily as the impoverished. It was not only the marginal or the

30. AD S-M, Tabel. Pont-St-Pierre, 19 November 1710, 13 February 1761.

31. AD Eure, 86 B 104, 17 September 1687, 17–31 August 1715, 9 April–26 June 1717.

32. AD S-M, Tabel. Pont-St-Pierre, 1660–66, 30 April 1661 (act signed 18 December 1660).

33. AD S-M, C 410, 411.

desperately poor nobles who were expected to follow closely the management of their properties or even to run them directly; rich nobles made similar claims.

Nobles' relations to their tenants, servants, and neighbors involved a complex mixture of mistrust and paternalism. Mistrust derived partly from the collision of owner's and tenant's economic interests, a collision that (we shall see) often led to violence. Mistrust also reflected a long tradition of doubt and resentment about the moral status of the market-oriented farmer, as someone who trafficked in a necessity of life and whose control of the food supply gave him undue power. But relations were also strained by the nobles' readiness to resort to violence in situations of all kinds and by their involvement in other forms of delinquency. In 1663 Jacob and Sandrin Rassent, *écuyers*, were incarcerated in Pont-St-Pierre for "carrying firearms, acts of violence, assaults." In 1685, Jean-Baptiste Bigot, his brother, and their servant beat up a sharecropper who had accused them of stealing his share of the harvest; the Bigots were accused of a similar theft in 1715 and again in 1717. The last episode culminated in an attempt by Bigot's son to shoot a neighbor, and the neighbor argued that these actions were "only a sequel and continuation of the crooked maneuvers and ill will of which they have not ceased to show signs for the last several years." Four years later the Bigots were again in court, this time accused of destroying the hedge between their land and that of a wealthy neighbor and of encroaching on his field.[34] In 1749 the son of Luc Lequesne, sieur de Sarcilly, a military officer who had retired to Romilly, was accused of a string of thefts from a neighbor and of then selling the stolen goods in Pont-St-Pierre. In 1764 a woman in Romilly declared that she was pregnant by the younger Lequesne, "who took advantage of her with promises of marriage." A year later Lequesne complained to the seigneurial court of Pont-St-Pierre that "none of the lawyers exercising in this jurisdiction has been willing to take the case of the sieur his son," and two months after that they were again in court, for having stolen wood.[35]

But manifestations of closeness with their neighbors also existed. One was the relationship created by godparentage. Thus when Jo-

---

34. Caillot, liasse 245, Haute Justice de Pont-St-Pierre; AD Eure, 86 B 104, Haute Justice de Pont-St-Pierre, Procédures criminelles, 17 September 1685; 106, 17 August 1715, 9 April 1717, 10 January 1722.

35. AD Eure, 86 B 108, Haute Justice de Pont-St-Pierre, Procédures criminelles, 28 July 1749; Plumitifs, 61, 3 November 1764, 10 May, 6 July 1765.

seph-Alexandre Rassent's son was baptized in la Neuville in 1747, the godfather was a "boy of the said parish," the godmother a "servant with the said lord Rassent"; two years later at the baptism of his daughter, the godfather was a "serving boy at the said lord Rassent's," the godmother a "serving girl" at the house of a relative.[36] In 1751, likewise, a girl in la Neuville was represented in a financial transaction by "madame de Beaufort her godmother residing in the said parish of la Neuville."[37] Marriage was another occasion for the display of such attachments. When a servant of Louis Bigot married in 1646, it was "with the advice, presence, and consent of the said sieur Bigot, her master."[38] Noble landowners were assumed to take a close and active interest in their tenants' lives. An episode from 1712 shows how widely this assumption permeated local life. At the market of Pont-de-l'Arche a local midwife encountered a woman from Pîtres. The midwife had begged her, so the woman later reported, "to see on her part madame de La Vallée and to tell her . . . to warn Jacques Le Tellier, her tenant farmer, to look carefully to his daughter, who was assuredly pregnant." The neighbor had performed the errand, and Madame de La Vallée immediately passed the message to Le Tellier.[39] In 1736, when the farmer of a nobleman of la Neuville came to blows with a laborer, it was the nobleman and his family who intervened; they lived next to their tenant farmer's house and had heard the altercation.[40]

For most nobles in the area around Pont-St-Pierre, such informal ties of patronage with servants and tenants were the essential component of "feudal" relations, for they held few seigneurial powers. Rolls of the *vingtièmes* in the later eighteenth century supply a picture of how lay lordships functioned at the end of the Old Regime and demonstrate the weakness of seigneurial power on even large estates in the region.[41] What follows is based on analysis of twenty-eight large lordships owned by laymen, from the years 1773–80,

36. BN, Carrés d'Hozier, 527, fols. 52, 53.
37. AD S-M, Tabel. Pont-St-Pierre, 1751, 11 October 1751.
38. AD S-M, Tabel. Pont-St-Pierre, 1641–46, 19 June 1646 (inserted after 26 April 1646).
39. AD Eure, 86 B 105, 23 July 1712.
40. Ibid., 107, 15 October 1736.
41. AD S-M, C 555, 556, 558. I have included in this analysis only those estates whose owners were described in the *vingtièmes* rolls as lords of their parishes; this procedure excludes estates whose seigneurial status was ambiguous, resting rather on their owners' pretensions than on legal realities.

TABLE 29. *Seigneurial Revenue as Percentage of Total Revenue*

Percentage of Total Income	Seigneurial Dues (Number of Estates)	Banalités (Number of Estates)
0	3	18
1–5.9	15	2
6–9.9	3	0
10–19.9	6	5
20–24.9	1	2
25 and above	0	1
Total	28	28

SOURCE: AD S-M, C 555, 556, 558.

from the cantons of Boos, Darnétal, and Maromme. This analysis throws into particular relief seigneurial sources of income, since these large estates held larger public powers and received more in seigneurial dues than their smaller neighbors. Thus the mean area of the domains—that is, the land that the estate-owners controlled directly—of these twenty-eight estates was just under 300 acres, far larger than the properties in la Neuville whose development was traced in Chapter 2; the median area was just over 200 acres. Mean income was 5,965 l., median income 4,288 l.; this was about twice the total income of typical noble households in these years.

Given this overrepresentation of large estates, the relative weakness of the seigneurial system that the tax rolls display is particularly striking. As table 29 shows, seigneurial dues had relatively little importance in these twenty-eight estates. Eighteen of the twenty-eight derived less than 6 percent of their total income from seigneurial dues, and twenty-one derived less than 10 percent; only one estate derived as much as 20 percent of its income from this source. Income from seigneurial monopolies—the *banalités*—followed an essentially similar pattern. Eighteen of these estates had no mills at all, and two others received only a small share of their total income from them. On the other hand, eight of the twenty-eight estates derived a substantial share of their total income from milling monopolies, in two cases about one-fifth of the total, in a third case about one-half.

Seigneurial rights were obviously far from defunct, and on a few estates they were very important. But this was not the typical case. Table 30 sets out the total income received by the twenty-eight estates from these different sources. Overall, seigneurial revenues

TABLE 30. *Distribution of Revenues, Twenty-eight Estates*

Type of Revenue	Income Received (%)
Seigneural revenues	
Dues	9.8
Banalités	6.9
Total	16.7
Domain revenues	
Farms	44.5
Forest	22.2
Other	16.7
Total	83.3

SOURCE: AD S-M, C 555, 556, 558.

made up less than one-fifth of the total income received by these estates, domain revenues about 83 percent.

Such averages, however, conceal the enormous variations that existed among these twenty-eight estates. The barony of Préaux, for instance, included a forest that spread over 2,000 acres and counted for more than two-thirds of the estate's total income; the lordship of St-Denis-le-Thibout included no farms and derived nearly 40 percent of its value from its woods. The lordship of Salmonville-le-Léage had no forest, covered only 70 acres of farmland, and received only 20 l. yearly in seigneurial dues—but it received over half of its total income from seigneurial mills.

In fact the typical estate looked rather different from the collective portrait presented by table 30. Eleven of the twenty-eight had no forest lands at all, and on seventeen of the twenty-eight seigneurial dues and mills together provided less than 10 percent of total income; on only five of the estates did they together produce as much as one-fourth of the total. On most of the estates the majority of income came from large farms, with lesser amounts coming from rentals of houses and small plots of land or from woodlands (see table 31). Dependence on seigneurial incomes certainly existed in late eighteenth-century upper Normandy, but such dependence was exceptional even in the case of large estates.

Smaller estates relied still less on seigneurial rents and other seigneurial sources of income. The *vingtièmes* roll of la Neuville-

TABLE 31. *Farm and Seigneurial Income*

Percentage of Total Income	Farm Income (Number of Estates)	Seigneurial Income (Number of Estates)
0	1	2
1–24		
1–5	0	12
5–9	1	3
10–24	2	6
Subtotal	3	21
25–49	4	4
50–100		
50–74	5	1
75–100	15	0
Subtotal	20	1
Total	28	28

SOURCE: AD S-M, C 555, 556, 558.

Chant-d'Oisel makes no mention of seigneurial rents there in the mid–eighteenth century, although the village included at that time a half-dozen substantial estates.[42] This did not prevent estate-owners from adopting seigneurial titles. Members of the Bigot family of la Neuville regularly called themselves "sieurs de Bolleville," although Bolleville was in fact a farm of about five acres, without seigneurial rights.[43]

But ownership of seigneurial rights was only one aspect of the lesser nobles' involvement in the seigneurial system. In Pont-St-Pierre during the sixteenth and early seventeenth centuries, the lesser

42. AD S-M, C 555.
43. For example, AD Eure, E 1264, Tabel. Pont-St-Pierre, 16 January 1726; AD S-M, Pont-St-Pierre, Terrier, 1605. Cf. Jean Gallet, *La seigneurie bretonne (1450–1680): L'exemple du Vannetais* (Paris, 1983), 595–603 and passim, for similar emphasis on the contrast between "sieuries" and older fiefs; for a very different view, emphasizing the importance of seigneurial rights, see Philippe Goujard, *L'abolition de la féodalité dans le pays de Bray* (Paris, 1978), and Guy Le Marchand, "La féodalité et la Révolution française: Seigneurie et communauté paysanne (1780–1799)," *Annales historiques de la Révolution française* 252 (October–December 1980): 536–58.

nobles profited from the seigneurial system in ways that were chiefly indirect: by serving as agents and dependents of the barony of Pont-St-Pierre and other large estates rather than by exercising their own seigneurial rights. The lesser nobles' involvement with the barony's seigneurial power was not a simple matter, for they were subject to many of the same seigneurial exactions as the commoners around them. Nobles and their tenant farmers found themselves arrested by the barons' officials for violations of the *banalités*.[44] Nobles might be arrested as well for violations of the barony's forest rights.[45] In these cases and in most other civil litigation, nobles found themselves in the barons' own courts, where their judges were baronial employees.

Through the mid–seventeenth century, however, the resentments that these exactions created were balanced by the opportunities that the barony offered to the lesser nobles. Seigneurial rights belonging to the barony and other large estates offered the lesser nobles employment as well as vexations. In the 1640s and 1650s, "Louis Bigot escuier" was "receiver general of the property and seigneury of Radepont"; in 1659 he was judge in the forest court of Longbouel, belonging to the barony of Pont-St-Pierre. "Me Jacques Moysant escuier sieur de Rougement" was likewise a judge in the barony's forest jurisdiction in 1607 and 1616. In the 1630s "Louis Le Chevallier escuier sieur des Ifz" held the same office. In the early sixteenth century "me Robert La Vache escuier" had been a forest judge for the barons of Pont-St-Pierre on another estate, the nearby barony of Heuqueville; in 1630 "Jehan La Vache escuier" was "maitre d'hostel de monsieur du Pont-St-Pierre." In 1600 "Jehan de Lux, escuier, licentié es loix, advocat," was seneschal of the fief of Cormeilles, in Romilly; in the 1640s "Ysaac de Lux escuier" was a personal attendant of the dowager of Pont-St-Pierre, and in 1657 he had become *procureur fiscal* of Pont-St-Pierre's High Justice. "Vallerien le Flamen escuier sieur des margottes" had been a sergeant for the Haute Justice of Pont-St-Pierre

44. AD S-M, Tabel. Pont-St-Pierre, 7 November 1646, settlement with "Monsieur Gueroult seigneur du Manoir sur Seine"; Caillot, liasse 246, "Moulins-banalités," 17 September 1654, sentence concerning seizure of "une charge de farine . . . appartenant a Pierre Hubert fermier dudit sieur Busquet . . ."; AD Eure, 86 B 102, "Police, 1702–1789," 19 October 1697, "sentence qui confisque un cheval et un sac de farine saisis sur M. Bigot venant moudre de moulin estranger."

45. See, for instance, AD Eure, 86 B 122, Haute Justice de Pont-St-Pierre, verderie: between September 1584 and April 1587, the barony's agents arrested an *écuyer* four times for forest violations and three times arrested servants of the abbess of St. Amand.

in the first decade of the seventeenth century.[46] Members of the Sauguin family, who (according to the testimony of the residents of la Neuville) "from time immemorial have lived nobly, without any *dérogeance,*" supplied in 1553 the "seneschal des fiefz terres et seigneuries du Becquet escorchebeuf la motte et malicorne pour monseigneur monsieur le baron de heugueville et du pont sainct pierre sr desd fiefs," and in 1601 they supplied a "receiver for my lord the baron du pont St. Pierre of la Neuville."[47] In 1580, "monsr Jehan de La Faye escuier sr de Lenart licen es loix" was the *bailli* of Pont-St-Pierre's seigneurial court; and in 1589 "Jacques Blanchart escuyer" was sergeant in the forest of Longbouel.[48] Service in such specific offices overlapped with less clearly defined roles within the barons' household, such as that of "noble homme Nicollas Benard escuier sr de Freauville at present residing in the château of Logempré" in 1585 or of the anonymous "gentilhomme" whom the Roncherolles promised to send with messages to a fellow conspirator during the League of 1576.[49]

These figures derived a complex of benefits from their service to such large estates as the barony of Pont-St-Pierre. Service conferred prestige as well as material benefits. When Vallerien Le Flamen's son married the daughter of another local nobleman in 1601, the marriage took place "with the advice and consent of *hault et puissant seigneur messire* Pierre de Roncherolles, knight of the order, lord and baron of Pont-St-Pierre, and of dame Charlotte de Moy, his wife," and both the baron and his wife signed the marriage contract.[50] Probably other forms of intangible support and patronage flowed to lesser nobles who were involved in running the large lordship, forms of support that are less clearly visible in the records.

But the material rewards of serving the barony had at least equal

46. AD S-M, Tabel. Pont-St-Pierre, 30 September 1645, May 1652 (exact date illegible), 5 August 1616, 9 October 1607, 23 April 1615, 18 August 1634, 23 May 1634; AD S-M, J, Chartrier de La Rivière Bourdet, no. 2643; Comptes, 1515–16; AD S-M, Tabel. Pont-St-Pierre, 21 September 1611.

47. Caillot, liasse 253, "Paroisse de Romilly, Ferme," 13 November 1553, *aveu* of Charles de Becdelièvre; AD S-M, Tabel. Pont-St-Pierre, 1600–1606, 1616–20, 23 March 1601. Through the mid–seventeenth century the Sauguins supplied a series of "verdier pour le Roy en sa forest de Longboel" (for example, ibid., 1647–50, 1 July 1649; 1655–59, 15 November 1656).

48. AD Eure, 86 B 2, Plumitif, 1580, 9 January 1580; 121, Verderie de Longbouel.

49. AD Eure, E 1260, Tabel. Pont-St-Pierre, 1585–86, 8 February 1585; BN MS français 3329, fol. 166r.

50. AD S-M, Tabel. Pont-St-Pierre, 1600–1607, September 1601.

Figure 11. The local nobles: Hunting (Bibliothèque de l'Arsenal, MS 1191, Livre d'heures de Louis de Roncherolles, fol. 56r; phot. Bibl. nat. Paris)

importance. Salaries for serving the barony of Pont-St-Pierre remained low throughout the Old Regime. In 1515–16, the sixteen
legal officials—attorneys, judges, and sergeants—whom the baron
employed divided a total of 70 l. in salaries: 10 l. for the *bailli* of the
High Justice, 5 l. for the principal judge in the barony's forest court,
2.5 l. for each sergeant, and so on. The barons gave only their
receiver a substantial salary, of 55 l.[51] For most officials there was
some improvement by the later sixteenth century; the barony's *bailli*
now earned 25 l., each sergeant 30 l., the chief judge of the forest
court 60 l.[52] Such salaries were still very low, but officials supple-
mented them with a share of the fines that the barony's judicial
system levied; and together these revenues might form a significant
addition to the modest incomes of the minor nobles.

There remained the hope of more substantial reward, for a for-
tunate handful of the barony's officials received significant grants
of land. This was a practice (as has been seen) that the barons of
Pont-St-Pierre persisted in well into the seventeenth century. In
1625, in two separate acts, Pierre de Roncherolles, baron of Pont-
St-Pierre, made over 25 acres of land at Touffreville and 24 acres at
Pîtres—the latter a part of the barony's *domaine non fieffé*. Both
grants went to lesser nobles in the baron's service, "Jehan de La
Vache escuier son me dhostel" and "Louis Le Chevallier escuier
sieur des Ifz verdier pour mond sieur en sa forest de Longbouel."
These were not outright gifts. Each was made in exchange for a
small ground rent and with the provision that the barons could
block any alienations of the property; and in fact in 1656 most of Le
Chevallier's grant reverted to the barons, who "considering the
poverty of the said lady," Le Chevallier's widow, acquitted her of
eleven years of unpaid rents and neglected maintenance.[53]

Political uses of property persisted in Pont-St-Pierre to the eve of
the Fronde; they remained a strong bond attaching petty nobles like
Le Chevallier and La Vache to the barons of Pont-St-Pierre. By the
early eighteenth century, however, the lesser nobles' relations to
such figures as the barons of Pont-St-Pierre had decisively changed.
One cause of change was an increasingly rigorous definition of nobility itself. Service as a seigneurial official had come to seem by the

51. Comptes, 1515–16.
52. Ibid., 1570–74.
53. AD S-M, Tabel. Pont-St-Pierre, 1625–32, 7 January 1625, 21 January 1625;
1655–59, 28 March 1656.

late seventeenth century incompatible with noble status, and Colbert's investigators disqualified families from nobility for having undertaken such service.[54] By itself this would have strained relations between lesser and greater nobles, by eliminating one of the principal bonds between them. But adding to the problem were the new economic calculations that large landowners began making in these years. After the mid–seventeenth century (for reasons that will be considered below, in Part Two) they were no longer willing to grant out parcels of their domains to loyal servants. Service to the large landowner no longer carried hopes of significant profits. The barons of Pont-St-Pierre continued to reside in the countryside well into the eighteenth century, but the material conditions that once had bound them to the lesser nobles no longer prevailed.

For these reasons, by the early eighteenth century relations of the lesser nobles to the seigneurial system were under increasing strain. The principal expression of tension was the lesser nobles' effort to establish their independence from the seigneurial authority of the barony—and at the same time to establish the reality of their own estates' seigneurial standing. The Busquet family, Rouennais *parlementaires* who owned a substantial estate in la Neuville, waged a ninety-year legal struggle with the barons of Pont-St-Pierre to free their property from the barony's milling monopoly, "for the conservation of the rights of his fief and of his vassals," as one Busquet put it. The struggle had begun in the 1650s; in 1743 one of the baron's officials reopened the question by arresting one of Busquet's "vassals" for having taken her grain elsewhere for milling. Busquet himself wrote to the baron's business agent in protest and announced that although "the woman it is said has obeyed, by going to Pont-St-Pierre for her milling, I shall forbid her to continue doing so."[55] Accompanying this suit was a longstanding struggle between the Busquets and the Roncherolles over the Busquets' efforts to acquire the title "lord of la Neuville," a title that the Roncherolles claimed as part of their barony.[56] Both the abbess of St. Amand and the cathedral canons of Rouen likewise undertook protests and lawsuits seeking to free their tenants from the barony's milling monopoly.[57]

But the most spectacular effort of this sort came from the local

54. Meyer, *La noblesse bretonne*, 48.
55. Caillot, liasse 246, "Moulins-banalités," 19 July 1651, 13 June 1652, 17 September 1654; liasse "Provisoire E 153," 14 December 1743.
56.   AD Eure, E 2392, Chartrier de Pont-St-Pierre, 84.
57. Caillot, liasse 246, 19 July 1651, 26 March 1735, and following.

nobility. A judicial complaint in 1714 reported that the sieur de Rassent, one of the three nobles resident in la Neuville in the early eighteenth century, "for a long time has been contesting" the *banalité* of Pont-St-Pierre "and prevents by his authority those subject to the *banalité* from obeying it." In an effort to expand this campaign, he recently "had decided to post notices on the door of the church of the said village of la Neuville, by which he makes it known that anyone who wishes to acknowledge him as seigneur, he will exempt from the said right of *banalité* and promises that he will . . . discharge them at his own expense." Rassent's campaign against the *banalité* culminated one July evening in 1714. Two baronial officials had arrested some residents of la Neuville as they returned from having their grain milled in Rouen. The residents protested that they were not subject to Pont-St-Pierre's *banalité* and insisted that Rassent represent their rights. When the party knocked at his gate, Rassent emerged immediately, armed with two pistols and followed by two other nobles and some servants, all of them armed. Rassent's words matched his menacing appearance: "You are certainly impudent, bugger of a dog, to come onto my land armed with a gun to arrest my vassals; all right, bugger, lower your gun." The official he was addressing indicated his eagerness not to offend Rassent and his readiness to return the flour that he and his colleague had confiscated, but Rassent was not appeased. He and his henchmen beat the official, then shot him; he died instantly, and his body was left on the ground in front of Rassent's house.[58]

Momentary passions had their part in this episode; so also did the widespread acceptance of violence and intimidation as methods for settling disputes within village society.[59] But underlying Rassent's violence was a fundamental political aim, of establishing his estate's independence from the barony's overlordship and broadening his own leadership over peasant "vassals." To attract such dependents, Rassent was ready to undertake the financial and legal risks of struggle with the barony. His campaign testifies to the ambiguous relationships that prevailed in the early eighteenth century between lesser nobles and the seigneurial system. The language of vassalage and the desire for seigneurial eminence—the impulses that had been manifested in the lesser nobles' efforts to acquire dovecotes and other marks of seigneurial status—were still powerful

58. Ibid., 14 July 1714.
59. These issues are discussed below, Chapter 4.

Figure 12. The urban landowner: The château of the Asselin des Parts, la Neuville-Chant-d'Oisel (Cliché CAPPONI © 1969 Inventaire général/SPADEM)

at the death of Louis XIV. But at the same time, the bonds between lesser and wealthier nobles had apparently ceased to function. The path to seigneurial eminence now involved the local nobles in opposing the barony rather than in serving it.

An additional set of changes encouraged this disaggregation of the nobility—the nobles' progressive disengagement from local life. The rolls of the capitation show the completeness of the process within the barony of Pont-St-Pierre. The capitation of 1703 listed four noble households within the barony, one in Pont-St-Pierre and three in la Neuville. By 1757 (the next year for which there are extant rolls) there were two noble households, the Roncherolles in Pont-St-Pierre and the Cottons in la Neuville; by 1774 there was listed only the marquis de Pont-St-Pierre; and by 1788 there was not a single noble household within the five principal parishes that made up the barony.[60] The nobility's disappearance from local life was obvious to

60. AD S-M, C 311, 343, 358, 390, Capitation des nobles.

TABLE 32. *Noble Households, Elections of Rouen and Gisors*

Election	1703	1757	1788
Rouen			
Rural noble households	154	105	55
Parishes with noble households	95	74	40
Gisors			
Rural noble households	74	45	42
Parishes with noble households	44	29	25

SOURCE: AD S-M, C 311, 343, 390.

contemporaries. The inhabitants of la Neuville undertook extensive repairs of their parish church in the 1770s and early 1780s and included in the project the construction of private benches that could be rented out "to gentlemen and nobles." But in 1786 the community complained that too many such benches had been constructed. "As for gentlemen residing in the parish, there is only M. Cotton des Houssayes, who has no fief at all; MM. du Veneur et de Chant-d'Oisel, who do possess each one a fief, do not reside there. . . . Thus, these messieurs have no need at all for the benches belonging to them, which have been made for the inhabitants of the parish, who alone have a right to them."[61] By the eve of the Revolution, their complaint suggests, the residents of la Neuville perceived the nobility as essentially outside the community, with no claim to a place in its ritual life

The nobility's numerical decline within the barony of Pont-St-Pierre was typical of upper Normandy. In the area around Rouen (table 32 shows), rural nobles were only about 40 percent as numerous on the eve of the Revolution as they had been in 1703. There had been 154 households of rural nobles in 1703, but there remained only fifty-six on the eve of the Revolution. Ninety-five parishes had included at least one noble household in 1703; in 1788 there were only forty such parishes. The nobles' numerical decline was somewhat less drastic in the election of Gisors, but it was impressive there too: a decline of 43 percent in both the number of noble households and the number of parishes that included resident nobles. This was the situation that Arthur Young expected when he undertook his travels through France in the 1780s, having been told and

61. Quoted by Jules Lamy, *Histoire de la Neuville-Champ-d'Oisel* (Rouen, 1950), 42–43.

having read "that nobody but farmers and labourers in France lived in the country"; and it was a reality that he often encountered, as in his description of the countryside around Nantes: "What a miracle, that all this splendour and wealth of the cities in France should be so unconnected with the country! There are no gentle transitions from ease to comfort, from comfort to wealth. . . . The country [is] deserted, or if a gentlemen in it, you find him in some wretched hole, to save that money which is lavished with profusion in the luxuries of a capital."[62]

Young's comments suggest a plausible explanation for the rural nobles' declining numbers, the pull of urban life with its amenities and entertainments. In upper Normandy, however, the urban nobility too became less numerous over the eighteenth century. During the first half of the century, the number of noble households in Rouen declined by about one-fifth, from 272 to 211; by 1788 there was an additional decline of 12 percent, to 176.[63] The nobility's decline was certainly less striking in the provincial capital than in the countryside around it, a total decline of just over one-third in contrast to the rural nobles' decline of nearly two-thirds. The contrast meant that by 1788 the upper Norman nobility was overwhelmingly an urban group. At the time of the Revolution there were more than three times as many noble households in the city as in the election's rural parishes. But the urban nobility was declining too in these years; the city's attractions may explain some of the rural nobility's decline, but they clearly are an incomplete explanation.

Economic changes offer a second explanation for the decline of the rural nobility, for the growing preponderance of the urban nobility over the eighteenth century was matched by changes in the rural nobility's economic structure. In the countryside around Rouen, it was the very poor and the relatively wealthy nobles whose numbers declined most sharply over the eighteenth century, those whose tax assessments indicated incomes of less than 1,000 l. and of more than 15,000 l. (see table 33). In 1703 the former had constituted over 40 percent of the rural noble households in the region; by the mid-eighteenth century they were 16 percent of the total in the rural

62. Arthur Young, *Travels in France During the Years 1787, 1788, and 1789,* ed. Constantia Maxwell (Cambridge, 1950), 5, 115–16. See also Pierre Goubert, *The Ancien Régime: French Society 1600–1750,* trans. Steve Cox (New York, 1973), 136, for stress on the nobles' nearly complete disappearance from the countryside by the end of the eighteenth century.

63. AD S-M, C 311, 343, 390. These numbers do not include members of Rouen's sovereign courts.

TABLE 33. *Capitation Payments, 1703–1788*

Election and Payment	1703	1757	1788
Rouen			
Less than 10 l.	41%	16%	26%
More than 179 l.	12%	3%	2%
Gisors			
Less than 10 l.	46%	11%	17%
More than 179 l.	12%	16%	12%

SOURCE: AD S-M, C 311, 343, 390.

election of Rouen, 11 percent in the election of Gisors.[64] Their relative importance increased somewhat in the years before the Revolution, but in 1788 they remained a small minority within the order. Wealthy nobles, on the other hand, had never been numerous in the upper Norman countryside, but there had been enough of them to constitute a powerful influence on the region's rural life: in 1703 there had been one noble household paying over 100 l. in capitation for every eight rural parishes in the election of Rouen. By 1788 this group had essentially disappeared from the countryside: only 2 percent of the election's nobility paid at least 180 l. in the capitation of 1788. Farther from the city, the situation was different. The wealthy nobility remained a stable presence in the election of Gisors, increasing slightly in numbers between 1703 and 1757, declining to their previous numbers by 1788.

As a result of these changes, the typical rural nobleman in each election was richer in 1788 than in 1703. The median tax payment in the election of Gisors had risen from 18.6 l. to 52 l.; the median in the election of Rouen had risen from 20.67 l. to 26 l. But these changes had not necessarily strengthened the nobility as an order. They reflected not economic improvement but the declining numbers of the poor nobility in the countryside, a nobility apparently unable to maintain its status in the conditions of the eighteenth century.

A statistical approach to the nobility's development over the eighteenth century suggests a third important fact about the order's place in the countryside: a large number of those nobles who remained

64. Possibly some of this decline was due to inflation, to intendants raising tax assessments in response to rising prices. There are no signs, however, that capitation assessments responded in this way to changing prices; and higher as well as lower tax assessments became less frequent during these years. I have therefore not attempted to "correct" these figures for inflation.

TABLE 34. *Turnover of Noble Households in the Elections of Rouen (Banlieue Included) and Gisors*

	Rouen		Gisors	
	New Surname	Old Surname	New Surname	Old Surname
1757	62 (58%)	45 (42%)	32 (71%)	13 (29%)
1788	24 (43%)	32 (57%)	23 (55%)	19 (45%)

SOURCE: AD S-M, C 311, 343, 390.

NOTE: Old families are defined as those whose surnames are present in the previous capitation roll, whether or not in the same parish; new families are those whose names are not present in the previous role of the election. Consequently, this table may underestimate the extent of geographical mobility.

there were relatively new arrivals to the parishes they inhabited. Geographical mobility can be measured only approximately, by measuring changes in the surnames listed in the capitation rolls (table 34). Changes in surnames need not indicate geographical mobility; they may, for instance, result from properties' changing hands because of marriage. Despite its uncertainties, however, table 34 displays a striking degree of fluidity among the rural nobles. In the rural election of Rouen, well over half of the names listed in 1757 had not been present in 1703, and there was a nearly equal degree of change between 1757 and the Revolution. In the election of Gisors, the change was even more dramatic: in 1757 nearly three-fourths of the names listed were new, and more than half of those listed in 1788 had not been listed in 1757. The eighteenth-century rural nobility was not only declining in numbers. Rural nobles were also typically recent arrivals to the parishes where they resided.

This group of changes—numerical decline, changing economic configuration, and a high rate of geographical mobility—had important implications for the nobility's role in local society. It is likely that these changes reduced the nobility's standing in the countryside by weakening its attachments to village life. The effect on the order's internal solidarity, however, must have been equally important. Mobility weakened the bonds of patronage that had previously united the nobility. So also did the disappearance of the order's poorest and wealthiest strata from the countryside. The presence of wealthy nobles in the countryside had provided nuclei around which gentry communities might form; the poor nobles had needed the resources that these patronage connections offered, and they had readily accepted dependence on their wealthier neighbors. By 1788 there were few potential patrons and a much smaller reservoir of potential clients. On average the nobility was wealthier, but its structure made internal unity more problematic than it had been in 1703.

To understand both the causes of the nobility's disappearance from the countryside and its effects, it is helpful to look closely at the nobles who resided within the barony of Pont-St-Pierre at the start of the eighteenth century. All had left the region by the time of the Revolution. The wealthiest of them, the barons of Pont-St-Pierre, had departed in the 1740s, drawn by the pleasures and high politics of Paris and Versailles; in 1765 they sold the estate itself, partly to meet the enormous debts that they had accumulated.[65] The development of urban tastes and the centralization of political power had decisively changed the family's relationship to the countryside, and their successors in Pont-St-Pierre held a very different position there. The barony passed first to a family of the high *noblesse d'épée*, whose principal interests were likewise Parisian, and then to a family of wealthy Rouennais magistrates. Neither family was a regular presence in Pont-St Pierre.

For the other families who had resided within the barony at the start of the eighteenth century, however, change was more complex. The Rassent family survived to the Revolution, when two of its members were military officers; both participated in the emigration.[66] By this time the family no longer had attachments to la Neuville. Its members resided near Dieppe on a property that they had inherited from another branch of the family, and their marriage alliances attached them to that region.[67] In part the move reflected economic troubles. In 1729 the sieur de Rassent complained to the intendant about his tax assessment, "in view of the losses that his late father sustained and that have forever diminished the petitioner's property." The problem, he explained, had been his father's investments during the Law system: "The losses that his late father underwent during his lifetime have prevented the petitioner from finding an inheritance after his death according to his hopes and . . . there remains for him very little property from his succession, which he has had to divide in two, having given half to the lady his sister."[68] In

65. See below, Chapter 5.
66. Frondeville, *Les conseillers*, 402–9.
67. BN, Carrés d'Hozier, 527, fols. 48, 52–54.
68. AD S-M, C 411, Capitation, 1728.

1742, shortly after the Rassents' departure from the area, they sold their estate in la Neuville to a Rouennais magistrate. The total price was 35,000 l., but the Rassents saw little of this money; all but 3,532 l. went to pay off their debts.[69] The Rassents were pushed from the region by their miscalculations in the economic adventures of the early eighteenth century.

Comparable difficulties beset all of the other noble families that had resided within the barony at the start of the eighteenth century. Like the Rassents, the Bigots survived into the late eighteenth century: a "Bigot de Bolleville" was among the nobles from the bailliage of Rouen who selected the order's representatives to the Estates General in 1789. But the Bigots had begun to sell land in the 1720s.[70] By the 1730s their principal property in la Neuville had passed to a family of Rouennais officials, and they had left the parish.[71] The Cottons' difficulties were clearer still. Between 1767 and 1771 members of the family—now residing chiefly in the nearby parish of Amfreville—sold about 7,000 l. worth of land in sixteen separate acts; several included hopeful provisions for the family to repurchase the properties it had alienated within one or two years.[72] Of the families of local nobility that resided within the barony during the eighteenth century, only the Landaults appeared to be relatively sheltered from financial crises; but in 1766 they sold "a small farm," for the sum of 2,100 l.,[73] and in the 1780s this was followed by much more serious sales: a total of six transactions, amounting to about 31,000 l. and involving the liquidation of most of the family's property in la Neuville.[74] These examples suggest that the essential factors shaping the local nobles' new relations to the countryside in the eighteenth century were economic. All of these families survived into the late eighteenth century; their departure resulted not from demographic failure but from economic troubles. Departure from the countryside followed a long series of land sales.

69. AD S-M, E, Leger, notaire à Rouen, 22 May 1742.
70. AD S-M, 4 BP 6009, "Liste par Bailliage de Messieurs de l'ordre de la noblesse . . ."; AD Eure, E 1264, Tabel. Pont-St-Pierre, 16 January 1726.
71. AD S-M, Tabel. Pont-St-Pierre, 21 July 1737.
72. AD S-M, Tabel. Pont-St-Pierre, 28 April, 25 May 1767; 3 March, 8 May 1768; 8 April, 20 May 1769; 21 February, 7 April, 5 May, 12 May, 27 May, 2 June, 23 October, 6 December 1770.
73. AD S-M, Tabel. Pont-St-Pierre, 1764–74, 26 October 1766.
74. AD S-M, Pont-St-Pierre, "Recettes des treizièmes, 1769–93," 1769 and following.

But more than economic situations changed in the eighteenth century; the lesser nobles' values and outlooks changed as well. It is possible to gain some understanding of these changes through the extensively documented example of Jean-Baptiste Cotton des Houssayes. Cotton was born in 1727, a member of one of the noble families that resided within the barony of Pont-St-Pierre. His family derived from the Rouennais bourgeoisie, had been ennobled by royal service in the later sixteenth century, and had resided in la Neuville-Chant-d'Oisel since the later seventeenth century; already at that time the Cottons' situation had been undistinguished, and the eighteenth century—as we have seen—brought further financial troubles. In these ways (as has been argued here) the Cottons were typical of the petty nobles of the Andelle Valley and of upper Normandy as a whole. Jean-Baptiste's own life and thought, however, were far from typical. His interest to the historian lies rather in the intellectual possibilities that his career shows were open to the poor provincial nobility in the eighteenth century.

Although he was born and baptized in la Neuville and retained connections with his family there, most of Cotton's life was spent elsewhere. He studied at the Jesuit College of Rouen, then became a priest and professor of theology at the college after the Jesuits had been expelled from it. He also became a canon in the Cathedral Chapter of Rouen and a member of the provincial capital's learned society, the Académie des Palinods; only one other landowner connected with the barony of Pont-St-Pierre—a councillor in Rouen's Parlement who owned property in la Neuville—was a member of the academy.[75] Cotton was also involved in the foundation of Rouen's Society of Agriculture and was named to the Academy of Caen. Despite these attachments to local society, a combination of ill health and clerical intrigues drove him from Rouen, and his last years were spent in Paris as librarian of the Sorbonne. He died in 1783, "after long and horrible sufferings," but in possession of two priories, his canonicate, and a personal fortune of more than 100,000 l.[76]

75. On Cotton's life, M. de Couronne, "Notice biographique sur la vie et les ouvrages de M. l'abbé des Houssayes," in *Précis analytique des travaux de l'Académie Royale des Sciences, Belles-Lettres et Arts de Rouen* . . . (Rouen, 1821), 5 (1781–93): 294–96, summarized in Edouard Frère, *Manuel de bibliographie normande* . . . , 2 vols. (Rouen, 1858), 1:290; on Rouen's academy, A. Héron, *Académie des Sciences, Belles-Lettres, et Arts de Rouen: Liste générale des membres* . . . (Rouen, 1903), 27, 29, 33, passim.

76. Couronne, "Notice," p. 296.

Cotton's life thus in part illustrates the opportunities that the Church still offered at the end of the Old Regime to sons of even the poor nobility. But his life also shows the weak links that might bind such a figure to his family and to the second order from which he had come. Cotton knew well his family background; in 1766 he was able to supply the baptismal records to prove that one of his nephews "has the necessary nobility to be received" as one of the noble students in Rouen's *séminaire de Joyeuse*.[77] To the end of his life, likewise, he retained some sense of connection to la Neuville; his testament left 6,000 l. to the parish as the endowment for a rosary.[78] But in every other respect his detachment from family, parish, and order appears to have been complete. His testament offered what was apparently a carefully thought-out expression of this detachment. In the words of his close friend Couronne (a Rouennais magistrate), "because the larger part of what he possessed was the fruit of his own savings, he believed that he had the right to dispose of it following the pleasure of his sensitive and religious heart"—and thus he left his fortune entirely to the public, with no mention of family.[79] Cotton's correspondence with Couronne, which survives for the years from 1776 to 1779, made the same point: "When I have returned to my family what I received from them, and even more, when I have restored the small patrimony that I had from my fathers, the rest—the fruit of my work—will go to support literature and the poor." Otherwise he made no reference to his family.[80]

Nor does the correspondence include reference to la Neuville or to any traditional attachment to the countryside. Cotton appreciated rural life—and indeed hoped to retire to the countryside—but his appreciation was that of an urban individualist. "I confess to you," he wrote to Couronne in 1777, "that a little abbey (or at least a priory) in my native land, which would procure for me a comfortable living and a rural retreat—which has always been and is now more than ever the sum of my desires—would make me nearly as happy as I could be in this world." Such a retirement, he thought, would allow him tranquil study and friendship and enable him to perform "those efforts of a philanthropy that I would make as enlightened as possible. . . . I would like at least to bring happiness to

77. BN, Pièces Originales, 874, fols. 10 and following.
78. Couronne, "Notice," 296.
79. Ibid., 295, 296.
80. BM, MS m30, fol. 34r, 19 September 1778; Cotton repeated this point the following spring, fol. 54v, 20 April 1779.

some village."[81] Cotton's view of the countryside combined worldly hopes of sinecures with a sentimental desire for rural calm and philanthropy, but return to an ancestral home apparently was not a part of his plan. He urged his friend to retreat to the countryside as well but added that "Paris or Rouen will draw you during the winter, for during the winter the countryside is sad, and moreover study demands communication."[82]

Cotton's view of the nobility itself was similarly detached. Certainly he took his birth seriously. In the midst of bitter intrigues among the cathedral canons of Rouen, he wrote to Couronne asking, "Is it agreeable—I appeal to your heart—to find oneself every day among cowardly enemies, as base in their sentiments as in their birth?"[83] "Why have I been honest, hardworking, and wellborn," he asked Couronne, for the archbishop "has never advanced any but *gens de néant.*"[84] Cotton offered such expressions of private annoyance less often, however, than calls for social equality—at least among the hardworking and enlightened. Thus he praised a fellow member of Rouen's academy for "the reform effected in 1756 by his efforts and those of several other academicians, animated as he was by the true spirit of literature. Then was seen to disappear from the academy every shadow of aristocracy, and that precious equality that is the soul of institutions consecrated to letters, that form of legislation suited only to wise men, was irrevocably established."[85] This was far from a call for democracy. Equality was for the wise, not for everyone. But Cotton's desire to shift the bases of inequality from birth to wisdom implied detachment from aristocratic values; and this view was linked in his thought with a profound dislike of idleness, the idleness both of the nobleman and of the beggar. Work was the foundation of society, and thus begging was a serious social danger, the preserve (in Cotton's words) of "a crowd of bad citizens (*mauvais citoyens*), enemies of work, and consequently of the fatherland."[86] Conversely, he had only praise for schemes to aid "those industrious

81. Ibid., fols. 9v–10r, 3 January 1777.
82. Ibid., fol. 25v, 22 January 1778.
83. Ibid., fol. 64r, 16 July 1779.
84. Ibid., fol. 50r, 6 April 1779.
85. Abbé Cotton des Houssayes, *Eloge historique de monsieur Maillet-Du-Boul-laye* . . . (Rouen, 1770), 14–15.
86. Abbé Cotton des Houssayes, ed., *Oeuvres de M. de Chamousset* . . . , 2 vols. (Paris, 1783), 1:lvii (Cotton supplied a 140-page introduction to his edition of the works of this Parisian magistrate); see also Daniel Roche, *Le peuple de Paris: Essai sur la culture populaire au XVIIIe siècle* (Paris, 1981), 93, on Chamousset's significance.

artisans, those small-scale merchants, in general all those men, precious to the state, who live from the daily fruit of their work."[87] He saw the peasantry in similar terms: "Providence"—so he wrote in praise of a fellow cathedral canon—"caused him to be born in the first Estate in the eyes of the wise man who calculates men in terms of their usefulness, the last where frivolity and luxury are concerned. His father . . . was a farmer."[88] For Cotton, work was the essence of citizenship, and he used powerful language to express this view. "No one is ignorant of the fact that a state is all the more powerful, the more it retains men in the *productive* class and the more consideration it gives to truly useful men."[89]

Despite his origins in the petty local nobility, then, Cotton presented views of his society that were critical of the nobility's claim to eminence; and he showed little sense of rootedness in the local society and family from which he came. Such detachment had its price, and Cotton's correspondence with his friend Couronne conveys a poignant sense of his anxieties as an isolated figure, whose main social attachments were friendship and work. "It is still morning," he concluded one letter in 1779, "I have just awakened after the most dismal dreams. I dreamed in particular that I was dead. Where then for me is *The art of procuring for oneself agreeable dreams?* It is a book of hygiene, which advises sobriety. I am sober, and I have horrible dreams. . . . oh peace, peace, when will I possess you! . . . I run after you, I call to you with great cries, I pursue you with my ardent wishes, and you do not arrive. . . . ah, my friend, sensibility is a sad gift of nature. . . . I seek happiness in work, it is there more than elsewhere. Let us pin down with work the existence that escapes us: here is a verse that one could place on the sundial of college, university, academy, and other places destined for work."[90] The ethic of work was a remedy to sadness and anxiety; at the same time, aware of his anxieties, Cotton greatly admired Rousseau and complained that "a cold and formal philosophy" dominated contemporary thinking.[91]

Despite his anxieties and his complaints, Cotton was also an enthusiastic and hopeful advocate of enlightened reforms: a believer

---

87. Cotton, *Oeuvres de M. de Chamousset*, 1:xxii.

88. Abbé Cotton des Houssayes, *Eloge historique de M. l'abbé Saas, Chanoine de l'Eglise Métropolitaine de Rouen . . .* (Rouen, 1776), 1.

89. Cotton, *Oeuvres de M. de Chamousset*, 1:lxxxiv.

90. BM, MS m30, fol. 68r, 15 August 1779.

91. Cotton, *Eloge historique de monsieur Maillet-Du-Boullaye*, 20.

in social progress and in the benefits that work could ultimately bring and a believer in the role of science as the guide to reform. He expressed these enthusiasms in both private correspondence and published writings. His particular scientific interest was in botany; in Paris he was a regular visitor to the king's garden, and for the Academy of Rouen he made long extracts and reports on foreign botanical publications.[92] "I love botany," he wrote to Couronne; "it amuses me, it exercises both the mind and the body; but I love above all to consider its usefulness to humanity."[93] Some of his specific hopes emerge from his praise for the Parisian magistrate and reformer Chamousset; Chamousset's "projects of humanity, of charity, and of patriotism," as Cotton described them, all tending "to the relief of suffering and miserable humanity," included the establishment of hospitals, health insurance schemes, plans to replace venal wet-nursing with fortified cows' milk, a penny post within Paris and plans for a national post.[94] But useful knowledge for Cotton extended beyond the sphere of public health. With his friend Couronne, Cotton planned to publish a "feuille économique et littéraire de Normandie" and to establish a public library in Rouen, and he had great hopes for the effects of a public chemistry course to be established in Rouen.[95]

Cotton described himself and his fellow reformers in the language of heroic citizenship. He described Chamousset as "this virtuous citizen, full of strength and courage for the public good,"[96] and he praised a fellow member of Rouen's academy in similar terms: "He felt the immense extent of our duties and obligations toward the Fatherland. The system that has become so common, of following one's inclinations, of living for oneself, of enjoying in sweet idleness the fruits of the labors of one's fellows, appeared to him a monstrous ingratitude."[97] To Couronne he wrote, "Yes, my friend, you are certainly right, it is singularly sweet to think that some good may result from the cares that one gives oneself and that one may

---

92. BM, MS m30, fol. 18r, 29 August 1777; MS m55, "Manuscrits de l'abbé Cotton des Houssayes sur le botanique."
93. BM, MS m30, fol. 18r.
94. Cotton, *Oeuvres de M. de Chamousset*, 1:lxxvii, xxiii, xxviii, xliv, cix.
95. BM, MS m30, fol. 10v, 3 January 1777.
96. Cotton, *Oeuvres de M. de Chamousset*, 1:xxvi. For the intellectual traditions from which such concepts of citizenship and virtue developed, see J. G. A. Pocock, *The Machiavellian Moment: Florentine Political Thought and the Atlantic Republican Tradition* (Princeton, 1975).
97. Cotton, *Eloge historique de monsieur Maillet-Du-Boullaye*, 21.

live on in the hearts of his fellow citizens. That thought alone ought to console one for the troubles one undergoes, for the eternal obstacles one encounters to accomplish the smallest good."[98] The path toward progress, toward the application of scientific knowledge to society, was beset by difficulties and failures. But with the effort went a comforting sense of membership in a band of the virtuous and a rarely shaken confidence that work would in the end benefit humanity.

Cotton thus offers an example of the essentially modern mental world that the local nobility might move in at the end of the eighteenth century.[99] This was scarcely a revolutionary outlook. Cotton moved easily between his reformist concerns and the system of ecclesiastical preferment and pluralism through which he had accumulated his fortune. Reform itself might involve dependence on the high aristocracy; to launch their planned *Economic and Literary Journal of Normandy*, Cotton urged Couronne to secure the patronage of the first president of Rouen's Parlement.[100] He took for granted paternalist controls over the peasantry. When he urged Couronne to retreat to the calm of the countryside, it was with the consideration that "there you will be the father even more than the master of your vassals";[101] and he urged that the government forbid peasants to leave the countryside for the cities.[102]

In all of these ways, Cotton was fundamentally comfortable with the way the Old Regime functioned. But in other ways he seems a modern man. His language was that of the Revolution, a language of citizenship, patriotism, virtue; and although this language often served to express conservative ideas, Cotton used it to express a real belief in the benefits that science and enlightened effort might bring

98. BM, MS m30, fol. 10v, 3 January 1777.
99. For similar emphasis on the nobility's ready adaptation to enlightened thought in the eighteenth century, see, for instance, Chaussinand-Nogaret, *La noblesse au XVIIIe siècle*, 9–21, 93–117; Daniel Roche, *Le siècle des lumières en province: Académies et académiciens provinciaux, 1680–1789*, 2 vols. (Paris and The Hague, 1978), 1:197ff.; Patrice Higonnet, *Class, Ideology, and the Rights of Nobles during the French Revolution* (Oxford, 1981), 39ff. For criticism of these views, Michel Vovelle, "L'élite ou le mensonge des mots," *Annales ESC* 29, no. 1 (January–February 1974): 49–72; Philippe Goujard, " 'Féodalité' et lumières au XVIIIe siècle: L'exemple de la noblesse," *Annales historiques de la Révolution française* 227 (January–March 1977): 103–18.
100. BM, MS m30, fol. 10v, 3 January 1777.
101. Ibid., fol. 25v, 22 January 1778.
102. Cotton, *Oeuvres de M. de Chamousset*, 1:lxxxiv; Cotton's language was that of liberty, but his point was authoritarian: "ce ne seroit pas blesser la liberté, ce seroit arrêter la licence qui fait quitter arbitrairement & sans raisons suffisantes une profession utile, honnête, nécessaire."

to society. His sense of his place in society appears likewise fundamentally modern. At a deep level he was an individual, with weak attachments to family, village, or order, and with the anxious sensibility of someone who had little confidence in such sources of identity.

Jean-Baptiste Cotton was hardly typical of the petty nobles who inhabited the barony of Pont-St-Pierre in the eighteenth century. His education, his life in the priesthood,[103] his membership in Rouen's academy and in the larger, more informal band of enlightened reformers set him sharply apart from other local nobles. But his life and thought illustrate the possibilities that the local nobles confronted in the later eighteenth century, both of involvement in the currents of the Enlightenment and of withdrawal from local life. We shall see below, in examining the Roncherolles, that this dual set of possibilities touched other nobles as well.

Cotton illustrates some of the psychological dimensions of what was the central theme in the nobility's eighteenth-century history in the Andelle Valley, its withdrawal from the countryside. To the historian, the most visible aspect of this process is economic. Withdrawal from the countryside resulted from impoverishment; all four of the noble families that resided in la Neuville-Chant-d'Oisel in 1700 were in significant financial trouble in the mid–eighteenth century.

Even before their eighteenth-century troubles began, however, the local nobles' position was a difficult one. A significant minority of the upper Norman nobles lived in genuine poverty; and few enjoyed either substantial wealth or familiarity with written culture that would sharply separate them from the villagers among whom they lived. Within the barony of Pont-St-Pierre, further ambiguities characterized the local nobles. Their claims to nobility were recent, and their establishment in the village was more recent still. Although their careers were military, they retained close connections with the lesser officials and lawyers of Rouen and the smaller cities of the region, the social background from which most had come.

Most important, by the early eighteenth century their relations

---

103. On the eighteenth-century clergy's complex response to the Enlightenment's ideas and projects, see Timothy Tackett, *Priest and Parish in Eighteenth-Century France: A Social and Political Study of the Curés in a Diocese of Dauphiné, 1750–1791* (Princeton, 1977), 86–95. See also Bien, "The Army in the French Enlightenment," for comparable ambiguities in eighteenth-century nobles' thought.

with the barons of Pont-St-Pierre were under considerable strain. Until about 1650 powerful considerations bound the lesser nobles to the barony; lesser nobles had served the barons informally and in seigneurial offices, and they had received significant material rewards for their service, including substantial grants of land. These relationships ceased after the mid–seventeenth century. What remained were sources of conflict between the barony and the lesser nobles. The nobles were subject to many of the same seigneurial vexations as their neighbors; but the more fundamental source of conflict was the lesser nobles' concern to establish the seigneurial dignity of their properties and thus to establish their properties' independence from the barony's overlordship. The sharpest challenges to the region's seigneurial structure came not from the peasant community but from the lesser nobles, acting on their neighbors' behalf. Already by the early eighteenth century, this breakdown of unity indicated the nobles' weakness in the countryside. The eighteenth century brought further weakness: financial troubles, withdrawal from the countryside, and—so the example of Jean-Baptiste Cotton suggests—detachment from the nobility's traditional values and assumptions.

IV

COMMUNITY AND CONFLICT

T he population was little more than a horde of ignorant, un-
educated peasants, quite incapable of administering local affairs. 'A French parish . . . is a congeries of huts and countryfolk as
inert as their huts' ": thus Alexis de Tocqueville, quoting Turgot.[1]
" 'The little parish of Saci . . . , since it has communal lands, gov-
erns itself as a large family' ": thus Albert Soboul, quoting Restif de
la Bretonne.[2] In their choice of citations, Tocqueville and Soboul
illustrate the two poles around which interpretations of the French
rural community have gathered. For Tocqueville, the village community of the Old Regime was a hollow institution; a vigorous communal life inherited from the Middle Ages had been destroyed by centuries of monarchical government and by the inequalities inherent in
feudalism, which freed the wealthiest parishioners from the sway of
village obligations. For Soboul, on the contrary, communal life remained strong through the Revolution, in part because of the very
strength of feudalism. Common opposition to the lordship united
villagers despite widely differing economic interests. Only when the
lordship disappeared in the Revolution did the community's disintegration begin, for the destruction of their feudal enemy left villagers
to confront their internal differences.

1. *The Old Regime and the French Revolution*, trans. Stuart Gilbert (Garden City,
N.Y., 1955), 49.
2. "Problèmes de la communauté rurale (XVIIIe–XIXe siècles)," repr. in *Problèmes
paysans de la Révolution, 1789–1848* (Paris, 1983), 187.

This chapter asks how the communities of the Andelle Valley functioned. It seeks to define the bonds that held communities together, to measure their strength, to determine how they changed during the Old Regime. This requires, first, examining the daily facts of communal life as they emerge from the records of village conflicts brought before Pont-St-Pierre's seigneurial justice. I shall then consider two focal points of communal solidarity: religious life and the exercise of communal economic rights. Finally, I shall briefly consider villager's political demands and assumptions on the eve of the Revolution.

Such an inquiry yields a complex view of the rural community and its evolution. In one sense, Tocqueville's vision applies well to the Andelle Valley, for communal life there was weak and only occasionally inhibited leading villagers' economic and political choices; poorer villagers had little power to enforce their vision of economic behavior on wealthy tenant farmers or village merchants. In other ways, however, Tocqueville's vision is deeply misleading. Communal life in the region was not a decaying inheritance from the Middle Ages but in many ways a creation of the Old Regime itself; during the later seventeenth and eighteenth centuries, it acquired new coherence and strength. From a very early date, furthermore, villagers proved capable of defending their interests in the complex ways that the early modern state demanded. They made use of the law, and they turned readily and effectively to alliances with representatives of the seigneurial system. In this respect, Soboul's vision of the peasant community is misleading as well. Around Pont-St-Pierre, the interplay of communal values and seigneurial power involved alliance and mutual influence as well as opposition. At the root of village life was the careful calculation of interests; as a result, village action rarely expressed simple or traditional oppositions between lord and peasant.

In order to understand how villages functioned, it is helpful to begin by examining conflict: that is, by examining cases in which communal relations were strained or broken. The records of Pont-St-Pierre's High Justice allow one view of the qualities and dimensions of local conflict from the late seventeenth century to the eve of the Revolution.[3] The High Justice of Pont-St-Pierre decided cases from the four villages most completely under the lordship's domination—

3. What follows is based on AD Eure, 86 B 105–10, Haute Justice de Pont-St-Pierre, Procédures criminelles. The functioning of Pont-St-Pierre's High Justice is discussed in greater detail below, Chapter 6.

TABLE 35. *Kinds and Chronology of Crime*

Year	Total Cases	Percentage Excès	Percentage Other Violence	Percentage Insults	Percentage Theft
1680–1719	60	61.7	5.0	5.0	16.7
1720–1759	50	64.0	12.0	6.0	10.0
1760–1789	33	66.7	3.0	0.0	15.2
Total	143	63.6	7.0	4.2	14.0

Pont-St-Pierre, la Neuville, Romilly, and Pîtres—and occasionally from more distant communities that fell partly under the barony's power. The court and its profits belonged to the barons of Pont St-Pierre, but the barons had little part in its operations. Their interests and those of the public were represented by a salaried attorney, the *procureur fiscal;* decisions were made by a salaried judge, normally a lawyer whose fitness for the position had been approved by the Parlement of Rouen. In theory the High Justice heard all criminal cases arising within the barony's confines, and it could decide cases of all degrees of gravity. The most serious cases were brought to the court's attention by the *procureur fiscal,* acting in effect as a public prosecutor; far more often the aggrieved party brought the case to court, with the aim of gaining reparations. Appeals in criminal cases went directly to the Parlement of Rouen, and in cases of any gravity appeal was automatic.

Apparently, only a few conflicts were serious enough to produce judicial inquiries in Pont-St-Pierre: 143 criminal inquests survive for the 110 years between 1680 and 1789, only one or two cases a year for four substantial communities. Possibly these records are incomplete, but they nonetheless make it clear that crime rarely seemed serious enough to provoke villagers to resort to the public authority of the seigneurial justice. To a large degree, the communities within the barony must have regulated their conflicts without recourse to the judicial institution most readily available to them.

When residents did appear before the seigneurial court, the records suggest, it was above all to deal with matters of personal violence; the problem of crime in these communities was essentially the problem of violent disorder. Table 35 summarizes the distribution of crimes that Pont-St-Pierre's judges investigated and demonstrates that neither the quantity nor the kinds of crime changed very much over the late seventeenth and eighteenth centuries.[4] Through the eighteenth century there remained about one or two cases each year, and the large majority of these cases continued to be matters of personal violence. About two-thirds were typically what the Old Regime called "excès," that is, cases of personal assault. A smaller percentage of crimes formed a penumbra around this basic form of violence: at the more trivial side, cases of personal insult; at the more serious side, cases of rape and homicide. In contrast to what historians have suggested about other Norman jurisdictions,[5] in Pont-St-Pierre there was no visible decline in the importance of violent crime or displacement of crimes against persons by crimes against property. *Excès* formed a slightly higher percentage of the total at the end of the eighteenth century than at the start, and theft was in fact slightly less important than it had been earlier. Serious forms of violence may have become somewhat less frequent during the century before the Revolution, but the numbers of such cases are too small to permit much confidence about even this. In the main, the impression that the figures leave is one of great stability over the century before the Revolution.

Together, theft and crimes of violence made up 89 percent of the cases that Pont-St-Pierre's seigneurial jurisdiction heard. Most of the remaining cases were closely related. Thus, ten of the 143 cases centered on personal malice: slander and vandalism. One of these cases involved encroachment on a neighbor's property. Four involved violations of baronial monopolies and market regulations. And a final case involved the concealment of pregnancy, a serious offense in the Old Regime because of magistrates' fears that this might lead to infanticide.

These crimes were evenly distributed among the communities that made up the barony. As table 36 shows, there was only a weak

4. Cf. Nicole Castan, *Justice et répression en Languedoc à l'époque des lumières* (Paris, 1980), 301–5, for emphasis on the rising number of crimes perceived in some eighteenth-century jurisdictions. The data in tables 35–40 are from AD Eure, 86 B 105–10.

5. See, for instance, B. Boutelet, "Etude par sondage de la criminalité dans le bailliage de Pont-de-l'Arche (XVIIe–XVIIIe siècles)—De la violence au vol: En marche vers l'escroquerie," *Annales de Normandie* 12, no. 4 (1962): 235–62, and the summary of recent research by Emmanuel Le Roy Ladurie, in Le Roy Ladurie, Hugues Neveux, and Jean Jacquart, *Histoire de la France rurale* (Paris, 1975), 2:547ff. For criticism of this emphasis, see T. J. A. Le Goff and D. M. G. Sutherland, "The Revolution and the Rural Community in Eighteenth-Century Brittany," *Past and Present* 62 (February 1974): 108 n. 33, and Steven G. Reinhardt, "Crime and Royal Justice in *Ancien Régime* France: Modes of Analysis," *Journal of Interdisciplinary History* 13, no. 3 (Winter 1983): 437–60.

TABLE 36. *Place of Crime*

Location	Number of Criminal Cases	Percentage of Total Cases	Criminal Cases/Population[a]	Accused Reside Elsewhere
Pont-St-Pierre	33	23	.36	17 (52%)
La Neuville	57	40	.22	13 (23%)
Romilly	27	19	.37	9 (33%)
Pîtres	22	15	.13	8 (36%)
Other	4	3	—	—

[a] Population based on Feux of 1713.

relationship between crime and place. To be sure, the level of crime when compared to the population was higher in the most nearly urban communities within the lordship, Pont-St-Pierre itself and the adjoining village of Romilly, than in the larger but more agrarian communities of Pîtres and la Neuville-Chant-d'Oisel; it was in the bourg that some of the most hospitable settings for disputes were located, cabarets, the market, and the river. But the level of dispute was not dramatically higher near the center of the lordship than at its periphery. What set the bourg apart from the outlying villages was the frequency with which its crimes involved outsiders. More than half of the crimes in Pont-St-Pierre involved figures from outside the community, who found themselves in the bourg because of its administrative and commercial functions. In Romilly and Pîtres, the other river communities in the lordship, about one-third of the conflicts involved outsiders. La Neuville's conflicts were chiefly internal; fewer than one-fourth involved actions by people from outside the village.

The bourg's pattern of criminal complaints was thus exceptional. Typically, crime within the barony—either violent or in the more muted forms of slander, insult, or vandalism—consisted of conflict between neighbors. These conflicts were usually acted out in public. Of the 132 criminal cases whose setting is clear from the interrogations, only thirty-six took place in private surroundings: houses (twenty-seven instances) or courtyards or barns (nine instances). The rest occurred in public: in cabarets (twenty-eight instances), in the fields (thirty-five), in the streets (eighteen), or more rarely in the cemetery, the woods, the church, the market, or along the river. Whatever violence may have taken place in private remained private. Its victims did not turn to the baronial authorities for protection or redress.

Conflict was so often public because the disputes that it grew out of so often involved interests rather than passions. Of course, the fact that more than one-fifth of all criminal cases arose in taverns suggests the role that simple intoxication might have in such conflicts. Further, the real motives of conflict are often invisible; the lawyers who ran the High Justice seem to have attached little importance to the discovery of motives, and thus in about one-fifth of the cases of violent assault (*excès*) no clear causes are visible.[6] When motives can be seen, however, violence typically combined utilitarian calculation with passion. A group of cases from 1709 illustrates the combination. Jacques Le François had been drinking in a house in Pîtres at one o'clock in the morning; without any reason (so ran his complaint to the High Justice), the cabaret owner suddenly attempted to force him out of his place; and when he sought to retain his seat, he was assaulted by the cabaret owner's family and eventually cut by a tankard. Here were the predictable elements of a drunken quarrel, a meaningless late-night explosion. Others involved in the case brought their own version of events to the High Justice, however. The cabaret owner himself complained that Le François and some companions had in fact forced their way into the cabaret and assaulted the tenant farmer of a local landowner; when the cabaret owner intervened, he too was beaten, and later his apple trees were found to have been vandalized. The landowner brought a third and more revealing complaint. He explained that a member of the Le François family had rented his properties at Pîtres on the basis of only a "nearly immemorial" series of unwritten leases. Now he had shifted the lease to a new group of tenants, which included the cabaret owner himself. Angry at having been displaced, the original tenants had harassed their successors repeatedly, and the landowner asked that the Haute Justice protect them.[7]

Clear economic issues thus underlay the apparently pointless violence between Le François and the cabaret owner. Whatever the role of drink and passion in their quarrel, the violence between them had clear instrumental qualities; it followed a series of acts of vandalism, and it was directed to defending important economic interests. At

6. See Yves Castan, *Honnêteté et relations sociales en Languedoc (1715–1780)* (Paris, 1974), for judges' reluctance to extend their inquiries beyond the basic facts of a case.
7. AD Eure, 86 B 106, 16 August 1709 and following.

TABLE 37. *Causes of Violence*

Motives	Number of Cases	Percentage of Cases
Dispute over specific interests	46	50.5
Long-standing conflict	7	7.7
Inheritance dispute	1	1.1
Grain riot	1	1.1
Resistance to law enforcement	3	3.3
Following judicial complaints	2	2.2
Following insults or accusation	5	5.5
Religious dispute	2	2.2
Intoxication/cabaret violence (no other cause mentioned)	8	8.8
Unknown	16	17.6
Total	91	100.0

stake were fundamental questions about the freedom that property-owners enjoyed in disposing of what they owned and the ability of tenant farmers to establish rights over the properties they worked.[8]

Most of the violent assaults that the High Justice investigated shared this quality. They arose in contexts of dispute about specific and rational interests. Violence was a means of advancing those interests, whatever elements of passion or drink were also involved. Table 37 summarizes the motives that emerge in the ninety-one cases of assault that came before the High Justice in these years. Many of these disputes had no clear motives, and others resulted just from the overheated atmosphere of the cabaret or from private drinking. A few resulted from more particular causes: the efforts of a *vicaire* to enforce observance of the Sabbath, accusations of Protestantism, revenge for accusations or insults, resistance to law enforcement. But the majority of cases involved specific economic motives. In these instances, violence followed disputes about property boundaries, grazing and gleaning rights, collection of the tithe, water

8. On the importance of such rights, see, for instance, Hugues Neveux, *Vie et déclin d'une structure économique: Les grains du Cambrésis (fin du XIVe–début du XVIIe siècle)* (Paris, New York, and The Hague, 1980), 329–36.

rights, inheritance, or the rights of tenants and owners.[9] Such specific causes of dispute are too various for ready tabulation, but they shared common elements: in different ways, all derived from efforts to define and defend property rights. Indeed, even cases of theft that came before the High Justice often arose from a larger context of dispute about inheritance, boundaries, and the like; this was true in nine of the twenty instances of theft that came before the court.

Who were the villagers accused of these acts of violence? Table 38 attempts a detailed answer to this question, both for all cases of crime brought before the High Justice and for cases of *excès*. The uncertainties of such attributions of status in criminal cases are well known; in Pont-St-Pierre and elsewhere, some of those accused of crimes probably inflated their social position in the hope of impressing their judges. But prevarication was unlikely to succeed in a setting of village conflict, when victims and witnesses were neighbors. Although table 38 doubtless includes errors, then, the main impressions that it conveys are accurate. The large majority of those whose status or professions were specified and probably a slightly smaller majority of all the accused were members of a village elite. They were farmers, millers, village merchants, cabaret- and hotel-keepers, sergeants. These groups were prominent in all forms of crime, and they were especially visible in cases of violence. Violence that was brought to the attention of the authorities was not chiefly the work of marginal or impoverished groups, although occasionally such figures appear in the criminal dossiers. The accused came above all from the groups that dominated local society.

This was so partly because of the nature of the disputes that provoked violence in the villages near Pont-St-Pierre. The leading groups in local society were those most likely to find themselves embroiled in the property disputes from which so many incidents of violence developed. But equally important were these groups' assumptions about violence and about their rights within the community. One such assumption was that the young might be given violent correction by anyone whom they had offended—an assumption that readily affected the treatment of other categories of social inferiors. The youthful victims of such correction might in fact be close to

9. Cf. James B. Given, *Homicide and Society in Thirteenth-Century England* (Stanford, 1977), 193–213, for emphasis on the purposive nature of medieval violence; on the other hand, Yves Castan, *Honnêteté et relations sociales*, 156ff., argues that economic interests were often only pretexts or justifications. See also Nicole Castan, *Les criminels de Languedoc: Les exigences d'ordre et les voies du ressentiment dans une société pré-révolutionnaire* (Toulouse, 1980), 327–29, for the interplay of interests and honor in criminal cases.

TABLE 38. *Status of the Accused*

Status	All Cases	Cases of Excès
Fermier, laboureur	26	18
Receveur	1	1
Miller	10	7
Merchant	8	7
Cabaretier-hotelier	6	4
Boucher, charcutier	3	2
Garde, sergeant	6	4
Subtotal	60	43
Bonnetier	2	1
Charon	1	1
Cordonnier	2	1
Mason	1	1
Tailleur	1	1
Tonnelier	1	—
Subtotal	8	5
Architecte	1	1
Avocat	2	1
Procureur	1	—
Bourgeois of Rouen	1	1
Ecuyer	7	3
Subtotal	12	6
Journalier, ouvrier	5	4
Vagabond	1	—
Berger	2	1
Chartier	2	2
Widow	2	1
Youth	1	1
Marinier	3	2
Domestiques, lacquais	2	2
Subtotal	18	13
Total	98	67
Unknown	54	24

adulthood. When a bourgeois of Rouen, the owner of a property in Romilly, learned that the son of a local *laboureur* had injured his dog, he beat the youth "so that he not continue to act in the same fashion in the future . . . as a form of correction"; the youth in fact was old enough to work on the road crew of the corvée.[10] In 1736 a *laboureur* in la Neuville found two cows grazing on his land and a youth of sixteen or seventeen guarding them. The *laboureur* and his servant gave the youth a beating, then took down his pants and whipped him, leaving him "for dead." Witnesses who encountered the youth shortly afterward made it clear that even at this age he was still "un pauvre petit malheureux," "un jeune garcon."[11]

Readiness to apply such correction extended to social inferiors of all ages. In this the wealthiest groups within the Third Estate were following the example of the first two orders. In 1768 the wife of a *laboureur* in la Neuville came upon the curé's horse in the middle of her oat field. As she was leading it off, the curé himself appeared, out for a walk with his niece. The curé demanded his horse; the woman replied that she would hand it over only if he accepted responsibility for the loss of her crops; and the curé thereupon flew into a violent temper, striking her and saying "you (*tu*) are a thief to say that you found my horse doing damage to your oats." The curé's niece sought to intervene, urging him, "My uncle, do not put yourself in a rage," but his response was "Je me fous d'elle."[12] Local nobles adopted a similar stance. When a son of the Bigot family sought to shoot a neighbor, his father defended him with the justification that he had been "insulted by peasants."[13]

Laboureurs and village merchants had a comparable sense of their position and rights. When a dispute over wages degenerated into a fistfight between a farmer and a day laborer in la Neuville, the farmer concluded his complaint with the pronouncement that "such an act on the part of a domestic day laborer is criminal, and there is a theft and attack (*assassinat*) on the person of his master."[14] When the crowd in Pont-St-Pierre's market complained that a grain merchant was driving up prices with his large purchases, he responded

10. AD Eure, 86 B 109, 12 October 1765.
11. Ibid., 108, 30 May 1736.
12. Ibid., 109, 18 July 1769. For an insightful reading of eighteenth-century villagers' quarrels with their priests, see Philip T. Hoffman, *Church and Community in the Diocese of Lyon, 1500–1789* (New Haven and London, 1984), 146–66.
13. AD Eure, 86 B 107, 9 April 1717. See also above, Chapter 3, for the problem of violence by the local nobility.
14. Ibid., 108, 15 October 1736.

"that he wanted it so. . . . bugger, in a week I'll have you eating it at a higher price than today."[15]

Such men expressed a similarly aggressive confidence in dealing with local authorities. A miller who had been warned that his violations of the baronial fishing monopoly would be prosecuted responded with typical disregard for local police powers "that the said plaintiff was a bugger and that he would kill him wherever he found him."[16] Another miller and his accomplice, accused of robbing passersby in la Neuville, were told by one victim that "it is not the intention of monsieur de Pont-St-Pierre that passersby be thus mistreated." The response was again characteristic: "I don't give a fuck about monsieur le marquis, and I don't care any more about him than about you, and if he himself passed by I'd stop him and his horses."[17] For the local nobility, of course, there was still less respect. A farmer of la Neuville, having accused a nobleman's son of stealing grain from his field, directed a long string of insults to the boy's father: "By God, bugger of a thief, you (*tu*) are certainly bold to have taken my wheat, you (*tu*) are a bugger of a thief." The nobleman's response that the farmer "ought to control himself and have respect for a man of quality" only elicited further profanity: "Go fuck yourself, bugger of a thief, I've no fear of you." At least to the nobleman, the social implications of the interchange were clear and important; "Such threats and insults offered by a peasant to a gentleman deserve corporal and civil punishment," concluded his complaint to the authorities.[18]

Violence within the barony of Pont-St-Pierre was thus linked to a series of assumptions and attitudes held by village elites—by curates and nobles as well as prosperous members of the Third Estate. Drink and ill temper certainly help to explain the readiness with which these groups employed violence in their quarrels. But more important was their sense of their place within local society: a sense that included disdain for public authorities and social superiors and belief in the right to discipline inferiors. The exercise of violence was an aspect of their standing and power within the community.

15. Ibid., 102, "Police, 1702–1789," 26 April 1735.
16. Ibid., 108, 18 August 1727.
17. Ibid., 106, 27 January 1708.
18. Ibid., 107, 17–31 August 1715. Cf. Olwen H. Hufton, "Attitudes Towards Authority in Eighteenth-Century Languedoc," *Social History* 3, no. 3 (October 1978): 281–302, for similar expressions of disrespect toward the nobility of southern France; more generally, see Yves Castan, *Honnêteté et relations sociales*, passim, for the pride that such statements imply.

TABLE 39. *Gender and Criminal Accusations*

	Male	Female	Both	Unknown/ Not Applicable
Accused	97 (67.8%)	5 (3.5%)	24 (16.8%)	17 (11.9%)
Victims	93 (65.0%)	23 (16.1%)	17 (11.9%)	10 (7.0%)

TABLE 40. *Victims' Status*

Victim	Number
Laboureur	24 (28.6%)
Miller	8 (9.5%)
Merchant	12 (14.3%)
Cabaretier	6 (7.1%)
Hotelier	2 (2.4%)
Ecuyer	1 (1.2%)
Sergeant	4 (4.8%)
Procureur	1 (1.2%)
Bourgeois	2 (2.4%)
Journalier	12 (14.3%)
Unknown	12 (14.3%)
Total	84 (100.1%)

The victims of crime were drawn from roughly the same leading groups within village society—although the victims included a larger mixture of the poor, the weak, and the female. Women were far more often victims than perpetrators of crime (table 39), and more victims than accused were drawn from the lower reaches of village social order (table 40). The victims included fewer *écuyers* and more *journaliers* than the accused, but the most visible groups among them were *laboureurs*, millers, and village merchants—the groups that were most prominent among the accused. The conflicts that came before the High Justice were mainly conflicts within this village elite; less often, they set this group against the poorer and less powerful villagers around them.

Against the power of the village elite, the authorities posed only a modest control. Seigneurial justice was not inaccessible to the village poor, but in fact much of what went on in the barony's villages remained impenetrable to the seigneurial apparatus. In 1710

Suzanne Vaillant and her father, a *laboureur* of la Neuville, were accused of incest and infanticide. Their crimes had been common knowledge in the village. One witness reported that "more than six months ago by common rumor (*le bruit public*) . . . she had learned that Suzanne Vaillant was pregnant and that in the beginning her father's servant had been suspected but that since then most people in the area said that it was the said Daniel Vaillant her father." Another witness made the same point: "For more than six months before her delivery, most people said that she was pregnant by her father." Most "gens du pays" might know of the situation, but not so the authorities. The curé of la Neuville heard rumors and did his best to learn the truth, but without success. Only when the Vaillants' maidservant came upon the infant's corpse did word reach the seigneurial judges. The maid spoke to the curé, and he conveyed the information to the court—by which time father and daughter had fled the region.[19] Given the authorities' inability to penetrate the community's life, there was little hope that judicial institutions might counterbalance the power of the village's wealthiest members.

Village conflict thus testified to the power and aggressiveness of a village elite of farmers, millers, and merchants. It affirmed rather than challenged village social hierarchies, and it did so in a public setting; and it made clear the scorn that farmers and merchants felt for their neighbors, whether nobles or commoners. The violence of the weak proves surprisingly infrequent in the records. There is no mention of barn burning, only a suggestion of witchcraft in the course of a case of theft, one instance of grain rioting in 1699, a second in 1789. In eighteenth- and early nineteenth-century England, the threat of violence was a means by which the laboring poor enforced respect for their needs on the well-to-do. Farmers and landowners, wrote William Cobbet in about 1830, "knew that they could not live in safety even in the *same village* with labourers, paid at the rate of 3, 4, and 5 shillings a-week";[20] and violence served to assure respect for traditional prices as well.[21] Violence apparently did not serve these functions in the villages around Pont-St-Pierre. Nor was the authority of the seigneurial structure a real counter-

---

19. AD Eure, 86 B 106, 21–31 May 1710. Cf. Le Goff and Sutherland, "The Revolution and the Rural Community," for similar emphasis on the reluctance of villagers to turn to the authorities.

20. *Rural Rides,* ed. George Woodstock (London, 1967), 48 (emphasis in original).

21. E. P. Thompson, "The Moral Economy of the English Crowd," *Past and Present* 50 (February 1971): 76–136.

weight to the village elite's power; farmers and merchants showed little respect for seigneurial officials, and a large share of what happened within the village was hidden from the officials.

What forces gave unity to the villages of the Andelle Valley? In la Neuville—which by the late seventeenth century contained two-thirds of the barony's population—some measure of fragmentation was inherent in village geography: as a *village-rue*, its houses scattered along the route des Andelys without reference to one another, their courtyards further enforcing separation, it offered few public spaces to serve as foci for communal feeling. Only a handful of houses around the parish church at the far northern end of the village formed an obvious public space, but the church was at a considerable and inconvenient distance for most villagers. In Pont-St-Pierre and the other principal villages within the barony, residential separation was less marked. There village geography had been determined by the defensive needs of the early Middle Ages and by the need to make use of water power. Houses were more closely grouped and public spaces more significant. In Pont-St-Pierre the marketplace gave an additional focus to communal life.

Other sources of unity were weak. One potential focus of village solidarity was the parish priest, but through the seventeenth century he was an uncertain presence. "For the past nine or ten years . . . ," complained the residents of la Neuville in 1653, "they have not seen any curé reside in the said parish, because it does not have the resources to maintain one: both because of the excessive pensions with which the said benefice is encumbered and because of all the tithes that the lords abbots of Lyre and St. Ouen take in the the said parish."[22] This situation had clearly improved by the eighteenth century, as reform movements created a new seriousness among the parish clergy, but reform brought its own problems. In 1730 the residents of la Neuville had a new complaint. The archbishop of Rouen had withdrawn the village's vicar because of accusations of Jansenism. The villagers begged that he remain with them, because he had "been there for the past four years, . . . exercising his functions to the edification of the entire parish; although it is composed of twelve hundred communicants and is very large in area, the said sieur Carrey has always done his duty perfectly well,

22. AD S-M, Tabel. Pont-St-Pierre, 1651–54, 9 March 1653.

walking day and night to minister to the sick, who have always been in his care because of the indisposition of the sieur incumbent of the said parish, and performing all the other functions of his ministry: preaching with edification, taking part in the mass, holding schools as regularly as possible."[23] The villagers themselves expressed awareness of the fragility of their bonds to one another, the result of la Neuville's large population and area. The vicar's tireless efforts had in some degree strengthened these ties, but the ecclesiastical authorities had abruptly ended his service in la Neuville.

Villagers' belief in the priest's centrality reflected his complex relationship with the community. Village priests might undertake varied roles in la Neuville, Pont-St-Pierre, and the surrounding communities. In 1558, when the commissioners from the Parlement assembled representatives of the villages around the forest of Longbouel in the course of a lawsuit over rights of usage, at least one of the communities was represented by a priest.[24] When parishioners died, the priest was normally entrusted with keys to the chest in which documents and valuables were kept.[25] More dramatic episodes, such as the discovery of a corpse in the street in la Neuville, typically resulted in a call to the curé as someone who could deal with the judicial authorities; he was the first to inspect the dead man's pockets, but "being . . . hurried to get to Rouen for his business," he left further dealings in the case to his vicar.[26]

Villagers might take a large role in selecting the vicars who served them. In 1646 the curé and parishioners of Boos, just to the north of la Neuville, arranged with another priest to serve as vicar "by the year, for as long as it pleases the said parishioners." Curé and parish divided responsibility for providing a modest stipend and held out the hope of a supplementary stipend from the Rouennais convent of St. Amand, the lord of the parish. In exchange the vicar was to perform a motley series of tasks: celebrating mass when the curé was absent, ringing the bells every day, sweeping out the church, joining the village confraternity when it attended burials, and teaching "the schools for the instruction of the youth," whose students were to pay him "raisonnablement."[27]

23. AD Eure, E 1264, Tabel. Pont-St-Pierre, 2 April 1730.
24. Caillot, liasse 230, "Forêt de Longbouel," fol. 4.
25. See the inventories listed in Appendix A.
26. AD Eure, 86 B 107, 3 March 1713.
27. AD S-M, Tabel. Pont-St-Pierre, 1641–46, 4 February 1646.

The community had a similar degree of independence at Pîtres. Its residents in 1654 appointed two representatives who would "arrange with a priest for them and in their names, as they see fit." The community authorized its representatives to assess each household in the parish for the support of the priest whom they eventually selected; and it gave them full powers to take legal action against the incumbent of the parish in the event that he refused "to accept or endure the said priest in the said parish or pay the sum at which he will be assessed" for the new priest's maintenance.[28] Three years later the parishioners of Pîtres were again hiring their own priest, who would serve as chaplain to the village's confraternity, say four masses each week, ring the church bells, "keep school and instruct the youth as best he is able, in exchange for a reasonable salary."[29] Here were villagers directly controlling their religious lives: insisting on their own choice of vicars, preparing for litigation should the incumbent curé oppose their selection, assessing themselves for the vicar's maintenance, and accepting the need for further contributions for the vicar's work as schoolmaster. The curé, named by the church authorities and maintained by the tithes, had chiefly an adversary role in the community's religious life.

These episodes, however, also illustrated the darker side of parish democracy. Villagers' ability to select vicars and set the terms of their service required the existence of a large, rootless ecclesiastical proletariat, whose members were ready to take on such unpromising positions.[30] Such figures did not always play an edifying role in local life, and even the more serious among them were only a temporary presence. In 1650 Jacques Maille, a priest in la Haye Malherbe, acknowledged a debt he had contracted six months earlier when he had been living in Amfreville-les-Champs. Maille had left six pieces of cloth with a publican in Pont-St-Pierre as payment for his "despence de bouche" at the tavern. Maille acknowledged, however, that "because of his need he had improperly taken [some of the cloths] from the curé of Radepont"; and he acknowledged his obligation to repay the publican for the losses that he had suffered as a result.[31] Maille's case combined all the elements that scandalized

28. Ibid., 1651–54, 1 March 1654.
29. Ibid., liasse without cover or title, 5 May 1657.
30. On the functions of a clerical proletariat in sixteenth-century France, see A. N. Galpern, *The Religions of the People in Sixteenth-Century Champagne* (Cambridge, Mass., 1976), 25–27.
31. AD S-M, Tabel. Pont-St-Pierre, 1649–51, 11 April 1650.

seventeenth- and eighteenth-century reformers: rootlessness, drink, poverty, and, as a direct consequence, theft and fraud.[32]

But even more respectable members of the clergy found themselves forced into an unsteady life. In 1658 a priest residing in Pont-St-Pierre asked that the notaries visit la Neuville and secure testimony about his morals from the parishioners there. When the notaries arrived, the parishioners explained that the priest had served the parish as vicar for four or five years but that the incumbent curé had recently decided to return to the village and "perform his functions of curé"; the vicar had thus been obliged to "withdraw and provide for himself in another locality."[33] His former parishioners spoke highly of the priest's service as vicar; there was no suggestion of the shiftless criminality that marked Maille's career. But like Maille, the vicar was forced to move on in search of other means of support.

Figures such as these would have been familiar not only because of their institutional roles but also because of their familial connections. Many local families were able to supply their sons with the education and the assurance of minimal support—50 l. yearly in the seventeenth and eighteenth centuries—that entry in the priesthood required; and they were willing to make this effort "so that his relatives and friends, living and deceased, may benefit from the prayers and devotions" of the future priest "and to move him and make him more capable and more inclined to pray God for them, their relatives living and dead, and their benefactors," as one early seventeenth-century contract expressed it.[34] Those who established such pensions for their sons came from a wide range of social positions: among them were a locksmith, a merchant butcher, and a *laboureur* of Pont-St-Pierre, a leather-worker of Pîtres, two *laboureurs* of la Neuville.[35] Such connections gave further strength to the communal bonds that centered on the vicar; family, piety, and community in some degree reinforced one another.

Neither Pont-St-Pierre nor la Neuville was able to take full control of its religious life, partly because of the very presence of seigneurial power. The choice of schoolmaster was left to the seigneurial and

32. On efforts to purify the rural clergy and the conditions that they encountered, see Hoffman, *Church and Community*, 48–52, 81–83, 98–103; and Jacques Bottin, *Seigneurs et paysans dans l'ouest du pays de Caux, 1540–1650* (Paris, 1983), 268–73.

33. AD S-M, Tabel. Pont-St-Pierre, liasse without cover or title, 7 July 1658.

34. AD S-M, Tabel. Pont-St-Pierre, 1619–24, 26 November 1622.

35. Examples from ibid., 1611–15, 1645–48, 27 December 1615; 1619–24, 26 November 1622; 1739, 11 July 1739 (Pont-St-Pierre); 1600–1607, 1616–20, 19 January 1605 (Pîtres); 1752, 22 October 1752; 1759, 9 February 1759 (la Neuville).

ecclesiastical authorities, the choice of vicar to the Church alone.[36] But these communities too had their confraternities, which made the parish church in some sense a center of independent religious life. In la Neuville statutes of a *charité* were established in 1658. Anyone could join for annual dues of 2 s. From the money that it collected, the *charité* was to pay priests for twice-yearly sermons and for members' funeral masses and to pay for shrouds for indigent members. But it was above all a ceremonial institution. All who joined were to march in members' funeral processions, with the twelve brothers of the *charité* wearing the capes of their office. Twice yearly there were processions around the church, and members were to march in parish processions as well.[37] Like the more extensive arrangements at Boos and Pîtres, these regulations gave villagers a degree of control over their religious lives, and they offered intense moments in which communal solidarity could be expressed and reinforced. Such organizations proliferated in the later seventeenth and eighteenth centuries. In 1762 Pont-St-Pierre's two parish churches included separate confraternities devoted to St. Peter, the Virgin, St. Anne, and St. Nicolas.[38]

This was one of several signs that religious life remained strong in the area to the end of the Old Regime.[39] There were numerous clerical vocations: in la Neuville, at least five young men became priests between 1778 and 1787.[40] Most of the books that the notaries listed after the deaths of the village's farmers were apparently "books of devotion"; literacy, as the church authorities had wanted, was at least partly an aid to piety rather than a distraction from it.[41]

36. AD Eure, E 2392, Chartrier de Pont-St-Pierre, 62 (1598); AD S-M, Tabel. Pont-St-Pierre, 1651–54, 9 March 1653; 1750, 11 May 1750.

37. AD S-M, G 1457, "Archévêché de Rouen: Statuts des confréries et charités"; Jules Lamy, *Histoire de la Neuville-Champ-d'Oisel* (Rouen, 1950), 125. More generally, see André Dubuc, "Les charités du diocèse de Rouen au XVIIIe siècle," *Actes du 99e Congrès National des Sociétés Savantes (Besançon, 1974): Section d'histoire moderne et contemporaine*, 211–36, and E. Veuclin, *Documents concernant les confréries de charité normandes* (Evreux, 1892).

38. AD Eure, E 1266, Tabel. Pont-St-Pierre, 9 May 1762.

39. Cf. discussions of dechristianization by Michel Vovelle, *Piété baroque et déchristianisation en Provence au XVIIIe siècle* (Paris, 1973); Dale K. Van Kley, *The Damiens Affair and the Unraveling of the Ancien Régime, 1750–1770* (Princeton, 1984), 50–51, 164–65; and Hoffman, *Church and Community*, 153–55.

40. Jules Lamy, *La Neuville-Chant-d'Oisel* (Darnétal, 1981), 18. On the problem of clerical vocations, see, for instance, Timothy Tackett, *Priest and Parish in Eighteenth-Century France: A Social and Political Study of the Curés in a Diocese in Dauphiné, 1750–1791* (Princeton, 1977), 43–54; Jean-Pierre Bardet, *Rouen aux XVIIe et XVIIIe siècles: Les mutations d'un espace social,* 2 vols. (Paris, 1983), 1:303–8.

41. See Appendix A; however, it is important to note that not all the books listed were pious, and that many books' titles were not given—they were described simply as "livres de peu de consequence."

In the course of the eighteenth century, there were other signs that the Church was strengthening its role as a center of communal life. Both Pont-St-Pierre and la Neuville rebuilt parish buildings in the 1780s. In each case, construction involved the assertion of communal pride and an aggressive stance toward the nobility and the privileged in general. The priest of St-Nicolas de Pont-St-Pierre noted in the parish registers that "the old presbytery . . . built of wood" was demolished in 1783 and replaced with one of brick and stones. The construction, he noted, had taken place "under the reign of Louis XVI, under the pontificate of Pius VII, M. the president of the Chambre des Comptes Caillot seigneur, the said sr Caillot de Coquéraumont having given all of the stone and brick, . . . and his goods having been assessed for the contribution like those of the other property-owners."[42] In la Neuville the parish church itself was extensively rebuilt during the following year, after twenty years of complaints about its dilapidated condition.[43] These efforts were expensive and not entirely voluntary; in la Neuville, both the archbishop of Rouen and the intendant pressured the community, and it was the intendant who sent an expert to the church to inspect its condition.[44] Nonetheless, these efforts suggest a concern with parish properties as public space, even a concern with giving public space a certain monumental quality: thus the shift from a parish house of wood to one of brick and thus perhaps the grandiloquence with which the priest described the change. Village and bourg participated, in small ways but proudly, in the rearrangement of public space characteristic of the late eighteenth century.[45]

During the eighteenth century the curés themselves were also more imposing figures than their frequently absentee predecessors. Nicolas de Graventerre was curé of la Neuville for nearly fifty years, from 1694 to 1742; and the inventory of his possessions at his death suggests a position within local society commensurate with this extraordinary stability. De Graventerre was prosperous: he owned two houses in Rouen, and he left at his death 5,676 l. in cash—the yearly income of a prosperous provincial nobleman. His surroundings reflected a certain degree of elegance: he owned a clock, a watch, several pictures, a mirror. He was strikingly well educated, with a

42. Archives Communales, Pont-St-Pierre, Registres paroissiaux, 1765–89, end of year 1783.
43. Lamy, *Histoire de la Neuville*, 41–43.
44. Lamy, *La Neuville*, 8.
45. See the discussion of urban space by Bardet, *Rouen*, passim; the same intendant—Crosne—was responsible for the church at la Neuville and for the most dramatic urban developments in late eighteenth-century Rouen.

library that included 431 volumes. The notaries described 174 of these simply as "books covered in calf and parchment"; but the rest of de Graventerre's reading was almost entirely clerical in orientation, with no signs at all of enlightened or skeptical philosophy. De Graventerre exemplified the local success of the Catholic reform movement. His library seems above all to have been a reference collection for educated commentary on the Bible (he owned a Greek New Testament) and for pastoral guidance.[46]

De Graventerre's successors could match neither his longevity in office nor his wealth; between his death and the Revolution there were five curés in la Neuville, serving on the average a decade each.[47] Nonetheless, they too seem to have been substantial figures within the village. De Graventerre's immediate successor, Michel Chaulin, shared urban origins with de Graventerre: one brother was a merchant in Paris, the other a merchant in Pontoise. He left almost no cash at his death and owned neither watches nor mirrors; in addition, he was involved in selling cider to his neighbors, a commercial role that must in some measure have diminished his standing within the parish. But his possessions were evaluated at the substantial sum of 2,000 l., and he too owned a large library, of 120 volumes. The library suggests an outlook somewhat less relentlessly clerical than de Graventerre's. There was no enlightened philosophy and the large majority of the books dealt with theology or pastoral practice, but there were also the works of Molière, a volume of the *Mercure galant*, a life of Turenne, and several volumes of Latin classics. There was also a mild suggestion of heterodox views: Chaulin owned a volume by the Jansenist Nicole, a significant choice in view of the concern about Jansenism that had been abroad in the parish in the previous generation.[48] The relatively high level of education that such figures as Chaulin and de Graventerre displayed doubtless helps to explain the development of literacy in eighteenth-century la Neuville. So also does the fact that, by the end of the Old Regime, a second figure had apparently joined the parish priest as a relatively stable fixture within the community: the schoolmaster. "Pierre Gruel Me dEcolle" apparently resided in la Neuville from 1754 to 1779.[49]

In all the parishes that clustered around Pont-St-Pierre, religious

46. For de Graventerre's dates of service, Lamy, *La Neuville*, 15; for his inventory, AD S-M, Tabel. Pont-St-Pierre, 12 December 1742.
47. Lamy, *La Neuville*, 15–16.
48. AD S-M, Tabel. Pont-St-Pierre, 11 May 1750.
49. AD Eure, E 1268, Tabel. Pont-St-Pierre, 16 January 1779.

life provided an increasingly important focus of communal experience in the eighteenth century. There were new buildings, new confraternities, a more serious and more frequently present clergy, and all of these strengthened the ties of parish life. In important respects, the parish community there had been a feeble institution through much of the seventeenth century. It was an entity in the process of formation over the later seventeenth and eighteenth centuries, not an inheritance from a more traditional past.[50]

Religion formed a first source of communal organization in Pont-St-Pierre and the surrounding villages. Defense of communal economic interests provided a second. But in this respect as well, village unity was an uncertain matter. Poor villagers might find themselves with an interest in the success of the seigneurial system, while the village might find itself closely allied with local nobles and even with the seigneur himself. The community was a shifting web of alliances rather than a monolith defined by geography.

A wide range of economic rights evoked villagers' collective concern, and conflicts about them arose intermittently throughout the Old Regime. The Crown created one strand of conflict by auctioning off marginal lands that had provided villagers with grazing and firewood[51] and by its growing concern to protect the quality of both royal and private forests.[52] Owners of private forests likewise became more aggressive in defending them, because these properties acquired a new economic importance in the sixteenth century.[53] The decline of peasant property from the sixteenth century was a final source of pressure on forest rights, for villagers' need for the firewood and pasturage that the forests supplied became increasingly urgent.

For all of these reasons, questions about rights of usage—over marginal lands, forests, and meadows—provided the most important public issues that the villages along the Andelle faced between the sixteenth and the eighteenth centuries. Disputes over these rights produced occasional episodes of violence in the region. In

---

50. For a contrary interpretation, emphasizing the corrosive effects of reformed Catholicism on communal rituals and institutions, see Bottin, *Seigneurs et paysans,* 280–87, and Hoffman, *Church and Community,* passim.

51. See above, Chapter 2.

52. Michel Devèze, *La vie de la forêt française au XVIe siècle,* 2 vols. (Paris, 1961), 2:57–138, 198–226, 320–41, describes this growing concern in the sixteenth century.

53. See below, Chapter 6.

1621, for instance, the Parlement of Rouen investigated "acts of violence and assaults alleged against several masked individuals armed with guns, swords, and sticks against some wood merchants who had purchased the cutting of several acres in the forest of La Londe," just north of Elbeuf.[54] Pont-St-Pierre itself was the scene of similar events in 1738. A gate leading to the château was found to have been broken in during the night, and a witness reported hearing "four or five persons who were speaking together and cursing one of Monsieur's guards, saying 'damned bugger of a guard, if we held you on this side of the gate, you and your damned bugger of a marquis, we'd pull your balls out by your mouth.' "[55]

More often, however, the villagers used litigation—with surprising tenacity and with some degree of success. Conflict over the forest of Longbouel began early in the sixteenth century, when the baron of Pont-St-Pierre complained to his own seigneurial court that villagers' use of the forest had diminished its value. Not surprisingly, the seigneurial court granted him what he requested: a "reformation" of the regulations governing use of the forest, so as to restrict villagers' rights to pasturage. The communities surrounding the forest responded with their own lawsuits and vandalism,[56] and thus began about 150 years of intermittent litigation.

The inhabitants of Pont-St-Pierre itself participated in these efforts, but from an advantageous position, for they held pasturage rights in the Crown's share of the forest of Longbouel;[57] this was yet another way in which the center of the lordship was shielded from the full effect of conflicts with the barons. Communities at the lordship's periphery depended mainly on their rights within the seigneurial forest and as a result found themselves in direct opposition to the lordship. By the mid–sixteenth century this involved nearly all of the villages surrounding the forest: when a commission of *parlementaires* in 1558 took testimony before an important measurement of the forest, it heard from attorneys for thirteen villages, along with several lords—secular and ecclesiastical—who believed their interests to be at stake.[58] By these efforts, the communities

54. AD S-M, 1 BP 5202, Parlement de Rouen, Tournelle, January–March 1621; 3 February 1621.
55. AD Eure, 86 B 109, 30 May–7 June 1738.
56. Pont-St-Pierre, unclassified, Sixteenth-century inventory of estate papers and acts, 20, 21 July 1514.
57. AN, KK 948: Arpentage, forêt de Longbouel, 1565.
58. Caillot, liasse 230, "Forêt de Longbouel, fols. 4ff.

were in fact able to retain substantial rights over the forest, although often at a significant price. They were allowed to pasture limited numbers of animals in the forest, in some instances in exchange for payments by each village household to the barony.[59]

The forest was the most important subject of dispute, but other issues also aroused communities to action. In 1577 the inhabitants of Pont-St-Pierre, Romilly, Pîtres, and Douville and the nuns of Fontaine Guérard fought the Crown's alienation of their common lands—unsuccessfully, for these lands became a central part of the estate of les Maisons in Pont-St-Pierre, the property of an important Rouennais official.[60] Starting in 1621, the same villages defended their title to a piece of meadow that the Rouennais monastery of St. Amand claimed as its property by virtue of a twelfth-century donation; and in about the same years they fought St. Amand to overturn yet another royal alienation of their common lands. In the 1640s the residents of Pont-St-Pierre sought to defend their rights against Fontaine Guérard, which had acquired some land that the villagers had used as common pasture.[61] In 1737 the residents of Pîtres gathered to defend their "right and possession to dry their linens and hemp on the edge of the river Seine," a right that they had held from "tout temps immémorial." Now the tenant of the land that they had customarily used for the purpose was seeking to limit their access to it; in response the community readied itself for a lawsuit before the Parlement.[62] In 1759 there was a similar conflict in Pont-St-Pierre, over the community's right to use a meadow that the baron of Pont-St-Pierre claimed as his exclusive property; again, the community pursued the possibilities of litigation.[63]

Such conflicts display two critical aspects of communal politics in the villages around Pont-St-Pierre. From the sixteenth century, in the first place, villagers were prepared to use the mechanisms of the law in their disputes with the lordship; litigation rather than savage rebellion was their characteristic response to the problem of commu-

59. AD Eure, E 2394 (agreement of 1558); Caillot, liasse 230 (agreement of 1572); AD S-M, G 2868, report on communal pasture of la Neuville, mid–eighteenth century.

60. AD Eure, E 2392, "Chartrier de Pont-St-Pierre," 90. On the development of les Maisons, see above, Chapter 2.

61. AD Eure, E 2392, 90–92, 67–69.

62. AD S-M, Tabel. Pont-St-Pierre, 1737, 26 May 1737.

63. AD Eure, E 1266, Tabel. Pont-St-Pierre, 31 January 1759; see also below, Chapter 6.

nal rights.[64] Second, the social dimensions of these conflicts were complex, in keeping with the complexity of the interests involved. Villagers could count on the financial and cultural resources of powerful allies. Fontaine Guérard allied with the villagers in 1577 in the attempt to recover alienated common lands but fought them in the 1640s over another question of pasturage. Even within the bourg of Pont-St-Pierre there might be important conflicts. In the mid–eighteenth century, the inhabitants of the parish of St-Nicolas had succeeded in assuring themselves of 30 acres of pasture, following a lengthy dispute with the barons; they now met to ask that the barons "prevent the residents of St-Pierre [the bourg's smaller parish] from coming to pasture their livestock in their new pasture."[65] Village nobles had an interest in maintaining rights of pasturage, which their large herds made especially profitable. Even the barons of Pont-St-Pierre might be involved on the side of the villagers: the Roncherolles had advanced the villagers the money that they needed to meet the legal expenses of their struggle with St. Amand—with the result that in 1659 it was the baron who took over the ownership of the disputed pastures.[66] Over the whole network of interests loomed the ambiguous presence of the Crown. In many ways the Crown's role was antithetical to villagers' interests. It was the Crown that sponsored sales of marginal lands, and the Crown's eagerness to conserve forest resources made it unsympathetic to villagers' grazing rights.[67] But royal officials listened seriously to villagers' complaints of seigneurial harassment and provided occasional relief. Jean Bodin, the royal commissioner who attempted in 1572 to reassert the Crown's rights to Norman forests, presented himself as a defender of the communities against the chicanery of the barons of Pont-St-Pierre; he begged the Parlement of Rouen "not to suffer that the king, the republic, and the poor customary users be denied their rights by the delays of litigation."[68]

Such complex and shifting alliances help to account for the

64. On the importance of the availability of legal methods for the evolution of village communities, see Robert Forster, *The House of Saulx-Tavanes: Versailles and Burgundy, 1700–1830* (Baltimore, 1971), 95–98; Hilton Root, "Challenging the Seigneurie: Community and Contention on the Eve of the French Revolution," *Journal of Modern History*, 57, no. 4 (December 1985): 652–81; and E. P. Thompson, *Whigs and Hunters: The Origin of the Black Act* (New York, 1975).

65. AD Eure, E 2392, 69.

66. Ibid., 91–92.

67. Devèze, *La vie de la forêt*, 2:118–38, 281–92.

68. Charles de Robillard de Beaurepaire, ed., *Cahiers des Etats de Normandie sous le règne de Charles IX* (Rouen, 1891), 280.

TABLE 41. *Village Assemblies, la Neuville-Chant-d'Oisel*

Year	Subject	Number Present	Percentage Who Sign
1618	Forest rights	24	67
1653	Vicariate	15	93
1655	Church repairs	18	78
1730	Vicariate	90	71
1787	Municipal assembly	30	100
1789	*Cahier*	29	100

SOURCE: AD S-M, Tabel. Pont-St-Pierre, 1600–1607, 1616–20, 17 June 1618; ibid., 1651–54, 9 March 1653; ibid., liasse without cover, title, 3 June 1655; AD Eure, E 1264, Tabel. Pont-St-Pierre, 2 April 1730; AD S-M, C 1111, "Subdélégation de Rouen, procès verbaux . . ."; AD S-M, 4 BP 6012, Bailliage de Rouen.

villagers' relative success in sustaining lengthy and expensive litigation. They could call on significant resources, and typically they were not alone in their struggles. Partly for these reasons, the state, with its courts, commissioners, and legal procedures, was not an alien or purely tax-collecting body to sixteenth- and seventeenth-century villagers. They could use it effectively to defend their situation. Even in cases where they ultimately failed to secure their aims, they were able to use litigation to delay change for generations.

Decisions about such matters of communal significance were taken by village assemblies, the inhabitants (in the notaries' formula) "having congregated and assembled at the issue of the great parish mass of the said parish in a state of community (*en estat de commun*)."[69] A few more or less permanent officials served in the villages of the Andelle Valley, for instance as guards in the fields. But it was in the assembly that the villages undertook the forms of communal action traced here: assuring their religious life, employing schoolmasters, defending rights to communal properties.

The assemblies were intermittent and sparsely attended events (table 41). Typically the "estat de commun" of la Neuville involved fewer than 10 percent of the village's households; only one of these meetings assembled more than thirty residents, and even in that instance only ninety of the village's three hundred or so households were represented. Political life in la Neuville was the business of a

69. AD S-M, Tabel. Pont-St-Pierre, 1600–1607, 1616–20, 17 June 1618; see Jean-Pierre Gutton, *La sociabilité villageoise dans l'ancienne France: Solidarités et voisinages du XVIe au XVIIIe siècle* (Paris, 1979), for excellent discussion of village assemblies and laws surrounding them.

minority only. Doubtless wealth helped to define this minority, but more striking was the role of culture. Those who took part in village meetings were overwhelmingly literate, even in the early seventeenth century when only a bare majority of *laboureurs* was literate; everyone who took part in drafting the village's *cahier de doléances* in 1789 was literate.[70] Those who spoke for the community, it appears, were those who were most at ease with the administrative world beyond the village. In some measure this accounts for the villagers' readiness to deal with this world on its own terms, to use the techniques that it offered for defending village interests.

The year 1789 offers a further view of these communities' relations with the political world around them. In that year Pont-St-Pierre and la Neuville, like communities throughout France, drafted lists of grievances in preparation for the Estates General.[71] Comparison of the lists that they compiled provides a striking view of rural political cultures and assumptions at the end of the Old Regime.

Pont-St-Pierre's *cahier* was a politically sophisticated document. It called for regular meetings of the Estates General, although without specifying the role that the institution was to play in the new constitution. It also called for important judicial and administrative reforms: in the courts, the forest administration, the fiscal system, the militia. It called for reform in the Church, the replacement of the tithe by governmental pensions for the clergy and the suppression of smaller monastic houses, whose properties were to be rented out for the state's benefit. Finally, it called for significant social changes: the replacement of milling monopolies by fixed rents, the end of restrictions on hunting, the unification of weights and measures throughout the country.

70. I find no evidence that these listings are incomplete, as argued by Marc Bouloiseau, "Election de 1789 et communautés rurales en Haute Normandie," *Annales historiques de la Révolution française* 142 (January–March 1956): 29–47. Cf. the similar suggestion of the role of literacy in village affairs in Abel Poitrineau, *La vie rurale en Basse Auvergne au XVIIIe siècle (1726–1789),* 2 vols. (Paris, 1965), 1:601. Cf. also the much higher rates of participation in village assemblies in Lorraine: Guy Cabourdin, *Terre et hommes en Lorraine (1550–1635): Toulois et Comté de Vaudémont,* 2 vols. (Nancy, 1977), 1:273–75.

71. AD S-M, 4 BP 6012, Bailliage de Rouen, Cahiers de doléances, Sergenterie de Pont-St-Pierre. I have found no earlier *cahiers* from the region comparable to the ones used by Roger Chartier and J. Nagle, "Les cahiers de doléances de 1614—Un échantillon: Châtellenies et paroisses du bailliage de Troyes," *Annales ESC* 28, no. 6 (November–December, 1973): 1484–94, and Jean-Marie Constant, "Les idées politiques paysannes: Etude comparée des cahiers de doléances (1576–1789)," *Annales ESC* 37, no. 4 (July–August 1982): 717–28.

As a center of trade and legal activity, Pont-St-Pierre produced a list of grievances that showed genuine awareness of the possibilities of significant political change. The *cahier*'s language too displayed political consciousness. It spoke of "citoyens," "humanité," and "le bien de la nation," and it made reference to the superiority of English laws—if only in the modest realm of sparrow hunting. Its demands were not radical. There was no denunciation of the nobility, no call for the abolition of the seigneury. But Pont-St-Pierre's demands were more revolutionary than those of the large majority of *cahiers*, and they displayed a clear understanding that change in the political system was possible.[72]

Yet this political liberalism was joined to fierce denunciations of economic freedom. The residents of Pont-St-Pierre sought to preserve their bourg's monopoly as a market by forbidding markets in farming villages.[73] They also wanted strict regulation of the grain trade. They condemned "the spirit of greed that has reigned and continues to reign more and more in the spirit of men bent on the trade in grains." The markets had lacked grain in 1789, they argued, precisely because of "the liberty that the farmer had to sell his grain at his farm," a liberty that they wanted brought to an end. And they concluded with a bleak reading of the means that would be necessary to control such behavior. "Pecuniary penalties . . . will never suffice to restrain the man lacking in humanity and guided by vile interest, only corporal punishment will be sufficient, and then barely, to hold him back." Although their language was enlightened, the residents of Pont-St-Pierre were expressing an old, essentially seigneurial view of economic life: that the "vile interest" of individuals stood in direct opposition to the public good, that only governmental force could defend public interests.

La Neuville's *cahier* presented a very different group of demands. It included little in the way of enlightened language: two of its articles spoke of "citoyens," but it presented no equivalent to Pont-St-Pierre's talk of the nation and of humanity. The residents of la Neuville made no reference at all to the Estates General, and they proposed only small and essentially local changes in the ecclesiastical and the legal systems: that *gros décimateurs* take a larger role in

---

72. For emphasis on the conservative stance taken in most *cahiers*, see George V. Taylor, "Revolutionary and Nonrevolutionary Content in the *Cahiers* of 1789: An Interim Report," *French Historical Studies* 7, no. 4 (Fall 1972): 479–502, and François Furet, *Interpreting the French Revolution*, trans. Elborg Forster (Cambridge, 1981), 40–43.

73. See above, Chapter 1.

supporting the priests who actually served the parish; that the arbitration of lawsuits be made easier, more rapid, and less expensive. In contrast to the residents of Pont-St-Pierre, they did not challenge the tithe itself or suggest the consolidation of religious houses. Their most substantial demands concerned the workings of privilege and the lordship: they wanted an end to the *banalités* and to the nobility's hunting monopoly, and they wanted equality of taxation.

In all of these differences, la Neuville displayed political values that were characteristically less advanced than those of the bourg. Yet the village's demands also suggested ways in which it was the more advanced community—more fully integrated, that is, into the market economy of the late eighteenth century. La Neuville's residents offered no complaints about the grain trade, indeed made no mention of it. On the contrary, they expressed a tranquil acceptance of the free market and of the property relations that it might create. The *cahier*'s first demand was for the measurement of landed properties, to prevent disputes about them and to ease property transfers. Its second demand was for common weights and measures throughout the kingdom: this reform, the villagers argued, "would ease matters for many citizens who, not knowing the difference that results from these measures, are prevented from knowing the prices in different regions; if these were the same everywhere, they would be able to know the price of this produce and merchandise and the profit that they could make by transporting them from one end of the kingdom to the other." Here was a striking assertion of the villagers' sense of their role in the national economy. They perceived themselves within a national framework, and they saw the potential profits that long-distance trade—"from one end of the kingdom to the other"—might bring them. Institutional obstacles now limited such opportunities, but once the king had eliminated them, the calculation of profit could form the basis of economic choice. Pont-St-Pierre's *cahier* had demanded that morality and political wisdom govern economic life; la Neuville's *cahier* proposed instead a governing role for individuals' calculations of profit within the setting of a national market.

La Neuville's *cahier* expressed a second concern that set it apart from Pont-St-Pierre's, an awareness of the problems of unemployment and industrial poverty. Four hundred residents of the village, so the *cahier* claimed, "complain that they lack work, . . . cotton spinning is their sole resource for gaining a livelihood in the area . . . [and] because of the high prices of foodstuffs and the lack of work brought on by the lack of trade, they can no longer provide for their own needs or those of their children." They asked that the king deal with this crisis and, in a later article, that a "bureau dospitalité" be established in the parish to care for its poor. Here too the residents of la Neuville showed their awareness of the market economy's hold on their village; they saw that a large fraction of the village was wholly vulnerable to "le mauvais commerce," was in fact dependent on the fluctuations of the market.

In 1789, then, the vision of a "moral economy," in which the community's interests took precedence over the free market, remained stronger in Pont-St-Pierre than in la Neuville. The market town was a center of relative political sophistication; its *cahier* asked for wide-ranging reforms in church and government and for a significant reduction in the role of privilege. Yet it was the village, not the market town, that had accepted the free market economy, in both its possibilities for profit and its difficulties.

The contrast reflected the divergent interests of bourg and village: the bourg eager to retain the monopolies that its seigneurial position gave it, the village increasingly involved in the currents of national economic life. The contrast also reflected the complexities of communal organization in the Andelle region. Neither bourg nor village was a tightly knit community. In each, local elites aggressively asserted their rights and standing against both their poorer neighbors and seigneurial authorities. The community as a whole does not seem seem to have been able to balance the power of local farmers and merchants by either the threat of violence or effective public authority.

Communal life derived most of its vitality from religious organization and from defense of common economic interests. Religious institutions became more solidly implanted over the last century of the Old Regime and thus formed a more effective base for communal life; the roving vicars who had intermittently supplied la Neuville's religious needs in the seventeenth century disappeared, and their place was taken by a series of well-educated, resident curés and vicars. Village confraternities developed in the seventeenth century, and they remained vital in the eighteenth.

Communal efforts to preserve economic rights likewise persisted through the eighteenth century. Communal rights remained a concern for both bourg and village in the *cahiers* of 1789, and they provoked occasional episodes of violence. But bourgeois' and villagers' assertions of their economic rights were dominated by litigiousness rather than violence. Villagers made ready use of the means that the developing state offered them. They were able to do so partly because the literate dominated village assemblies and partly because of the alliances available to them; lesser nobles, monastic houses, even the barons of Pont-St-Pierre themselves found their interests in occasional conjunction with those of the village and assisted villagers in their litigation. In these episodes, the community functioned not as a unifed, tradition-bound entity but as a shifting set of alliances. In most instances, the lordship of Pont-St-Pierre confronted not the community as a whole, but a narrow ruling group within it: farmers, merchants, and local nobles in la Neuville, merchants and petty officials in Pont-St-Pierre.

In the course of the eighteenth century, the balance within this ruling group shifted in favor of the village's farmers and merchants. With the disappearance from the region of the local nobility, they were clearly the wealthiest group in the region. It is not surprising that their views were in close accord with those of the liberal revolution launched in 1789.

II

THE RONCHEROLLES
AND THEIR ESTATE

V

THE RONCHEROLLES

For more than three centuries—from the early fifteenth century until 1765—the barony of Pont-St-Pierre belonged to the
Roncherolles family. Over these years, the family and the household
that surrounded it conducted an evolving dialogue with the communities whose structures have concerned us thus far, a dialogue
that was fundamental to the character of each. The institutional
framework of this relationship, the seigneurial system, will be the
subject of the following chapter. In this chapter, I consider the
family itself: its history, values, patterns of consumption, successes
and failures.

An elementary fact underlay relations between the Roncherolles
and the villagers around them. In their dialogue with the larger
community, the Roncherolles by themselves controlled resources
that approximately equaled the total resources of the two thousand
or so villagers, bourgeois, and petty nobles who were their inter-
locutors. A tax roll of 1776, the *imposition territoriale*, lists with considerable accuracy the net landed incomes of all landowners in la
Neuville, nobles and religious institutions included; the total income
thus taxed amounted to 41,591 l. By the later seventeenth century
the marquis de Pont-St-Pierre was already thought to have a total
income of about 40,000 l., and by about 1780 the yearly revenue of
the barony of Pont-St-Pierre by itself was over 50,000 l.—this in
addition to the other sources of income that the lords of Pont-St-

Pierre enjoyed.[1] With such resources at their disposal, the Roncherolles' presence in the countryside was a fundamental economic fact for the villagers nearby. The Roncherolles took for themselves a large share of the area's total agricultural production; their spending habits could deeply affect the local economy; their paternalism might shape local careers; their local political power had an enormous economic force behind it.

Comparable situations could be found throughout upper Normandy. Contemporaries recognized the Roncherolles as one family among a distinctive group within the nobility. "There are at present more than two thousand gentlemen in the généralité of Rouen," wrote Rouen's intendant in 1698, but among them "the names that seem to be the most distinguished" numbered only fifteen; the Roncherolles were the first family that the intendant listed among these fifteen. "All of these families," he continued, "possess important fiefs and properties; but the largest and most valuable of these are in the hands of persons of the greatest elevation, indeed they are to be counted among those great properties that have given their names in the most distant centuries to perhaps the most illustrious houses of the kingdom." Among them were such families as the Harcourts, Longuevilles, Guises, and Montpensiers.[2] The intendant thus defined a three-part structure of the upper Norman nobility: a large mass of mere gentlemen, a group of about fifteen families that enjoyed substantial wealth and influence on a provincial level, and a handful of great nobles who held the province's largest properties and thus had some interest in its affairs. The Roncherolles were thus neither typical of the order as a whole nor members of the great courtly aristocracy that dominated the Old Regime's political life. But they were leading representatives of the middling group within the intendant's schema, those families whose standing and means allowed them to dominate provincial life.

---

1. AD S-M, C 582, no. 114: "Généralité de Rouen . . . , imposition territoriale," 30 August 1776 (there is no equivalent listing for Pont-St-Pierre itself). On the marquis's income in the late seventeenth century, G. A. Prévost, ed., *Notes du premier président Pellot sur la Normandie: Clergé, gentilshommes et terres principales, officiers de justice (1670–1683)* (Rouen and Paris, 1915), 243. On the barony's eighteenth-century income, see below, Chapter 6; the barony's yearly worth at this point was greater than the value of a typical lesser noble's estate at la Neuville.

2. BM, MS Martainville Y 40, "Mémoire concernant la Généralité de Rouen. Dressé par M. de Vaubourg, Me des Requêtes Intendant en lad. Gnalité. 1698," fol. 12. Cf. the very similar assessment by his predecessor, Voysin de la Noiraye: Edmond Esmonin, ed., *Voysin de la Noiraye: Mémoire sur la généralité de Rouen (1665)* (Paris, 1913), 72–78.

SUCCESS AND FAILURE

Through most of the Old Regime, the Roncherolles' history was a story of success, illustrating the possibility that the nobility might be a rising rather than declining group in the early modern period.[3] The family had apparently been connected to Pont-St-Pierre since the mid–thirteenth century. Members of the family had been buried in the nearby priory of the Deux Amants from 1249 on, and a "Guillelmus de Ronceroles" held a small amount of land at Pont-St-Pierre itself in 1281;[4] forty years later a "Johanne de Roncerolis" was a jailor at nearby Pont-de-l'Arche and an agent of the *bailli* of Rouen, Pierre de Hangest—whose family owned the lordship of Pont-St-Pierre.[5] The Roncherolles were both feudal tenants and subordinates within the royal bureaucracy of the Hangests,[6] and the connection was critical to the family's eventual rise. In 1385 Isabelle de Hangest was the widow of "mre Jean de Roncherolles chevalier," lord of Roncherolles; by 1408 she had inherited the properties of her brother, "feu noble et puissant seigneur messire Jean de Hangest, seigneur de Heuqueville, chevalier conseiller et chambellan du Roi, et maître des arbalétiers de France," titles that testified to the Hangests' importance within the kingdom and the superiority of their status to that of the Ronche-

3. Cf. Jean-Marie Constant, "Gestion et revenus d'un grand domaine aux XVIe et XVIIe siècles, d'après les comptes de la baronnie d'Auneau," *Revue d'histoire écono mique et sociale* 50, no. 2 (1972): 165 202; James B. Wood, *The Nobility of the Election of Bayeux, 1463–1666: Continuity Through Change* (Princeton, 1980); Pierre Charbonnier, *Une autre France: La seigneurie rurale en Basse Auvergne du XIVe au XVIe siècle*, 2 vols. (Clermont-Ferrand, 1980); J. Russell Major, "Noble Income, Inflation, and the Wars of Religion in France," *American Historical Review* 86, no. 1 (February 1981): 21–48; and James Lowth Goldsmith, *Les Salers et les d'Escorailles: Seigneurs de Haute Auvergne, 1500–1789* (Clermont Ferrand, 1984), for similar arguments; for a contrary view, Guy Bois, *Crise du féodalisme: Économie rurale et démographie en Normandie orientale du début du XIVe siècle au milieu du XVIe siècle* (Paris, 1976), and Manfred Orlea, *La noblesse aux États généraux de 1576 et de 1588* (Paris, 1980).
4. AN, 3 AP 50, Fonds Nicolay, no. 2: "Généalogie de la maison de Roncherolles"; Léopold Delisle, *Cartulaire normand de Philippe-Auguste, Louis VIII, Saint Louis, et Philippe-le-Hardi* (Caen, 1882; repr. Geneva, 1978), 249, no. 976, summarized in Robert Carabie, *La propriété foncière dans le très ancien droit normand (XIe–XIIIe siècles): 1. La propriété domaniale* (Caen, 1943), 200.
5. E. Boutaric, ed., *Actes du Parlement de Paris: Première série, de l'an 1254 à l'an 1328*, 2 vols. (Paris, 1863–67), 2:449, no. 6799; Joseph R. Strayer, *The Royal Domain in the Bailliage of Rouen* (Princeton, 1936; rev. ed., London, 1976), 50 n. 1, 254.
6. See Philippe Contamine, *Guerre, état, et société à la fin du moyen âge: Etudes sur les armées des rois de France, 1337–1494* (Paris and The Hague, 1972), 168–70, for the complex links between captains and followers at this period.

rolles; and at Isabelle's death the Hangest properties passed to her Roncherolles descendants.[7]

The Hangest inheritance lifted the Roncherolles out of the merely chivalric nobility and placed them among the province's leading baronial families. The contrast was evident in economic terms. In 1416 a royal inquest established the value of the lordship of Roncherolles itself at 310 l. annual revenue; in the same years the properties that Isabelle de Hangest inherited were worth 1,300 l. yearly, over four times as much.[8] But it was long before the Roncherolles could enjoy these properties and the position that accompanied them. In 1415 Guillaume de Roncherolles was killed in battle against the English.[9] Three years later Isabelle de Hangest had fled the region, and Henry V granted her properties to one of his English followers; in 1428 the properties passed to another English captain.[10]

Even the expulsion of the English did not establish the family in secure possession. The French recovery of Normandy was followed by a series of wardships, in which the Roncherolles' properties were systematically exploited by the courtiers who governed them. In 1449, even before the final peace settlement with England, Charles VII gave the wardship of the young Pierre de Roncherolles to Jehan de Brézé, a relative of one of his most beloved *mignons*. The Crown seized the Roncherolles' estates in the course of this process, and thereafter both the properties and the heir himself passed from hand to hand: first to a maternal grandfather and an uncle, a year later to the Châtillons, another important family at Charles VII's court.[11] These events exposed the family to the greed of courtly aristocrats, and they stimulated conflict and instability within the family itself. In 1487 Pierre de Roncherolles—now grown to adulthood—launched a lawsuit against his uncle and erstwhile guardian. His uncle and grandfather, he claimed, had kept an undue share of his income

7. BN, Pièces originales, 2539. On Hangest, M. Vallet de Virville, ed., *Chronique de la Pucelle, ou Chronique de Cousinot suivie de la chronique normande de P. Cochon . . .* (Paris, n.d.), 95, 115, 134, 325.

8. BN, Pièces originales, 2539; below, p. 234.

9. Ibid.

10. "Rôles normands et français . . . ," Mémoires de la Société des Antiquaires de Normandie (1858), 23:101, no. 620; Paul Le Cacheux, ed., *Actes de la chancellerie d'Henri VI concernant la Normandie sous la domination anglaise (1422–1435)*, 2 vols. (Rouen and Paris, 1908), 2:361.

11. For these wardships, Pont-St-Pierre, Sixteenth-century inventory of estate papers and acts (unclassified). For the position of the Brézés and the Châtillons, M. G. A. Vale, *Charles VII* (Berkeley and Los Angeles, 1974), 88–89, 103, 110.

during his minority and had failed to keep adequate records of their administration.[12]

The Roncherolles had been directly affected by the major disasters of the fifteenth century. Members of the family had been killed in battle, and English invaders had seized their properties; the family's weakness after 1453 had brought internal conflicts and exploitation by the great aristocracy. In addition, two generations of warfare and population decline had drastically reduced the worth of the family's properties. At the end of the Hundred Years' War, the barony of Pont-St-Pierre produced about one-third the income that it had produced in 1398–99.[13] These are among the disasters that historians have seen as a crisis of feudalism, a fundamental threat to the nobility's position.[14] For the Roncherolles the crisis was real, but it had little effect on their ability to prosper over the long term. During the century of relative internal peace that followed 1453, the family managed to retain the properties inherited from Isabelle de Hangest and to acquire new ones. These acquisitions allowed the family to undergo without difficulty the only major inheritance division of its history, in 1570. The family divided into four branches. The eldest son retained the barony of Pont-St-Pierre, the centerpiece of the Hangest inheritance; his younger brothers became the lords of Maineville, Roncherolles, and Heuqueville, all of them substantial lordships set between the Andelle and the Epte, the eastern border of Normandy (see map 1).[15]

Prosperity continued through the seventeenth century, but not without momentary difficulties and anxieties. In 1606 another Pierre de Roncherolles wrote to his father-in-law about his need for funds: "My affairs have been explained to me in terms so distant from what I had imagined that in truth . . . I judge it necessary for me to find [a loan] or else cut back and never speak of leaving the house. . . . it's been nearly a year that I have not touched 200 écus."[16] His father-in-law did indeed arrange a loan, and Pierre wrote back that the money "will bring if it pleases God an order into our house, which we cannot regulate without money; what is past is not without bad management, I confess it, but I've learned something from

12. BN, Pièces originales, 2539; cf. Bernard Guenée, *Tribunaux et gens de justice dans le bailliage de Senlis à la fin du moyen âge (vers 1380–vers 1550)* (Paris, 1963), 57, 392–98, for the explosion of litigation that followed the Hundred Years' War.

13. See below, Chapter 6.

14. Robert Boutruche, *La crise d'une société: Seigneurs et paysans du Bordelais pendant la Guerre de Cent Ans* (Paris, 1947); Bois, *Crise du féodalisme*.

15. AD S-M, E, Tabel. de Rouen, Héritages 2e série, June–July 1570, 20 July 1570.

16. AN, 3 AP 20, no. 8, n.d. [1606].

TABLE 42. *The Roncherolles' Purchases and Sales of Land,*
1548–1625

Year	Sales	Purchases
1548		Half of barony of Pont-St-Pierre (15,000 l.)
1569		"Héritages," near Gournay (value unspecified)
1570		Fief of la Neuville (2,300 l.)
1580		Fief des Minières (7,000 l.)
1580		Fief of Dampierre (value unspecified)
1580		Fief of Vimont (value unspecified)
1610		Fief of Calleville (21,200 l.)
1618		Seigneurie of Plessis, Ecouis, and Bec (100,000 l.)
1625	Houses and fief (18,000 l.)	

SOURCE: BN, Pièces originales, 2539, 31 March 1627; AD Eure, E 2392, Chartrier de Pont-St-Pierre, 7.

it—to my cost—so much so that with the grace of God we are well resolved to look out for ourselves more closely."[17]

Pierre seems indeed to have learned to watch over his affairs. An inventory of the papers left at his death in 1627 permits a balance sheet of the family's sales and purchases of land in the previous eighty years (table 42). Between 1548 and 1627, the Roncherolles bought eight fiefs and sold one. Most of their purchases were small, and some involved chiefly honorific concerns; this was the case in the purchase of half of Pont-St-Pierre itself, a purchase that apparently involved no land at all, and in the purchase of the Cathedral Chapter's rights in la Neuville-Chant-d'Oisel. But there was also one very large purchase, that of the fief of Ecouis for the sum of 100,000 l., and some of the other fiefs seem to have been substantial. Neither the inheritance division of 1570 nor the momentary difficulties of the early seventeenth century interrupted the family's accumulation of property.

The Roncherolles' acquisitions during the late sixteenth and early seventeenth centuries strengthened their domination of the region to the south and west of the Andelle. With them the family received a

17. Ibid., no. 10, 4 April 1606.

series of honorific distinctions within the province. In 1577 Henry III
named the barons of Pont-St-Pierre "conseillers nés" of the Parlement
of Rouen, with a full voice in its deliberations. In 1684 the family
received royal letters creating a marquisate of Pont-St-Pierre from the
fiefs that it had accumulated.[18] To these formal distinctions was joined
a more informal "credit" within the region. When the first president
of Rouen's Parlement drew up a list of the "principal gentlemen of
the province who ordinarily reside there and enjoy influence there
(*qui y sont acréditez*)" in the 1670s, the Roncherolles supplied two of
the seven families that he named in the bailliage of Gisors. The marquis de Maineville, with an income of about 19,000 l., was "fort
acrédité dans son canton"; the marquis de Pont-St-Pierre, "riche de
40 m. l. t. de rente," was "fort acrédité et considéré." The president
also noted a member of the third branch of the family, the marquis de
Roncherolles, as one of the principal gentlemen of the vicomté
d'Andely.[19] Together these three branches of the family controlled
incomes that were fifty times as great as those of their ancestor Isabelle de Hangest in the early fifteenth century. Through the interven-
ing centuries of invasion, civil war, and periodic agricultural depression, the family had continued to prosper.

Trouble came not in these periods of crisis but in the peace and
prosperity of the eighteenth century. Several kinds of change rapidly undermined the apparently stable position of local dominance
that the president Pellot had described in the 1670s. The first of
these was a precipitous decline in the family's numbers (a process
that we will consider in more detail below). From the 1680s on,
successive branches of the Roncherolles died out in the male line.
The last marquis de Maineville died in 1683; "seeing himself child-
less at a very advanced age and wishing to restore to the senior
branch of his house the properties that had left it," he willed his
properties to his nephew, the marquis de Pont-St-Pierre. The last
marquis de Roncherolles died in 1728. His properties left the family,
passing with his daughter to René-Nicolas de Maupeou, the future
chancellor. A third branch, the descendants of the barons of Heuqueville, survived into the nineteenth century, but the barony of
Heuqueville itself had been sold in the mid–seventeenth century.[20]
The family's senior branch, that of the marquis de Pont-St-Pierre,

18. BN, Pièces originales, 2539.

19. Prévost, *Notes du premier président Pellot*, 7–8, 242–44.

20. La Chesnaye-Desbois, *Dictionnaire de la noblesse* . . . , 15 vols. (Paris, 1770–86),
s.v. "Roncherolles."

likewise survived the Old Regime but died out early in the nine-teenth century.[21] The Roncherolles were victims not of the Revolu-tion but of long-term demographic trends.[22]

The impact of numerical decline was reinforced by a second change, the family's withdrawal from provincial life and its increas-ing attachment to Paris. The Roncherolles' position had never been exclusively provincial. Military service and governorships had drawn its members away from Normandy, and several of their marriages had been with prominent Parisian families. But in the course of the eighteenth century, such occasional involvements outside the prov-ince were replaced by permanent residence in Paris. Already in 1708, when the marriage contract for one of the daughters of the marquis de Pont-St-Pierre was drawn up, the signing took place "in the residence of the said lady" in Paris, rue du Bac.[23] Forty years later, her brother, who had become marquis, made over his Norman properties to his two sons and retired to an apartment in a Parisian seminary.[24]

This evolution was completed in the 1750s and 1760s. The family's last period of extended residence in Pont-St-Pierre was in 1746–47. Thereafter they appeared in Normandy for visits of only a few days,[25] and the château of Pont-St-Pierre was allowed to fall into increasing dilapidation: in 1765 it was estimated that 30,000 l. would have to be spent on repairs.[26] The Roncherolles also began in these years to sell off their Norman properties. In 1756 the marquis sold a substantial part of Pont-St-Pierre's forest, one of the estate's principal resources; in 1759 he sold much of the land attached to the lordship of Marigny; in 1765 he sold the rest of Marigny along with the barony of Plessis-Ecouis; and in the same year he sold Pont-St-Pierre itself, retaining only the titles marquis de Pont-St-Pierre and *conseiller né* in the Parle-

21. Ibid.; BN, Pièces originales, 2539, 18 November 1777; AD S-M, Tabel. Pont-St-Pierre, 1764–73, 12 March 1765; AD S-M, 16 J 119 bis; E. de Magny, *Nobiliaire de Normandie* (Paris, Rouen, and Caen, n.d.), 223–24.

22. This question is discussed in more detail below. On the demography of the French nobility, see, for instance, Louis Henry, "Ducs et pairs sous l'ancien régime: Caractéristiques démographiques d'une caste," *Population* 5 (1960): 807–30; Robert Forster, *The Nobility of Toulouse in the Eighteenth Century* (Baltimore, 1960), 128–29; Jean Nicolas, *La Savoie au XVIIIe siècle: Noblesse et bourgeoisie,* 2 vols. (Paris, 1978), 2:767–74.

23. AN, Minutier Central, LXVI, 319 (Boutet, notaire au Châtelet), 17 April 1708.

24. Ibid., XCI, 907 (Aléaume, notaire à Paris), 15 July 1754; Caillot, liasse 5, "Délaissement de Mre de Pont St. Pierre à ses deux fils . . . ," 30 April 1745.

25. See below, pp. 196–97.

26. AD S-M, Tabel. Pont-St-Pierre, 1764–73, 12 March 1765.

ment of Rouen.[27] By this point the family had almost entirely broken with its provincial past.

Conversely, in these years the Roncherolles strengthened their attachments to Paris and to the royal court. The marriage in 1752 of Claude Thomas Sibille de Roncherolles symbolized this effort. By this time, the forty-eight-year-old Claude Thomas Sibille was himself a figure of some importance in the royal army, a "lieutenant général des armées du Roi, brigadier des gardes du corps de Sa Majesté." His bride was Marie Louise Amelot, heiress to a substantial ministerial fortune and relative of several other important Parisian officials; the marriage contract was witnessed by the king and queen, the dauphin and dauphine, the princes of Orléans, Condé, and Conti, and other leading figures at court.[28] The couple was to reside with the bride's mother during the first six years of the marriage and to receive half of a pension that she held from the king.[29] As the Roncherolles sold their Norman properties, they turned to the resources and connections of Paris and the court.[30]

The final element in the Roncherolles' eighteenth-century history was debt, of a degree unknown to earlier generations. Financial difficulty was evident first in the case of the junior branch of the family, that of the marquis de Roncherolles; in 1703 the marquis's widow based a request for tax relief on the fact that she and her children owned no fief and that her minor son was a "pensioner of the king."[31] The troubles of the senior branch, that of the marquis de Pont-St-Pierre, became obvious in its liquidation of its Norman estates in the decade after 1756. In all the family sold about 900,000 l.

27. AD S-M, Tabel. Pont-St-Pierre, 1756, 1 September 1756; 1764–73, 12 March 1765; AD S-M, C 1679, "Registre du controlle des ensaissinements," 30 November 1765; AN, Minutier Central, LIII, 390 (Le Pot d'Auteuil, notaire à Paris), 19 June 1764.

28. This was not extremely rare in the mid–eighteenth century; families that wanted the royal signature on their marriage contracts paid for the honor. See Robert Forster, *Merchants, Landlords, Magistrates: The Depont Family in Eighteenth-Century France* (Baltimore and London, 1980), 111.

29. AN, Minutier Central, LXVII, 580 (Hurtrelle, notaire à Paris), 3 March 1752.

30. On the tendency of Parisian nobles to trade land for *rentes* and other liquid resources, Robert Forster, "The Survival of the Nobility during the French Revolution," *Past and Present* 37 (July 1967): 71–86.

31. G. A. Prévost, ed., "Documents sur le ban et l'arrière ban, et sur les fiefs de la vicomté de Rouen en 1594 et 1560, et sur la noblesse du bailliage de Gisors en 1703," *Mélanges, Société de l'Histoire de Normandie*, 3d series (1895): 381. On the ease with which eighteenth-century nobles might contract enormous debts, see Robert Forster, *The House of Saulx-Tavanes: Versailles and Burgundy, 1700–1830* (Baltimore and London, 1971), 109–38.

of property in these years. The largest sale, that of Pont-St-Pierre itself for 567,072 l., illustrated the extent of its indebtedness. By the terms of the sale, the Roncherolles received just over 85,000 l. in cash; the buyer was to pay the remaining 481,396 l. directly to the Roncherolles' creditors. Some of their debts resulted from obligations that aristocratic families had always needed to confront: dowries for daughters and sisters, lifelong pensions (*douaires*) for widows. Nonetheless, the fact that the Roncherolles could accumulate debts of about half a million livres—ten times their yearly income—illustrates the dangers that the eighteenth century posed for aristocratic families. In fact the Roncherolles survived these dangers. But the price of survival was the almost total liquidation of the family's landed inheritance.

ARMS, POLITICS, AND THE SOCIAL HIERARCHY

The Roncherolles' history between the fourteenth and the eighteenth centuries involved several distinct phases, but the common theme of service in the royal armies gave an important degree of unity to the family's development. From the fourteenth century to the end of the Old Regime, almost all men in the family had some experience of military service; the only exceptions were those who entered the Church. This was more than simply a professional choice. In fundamental ways the "profession of arms"[32] shaped the Roncherolles' view of themselves and of their order, and it determined many of their political choices.[33] "During my stay at Rouen," wrote Michel de Roncherolles to the minister of war in 1755, ". . . I learned of the rupture between us and the English; it looks like this will have consequences, in which I would be inconsolable not to participate."[34] It was not surprising that warfare seemed a way of life to Michel de Roncherolles. He had begun his military service at the age of seventeen, and at the age of twenty-four he was leading a

32. The expression of an early seventeenth-century president in the Parlement of Rouen; see Jonathan Dewald, *The Formation of a Provincial Nobility: The Magistrates of the Parlement of Rouen, 1499–1610* (Princeton, 1980), 103.
33. For discussions of the importance of military activity in the nobles' thinking, see Dewald, *The Formation*, 106–9; Arlette Jouanna, *Ordre social: Mythes et hiérarchies dans la France du XVIe siècle* (Paris, 1977), 140–79.
34. Service Historique de l'Armée de Terre, Vincennes, A 1 3418, fol. 70r (30 July 1755).

regiment in action; his younger brother had begun serving at the age of sixteen.[35]

A century and a half earlier, Pierre de Roncherolles explored some of the links between military service, politics, and the social order in his speech at the opening of the Estates General of 1614.[36] Roncherolles' speech was a characteristic expression of the early seventeenth-century nobility's irritation with other elements of society; indeed the main points that he was to discuss had been set out for him by the president of the Chamber of the Nobility.[37] Roncherolles began by stressing the king's absolute power, but he moved quickly to pointing out the practical advantages of careful consultation with the people: "these three Estates . . . ," he said, "can be called the tongues of the gods, since this voice of the people is ordinarily His [sic] own voice."[38] Consultation would supply the basis for reform by the king's authority "of some disorders that have slipped into this state since a certain time."[39] Above all, in Roncherolles' view, there was the problem of the nobility itself. It was necessary that the nobility recover "its initial splendor: That nobility, previously so exalted, now so pushed down, by a few members of the lower order. . . . Let them learn that although we are all subjects of the same king, we are nevertheless not equally treated. They will soon see the difference that there is between them and us: they will see it and remember it, if they please. It is this nobility, sire, that is every day prepared to risk a thousand lives, if it had them, for the service of its prince and that will never spare its blood for the defense of its fatherland. It would be much more at its ease and would hold itself more honored to give you proof of its affection with sword in hand in the midst of danger than in giving you this feeble expression, so common to the other orders."[40]

Roncherolles' speech expounded commonplace ideas: that the nobility suffered from the exaggerated pretensions of the Third Estate; that social stability demanded clear differentiation between the orders, and that the orders not be treated equally; that what distinguished the nobility from the rest of society was the use of arms

35. Pinard, *Chronologie historique militaire*, 8 vols. (Paris, 1760–68), 5:431–32, 507–8.

36. Messire Pierre de Roncherolle, *Harangue prononcée en la salle du petit Bourbon, le 27 Octobre 1614, à l'ouverture des Estats tenus à Paris* . . . (Paris, 1615). For brief discussion of the speech, Jouanna, *Ordre social*, 207.

37. Professor J. Michael Hayden kindly supplied me this information.

38. *Harangue*, 8.

39. Ibid., 11.

40. Ibid., 11–12.

rather than words, "so common to the other orders." Such anxieties about the nobles' position were regularly included in the grievances of the Estates of Normandy in the late sixteenth and early seventeenth centuries. The *cahier* of 1598 spoke of a "nobility impoverished and diminished by the length of the wars, inherently free, according to its ancient rights of exemption, seeing itself . . . rendered subject to taxation" because of the levies that the nobles' tenant farmers paid and that they themselves paid on salt. A year later the nobles again described themselves as "needy and impoverished by the length of the wars, in which they had spent what they had and what their friends had, to meet their expenses with His Majesty and in the armies." In 1607 the Estates proclaimed that "there remains to the nobility as a mark of its quality only the sword and the courage to give life itself in the service of its prince"; and a year later they fixed responsibility for this decline on the royal officials: "It is a strange thing that in Normandy there are officers of Your Majesty who, against the duties of their office, pursue nothing but tax contracts to ruin the nobility and the people."[41]

Such views mark both Roncherolles and the Norman nobles whom he represented as conservatives within the spectrum of seventeenth-century social thought.[42] But Roncherolles' speech is striking also for its silence about racial foundations for the nobility's special position. Not inherited racial characteristics but military activity defined the nobles' special position and justified the special consideration that they demanded from the Crown. This view too was typical of seventeenth-century upper Normandy. The Estates of Normandy seem not to have complained at all about ennoblement before the 1590s, despite its frequency over the sixteenth century.[43] But in 1593 they did complain, asking the king "to be willing to admit to the privilege of nobility only those who have acquired it

---

41. Charles de Robillard de Beaurepaire, *Cahiers des Etats de Normandie sous le règne de Henri IV . . .* , 2 vols. (Rouen, 1880–82), 1:107, 132; 2:118, 140.

42. Jouanna, *Ordre social,* passim.

43. On the relative frequency of ennoblement—both legitimate and illicit—in Normandy, Edmond Esmonin, *La taille en Normandie au temps de Colbert (1661–1683)* (Paris, 1913), 201–21; J.-R. Bloch, *L'anoblissement en France au temps de François Ier* (Paris, 1934); Roland Mousnier, *La vénalité des offices sous Henri IV et Louis XIII* (2d ed., Paris, 1971), 565–66; Wood, *The Nobility of the Election of Bayeux,* 43–68; Comte d'Arundel de Condé, *Anoblissements, maintenues, et réhabilitations en Normandie (1598–1790): La noblesse normande sous l'ancien régime* (Paris, 1981). For a view of ennoblement from a national perspective, Ellery Schalk, "Ennoblement in France from 1350 to 1650," *Journal of Social History* 16, no. 2 (December 1982): 101–10.

and won it by the virtue of arms."[44] Three generations later, in 1660, an anonymous memoir analyzed the problem of new nobles in the province; and like Pierre de Roncherolles and the Norman Estates, its author made the question of military service the focus of his discussion. "There had already been concern about the quantity of nobles introduced by the privilege of ennoblement given to the officials of the sovereign courts since the reign of Henry IV," he wrote. "Only those ennobled by service of arms have been willingly accepted, because that recompense for services is only a replacement for the nobility that perishes in such service." In this observer's view, the nobility did not object to ennoblement itself. Ennoblement was accepted as a reward for military service but resented when it rewarded service in the sovereign courts. An economic contrast sharpened this distinction. When the Crown sought to tax recent *anoblis*, those ennobled for military service "find themselves with no possibility of paying their taxes, whereas the others—rich, powerful, and *gens de plume*, who have their connections with the financiers—will arrange their affairs so that those who obtained their ennoblement by their blood will suffer and those whom the people have an interest in seeing suppressed will be maintained with no profit for the king." Like Pierre de Roncherolles a half century earlier, this analyst expressed little concern about the nobility's claim to inherited superiority. Whether from new families or old, the genuine nobles were those who based their claim to nobility on military service; and resentment at the officials' claims to equal status was all the sharper because of their perceived economic superiority.[45]

Military service defined the nobles' understanding of their place in society and created a complex relationship between the nobles and the Crown. Despite Pierre de Roncherolles' royalist sentiments in 1614, the family had a stormy political past. From the 1570s Pierre's father had been in correspondence with Jacques d'Humières, the governor of Péronne and one of the creators of the Catholic League. Roncherolles mobilized family and friendships in the cause of the League. One of his brothers, the baron de Maineville, was an intimate of the duc de Guise and negotiated for Guise interests at court; eventually he would die heroically for the League cause at the battle of Senlis. Roncherolles passed along to Humières the news that Maineville sent him, and he reported conversations with Car-

44. Robillard de Beaurepaire, *Cahiers . . . règne de Henri IV*, 1:16.
45. AN, KK 1083: Normandie, Lettres et mémoires . . . 1643–60, fol. 599r, "Memoire a V. E. sur quelques levées qui s'establissent en Normandie," late 1660.

rouges, the governor of Rouen, as well; Carrouges was one of the Crown's most trusted representatives in Normandy, but Roncherolles reported him to be "well disposed to apply himself in this effort. God grant that all of this succeed to the contentment of so many *gens de bien*."[46] By the 1580s Roncherolles had become governor of Abbeville, in Picardy itself. His position created a close attachment to the provincial governor, the *ligueur* duc d'Aumale, and his efforts on behalf of the League acquired new effectiveness. He sought to arouse the city's population against its royalist town government; and with the death of Henry III he took a leading role in turning the city over to the League forces.[47] Roncherolles' relations with Aumale and with the League itself became more entangled as the war of the League dragged on. In late 1591 Aumale arrested him and his brother the baron de Heuqueville, who had held the fortress of le Crotoy on the Picard coast; the Roncherolles were accused of negotiating with the royalists and were only released three months later.[48]

The League brought the Roncherolles into dramatic conflict with the Crown. The family's later history was more placid, but other tensions arose from their understanding of their role as warriors. At times the efforts of royal officials and judges to establish internal peace and military discipline met with nobles' indignation. In 1654 the marquis de Roncherolles—Pierre de Roncherolles' nephew—wrote indignantly to the duc d'Epernon, governor of Burgundy: "I have been advised that my lords of the Parlement have established a commission to investigate some disorders of my regiment in order to make me pay for them from what is due me in Burgundy. I am confident that they will not thus violate their honor (*ne reviendront a leur honneur*), being assured that Your Grace will do me the honor of protecting me."[49] The Norman nobles insisted also that their military service be voluntary rather than obligatory. An observer noted in 1652 that in Normandy the compulsory *arrière ban* "is these days a

46. BN, MS Français 3329, 9, 26 May 1577; Orlea, *La noblesse aux Etats généraux de 1576 et de 1588*, 36, 43; on the special intensity of noble politics in Picardy at this time, ibid., 48. On Carrouges, Philip Benedict, *Rouen During the Wars of Religion* (Cambridge, 1981), 117–18.
47. See F.-C. Louandre, *Histoire ancienne et moderne d'Abbeville et de son arrondissement*, 2 vols. (Abbeville, 1834–35), 2:307–15.
48. Ibid., 2:323.
49. BN, MS Français 20478, fol. 137r, 24 June 1654, letter from P. de Roncherolles, Rethel, to duc d'Epernon, Paris.

term of infamy for those who would have to serve, because it is obligatory and required."[50]

In place of requirements to serve, the mid-seventeenth-century Norman nobles demanded that the Crown demonstrate its need and appreciation for their services. Service was to follow respectful negotiation between Crown and nobles. Mazarin's Norman correspondents during the Fronde repeatedly urged him to be alert to this aristocratic vanity and to the rebelliousness that might result if the nobles felt that they were neglected. In 1649 one of Mazarin's Norman agents asked him to assure those who fought for the king in one of the battles of the Norman Fronde "that their efforts will be remembered at the first opportunity, so that they will see that much will be made of them after the peace; they are few in number, and if there is some way to confirm their privileges or to give them some other recompense, this would have a great effect on the whole province."[51] Another observer enlarged this advice at the end of the Fronde: it was important, he wrote to Mazarin, "that the nobility know that the king has confidence in it and recognizes its loyalty. . . . He has called them all to join him, and thus they may hope to be sustained by the king, against all the rumors that have been spread by enemies of the state to the effect that the king has no confidence in his nobility."[52] Like Pierre de Roncherolles in his speech to the Estates of 1614, these observers saw in the nobility a complex mixture of royalism and independence. They too conveyed the nobles' sense of being threatened by other social groups; they too saw the nobles' continued self-confidence in the face of these threats as deriving from the king's approval and appreciation. But the Crown's support could have meaning only if it came with an acknowledgement of the nobles' fundamental independence—their right to choose to serve the king.

Such views took concrete form in the nobles' incessant demands for military and governmental positions. "I will not provide Your Eminence with a full list of those who ask for employment," wrote another of Mazarin's Norman correspondents in 1652—as preface to a request that a friend be given command of a regiment.[53] Another

---

50. AN, KK 1083, fol. 471r, "Mémoire touchant la convocation de la noblesse pour aller servir le Roy," ca. 30 July 1652. See also Contamine, *Guerre, état, et société*, 397–98, for mockery of the *arrière ban* in the sixteenth and seventeenth centuries.
51. AN, KK 1083, fol. 141r, Bougy to Mazarin, 16 March 1649.
52. Ibid., fol. 470r–v, "Mémoire touchant la convocation . . . ," ca. 30 July 1652.
53. Ibid., fol. 365r, M. de Granery to Mazarin, 11 March 1652.

correspondent described for Mazarin the countryside around Rouen in 1649, "where several gentlemen have been solicited by M. de Longueville and have nonetheless assured me for the most part of their fidelity to the king's service. I have allowed them to hope that Your Eminence would soon send me cavalry and infantry commissions in order to keep up that hope and to maintain them in their duty."[54] The marquis de Roncherolles at this time was both a political observer for Mazarin and a leader of the royal armies in Normandy, and he offered the same advice. "My lord of Longueville has sent some of his followers into this province to seek gentlemen to join his party, and they are offering money. . . . I hope that with God's help the Normans will not have so little zeal for the service of the king, having already found a great quantity of my friends who are ready to take employment. . . . it is useful, if I dare say so to Your Eminence, to give employment to the nobility in order to divert it from being carried away by wicked persuasions."[55]

Roncherolles himself, of course, was among those asking for positions. As an officer in the royal army, he already held a commission, but he also had his cousins to provide for. Five days after he stressed in general terms to Mazarin the importance "of giving employment to the nobility," he wrote to express his pleasure at a commission sent to his cousin Pierre de Roncherolles, baron de Maineville.[56] Ten days after that he again wrote Mazarin, begging him "very humbly to be so good as to give a commission as *mareschal de bataille* to monsieur de Heuqueville. . . . he is my first cousin and a man of merit, who has been strongly tempted by monsieur de Longueville and who enjoys credit in the province—everyone can testify to it to Your Eminence. He is here with monsieur the comte [de Harcourt, the commander of the royalist army in Normandy], awaiting your orders."[57] The fourth branch of the family, that of the barons of Pont-St-Pierre, lacked an adult male, hence Roncherolles' failure to ask for employment for them as well. Requests like these implied a large degree of fluidity in the political commitments of noble families such as the Roncherolles. Roncherolles sought to advance his cousins' careers and fortunes, but he also made it clear that one of these cousins had been "strongly tempted" by the *frondeurs*. The family's solidarity on either side could not be taken for granted.

54. Ibid., fols. 42v–43r, Heudicourt to Mazarin, January 1649.
55. Ibid., fols. 28v–29r, M. de Roncherolles to Mazarin, Rouen, 13 January 1649.
56. Ibid., fol. 44r, Roncherolles to Mazarin, 18 January 1649.
57. Ibid., fol. 64r, Roncherolles to Mazarin, 28 January 1649.

Nor could the solidity of ties of patronage and fidelity to the great nobles. The duc de Longueville was the governor of Normandy and of several towns within the province. He was one of the province's greatest landowners, a position that his family had held since the fifteenth century, and he was widely thought to be among the most successful of the great nobles in mobilizing provincial loyalties. La Rochefoucauld thought Longueville a political incompetent but nonetheless believed that "his long residence in Normandy had made him master of the Parlement, of most of the nobility, and of several fortresses of that province."[58] The duchesse de Nemours, Longueville's admiring daughter, echoed this judgment: "M. de Longueville had a power in Normandy such as no subject has ever equaled. The entire province was ready blindly to follow his will whatever it might be, and to enter the party that he wished to place them in."[59] In fact, as Mazarin's correspondents made clear, the good will and power that Longueville enjoyed in the province had not established a fixed system of loyalties to him. Longueville's agents, like Mazarin's, had to negotiate with offers of cash and positions to attach nobles to their party.

This did not mean that the Norman nobles lacked respect for *les grands*. Observers assumed that such respect might be a powerful political force. "There is a need for the presence of a man of high condition," wrote Roncherolles to Mazarin, in the course of discussing how the Norman nobles might be mobilized in the royalist cause.[60] Others offered similar advice. Thus an anonymous observer, writing to Mazarin in 1649: "I also believe that it is necessary to send a person of high standing (*grande condition*) to Normandy, such as M. de Nemours or M. de Joyeuse . . . and to have him accompanied by two or three men of the province who are known to be the most devoted and able to serve according to the sentiments of the court."[61] The great aristocracy mattered in Normandy: it was believed that its very presence offered one means "to remedy the disorders that might arrive." But for most nobles a diffuse respect for the great appears to have been more significant than specific ties of fidelity.

A further element that conditioned the political choices of the

58. *Oeuvres complètes*, Bibliothèque de la Pléiade (Paris, 1964), 82.

59. *Mémoires*, in Joseph-François Michaud and Jean-Joseph-François Poujoulat, eds., *Nouvelle collection des mémoires relatifs à l'histoire de France* (Paris, 1854), 23:654.

60. AN, KK 1083, fol. 44r, Roncherolles to Mazarin, 18 January 1649.

61. Ibid., fol. 73v, anonymous memoir "Pour remedier aus désordres qui peuvent arriver en Normandie," 1649.

Norman nobility was the existence of a vigorous community of gentlemen; and this too tended to weaken ties of fidelity to the great aristocracy. In the mid–seventeenth century, both the nobles them-selves and the officials who sought to control them seem to have taken for granted the political importance of such bonds among the provincial gentlemen. It was in such terms, it has been seen, that the marquis de Roncherolles recommended that his cousin the baron de Heuqueville be given a military command: Heuqueville's "credit in this province" was an important reason for Mazarin to secure his support. The issue of "credit" was likewise important to the presi-dent Pellot in his report to the central government on the state of the province in the 1670s. The marquis de Maineville (we have seen) was "greatly accredited in his canton"; the marquis de Pont-St-Pierre was "greatly accredited and considered."[62] Pellot's contempo-rary the intendant Voysin de la Noiraye used similar language: Mai-neville was for him also a "gentleman of birth and credit," and in general he sought to identify for the government the nobles who enjoyed "credit among the nobility and the peoples."[63] The inten-dant of Caen made the same point about the lower Norman nobility in 1666: "The nobility here has very strong connections one with another, and at the slightest matter that concerns one gentleman, it rides to the rescue (*monte à cheval*)."[64]

During much of the late sixteenth and early seventeenth centu-ries, this political community led a somnolent existence. In 1595 only seven or eight nobles from the bailliage of Rouen took part in voting for representatives to the provincial Estates, and in 1598 there were no nobles at all. In 1603 the first president of Rouen's Parlement, Claude Groulart, complained that "the deputies to the Estates were never so weak." A year later he was gloomier still: "It seems that they have chosen the weakest in every Estate, even worse than last year." Five nobles took part in this election, along with fifty-five ecclesiastics and a "great number" of bourgeois.[65]

But during the Fronde this provincial community took on surpris-ingly effective political life. In 1652 another of Mazarin's correspon-dents reported to him: "I found some of the leading [nobles] of the

62. Above, p. 165.
63. Esmonin, *Voysin de la Noiraye*, 72–78.
64. Esmonin, *La taille en Normandie*, 213.
65. Robillard de Beaurepaire, *Cahiers . . . règne de Henri IV*, 1:223, 272; 2:202, 227, 229. For emphasis on the vitality of provincial politics in the sixteenth century, see J. Russell Major, *Representative Government in Early Modern France* (New Haven and London, 1980), esp. 51–177.

bailliage of Evreux gathered at the home of M. de Feugerolles. . . . they had decided to meet there to prevent any levies of troops in the province and they showed me a statement that nearly three hundred gentlemen have already signed."[66] Their manifesto offered a strong statement of provincial independence from the intrigues of the great aristocracy. These gentlemen had "been warned that some close servants of the princes leagued against the king plan to raise troops against the service of His Majesty and to the detriment of public peace." They promised "by their word as gentlemen" to assemble as many men as possible to attack any such agents of the princes; and they promised to assemble in defense of any of their number who found themselves under attack. The group was seeking to expand the movement into adjoining areas of the province, although in the pays de Caux their success was limited by the number "of those who belong to M. de Longueville."[67]

In this case the provincial community of nobles stood in direct opposition to the great aristocracy and in support of the royal cause. Some observers urged the Crown to make more use of such communities. In 1652 it was suggested that the Crown mobilize the nobles for military service by means of formal assemblies of the nobility, at which the nobles could elect their own captains. "By this organization," it was argued, "the entire nobility will gradually engage itself in [the king's] service; each man who enjoys some distinction will make an effort to enter this election, simply from jealousy of his neighbor, who might surpass him in credit."[68] Even jealousies within the nobility, on this view, might encourage unity in the royal cause.

But in the atmosphere that followed the Fronde, the Crown was unlikely to encourage nobles to gather together. In 1658, six years after the royalist union of nobles in the bailliage of Evreux, another such union drew severe repression. Some 350 nobles from all parts of the province were reported to have gathered in lower Normandy. They called for a meeting of the Estates General and a reduction in the role of tax farmers; and they repeated the provincial Estates' complaint that the Crown had gone "so far as even to attack their quality and to make them pay by indirect ways like the commoners." Such complaints were not novel, but the government responded with extreme severity, especially as the movement devel-

66. AN, KK 1083, fol. 348r, Bertaud to Mazarin, 26 February 1652.
67. Ibid., fol. 441r–v, "Union de la noblesse," signed 1 February 1652.
68. Ibid., fol. 470v, "Mémoire touchant la convocation . . . ," ca. 30 July 1652.

oped increasingly clear ties with the exiled *frondeurs*. One leader was executed and the properties of a dozen others were confiscated before a royal pardon concluded the matter in 1662.[69]

In the years after the Fronde, the Crown sought in other ways to put an end to the nobles' potential for political unity. The last meeting of the provincial Estates came in 1658; to the end of the Old Regime, the Norman nobility was without this focus of political organization and discussion. Three years later Colbert began in earnest his investigation of the nobility, with the intent of punishing those who had usurped noble status without clear titles from the Crown. His explicit hope was to reduce the weight of the nobility within the province, "to cut away an almost infinite number of nobles that the disorder of the times and the foreign and internal wars have introduced."[70] Throughout France, these investigations created tensions and disunity within the nobility, as families found their status threatened and as rivalries among them intensified.[71] The combined effect of repression and investigation was to give the nobility's politics an exclusively urban focus; by the eighteenth century, only the sovereign courts could claim a political role in the province. Governmental officials continued to monitor the "credit" that leading nobles enjoyed in the countryside, but after 1659 the provincial political community had ceased to matter.

NOBLES AND THE CROWN: THE PRACTICAL REALITIES

By the early seventeenth century, the Norman nobles appear to have been profoundly royalist in their assumptions. They anxiously endeavored to secure the king's confidence and support; they feared being ignored by him and harassed by his officials. But the nobles also wanted the Crown to treat their service as freely offered rather than compulsory, and they had important alternative loyalties, to the family, the provincial community, and *les grands*.

To understand the nobles' choices among these loyalties, we need to turn from the values and ideas that have been considered thus far

---

69. Arsène Legrelle, "Les assemblées de la noblesse en Normandie (1658–1659)," *Mélanges, Société de l'Histoire de Normandie* 4 (1898): 334; Jean-Dominique Lassaigne, *Les assemblées de la noblesse de France aux XVIIe et XVIIIe siècles* (Paris, n.d.), 85–127.

70. Esmonin, *La taille en Normandie*, 206.

71. See Jean Meyer, *La noblesse bretonne au XVIIIe siècle* (abr. ed., Paris, 1972), 43–59.

to the concrete realities of their politics. At the Estates General of 1614, Pierre de Roncherolles expressed aristocratic fears of monarchical neglect, but in financial terms he and his fellows had little cause for complaint. The military positions that these nobles held were very well paid. In the 1560s Pierre's grandfather was paid at the rate of 225 l. for six weeks' service in his position as *capitaine de cinquante hommes d'armes des ordonnances du roy*, a rate of 1,950 l. for a full year's service. In the 1570s his father too was a cavalry captain, embarked on an impressive career: he received 300 l. for each quarter's military service; in 1579 he became *gentilhomme ordinaire de la Chambre du Roy*, with a pension of 600 l.; two years later he became governor of the fortress of Abbeville in nearby Picardy, with an annual income (by 1600) of 1,000 l.; and in 1586 he received the hereditary office of seneschal of Ponthieu. Pierre himself received further honors and revenues following his participation in the Estates General of 1614–15: he was named councillor of state in 1615 and received a pension of 3,600 l. in 1619.[72]

At his death in 1627, Pierre de Roncherolles was receiving something like 5,000 l. yearly from the Crown.[73] His nephew the marquis de Roncherolles was even more successful in the royal service. Having loyally served Mazarin during the Fronde, he rose in the 1650s to become a lieutenant general and the governor of the frontier town of Landrecies. The governorship brought him an official income of nearly 8,500 l. yearly, and in 1656 the Crown gave him the right to sell it for 120,000 l. or hand it on to his son, as Roncherolles in fact chose to do.[74]

A military governorship of this kind offered wide powers and ample scope for profiteering, and in the marquis de Roncherolles' case we catch a glimpse of what these might mean. As governors of Landrecies, Roncherolles and his son had control over seventeen villages in addition to the city itself, and they used their powers to the fullest. In 1673, as the Dutch war raged, Louvois himself wrote in a fury to Roncherolles, following accusations "that you send calves to the villages of your government that you have fattened at the inhabitants' expense until they are grown to oxen; that you

72. BN, Pièces originales, 2539.
73. This can only be a rough estimate. The sources include only fragmentary information on the family's positions and pensions; they do not specify interruptions, and they say nothing about the expenses that military service must have entailed. On the other hand, they rarely mention the illicit or occasional profits of these positions.
74. BN, Pièces Originales, 2539.

demand forced labor from the inhabitants of the city and collect [some of this] in cash. . . ; that you do not give the guards all the wood necessary. . . , using the surplus for your own profit; that you lease lands from the city, the Church, and the hospital, and that they have all the trouble in the world in being paid. . . . I do not believe that it should be necessary to tell you that it does not at all suit the dignity of a governor to become the tenant farmer of individuals, and that even were you to satisfy those to whom the lands belong, it is still beneath your dignity to involve yourself in this kind of business."[75] A military governorship combined wide legal authority with the de facto power of armed force, and power led easily to profit.

Such enterprises probably represented an extreme instance of the opportunities that a governorship offered. But the marquis de Roncherolles' exploitation of his position indicated clearly the resources that a successful military career could bring. In this instance, the profits of royal service dwarfed the 10,000 l. or so that the marquis received from his estates in the later seventeenth century. Pierre de Roncherolles derived a larger income from Pont-St-Pierre and his other estates, probably about 20,000 l.,[76] and he received less from the Crown; service to the state probably added about 25 percent to his income.

These estimates are approximate, but they suffice to establish an important comparison: these two Roncherolles relied more heavily on revenues from the state than all but a few of the provincial *noblesse de robe*. Even in the late seventeenth century, according to the intendant Voysin de la Noiraye, the typical councillor in the Parlement of Rouen earned about 1,200 l.[77] A few councillors earned considerably more, and so did the Parlement's presidents and leading members of Rouen's Chambre des Comptes, the province's principal financial court. Nonetheless, in the early seventeenth century only the Parlement's first president, the most important judicial figure in the province, received an income from the Crown comparable to Pierre de Roncherolles'. The marquis de Roncherolles, who rose higher in the royal armies and took a larger role in seventeenth-century politics, probably earned considerably more than the first president and several times as much as a typical councillor. Royal service

75. Service Historique de l'Armée de Terre, Vincennes, A 1 313, no. 372, 19 December 1673 (copy).
    76. Below, p. 234.
    77. Quoted Mousnier, *La vénalité*, 462–63.

probably also counted for a larger share of the Roncherolles' incomes; there were only a few *parlementaires* in early seventeenth-century Normandy who relied on their offices for one-fifth of their total income, as Pierre de Roncherolles did.[78]

Nor were the Roncherolles exceptional in the profits that they drew from the state. A list of pensions paid to "divers gentilshommes ordinaires de la chambre entretenus par sa majesté" from the early seventeenth century includes 183 names. One hundred of these gentlemen received at least 1,500 l. yearly, and the median pension was 2,000 l.[79] Governors of the dozens of small cities and fortresses throughout France typically received yearly salaries of 2,000–3,000 l. for their service.[80] The great aristocracy and the king's favorites, of course, might receive much larger sums. In the reign of Louis XIII, the typical provincial governor received about 60,000 l. in pensions and salaries.[81] Provincial nobles like the Roncherolles had no hope of such sums. But for several hundred provincial families like them, positions in the king's chamber, city governorships, pensions, and service in the army offered participation in the profits of absolutism.

The Roncherolles were connected in a second way to the developing absolutist state: by marriage alliances with some of its principal architects. This was a new development in the seventeenth century. Before 1600 the Roncherolles' marriages had allied them almost exclusively with other families of the substantial provincial gentry. Thereafter marriages with important official families became common. Of eleven marriages by heirs of the family's four branches during the seventeenth century, four were with the daughters of high officials: a first president in the Bureau des Finances of Rouen, a first president in the Chambre des Comptes of Paris, a master of requests, and a *contrôleur général des finances*. A fifth marriage was with the niece of a *contrôleur général*.[82]

These marriages brought the Roncherolles into close connection with Paris and the absolutist state, for the family showed little interest in alliances with provincial officialdom. Marriage alliances provided the foundation for a complex set of exchanges. Pierre de Roncherolles

78. Discussion in Dewald, *The Formation*, 130–58.

79. BN, Mélanges Colbert, 325: "Pensions de gens de qualité et autres personnes qui ont titre," fol. 15v–19v.

80. BN, Mélanges Colbert, 324, "Gouverneurs de provinces et places."

81. Robert Harding, *Anatomy of a Power Elite: The Provincial Governors of Early Modern France* (New Haven, 1978), 139.

82. La Chesnaye-Desbois, *Dictionnaire*, s.v. "Roncherolles."

turned to his father-in-law, the first president in the Chambre des Comptes of Paris, in matters both great and trivial: in 1604 for legal advice, in 1606 for intervention to forestall a royal investigation of his forest properties, to arrange a loan in Paris, and "to send me some fine fruit and other little things that are necessary" for celebrating the baptism of his daughter.[83] Pierre's wife wrote at about the same time to her father's secretary thanking him for a gift of olives and asking that he send other Parisian luxuries, a silver bowl, some bonnets for her children.[84]

The relationship involved affection and culture as well as utility. Pierre wrote to his father-in-law of his efforts "to prepare a room for you for when it pleases you to do us the honor of coming to visit your granddaughter" and eleven days later confided his anxieties when the infant fell ill: "I will tell you the news of your grand-daughter, which is such as we could desire and far better than we had hoped. God has wanted in this to test our patience, which on my side has not been so virtuous as one ought to want, but our lord has given me the grace of willingly taking her into his hands. . . . My brother [a priest] came here . . . having some pity for our afflic-tion, and I believe that his prayers have greatly helped his niece. We must thank God for all and satisfy the vows that we have made for her."[85] The daughter survived her illness, and a few years later wrote to her grandfather herself, "out of regard rather for the obedi-ence that I owe to your commands than with any hope that I have of pleasing you by my progress in writing. I will nonetheless do all that I can to render myself more learned (*scavante*) since I recognize that in making myself more able, I can promise myself some advanta-geous part in the honor of your good graces." The granddaughter of the president de Nicolay was expected to be "scavante." Soon there-after she wrote to her grandfather assuring him of the good health of her brothers and "of the effort that my good papa and mama take to raise us all in the complete obedience that we owe you."[86] Con-versely, the president de Nicolay kept among his papers a copy of Pierre de Roncherolles' speech to the Estates General of 1614.[87]

Marriages with the high *noblesse de robe* meant involvement with

83. AN, 3 AP 17, Fonds Nicolay, no. 206, 21 April 1604; no. 211, 24 October 1606 (Courson to Nicolay); 3 AP 20, no. 8, n.d. [1606]; no. 10, 4 April 1606.
84. Ibid., no. 52, n.d. [about 1608].
85. Ibid., no. 11, 7 April 1606; no. 13, 18 April 1606.
86. Ibid., nos. 53, 54, n.d.
87. AN, 3 AP 50.

the officials' cultural assumptions as well as use of the officials' political and financial resources. The alliances meant also that Parisian officials had a large role in shaping the family's history in more specific ways. After Pierre de Roncherolles' death in 1627, the family's affairs were largely in the hands of his widow, Marie de Nicolay, whose brother had by now replaced their father as first president in the Chambre des Comptes of Paris. It was she who arranged leases of the family's properties;[88] when her daughter married, the arrangements were signed in the Parisian house of Marie's brother-in-law Mathieu Molé, king's attorney in the Parlement of Paris and soon to be its first president;[89] when disputes over financial matters set Marie against her Roncherolles in-laws, the intendant of Rouen was one of the mediators who brought an end to the conflict.[90]

The Roncherolles could look on the absolutist state as a beneficial and familiar institution. They served in its armies and governorships throughout the Old Regime and were well paid for their efforts, better paid than most members of the *noblesse de robe*. Marriage alliances linked them to some of the most powerful officials of the seventeenth-century state. The seventeenth-century Roncherolles dealt on familiar terms with the architects of absolutism and could turn regularly to them for assistance. In these circumstances, the state could not be an alien institution. The Roncherolles' attachments to it were too numerous and too direct for that.

But the state was not only an ally. It could be intrusive, and its intrusiveness increased over the sixteenth and seventeenth centuries. Pressure from the state did not in the long run weaken the family's financial situation, although at specific moments its effects might be dire. Rather, the state's efforts tended to undermine the public powers that the Roncherolles exercised as landowners and thus to change the nature of landowning and of the Roncherolles' relations to the countryside.

Pressure from the state eventually touched every one of the public powers that the Roncherolles exercised as barons of Pont-St-Pierre. In 1537 the Parlement of Paris ordered the seizure of the barony's High Justice and briefly incorporated its rights into the royal domain; the king's attorney had argued that they had been usurped.[91] The Ron-

88. AD S-M, E, Caillot, liasse 252, "Paroisse de Romilly, Baux."
89. AN, T 153/83: confiscated papers, Choiseul-Gouffier, 12 April 1628.
90. AD S-M, E, Tabel. de Rouen, Héritages 2, 24, 25 December 1646.
91. Pont-St-Pierre, Inventory, 8 January 1536 (O.S.).

cherolles apparently fended off these efforts without great difficulty, but there soon followed a more serious struggle with the Crown over the estate's forest rights. From the beginning of the sixteenth century (as has been seen), the Roncherolles had sought to restrict the rights of communities around the forest of Longbouel to graze their animals and gather wood in it.[92] The Crown and its judges were intermittently sympathetic to the villagers' concerns, and this in itself was a problem for the Roncherolles. But the state had also its own aims, and these were far more threatening. It wanted to protect forests throughout France from the depredations of profit-minded owners; it wanted to reclaim usurped portions of the royal domain; it wanted to enforce a specifically Norman custom, the right of *tiers et danger*, which gave the Crown a share of all forest revenues in the province.[93] From the mid–sixteenth century on, the Roncherolles found themselves at the center of all of these concerns. Jean Bodin, the Crown's agent for a major "reformation" of the Norman forests in the 1570s, argued that the Roncherolles were both destructive users of the forest they controlled and unfounded in their claim to own it. By their charcoal burning, so he claimed, they had destroyed two leagues' worth of forest;[94] and he claimed to have "fully verified that the said lord of Heuqueville [Roncherolles] has absolutely no right in the said forest. . . . The king, the republic, and the poor customary users," he concluded, were all "frustrated of their rights" by the Roncherolles' legal maneuvers and delays.[95]

Bodin's denunciations were unavailing, for his investigations had alienated the province's magistrates along with its nobility. The Parlement of Rouen refused to heed his pleas for expeditious judgment of Roncherolles' case, and when he sought to leave the province the court's officials seized his documents and even his clothing.[96] A few years later the Estates of the province attacked Bodin as a "capital enemy of this province."[97] Bodin's failure illustrated the potential force of the provincial community when genuinely united and the absolutist state's need for the services of the local judiciary.[98]

92. Above, Chapter 4.
93. See Michel Devèze, *La vie de la forêt française au XVIe siècle*, 2 vols. (Paris, 1961), 1:173–75; 2:98–99, 105–7.
94. Ibid., 1:242. Bodin was apparently unrelated to the political philosopher, his contemporary: ibid., 2:212.
95. Charles de Robillard de Beaurepaire, ed., *Cahiers des Etats de Normandie sous le règne de Charles IX* (Rouen, 1891), 279–80.
96. Ibid., 276–78, 280.
97. Quoted in Devèze, *La vie de la forêt*, 2:215.
98. See Roland Mousnier, "Trevor-Roper's 'General Crisis': Symposium," repr. in Trevor Aston, ed., *Crisis in Europe, 1550–1660* (Garden City, N.Y., 1967), 103–11.

But his failure did not prevent later investigators from raising precisely the same questions about the Roncherolles' rights. In 1605 a financier acquired the right to inspect titles to former crown lands that had been alienated or engaged. He brought to the task a conviction that the Roncherolles' local power needed to be controlled and that the state needed to act more vigorously than it had in the past to recover its properties. "We find him," he wrote to the president de Nicolay about his son-in-law, Pierre de Roncherolles, "to have advantaged himself more by the authority that he has in this region than by any title that he can present"; investigation by officials from outside was essential "to supplement the too respectful officials of the area, who ought long ago to have dealt with this."[99] The investigators ultimately concluded "that the half of the forest of Longbouel belonging to the lord of Pont St-Pierre . . . was alienated crown land."[100] The Roncherolles apparently established the legitimacy of their rights again, but in the 1630s there were new investigations; in 1639 royal commissioners ordered the seizure and sale of the forest, as lands that had been improperly taken from the royal domain. The matter continued until 1641, when the Roncherolles again resumed possession.[101] A generation later Colbert's commissioners began their work of examining titles to forest properties. Their efforts dragged on over fifteen years, during which the Roncherolles were prohibited from taking any wood from the forest—this at a time when the forest was Pont-St-Pierre's most valuable resource. In 1684 the Roncherolles were finally reestablished in their ownership of the forest, and they were freed as well from the Crown's claim to tax all forest revenue in Normandy; but this came only after the payment of a substantial tax, initially set at the enormous sum of 41,260 l., ultimately reduced to 5,500 l.[102]

Colbert's reforms also affected the political status of the forest. His Forest Code of 1669 was directed to preserving forest resources, and to this end it established a long series of rules governing the exploitation of the forests. Royal judges could intervene whenever they

99. AN, 3 AP 17, no. 211, 24 October 1606.
100. AD Eure, E 2392, Chartrier de Pont-St-Pierre, 23ff. These documents give very little information on how the cases were settled and no information about what costs they created for the Roncherolles.
101. Ibid., 28–29.
102. Caillot, liasse 9, printed "Quittance du Garde du Trésor Royal pour servir au Recouvrement des Taxes ordonnées estre payées pour l'extinction du Droit de Tiers & Danger de tous les Bois de la Province de Normandie." On the burden that the *tiers et danger* potentially represented, see Devèze, *La vie de la forêt*, 1:173–75. For a critical assessment of Colbert's policies, see Daniel Dessert, *Argent, pouvoir, et société au Grand Siècle* (Paris, 1984), 325–28.

thought that the owners themselves were responsible for violations. In other cases they could intervene whenever called on by either party in a case, provided only that they notified the seigneurial judge.[103] These provisions effectively undercut seigneurial jurisdictions by allowing royal officials to intervene in forest matters almost at will. In Pont-St-Pierre, Colbert's legislation in fact seems to have brought an end to the barony's once thriving, profitable, and oppressive forest jurisdiction. As late as 1654 this court—the *verderie*—had been an independent institution, with judge, clerk, and sergeants all separate from those of the seigneurial court proper. In 1654 the forest court handed out 234 fines, worth just over 688 l.[104] By the mid–eighteenth century, however, it was apparently moribund; a single official served as both forest judge and judge of the barony's principal court, the High Justice.[105]

For more than a century, then, the Roncherolles' forest properties—their most valuable single resource—were under ongoing pressure from the Crown, pressure that was both financial and political. From the late seventeenth century, the Crown exerted similar pressure on other aspects of the public authority that the Roncherolles claimed as estate-owners. Colbert's agents took a lengthy and critical look throughout the province at seigneurial claims to exercise judicial powers.[106] Barely one month after the promulgation of the Forest Code in 1669, the Parlement of Rouen undertook a similar investigation of seigneurial markets in Normandy, requiring that all who levied market tolls present their titles to these rights.[107] In 1696 there was a new investigation of market rights, at the end of which the Roncherolles paid 300 l. for the confirmation of their rights in the two lordships of Maineville and Pont-St-Pierre.[108] In 1739 there was yet a third inquiry, and it too concluded with the Roncherolles' paying for the confirmation of their claims.[109] The family's right to

---

103. François Isambert et al., *Recueil général des anciennes lois françaises depuis l'an 420, jusqu'à la Révolution de 1789,* 29 vols. (Paris, 1821–33), 18 (August 1661–December 1671): 222 (title 1, art. 11, 13).

104. Caillot, liasse 9.

105. For example, AD Eure, 86 B 103, "Réceptions de procureurs, greffiers, tabellions . . . 1683, 1710–1784," 7 May 1763. The decline of the barony's High Justice is discussed in detail below, Chapter 6.

106. Robert d'Estaintot, *Recherches sur les hautes justices féodales existantes dans les limites du département de la Seine-Inférieure* (Rouen, 1892).

107. AD Eure, E 2392, Chartrier de Pont-St-Pierre, 41–49.

108. Caillot, liasse 237, "Droits en général," receipt of 6 August 1696.

109. Ibid., "Quittance du Trésorier des Revenues Casuels," 2 October 1739.

appoint notaries in Pont-St-Pierre was also questioned in the early eighteenth century; yet again the Roncherolles' claim was confirmed, by a decision of the Conseil d'Etat in 1717.[110] None of this pressure imposed a significant financial burden, nor were the lordship's market and judicial rights important to its overall value. But their honorific importance was substantial. The state repeatedly challenged the Roncherolles' claims to authority within the region.

Relations between such families as the Roncherolles and the Crown were thus deeply ambiguous. For the Roncherolles and their fellows, political life took place within a framework that was essentially monarchical rather than feudal or provincial. An important element of their definition of themselves as an order was their service to the Crown, service of a kind that other orders in society could not offer. Early in the sixteenth century, Louis de Roncherolles had chosen to have himself portrayed with his patron St. Louis standing over him (see fig. 13), an effort to link the family with the great traditions of the monarchy.[111] By the 1570s the family's financial dependence on the Crown was considerable, and after 1600 the family began a series of brilliant marriages with leading figures in the royal bureaucracy. Even the Roncherolles' moment of rebelliousness during the later phases of the Wars of Religion was set primarily in a context of royal service rather than of feudal independence; Pierre de Roncherolles' most dramatic efforts on behalf of the Catholic League came in his capacity of royal governor of Abbeville rather than at his territorial base on the Andelle.

The Roncherolles were part of the state, but they were also its victims, increasingly so as the seventeenth century progressed. The Crown challenged virtually all of the political powers that the Roncherolles exercised as seigneurial lords, and it repeatedly challenged their right to their most valuable property in Pont-St-Pierre, their forest. On balance, they probably gained more than they lost from the state, although they suffered significant economic losses in the seventeenth century. More important in the long run, pressure from the Crown changed the nature of lordship itself by making its political

---

110. AD Eure, E 2392, 56.
111. Bibliothèque de l'Arsenal, MS 1191, "Livre d'heures de Louis de Roncherolles," fols. 102v–103r; this picture is reproduced and discussed in Georges Ritter and Jean Lafond, *Manuscrits à peintures de l'école de Rouen: Livres d'heures normands* (Rouen and Paris, 1913), 28, 58, plate 76.

Figure 13. Louis de Roncherolles and St. Louis (Bibliothèque de l'Arsenal, MS 1191, fol. 102v; phot. Bibl. nat. Paris)

dimensions expensive to exercise and defend. Absolutism challenged the estate's functions as a political entity.[112]

NOBLE VALUES AND THE ENLIGHTENMENT

A history of the Roncherolles' reading habits can begin only at the start of the eighteenth century. Two inventories after death, one for the marquis de Pont-St-Pierre, the other for his cousin the marquis de Roncherolles, supply views of the family's level of culture at that time. In both cases, the literary culture that the notaries encountered was meager. Pont-St-Pierre was inventoried in 1700 at the death of Claude de Roncherolles. In all the notary encountered thirty books: "some histories, others memoirs, others devotional." Claude de Roncherolles had used writing, to be sure; the notary found a desk "with several drawers filled with personal letters." But he apparently had little interest in literature and none at all in its more difficult forms; there is no reference to the classical authors, legal treatises, philosophy, or fiction that formed a large part of the libraries of contemporary lawyers and officials.[113] Roncherolles' library suggested an outlook that was distant indeed from that of members of the *noblesse de robe*—some of them his in-laws.

A similar impression is conveyed by an inventory drawn up a generation later in 1728, at the death of the last marquis de Roncherolles.[114] The château of Roncherolles included some signs of cultivation: there were eight maps hanging in a hallway, a bookcase with the scores of ten operas, and four globes—two of them celestial, two terrestrial—in the bedroom of Roncherolles' wife. But the notary

112. For emphasis on the "centralized feudalism" that the state offered the nobility, see Bois, *Crise du féodalisme*, 364; for other recent studies emphasizing partnership between the nobility and the Crown in constructing the absolutist state, see Dessert, *Argent, pouvoir, et société*, 342ff., and William Beik, *Absolutism and Society in Seventeenth-Century France: State Power and Provincial Aristocracy in Languedoc* (Cambridge, 1985), 279–339. For contrary emphasis on the modernity and seriousness of the nobility's opposition to absolutism, see Richard Bonney, *Political Change in France under Richelieu and Mazarin, 1624–1661* (Oxford, 1978), 284ff., and "The French Civil War, 1649–53," *European Studies Review* 8, no. 1 (1978): 71–100.

113. AD S-M, Tabel. Pont-St-Pierre, 3 April 1700; cf. Henri-Jean Martin, *Livre, pouvoirs, et société à Paris au XVIIe siècle*, 2 vols. (Geneva, 1969), 1:481 and passim, for the importance of *parlementaire* libraries in the seventeenth century, and François Bluche, *Les magistrats du parlement de Paris au XVIIIe siècle (1715–1771)* (Paris, 1960), 289–96, for the eighteenth.

114. AD Eure, 2 B 40, Bailliage des Andelys, "Appositions de scellés," 23 August 1728.

mentioned only one book, an atlas. Like his cousin at Pont-St-Pierre, Roncherolles seems simply not to have read books.[115]

By the mid–eighteenth century, however, a transformation in mental habits had taken place among the Roncherolles; they had entered literary culture. The change came on a larger scale but only slightly in advance of the similar cultural change that the family's seigneurial subjects experienced in the mid–eighteenth century.[116] Michel de Roncherolles, marquis de Pont-St-Pierre, died in 1754, a half century after his father Claude. A decade before his death he had divided his estate between his two sons and retired to an apartment in a Parisian seminary,[117] rented for the relatively modest sum of 550 l. yearly.[118] The inventory of his possessions[119] concerns only what he had in this apartment; this fact limits the inventory's usefulness in several ways, but it does mean that what the notaries found was probably what Roncherolles had chosen to take with him into retirement. And among what he had chosen was a library of some twelve hundred volumes.

The notary did not list titles for every volume in this library. But he did list all of the larger volumes and many of the smaller ones, and thus his catalogue permits an understanding of Roncherolles' intellectual interests. It shows, first, that Roncherolles was a seriously pious man—not surprisingly, in view of his choice to reside in a seminary. His library included three translations of the Bible, a book of "figures of the Bible," and five books of theology and devotion. There was also the Jesuits' *Dictionnaire de Trévoux,* and Roncherolles' papers included a subscription to its supplement—one indication of his ongoing interest in theological matters. The inventory included other signs of piety. Throughout the apartment were paintings and engravings "representing various devotional subjects," otherwise unspecified; in his bedroom were bronzed plaster statues of the Virgin and St. John. But his interest in religion was not narrowly orthodox. The list of his books included Calvin's *Dis-*

---

115. Other discussions of nobles' reading habits include Jean Meyer, *La noblesse bretonne,* 311–20, and "Un témoignage exceptionnel sur la noblesse de province à l'orée du XVIIe siècle: Les 'avis moraux' de René Fleuriot," *Annales de Bretagne* 79, no. 2 (June 1972): 315–47; Nicolas, *La Savoie,* 2:1000–12; a forthcoming study by Kristin Neuschel will examine nobles' literacy in the sixteenth and seventeenth centuries.

116. See above, Chapter 1.

117. Caillot, liasse 5, "Délaissement de Mre de Pont-St-Pierre à ses deux fils . . . ," 30 April 1745.

118. AN, Minutier Central, XCI, 907 (Aléaume, notaire à Paris), 15 July 1754.

119. Ibid.

sertation de l'Ecriture sainte, and another source shows that he owned the "plaidoyers de mr Arnauld."[120] In fact works of enlightened philosophy were as numerous as works of theology. He owned Bayle's *Dictionnaire,* the works of Rousseau, Montaigne's *Essais,* and a French version of Pope's *Essay on Man,* which the family's accounts show him arranging to have bound in 1738: another indication that these books were actually used.[121] Michel de Roncherolles illustrates the ease with which the mid-eighteenth-century nobility might combine an interest in skeptical and enlightened thought with a commitment to conventional religious doctrine.[122]

But the main interests that his library displayed were neither pious nor philosophical. Well over the half of the titles listed in the inventory concerned either history (38 percent of the known titles) or geography and travel (17 percent). Roncherolles' interests included ancient history (three titles), ecclesiastical history (five titles), and above all the history of France (nine titles). Again, the family's accounts show the seriousness of these interests. Three volumes of "mémoires secrètes" were among the books bound in 1738; in 1747 there was the purchase of "3 almanachs chronologiques et historiques"; in 1748 the family's business agent noted that he had "paid to Gille, the worker, 12 sous for a very ancient silver coin that he found in the ravine and which I have sent to my lord the marquis."[123] Roncherolles' interest in geography and exotic lands was equally impressive. The list of his books began with a ten-volume geographical dictionary, evaluated at the impressive sum of 110 l., and along with this there were books on the geography of France, Japan, Syria, the Levant, and China, as well as travel narratives and a book on "the sovereigns of the world."

Michel de Roncherolles' literary interests thus stood in complex relationship to the culture of his father and cousin in the early eighteenth century. On the one hand, Michel was involved in a much larger literary culture than they. Reading books was for him an ordinary pursuit, as it had not been for them. But the main subjects of Michel's culture were the same as theirs: like his father and

120. Caillot, liasse 1, Comptes.
121. Ibid., 1738.
122. On the nobility's openness to Enlightenment thought, see Nicolas, *La Savoie,* 2:925–1049; Daniel Roche, *Le siècle des lumières en province: Académies et académiciens provinciaux, 1680–1789,* 2 vols. (Paris, 1978), 1:189–233; Guy Chaussinand-Nogaret, *La noblesse au XVIIIe siècle: De la féodalité aux lumières* (Paris, 1976). See also above, Chapter 3, for further discussion of these issues.
123. Caillot, liasse 1, Comptes, 3 April 1747; Comptes, 1743ff., May 1747, June 1748.

cousin, he read about history, geography, and the Christian religion. The gaps in his library were similar as well. Ancient literature was sparsely represented: there was only Aristotle in Latin, Ovid and Theophrastus in French. Save for Montaigne, there was no classical French literature. Most striking, there were no books at all dealing with the law. Roncherolles apparently took with him to Paris none of the summaries of customs, legal handbooks, introductions to Roman law, and legal dictionaries that the seventeenth and eighteenth centuries produced in such profusion. Of course the incompleteness of the inventory may account for some of these gaps, but legal books in particular were likely to be large and expensive, and the notary listed all titles of the larger formats. In fact the Roncherolles did occasionally buy legal books, but their purposes in doing so were purely practical. In 1743 Michel de Roncherolles' business agent reported spending 8 l. "for a quarto book entitled *Mémorial des eaux et forests*, which I bought to help in the business before the Table de marbre [the royal forest court], this being a book always very useful for drawing up the cartulary." Later in the same year he reported spending 14 l. "for the *Conférence sur les ordonnances* by Bernier, in two quarto volumes, a book necessary for the cartulary."[124] The Roncherolles might read legal manuals (or insist that their agents do so), but they did so for utilitarian ends, in pursuit of property rights. Michel de Roncherolles did not take such books with him when he retired from managing his estate. His apparent lack of interest in law or the legal study of institutions, together with his tepid interest in the ancient world and its institutions, indicates that even in the mid–eighteenth century the Roncherolles' culture remained very distant from that of the *noblesse de robe*. The contrast was no longer what it had been at the start of the eighteenth century, a contrast between robe learning and military indifference to literary culture. Nor was it a contrast between enlightened and conservative modes of thought; despite his piety, Michel de Roncherolles was interested in seventeenth-century skepticism and eighteenth-century enlightenment. Rather, the contrast was between the legal, institutional, and classical orientations of the *noblesse de robe* and Roncherolles' historical and geographical interests. The contrast between robe and sword retained some of its cultural force even in the mid–eighteenth century.[125]

---

124. Caillot, liasse 1, Comptes, 3, 4.
125. See Bluche, *Les magistrats,* 289–96, for the continuing importance of legal books in eighteenth-century robe libraries.

PATTERNS OF CONSUMPTION: THE FORCE OF THE MARKET ECONOMY

Changes in the Roncherolles' culture paralleled a second group of changes, in their habits as consumers. By the 1740s there had taken place what may be described as an urbanization of their spending habits; even when the family resided in the countryside, that is, it selected ordinary goods from the offerings of a regional market economy, and it sought out a wide range of more sophisticated goods as well. In buying as well as in reading, the Roncherolles were experiencing changes similar to those experienced by their rural subjects. At the top and the bottom of society, the eighteenth century brought a dramatic reduction in the countryside's isolation from urban purchasing patterns.

Both the dimensions of the change and some of its costs were illustrated in July 1748, when the Roncherolles' often harried business agent prepared for the arrival of the comte de Roncherolles, Michel's son and the owner of Pont-St-Pierre following Michel's retirement. "My lord the comte having told me that he was to arrive," the agent noted in his account of expenditures, "I sent Fleury [a servant] to Gournay to purchase poultry; he brought back twenty-two chickens, six ducks, and seven turkeys." By the 1740s, Gournay had become famous as a specialized center of livestock, marketing the widely appreciated production of the pays de Bray; presumably it was because of Gournay's national reputation that the agent sent there for poultry. But this was an expensive errand. Gournay is 40 kilometers from Pont-St-Pierre; servant and horse took two days traveling there and back, and their cash expenses added about 18 percent to the cost of the poultry itself.[126] Fleury's errand was not an exceptional luxury. The mid-eighteenth-century Roncherolles supplied almost none of their needs from the production of their estate. For goods of any sophistication, they turned to specialist producers.

Ordinary goods could be purchased in Pont-St-Pierre. During an extended stay in Pont-St-Pierre in the winter of 1746–47, the comte bought a large amount of meat and most of the household's bread from local merchants. Yet even basic necessities might come from a much wider range of suppliers. The comte regularly bought bread in

---

126. Caillot, liasse 1, Comptes, 1 July 1748. On the pays de Bray, Jules Sion, *Les paysans de la Normandie orientale: Pays de Caux, Bray, Vexin normand, Vallée de la Seine* (Paris, 1909; repr. Brionne, 1981), 244–50.

Rouen and cider in Bonnemare and la Neuville. He sent servants to purchase cheese in Neufchâtel, another of the famous centers of the pays de Bray, and he bought a surprising range of vegetables in Rouen: mushrooms, cauliflower, artichokes. The most elegant foods came only from the city: coffee from Paris, oysters from Rouen, along with lemons, oranges, marzipan, *poulardes, cannetons,* and so on. Most striking as an indication of the assumptions underlying these purchases is the fact that the comte regularly had meals prepared by Rouennais cooks and sent to Pont-St-Pierre. In 1748, for instance, the business agent noted that he had paid 41 l. 10 s. "to the sieur Noyer caterer in Rouen . . . for having sent fish together with a capon and a duck by order of my lord the comte; M. de Flavacourt and M. Simon, the lawyer, with his company, having been in Pont-St-Pierre." Late in 1747 there was a purchase of fourteen pounds of melted butter, along with the artichokes that the butter was to grace, again from Rouen. Roncherolles' favorite cook appears to have been the sieur Agis, who at one point had been in the family's service. By the 1740s Agis worked for another family, but Roncherolles continued to order dishes from him: fish that was sent to Pont-St-Pierre in June 1747, fish and vegetables sent there eight days later, and so on.[127]

These examples indicate the connection between the Roncherolles' dependence on specialized suppliers and the refinement of their culinary tastes in the eighteenth century. In this regard the Roncherolles were in a very different situation from the nobility of more backward areas such as the Auvergne, where (as Pierre Charbonnier has recently shown) aristocratic diet remained almost entirely unchanged from the Middle Ages through the eighteenth century.[128] By the mid–eighteenth century, in contrast, the Roncherolles enjoyed a diet that was varied and sophisticated (see table 43). In contrast to medieval habits, vegetables and fruits held a prominent place in it. The comte de Pont-St-Pierre's interest in supplying himself with fruits is suggested also by his efforts to construct a *melonnière* in Pont-St-Pierre.[129] Although bread was a large expense and a large share of his expenditure for meat was for undifferenti-

---

127. Caillot, liasse 1, Comptes, 26 September 1748; Comptes, 1743ff., 1746–48, passim.

128. Charbonnier, *Une autre France*, 1:129–50; for other examples, see also Lawrence Stone, *The Crisis of the Aristocracy, 1558–1641* (Oxford, 1965), 555–62; Andrew B. Appleby, "Diet in Sixteenth-Century England: Sources, Problems, Possibilities," in Charles Webster, ed., *Health, Medicine, and Mortality in the Sixteenth Century* (Cambridge, 1979), 97–116.

129. Comptes, 1743ff., September 1747.

TABLE 43. *Expenditures on Food and Drink, October 1746–December 1747*

Category	Expenditure (l.)
Meat and poultry	1,478.8 (36.5%)
Fish	253.0 (6.3%)
Oysters	54.2 (1.3%)
Vegetables and fruit	627.2 (15.5%)
Bread	447.6 (11.1%)
Dairy, eggs	47.9 (1.2%)
Condiments, *confitures*	90.5 (2.2%)
Sweets	17.5 (0.4%)
Cider	80.0 (2.0%)
Wine	793.2 (19.6%)
Coffee	9.9 (0.2%)
Mixed or unclear	146.7 (3.6%)
Total	4,046.5 (100.0%)

SOURCE: Caillot, liasse 1: "Registre de recette et dépense."

ated "viande" supplied by a butcher in Pont-St-Pierre, he also sought out regional specialties: *cannetons, poulardes, veau de rivière, langue de veau.* On average the household consumed a dozen oysters every day and a half, following a mode established in Paris fifty years earlier, a mode that had led to the development of rapid commerce between the Breton coast and the main cities of the country.[130] The comte's interest in gastronomic specialties also extended to wine. Wine accounted for nearly 20 percent of his total expenditures for food and drink during 1746–47, and the total was so high because he nearly always bought specialized vintages: Champagne, Hermitage, Chambertin, Auxerre.[131] The comte himself took an interest in selecting his wines; in 1747 he attended the Rouennais fair and bought several casks of wine there.[132]

The comte's expenditures for food provide an especially clear example of a larger phenomenon, a delight in the availability of specialized products and services, a refusal of local self-sufficiency. The family regularly sent its servants to Rouen to bring back skilled artisans: cabinet makers and turners to make furniture, a painter

130. Jean Meyer, *La vie quotidienne en France au temps de la Régence* (Paris, 1979), 136; see also ibid., 135–39, for the development of culinary sophistication in regency France.
131. See Nicolas, *La Savoie*, 2:958–59, for similar developments.
132. Comptes, 1743ff.

and an upholsterer for improvements of the château itself. More surprising is the comte's equal readiness to turn to Rouennais specialists for the care of his orange trees, which he had acquired in 1739. The care of these was confided to "the sieur Coquerel, master gardener of Rouen," who regularly appeared at the château and in the family's accounts: "for the orange trees, . . . for having listed them," "for having inspected the orange trees," "for nine days that he spent working on the orange trees that were dying and for having trimmed them."[133] The comte treated Pont-St-Pierre as an extension of the city, to which urban goods and workers could easily and frequently be called.

He could do so partly because of Pont-St-Pierre's situation. Rouen had never been very difficult to reach from Pont-St-Pierre, and the eighteenth century brought an easing of communications in Normandy as elsewhere in France.[134] We have seen what this development meant for ordinary villagers, whose involvement in the regional market increased dramatically in the eighteenth century.[135] But even in the eighteenth century the cost of sending a servant to Rouen—whether "pour les provisions," as the accounts put it, or to bring back urban artisans—remained significant; the expenses of the trip amounted to more than a servant's daily wage and maintenance. Other forms of communication also meant real expense. Over seventeen months between 1737 and 1739 the Roncherolles accumulated a bill of 406 l. 12 s. to the "courier et facteur des lettres de la poste d'Ecouis" for their letters, and the family owed money to other postal services as well.[136] For the Roncherolles, the reduced costs of transportation that the eighteenth century brought appear to have been less important than their own growing demand for such services. Transportation remained expensive; what was new was the family's delight in such services.

The family's comings and goings in the 1740s convey a sense of their own readiness to travel (table 44). During the five years from 1744 to 1749, the comte de Pont-St-Pierre paid seven visits to his estate—but only two of these visits, his period of extended rural residence in 1746 and 1747, lasted as long as three weeks; his other visits lasted eleven days, twenty days, and in one case a single night.

---

133. Ibid.
134. C. E. Labrousse and Fernand Braudel, eds., *Histoire économique et sociale de la France,* vol. 2, *1660–1789* (Paris, 1970), 166–86.
135. Above, Chapter 1.
136. Caillot, liasse 1, Comptes, 130.

TABLE 44. *The Roncherolles' Travels, 1744–1749*

Date	Activity
13 February 1744	The comte de Pont-St-Pierre arrives in Rouen from Paris.
19 February 1744	The comte's brother arrives in Rouen.
22 February 1744	Both depart for Paris. "Et mr. le Comte n'a fait que coucher à Pont-St-Pierre."
25 March 1745	The comte arrives at Pont-St-Pierre from Paris.
4 April 1745	The comte returns to Paris.
16 December 1745	The comte arrives from Paris.
26 December 1745	The comte returns to Paris.
23 October 1746	The comte's luggage, servants, and horses arrive in Pont-St-Pierre from Valenciennes.
29 October 1746	The comte himself arrives from Paris.
20 March 1747	The comte returns to Paris.
31 May 1747	The comte arrives from Paris.
7 June 1747	The marquis de Pont-St-Pierre (the comte's father) arrives from Paris.
22 December 1747	The comte returns to Paris.
15 September 1748	The comte arrives from Paris.
3 October 1748	The comte returns to Paris.
23 March 1749	The chevalier de Pont-St-Pierre (the comte's brother) arrives from his estate at Cisé.
25 March 1749	The comte arrives from Paris.
13 April 1749	The comte returns to Paris; the chevalier departs for Rouen and from there to Cisé.

SOURCE: Caillot, liasse 1.

Both the Roncherolles' restlessness and their involvement in a national market economy were new in the eighteenth century. To be sure, they had never been isolated local lords. In the fifteenth century Pierre de Roncherolles had been raised and educated in Paris and had traveled to visit maternal relatives in Brittany.[137] In the sixteenth century the family's military positions had required travels throughout France and to Italy.[138] Later in the century there was travel to Italy for pleasure; the Roncherolles were among those

137. Comptes, 1454–56, 1458–60.
138. See *Les mémoires de messire Martin Du Bellay*, in Claude-Bernard Petitot, ed., *Collection complète des mémoires relatifs à l'histoire de la France* . . . (Paris, 1821), 17:442, for the death of Adrien de Roncherolles in a siege near Milan.

French nobles whose exposure to Italian vices so worried Montaigne and La Noue.[139]

Neither poverty nor geography isolated the Roncherolles. Nonetheless, in the sixteenth and seventeenth centuries the family appears to have pursued an ideal of autarchy similar to that of more backward parts of France.[140] This was an ideal that reflected widespread fears among the French nobles of the seductions of the marketplace. The Breton nobleman René Fleuriot advised his son in about 1600: "It would take me a large book to list a number of others who have followed the path of those poor miserable prodigals who consume in three months what ought to last them a year, so much so that it was necessary to mortgage their land . . . and thus, from expedient to expedient, the property is reduced to nothing. To avoid this, you must acquire the provisions for your household . . . each in its season, or else buy them at double the price, coming [to market] from day to day, as do several great lords of our region as elsewhere, who by this means consume their great properties and are always in arrears."[141] To such observers, the market was a threat to the family's continuity and to social stability more generally.

To avoid these dangers, the sixteenth- and seventeenth-century Roncherolles supplied as many of their needs as possible without recourse to the market. Instead, they used the resources of the estate itself. Thus wine came from their own vineyards in Pont-St-Pierre; some of those who worked on the vineyards, moreover, could be paid not in cash but in wheat from other parts of the estate. Through the sixteenth century, the barony's seigneurial dues assured a steady supply of poultry for the barons' kitchen. Substantial amounts of wheat were delivered as well, to the "baker of my said lord"; the household produced its own bread. At their house in Maineville, which burned down in 1536, there had also been the equipment for brewing beer. The foods that the household needed to purchase were mainly meat, fish, and beer. The family's accounts from the sixteenth century do not specify all such purchases, but they make no mention at all of purchases of vegetables or fruit.[142]

The Roncherolles' diet became considerably more varied in the

---

139. Comptes, 1570–71.

140. Emmanuel Le Roy Ladurie, "La verdeur du bocage," repr. in *Le territoire de l'historien,* 2 vols. (Paris, 1973–78), 1:187–221, and Madeleine Foisil, *Le sire de Gouberville: Un gentilhomme normand au XVIe siècle* (Paris, 1981), 141–43; more generally, Otto Brunner, "Das 'Ganze Haus' und die alteuropäische Ökonomik," in Brunner, *Neue Wege der Verfassungs- und Sozialgeschichte* (2d ed., Göttingen, 1968).

141. Meyer, "Un témoignage exceptionnel," 140.

142. Comptes, 1515–16, 1570–74; below, p. 200.

seventeenth century. Sugar, oil, almonds, grapes, lemons, oranges, and oysters all were regularly purchased in the 1660s. Butter appears to have become much more important in the family's diet, and there were occasional purchases of such fruits as raspberries. But even in the 1660s there was nothing like the culinary variety of the eighteenth century, and the family continued to depend heavily on what the estate itself could produce. The accounts do not mention the purchase of any vegetables or the use of the urban culinary specialists who were to become so important in the eighteenth century; there were only occasional purchases of wine. As a result, the family's dependence on the market for its food supplies remained very limited. In 1664, a year in which the marquis de Pont-St-Pierre resided almost continuously at his estate, his receiver listed expenses of only 335 l. for food and drink, one-tenth what the marquis's grandson spent eighty years later. The family's accounts offer other indications of the continuing importance of self-sufficiency in the 1660s. When the marquis and his "people" went to Rouen, the receiver sent them cider and hay for their provisionment. Expenses for sending letters were minuscule: 4 s. in 1663, 33 s. in 1664.[143]

Self-sufficiency thus seems to have remained a cultural ideal into the late seventeenth century. The Roncherolles traveled widely and were in close touch with Parisian fashions; Pont-St-Pierre itself was close to one of the largest cities in France. Nonetheless, through the 1660s the Roncherolles sought to draw as much of their subsistence as possible from what the estate itself supplied. This model of economic behavior yielded only in the eighteenth century, but its disappearance then—insofar as the Roncherolles were concerned—was almost complete; by the 1740s the family turned to the regional market for even the most basic supplies. Like their rural neighbors, the Roncherolles had become more alert to the specialized offerings of the marketplace, more eager for delicacies that could not be found locally. But the Roncherolles' habits as consumers also reflected a more concrete set of realities, having to do with the organization of the household and the family. The Roncherolles' family organization too underwent large changes in the eighteenth century.

THE HOUSEHOLD AND THE FAMILY

In 1536 the Roncherolles' château in Maineville burned down. Because the family claimed to have lost important documents in the

143. Comptes, 1663ff.

fire, a royal inquest was held about the château's contents and organization. The result for the historian is a suggestive view of how
the Roncherolles' household functioned at the start of the sixteenth
century.[144]

The château in Maineville was an imposing collection of buildings. The main edifice was about 106 feet long and 31 feet wide,
constructed of stone and covered with tile. On its ground floor were
a "grand' salle de commun," two bedrooms, the kitchen and its
appendages. Above these were four more bedrooms, one of them
belonging to the baron of Pont-St-Pierre himself. A third floor included four more bedrooms and four towers, one at each corner of
the house. In one of the bedrooms lodged the baron's oldest son
and his wife; and he had outfitted the tower next to his bedroom "to
collect and hold there as in a study all of the writings, letters, and
documents mentioning and having to do with the family's property
and revenue." Next to this main building was a small brewery building, abutting an older building that had been the original château.
This building was only slightly smaller than the main building, and
in 1536 was still sufficiently habitable that the family could lodge
there after the main house was destroyed; a chapel was located in
this building. Along a third side of the property ran a wooden
gallery, and the whole collection was surrounded by moats twelve
to fifteen feet wide.

This massive group of buildings represented a center of both
patriarchal authority and gentry sociability. Louis de Roncherolles
had built the main residence at some point after 1520. Having built it
(so witnesses explained to the royal investigators), he "wished and
ordered that the lord of Châtillon, his oldest son and presumptive
heir," live with him in Maineville; and Châtillon, "obeying the will
of the said sieur Louis," established his residence in the top of the
house. The house thus effectively symbolized the family's unity and
continuity. It also symbolized the Roncherolles' importance within
the nobility. "At the said place," reported another witness, "a great
quantity of nobles have been accustomed to come to see the said
lord baron"; and he had arranged six bedrooms in his new building
"in order to receive them to sleep and to rest."

Finally, Louis de Roncherolles' house in Maineville was a center
of local loyalties. One of the witnesses prefaced his description of
the house by explaining his longstanding involvement in the Ron-

144. AD Eure, E 2393, Chartrier de Pont-St-Pierre, January 1535 (O.S.).

cherolles' affairs. *"Discrète personne* master Jean Le Seneschal, priest,"
was thirty-six years old at the time of the château's destruction. He
explained that his father had "been in the service of the late revered
madame de Châtillon, and before her widowhood [he had been] a
servant of messire Pierre de Roncherolles, baron of Heuqueville and
of Pont-St-Pierre [madame de Châtillon's husband], and then afterward under monsieur Louis de Roncherolles, presently baron of the
said place [Pierre de Roncherolles' son]. The said service was as the
agent and receiver of [the baron's] High Justice and chatellany of
Maineville; and for the past fifteen or sixteen years, . . . since he has
returned from his studies, he has been about the house and château
of Maineville, where the said sieur Louis came to reside." The Le
Seneschal family had been in the Roncherolles' service for two generations, over a period of at least thirty years (Pierre de Roncherolles
had died in 1503). Clearly they were a substantial family. They had
the resources and expertise needed to manage a substantial estate,
and they could allow Jean Le Seneschal to pursue his education and
enter the priesthood. But the family's resources did not prevent its
dependence on the Roncherolles' household; Jean Le Seneschal had
been in the Roncherolles' service during the entire fifteen or sixteen
years of his adult life.

Such solid attachments to local society remained characteristic of
the Roncherolles' household well into the seventeenth century. The
early seventeenth-century household included a priest—"chaplain
of monseigneur le baron"[145]—and occasional soldiers under the
baron's command.[146] There were also lesser nobles, with more or
less permanent attachments to the household: in 1634 "damoiselle
Anne de Boisgaultier," in 1647 "Isaac de Lux escuier," whom the
baron's widow described as "son gentilhomme" and who by 1657
had become the barony's *procureur fiscal.*[147] As we have seen,[148] in the
early seventeenth century such lesser nobles could hope that concrete benefits would follow from their loyalty; the barons granted
both land and seigneurial rights to local nobles in their service.

Most important, the early seventeenth-century household included servants with solid connections within the bourgeoisie of

145. AD S-M, Tabel. Pont-St-Pierre, 1600–1607, 1616–20, 2 July 1607.
146. Thus "Jacques Vallée homme darmes soubz la charge de monseigneur . . .
estant de present aud lieu de Pont St Pre": AD S-M, Tabel. Pont-St-Pierre, liasse
without cover or title, 28 March 1637.
147. Ibid., 18 July 1634; 13 January 1647; 30 May 1657.
148. See above, Chapter 3.

Pont-St-Pierre and the surrounding villages. "Honorable homme Marin Le Duc, homme de chambre de monsieur le baron" during the first decade of the seventeenth century, illustrates the complex ways in which domestic service bound members of the local elite to the baronial household.[149] The notaries' readiness to give Le Duc the title "honorable homme" is itself significant, for the title was normally applied in these years to merchants and others of clear bourgeois standing; there was plainly nothing demeaning about being the baron's *homme de chambre*. Le Duc also owned livestock (a cow, a heifer, a sow, and twenty-six sheep) and land; on entering the baron's service, he rented out his few acres of land in Romilly for 76 l. in cash and twenty-six pounds of flax. He had been married, and as he entered the baron's service he arranged with a brother-in-law to care for his daughter; the notaries described the brother-in-law as an "honneste personne," another title implying respectable social position, and both he and Le Duc were sufficiently literate to sign the contract. Two years later Le Duc remarried. His bride was the widow of a merchant in Pont-St-Pierre, and the marriage contract was signed at the château. The baron and one of his cousins signed the contract, along with several members of Pont-St-Pierre's bourgeoisie. Le Duc died in 1616. By that time he had left the Roncherolles' household to become a hotelkeeper in the bourg of Pont-St-Pierre. Such figures were among the most prosperous of Pont-St-Pierre's bourgeoisie,[150] and his family remained aware of its standing: his widow promised to supply his daughter with a trousseau "appropriate to the daughter of *une telle maison.*" But the connection with the baron's household remained. The contract naming guardians for Le Duc's children was drawn up at the château of Pont-St-Pierre, and Pierre de Roncherolles signed it as a witness.[151]

Marin Le Duc was typical of the Roncherolles' servants in the early seventeenth century. Like him, they were nearly all literate. Table 45 sets out male servants' ability to sign their names from the early

149. For discussions of the cultural and social functions of domestic sevice, Daniel Roche, *Le peuple de Paris: Essai sur la culture populaire au XVIIIe siècle* (Paris, 1981), 131–241; J.-P. Gutton, *Domestiques et serviteurs dans la France de l'ancien régime* (Paris, 1981), 169–201; Sarah C. Maza, *Servants and Masters in Eighteenth-Century France* (Princeton, 1983), 49–53; and the more skeptical view of Cissie Fairchilds, *Domestic Enemies: Servants and Their Masters in Old Regime France* (Baltimore and London, 1984), 111–19.

150. Above, Chapter 1.

151. On Le Duc's career, AD S-M, Tabel. Pont-St-Pierre, 6, 8 December 1604, 16 November 1607, 11 February, 13 March 1616.

TABLE 45. *Ability to Sign, Roncherolles' Male Servants*

Years	Sign	Mark	Total
1603–1623	5	0	5
1663–1692	5	1	6
1704–1763	5	2	7
Total	15	3	18

SOURCE: Tabel. Pont-St-Pierre.

seventeenth century. It shows that virtually all of the family's male servants were literate throughout the period; if there was any change, it was in the direction of an eighteenth-century decline in servants' literacy. The barons' household was doubtless the only social category in the region of Pont-St-Pierre that could claim complete male literacy at the start of the seventeenth century. In part such rates of literacy derived from the specific needs of domestic service: for accounts, messages, plans. Among the effects found at the death of the Roncherolles' gardener in 1724 were "one lot of cardboard and blank paper with several drawings" and "about four quires of ordinary paper with a register of the deceased's expenses and receipts, and in particular for monsieur the marquis de Pont-St-Pierre."[152] But literacy also reflected the servants' backgrounds. In the early seventeenth century, the Roncherolles' servants included "honorable homme Symon Hettier," a "vallet de chambre de monseigneur"; "honneste personne André Gaucher," described as a "servitteur domestique"; and "Jehan La Vache escuier maistre d'hostel."[153] The notaries used such titles to convey their sense of the substantial social position that these servants occupied.

Servants' marriages provided an occasion for the Roncherolles to display both the authority that they exercised over the household and their paternal support for those whom they employed. Of six servants' marriage contracts from 1606 to 1665, five were signed in the Roncherolles' presence: "in the presence and with the consent" of the baron, as one contract expressed it.[154] Four of the six contracts included substantial contributions from the Roncherolles: 150 l., 300 l., 400 l., and in the fourth case proprietary rights to a seigneu-

152. Ibid., 10 February 1724.
153. Ibid., 12 May 1603, 15 October 1617, 7 May 1619, 23 May 1634.
154. Ibid., 16 February 1664.

rial office.[155] Such gifts were a public statement of the Roncherolles' willingness—and ability—to help their dependents. They suggested as well that loyalty was not to end when the servant left the Roncherolles' service.

For during the seventeenth century, the family's relations with its domestic servants were only an especially clear manifestation of a larger paternalism. Through the 1660s the family employed about ten agricultural laborers, who might occasionally receive the Roncherolles' gifts; in 1665 the Roncherolles' receiver noted in his accounts that "I gave by order of Monsieur 71 l. 10 s. to François Le Hec of Pîtres, father of the plowman of the *basse cour,* as a loan to help in his affairs and avoid the seizure of his property."[156] Seigneurial officials likewise received gifts: of land (as discussed above) or of money at marriage.[157] Most important, the Roncherolles offered their patronage to some local figures who had no immediate connection to the household, although some were former servants. Such patronage connected the Roncherolles to families in the bourgeoisie of Pont-St-Pierre itself and of surrounding villages. Between 1612 and 1630, the Roncherolles witnessed at least six marriage contracts of couples who were not in their service, and five of these contracts were signed at the château. In some of these marriages the Roncherolles' financial contribution was trivial: a gift, for instance, of 30 l. to the groom "to advance him in some way in his craft of leather working."[158] In other cases there were substantial gifts: 600 l. to one bride "in recognition of the services" that she had performed for the late madame de Pont-St-Pierre; 150 l. to another, likewise "in consideration of the good and pleasing services" that she had performed.[159] Such patronage extended beyond material gifts. In 1608 Marie de Nicolay wrote to her father's secretary in Paris, asking that he help "the boy bearing the present message, whom I have had instructed in the craft of carpentry. I wanted him to see a little of the masters in Paris after finishing his apprenticeship; that is why I have sent him to you, to try to place him with a good master where he can earn some money. If you can, let it be with the master who works for my father or else with

155. Ibid., 16 September 1606; 6 January 1617; 4 December 1623; 5 January 1663; 16 February 1664; 8 December 1665.
156. Comptes, 1663ff., fol. 62v.
157. AD S-M, Tabel. Pont-St-Pierre, 4 July 1617.
158. Ibid., 16 September 1624.
159. Ibid., 14 May 1612, 16 Janaury 1622. The remaining examples are drawn from ibid., 5 May 1618, 16 January 1623, and 10 January 1630.

his son, because I know that he can still learn something from them." To assure the success of her plan, Marie promised to assume financial responsibility for the boy's good conduct.[160] In this instance, the baronial household governed geographical as well as occupational mobility.

Gifts and assistance gave the Roncherolles influence over leading *roturiers* throughout a region extending well beyond Pont-St-Pierre. In 1630, for instance, the Roncherolles participated in the marriage of their former servant Geneviève Ingoult to a surgeon; the contract was signed in the château in Pont-St-Pierre, and the Roncherolles gave the couple 300 l. The bride was literate and her dowry was large, both signs of her family's elevated social position. Her brother was a sergeant in the Roncherolles' High Justice of Ecouis, in the Vexin; the Roncherolles had witnessed his marriage contract as well. Another brother was a curé in Amfreville-les-Champs, a few miles from Pont-St-Pierre, and their father was a royal sergeant in the nearby bailliage of Gisors.[161] Paternalism gave the Roncherolles attachments to an entire clan of locally powerful members of the Third Estate.

The Roncherolles' household remained large through the early eighteenth century. In 1703 Michel de Roncherolles had ten servants in Pont-St-Pierre, more than any other nobleman in the rural election of Rouen.[162] Like the family's servants in the seventeenth century, Michel's servants held an imposing place in local society. His gardener left at his death in 1724 coins worth 117 l., banknotes worth 310 l., two wigs, two guns, and a number of small articles of silver.[163] The *maître d'hôtel* controlled sufficient resources that he could lease the baronial sales taxes levied at the market of Pont-St-Pierre for the impressive sum of 600 l. yearly.[164] The Roncherolles' servants displayed marks of status and undertook business arrangements comparable to those of the local bourgeoisie.

But important changes had begun, and they intensified as the eighteenth century advanced. First, by the early eighteenth century the Roncherolles' servants were recruited from a wider geographical area[165]—naturally enough, in view of the family's own movements

160. AN, 3 AP 20, Fonds Nicolay, no. 41, 2 December 1608.
161. Ibid., 29 January 1624, 10 January 1630.
162. AD S-M, C 311, Capitation, 1703.
163. AD S-M, Tabel. Pont-St-Pierre, 10 February 1724.
164. Ibid., 19 December 1704.
165. Ibid., 20 October 1716, 10 February 1724, 29 October 1763.

during the eighteenth century. Servants' wider recruitment meant that they had fewer connections with local society, and their presence in the household offered the Roncherolles less local influence. Second, the Roncherolles themselves seem simply to have taken less interest in their servants' affairs. Among four servants' marriage contracts from the eighteenth century, the Roncherolles signed only one—and that came early in the century; they signed none of the three contracts drawn up between 1753 and 1762.[166] Detachment is suggested as well by the testament dictated in 1755 by a "former governess of madame la marquise de Pont-St-Pierre." She resided in the château of Pont-St-Pierre, asked to be buried in the bourg's parish church, left money to the local poor and a silver bowl to the marquis's *valet de chambre.* But she made no mention of any of the Roncherolles themselves, and apparently none of the family was present as she drew up the testament.[167]

Third, there was a sharp decline in the number of the Roncherolles' servants as the eighteenth century progressed. Partly this reflected economic changes. By the 1740s the Roncherolles no longer employed agricultural laborers to perform the tasks of the château's *basse cour;* and for domestic tasks they turned increasingly to specialists from outside the household. Messages could be sent by the royal post rather than by servants, even laundry could be sent to a laundress in the bourg. Eighteenth-century fashion likewise encouraged families to maintain fewer servants and to seek greater privacy. Handbooks emphasized the dangers and vexations of excessive contact with servants, and employers sought to keep them out of sight.[168] The Roncherolles apparently felt these currents in the society around them; when the marquis de Roncherolles retired to his Parisian apartment in 1745, he kept with him only a cook and a *valet de chambre.*[169]

When the Roncherolles themselves discussed the decline in their household's scale, however, they explained the change in different terms. Finances and the organization of the family itself had the critical roles, as they saw it. Michel de Roncherolles explained his situation in a complaint to the intendant in 1729. He asked that the

---

166. Ibid., 20 July 1761, 18 February 1762; AD Eure, E 1264, 22 November 1724; E 1265, 21 May 1753.

167. AD S-M, Tabel. Pont-St-Pierre, 2 January 1755.

168. Discussed by Maza, *Servants and Masters,* 252ff., and Fairchilds, *Domestic Enemies,* 13–20 and passim.

169. AN, Minutier Central, XCI, 907, 15 July 1754.

intendant reduce his taxes, because (as he explained) "he has been obligated to give to Monsieur his son the regiment of the Cravattes, of which he is colonel and to establish him, which has required that he cede to him half of his property; moreover he has also given to his [younger] son, the chevalier, a commission as guidon in the gendarmerie"; and these expenses, together with the marriage of his daughter "leave him the enjoyment of only the smallest part of his revenues . . . , having even been obliged to cut back the larger number of his domestics."[170] Michel's complaint concerned both hard economic realities and more diffuse social changes. The family's resources were in fact strained in the mid–eighteenth century, and Michel's sons eventually would have to sell Pont-St-Pierre in order to meet their obligations. By themselves these problems would have encouraged the family to reduce the number of its servants, and eighteenth-century military careers added to the burden, for commissions had to be bought and regiments outfitted.[171]

But the chief problem that Michel de Roncherolles faced was the need to secure independent establishments for each of his sons. It had become important that each generation hold an independent position, despite the strains that this demand placed on the family's resources. This was in sharp contrast to the behavior of Michel's ancestor Louis de Roncherolles at the start of the sixteenth century: Louis had compelled his oldest son to reside with him in his new château in Maineville, and this patriarchal relationship had formed the core of the larger patriarchy of the household. In the mid–eighteenth century it was the patriarch himself who ultimately retreated to the privacy of a Parisian apartment. The eighteenth-century Roncherolles sought privacy not only from servants but from one another as well.[172]

The sharpest manifestation of the family's changing organization

170. AD S-M, C 411: "Intendance de Rouen. Capitation. Requêtes des contribuables. . . ."

171. For the costs of commissions and the other costs of service, Forster, *The House of Saulx-Tavanes*, 42–43; André Corvisier, "Un officier normand de Louis XV," *Annales de Normandie* 9, no. 3 (October 1959): 191–216; Corvisier, *L'armée française de la fin du XVIIe siècle au ministère de Choiseul: Le soldat*, 2 vols. (Paris, 1964), 2:159–171; Louis Tuetey, *Les officiers sous l'ancien régime: Nobles et roturiers* (Paris, 1908), 134–36; Emile G. Léonard, *L'armée et ses problèmes au XVIIIe siècle* (Paris, 1958), 171–74. For the social implications of this situation, David Bien, "La réaction aristocratique avant 1789: L'exemple de l'armée," *Annales ESC* 29, no. 1 (January–February 1974): 23–48, and no. 2 (March–April 1974): 505–34.

172. Cf. Forster, *The House of Saulx-Tavanes*, 50, for the refusal of the eighteenth-century Saulx-Tavanes to live in a single establishment.

TABLE 46. *Family Size of Married Male Roncherolles*

Year of First Marriage	Number of Marriages	Total Children	Mean Children	Number of Religious
1452–1571	4	27	6.75	5 (19%)
1575–1669	12	72	6.00	22 (31%)
1699–1728	7	15	2.14	1 (7%)

SOURCE: La Chesnaye-Desbois, *Dictionnaire de la noblesse* (Paris, 1770–86), s.v. "Roncherolles."

was its size. Table 46 presents the number of children produced by the male Roncherolles who married, from the mid–fifteenth to the early eighteenth century; it includes all branches of the family. It shows a small decline in family size during the later sixteenth and seventeenth centuries, followed by a precipitous decline during the early eighteenth century. There took place as well a dramatic increase in religious vocations among the Roncherolles' children during the seventeenth century, followed by a sharp decline in this measure of religious fervor during the early eighteenth century. Religious fervor and smaller numbers of children combined to produce the family's near disappearance in the eighteenth century. By the Revolution the senior branch of the family included only three individuals, and two other branches had disappeared altogether.

From the last third of the seventeenth century, contraception was widely practiced within the upper Norman bourgeoisie,[173] and contraception doubtless explains part of the decline in the Roncherolles' numbers. At least as important, however, were changes in the family's organization. Michel de Roncherolles, in his complaint of 1729, had described one form of his family's fragmentation: each generation's insistence on having its own establishment. A comparable atomization affected relations between spouses as well. An especially raucous example of family breakdown was provided by the marital disputes of "messire Marie-Charles-François de Roncherolles," heir of the barons of Heuqueville and Michel de Roncherolles' cousin.[174] In 1727 Roncherolles had married a fourteen-year-old heiress. His motives, so the bride's lawyer later claimed, had been crudely financial: "The sieur de Roncherolles courted this alliance

173. Jean-Pierre Bardet, *Rouen aux XVIIe et XVIIIe siècles: Les mutations d'un espace social*, 2 vols. (Paris, 1983), 1:263–303.

174. What follows is based on the printed lawyers' arguments in BN, Pièces Originales, 2539, fols. 60ff.

because of the lure of the fortune that he would find in marrying a girl of this standing, which alone could set off his own birth and sustain his house." Once again, according to the lawyer's argument, the Roncherolles' eighteenth-century financial troubles led to changes in the household itself, for after seven years of unhappy marriage the couple separated. A brief reconciliation, the conception of a son, and a new separation followed. Four years later this cycle was repeated and a second child was conceived; the couple separated before her birth. Roncherolles' dispute with his wife lasted twenty years in all; at one point it included his accusing her of infanticide, one of the most severely prosecuted crimes in early modern France. Following extensive litigation, the Parlement of Rouen condemned the bride to imprisonment in a Parisian convent. Roncherolles was ordered to pay her a substantial pension but otherwise retained control of her properties. The bride's lawyer argued that this had been his goal from the outset: he had been interested only in the bride's fortune and had mistreated her once he controlled it. Roncherolles himself argued that his bride was deranged, and he supplied plausible instances. But even his comments in his own defense illustrated the family's disorganized state. "In the month of October 1740," he wrote, "I learned that my wife had brought my son to Boussigny, a half a league from Planqueray, where my father resided. I was delighted. It was a favorable moment for giving a name to my son, who for four years had remained nameless. The name was to be given him by the comte de Roncherolles, my father. It was the wish of nature and of the family."[175] Roncherolles' invocation of patriarchal values contrasts with his apparent indifference to his son and heir. The child was left nameless and unbaptized during the first four years of his life and was left in the care of an apparently lunatic mother as well.[176]

This was an extreme instance of family breakdown, but it was not the only separation that the Roncherolles underwent in the eighteenth century. The marquis de Pont-St-Pierre and his younger brother both were separated "quant aux biens" from their wives in the later eighteenth century, the first after having two daughters, the second after having two sons and a daughter.[177] Separations of

---

175. Ibid., fol. 101v. See also AD S-M, C 53, "Police administrative," 5 May 1744.
176. Cf. Lawrence Stone, *The Family, Sex, and Marriage in England, 1500–1800* (New York, 1977), part 2, for emphasis on the links between patriarchal family organization and indifference to children.
177. AD S-M, 16 J 119 bis, Roncherolles: 10 Fructidor An XII, copy of act of 18 October 1788; La Chesnaye-Desbois, *Dictionnaire*, s.v. "Roncherolles."

this kind owed much to the peculiarities of the individuals involved and of the situations in which they found themselves. For the Roncherolles, however, these particular episodes had larger importance. In the late eighteenth century, marital breakdowns threatened the family's ability to reproduce itself. Equally important, these events still further undermined the family's ability to function as a powerful clan in the countryside. Several small, isolated, mobile households had replaced the imposing patriarchy of the early sixteenth century.

Well before 1765, when the Roncherolles finally sold Pont-St-Pierre and turned their full attention to Paris, the family had given up its dominance of local society. I have sought here to demonstrate the radical quality of the family's eighteenth-century divorce from Pont-St-Pierre and the surrounding villages and to show how starkly this situation contrasted with that of earlier periods. Far into the reign of Louis XIV, it seems, the Roncherolles' household had been a focal point of local society. It had been the most obvious center of literacy in the area; from the early seventeenth century virtually all the Roncherolles' male servants could write. It had also provided a large range of employment, and it had drawn into its employ members of substantial local families, both petty nobles and local bourgeois. Passage through the barons' household was apparently a normal stage in the modest careers that Pont-St-Pierre's commercial and artisanal life offered.

The household's scale and functions changed rapidly after 1700. The Roncherolles themselves were less numerous, and they were more independent of one another. Fashion and financial pressures likewise reduced the household's scale and its involvement with local society. In contrast to their ancestors' practices, the eighteenth-century Roncherolles made little use of the goods that Pont-St-Pierre itself offered. Instead they turned to the pays de Bray for poultry and cheese, to Rouen for wine, to Paris for coffee. The fashion of regional specialties had replaced an ethic that had been deeply felt in the sixteenth and seventeenth centuries, an ethic that emphasized the dangers of the market; autarchy had seemed a source of stability then, an assurance of the family's continuity.

In fact the Roncherolles' eighteenth-century experience suggests the wisdom of such advice, for the family's transition to the market economy was an uneasy one. By the mid–eighteenth century it was almost hopelessly in debt, and its principal estates had to be sold. The sparseness of the family's papers prohibits a full explication of these troubles; possible extravagances in Paris or at court are simply hidden from view, and the personal idiosyncracies that led to debt emerge only dimly. Nonetheless, it is instructive to contrast the family's ability to survive earlier crises with its eighteenth-century disarray. The Roncherolles had managed to deal with the endemic warfare and political crises of the early modern period, and they had survived both depression in the fifteenth and seventeenth centuries and inflation in the sixteenth. Survival was possible, it seems, partly because the patriarchal household sheltered the family from some of the effects of the market economy. Full exposure to the market came only in the eighteenth century, and its effects were immediately unsettling. For the Roncherolles, it seems, the psychology of the marketplace—the demand for specialized goods, the insistence on overcoming distance—developed more rapidly than the means for satisfying these wants; transport remained expensive, the family's income remained about what it had been in the late seventeenth century. In this instance, practical realities lagged well behind wants and assumptions.

By comparison, the family's adaptation to political change appears in certain respects to have been relatively easy. An important share of its income came from service to the state, and from an early date ideas of service to the Crown were deeply important to their understanding of what nobility meant. Alternative foundations for political action were weak; neither the provincial community of gentlemen nor the patronage networks of the great aristocracy had comparable psychological importance, although at moments of crisis each might play a considerable role. From the start of the seventeenth century, moreover, the Roncherolles frequently married daughters of important official families. Long before Louis XIV, the Roncherolles were integrated into the centralized state: intellectually, personally, financially.

But the state also shaped the family's development in new directions. Historians have traditionally emphasized the tensions between the centralizing demands of the early modern state and the aristocracy's exercise of seigneurial powers; and in Pont-St-Pierre this tension was real. The state questioned all of the public powers that the Roncherolles exercised in Pont-St-Pierre and seriously limited some of them. Such efforts had significant financial effects in the short term. Important revenues were blocked, sometimes for years, and there were substantial legal costs. But the most important effect was on the character of the Roncherolles' place in the countryside. The state's efforts were devoted to questioning, ultimately to paring away, the family's extra-economic role. The maintenance of seigneurial authority was made to be expensive and vexatious, even for rights that the Crown ultimately allowed to stand.

Like the market economy, then, the state worked to undermine rural paternalism: to limit the kinds of controls that the Roncherolles could apply to the villagers and bourgeois around them. This was a nearly continuous process during the Old Regime; royal judges began to question the Roncherolles' rights early in the sixteenth century, and their efforts persisted over the next two centuries. But its effects were most clearly visible from the late seventeenth century, and they coincided with a related tendency (discussed above), the growing eagerness of lesser nobles to free themselves from the barony's seigneurial demands. By the mid–eighteenth century, the Roncherolles' authority in the countryside had been decisively weakened.

VI

THE LORDSHIP OF PONT-ST-PIERRE

Previous chapters have considered the informal powers that the Roncherolles exercised along the Andelle Valley: powers that derived from their "credit" among the local nobles, from the character of their household, from the scale of the resources that they commanded and the impact that these had on local economic life. The present chapter examines more formal kinds of domination. It examines the Roncherolles' property rights in Pont-St-Pierre and the political powers that these conferred. It seeks to show how a large seigneurial property functioned and evolved over the Old Regime, and how it affected local life.

Two arguments underlie this examination. First, it will be argued here that changes similar to the ones seen in earlier chapters affected the Roncherolles' exercise of seigneurial power. At the formal level of the seigneury as well as at the more informal level of household administration, the Roncherolles' hold on local society diminished sharply over the Old Regime; and this evolution—like changes in the Roncherolles' household—was in the direction of increasing adaptation to a market economy. However—and this is the second of this chapter's principal arguments—Pont-St-Pierre's adaptation to the market economy was neither complete nor easy. To the end of the Old Regime, elements of the seigneury stood in the way of a free market economy and brought the barony into conflict with local merchants and farmers. Pont-St-Pierre's evolution illustrates the seigneurial system's ambiguous responses to economic change.

213

THE ESTATE IN 1600

In 1600 Pierre de Roncherolles presented to the Crown the feudal homage that every fief holder was supposed to offer his suzerain. As part of this acknowledgement of dependence, he drew up an extensive description of his barony of Pont-St-Pierre.[1] The barony included, first, the château itself, built of stone, with a slate roof, a moat, and a drawbridge. This had been constructed at some point after 1377; the original château had been destroyed during the early phases of the Hundred Years' War, but its ruins survived in 1600 as a reminder "of the ancient wars."[2] A mid-sixteenth-century picture confirms the impression of military functionalism that the drawbridge suggests (fig. 1, p. 24), but by then the moat's functions were chiefly decorative, to supply water to the gardens around the château. Near the château was an enclosed courtyard of farm buildings: barns, an apple press for making cider, a pigeon house. An enclosed park of about eight acres, part of it woods, part of it arable, surrounded the whole. A traveler described the scene in about 1640: "The château of Pont-St-Pierre is rather impressive from the exterior because of the main buildings with their pointed towers at the corners, the whole covered with slate. The interior is of irregular curves and is not very impressive. There are fine ditches full of water, and the Andelle is all about. . . . Thus the château is between the meadows and the river, and the wooded hillsides are to the south."[3]

The barony's second major component, and in 1600 its most valuable, was its share in the forest of Longbouel, which stretched along the hillsides to the north of the Andelle. A measurement in 1558 established the barony's share of the forest at 1,356 arpents (about 850 acres), the Crown's share at 2,200 arpents.[4] This was small in comparison with other forests in upper Normandy. In the mid–seventeenth century, the forest of Rouvray included 8,300 arpents and the forest of Roumare 9,013 arpents; up the Andelle from Pont-St-Pierre, the forest of Lyons included nearly 22,000 arpents.[5] Despite its relatively small scale, however, the barony's forest was far

1. Pont-St-Pierre, Aveu, 10 July 1600.
2. Ibid.; AD Eure, E 2392, Chartrier de Pont-St-Pierre, 1.
3. Chanoine Porée, ed., *Du Buisson-Aubenay, Itinéraire de Normandie* (Rouen and Paris, 1911), 59.
4. Caillot, liasse 230, arpentage, 1558.
5. Edmond Esmonin, ed., *Voysin de la Noiraye: Mémoire sur la généralité de Rouen (1665)* (Paris, 1913), 116–17.

Figure 14. *The château of Pont-St-Pierre (Cliché MIOSSEC © 1974 Inventaire général/SPADEM)*

more important both in area and in value than its farmland. In 1600 there were only 25 acres of meadow and about 70 acres of arable. The barony also included three grain mills, two of them in the bourg of Pont-St-Pierre and driven by the Andelle, the third a windmill in la Neuville recently constructed (in the words of the *aveu*) "as an aid and relief for our subjects," who would otherwise have been forced to bring their grain to Pont-St-Pierre. Unlike most seigneurial mills in upper Normandy, these mills enjoyed the profitable right of *banalité:* all residents of the barony, nobles as well as commoners, were required on pain of confiscations and fines to bring their grain to one of these three mills.

Third, the barony possessed an array of more specifically seigneurial rights. It enjoyed the right to hold a market every Saturday and the right to insist that all commercial transactions within the barony's limits take place there; violations of this monopoly too could be punished with fines and confiscations. The barons could hold fairs in Pont-St-Pierre twice each year, and at both fairs and markets they could charge fees for measuring grain and taxes (the *coutumes*) on most transactions.[6] The barony owned the Andelle River itself from the convent of Fontaine Guérard just upstream to what contemporaries called "the Gullet of the Andelle," its juncture with the Seine.[7] On the basis of this ownership, the barons exercised a series of lucrative rights: they monopolized fishing in the river; they charged fees on the timber that was floated downstream every year from the forest of Lyons; they charged a tax on wine that was brought across the river and on boats loading timber at the juncture with the Seine.

The barony included two seigneurial justices in 1600. Because the baron owned part of the forest of Longbouel, he had the right to employ a *verdier* to try infractions of his property rights there, in particular illicit grazing and woodcutting. Because he owned the right of high justice, he employed a *bailli* to decide all civil and criminal cases that arose within the barony's limits: crimes subject to capital punishment, cases in which the baron himself was a litigant, issues concerning the barony's seigneurial rights, appeals from decisions by the baron's *verdier*—these all came before the *bailli* of the High Justice. The *bailli* had in addition a wide range of what the Old Regime called police powers: powers to regulate trade, public hygiene, and such threats to public morality as taverns and billiard tables.

Finally, there was the barony's role as feudal and seigneurial overlordship. Five fiefs were subordinate to the barony of Pont-St-Pierre in 1600. One of them was the fief of Roncherolles itself, the family's original home, now held by its junior branch, and another had fallen into the baron's own possession; the three others retained an independent existence. More important than these essentially honorific dependencies, several hundred peasant tenants held their land from the barony in exchange for permanently fixed rents, the *cens* and *rentes foncières*. In contemporary legal theory, two sets of property rights applied to such tenures. Their tenants could sell them, transmit them to their heirs, and otherwise treat them as their own; but the barony also had property rights to them, deriving from the theory that seigneurial tenures had been permanently leased rather than

6. In the eighteenth century local merchants certified that "since time immemorial" the *coutumes* had amounted to 5 s. for each horse or colt, 4 s. for each cow or pig, 5 s. for each sack of wheat, 1 s. for each *boisseau* of other grains: Caillot, liasse 237, "Pont-St-Pierre, droits en général," 1768.

7. Porée, *Du Buisson-Aubenay*, 55.

sold. Thus the Norman law allowed seigneurial lords to intervene when tenures were sold and, by matching the purchase price, to reintegrate what had formerly been tenures into their domains.[8] The barony had tenants in eight of the parishes around the forest of Long-bouel, and their rents were set in a mixture of grain, poultry, and money. These rents were more than simple financial transactions. In practical terms they defined the limits of the barony's other powers; where the barony collected rents, there it could most easily enforce its rights of *banalité*, justice, and regulation.

CONTINUITY AND CHANGE

All of the elements that Pierre de Roncherolles described in his *aveu* of 1600 survived to the French Revolution. But the central theme in the barony's history over the early modern period was change in the relative importance of its constituent elements. Tables 47 and 48 and figure 15 present two views of this process. They display a fundamental transformation in Pont-St-Pierre's character between the late fourteenth century and the end of the Old Regime: from an essentially seigneurial property, in which rights of justice, monopolies, and fixed rents counted for as much as 92 percent of total income, to a property whose central resources involved production for the free market. In the eighteenth century, three fourths of Pont-St-Pierre's income came from short-term leases of domain lands and mills and from sales of timber and hay. By this point fixed rents amounted to about 3 percent of total value, judicial rights to about 1 percent; in the late fourteenth century these together had counted for more than three-fourths of the barony's total value.

Only two elements in the seigneurial economy of Pont-St-Pierre showed some signs of continuing vitality in the eighteenth century. Over the seventeenth and eighteenth centuries, the barony's taxes on commercial transactions, its *coutumes*, increased in value as commercial transactions became more frequent around Pont-St-Pierre;[9] and its grain mills profited from the growth of population within the barony's limits. But even these sources of income lost importance

8. For the jurisprudence surrounding the Norman lordship, see Josias Bérault, *La coutume reformée du pays et duché de Normandie . . .* (Rouen, 1614), 152–278, and David Houard, *Dictionnaire analytique, historique, étymologique, critique et interprétatif de la coutume de Normandie*, 4 vols. (Rouen, 1780), 2:344–493.

9. See above, Chapter 1.

TABLE 47. *Sources of Seigneurial Income, 1398–1780*
(percentage of total income)

Years	Rentes	Coutumes	Justice	Banalités	Total
1398–1399	63	[a]	15	14[a]	92
1414–1415	50	[a]	14	18[a]	82
1454–1455	50	4	12	8	74
1455–1456	46	6	10	16	78
1458–1459	46	5	8	14	73
1459–1460	48	6	9	15	78
1460–1461	46	6	9	14	75
1461–1462	48	7	8	14	77
1465–1466	38	5	13	10	66
1466–1467	39	5	8	15	67
1477–1478	50	4	8	16	78
1479–1480	51	3	8	16[c]	78
1480–1481	44	3	22	14	83
1481–1482	50	3	20	16	89
1482–1483	41	5	9	18	73
1506–1507	29	4	19	10	62
1513–1514	36	13[b]	11	12	72
1515–1516	37	16[b]	12	13	78
1521–1522	43	16[b]	7	11	77
1558–1559	14	3[b]	2	10	29
1560–1561	19	4[b]	3	12	38
1570–1571	11	2[b]	1	5	19
1571–1572	5[c]	1	2	3[c]	11
1572–1573	14[c]	2	0	7	23
1573–1574	12[c]	3	1	10[c]	26
1740	3	5	1	14[b]	23
1765	7	5	1	17[b]	30
1780[d]	3	2	unknown	6	11

SOURCE: Comptes; Tabel. Pont-St-Pierre.

[a] Included in lease of banal mills.

[b] Includes dues charged on wood floated on the Andelle.

[c] Estimate based on previous year's revenues.

[d] Estimate based on incomes over several years in the late 1770s and 1780s.

TABLE 48. *Sources of Domain Revenues, 1398–1780*
(percentage of total revenue)

Years	Farms [and] Meadows[a]		Woods	Fulling Mills	Total
1398–1399	0	4	4	0	8
1414–1415	0	5	12	0	17
1454–1455	5	8	13	0	26
1455–1456	5	8	10	0	23
1458–1459	4	9	13	0	26
1459–1460	2	8	12	0	22
1460–1461	3	9	14	0	26
1461–1462	3	6	15	0	24
1465–1466	12	5	17	0	34
1466–1467	11	9	13	0	33
1477–1478	0	6	15	0	21
1479–1480	0	6	14	0	20
1480–1481	0	5	12	0	17
1481–1482	0	5	7	0	12
1482–1483	0	8	20	0	28
1506–1507		10	28	0	38
1513–1514		8	21	0	29
1515–1516		7	15	0	22
1521–1522		4	20	0	24
1558–1559		14	58	0	72
1560–1561		12	51	0	63
1570–1571		7	75	0	82
1571–1572		4	86	0	90
1572–1573		4	73	0	77
1573–1574	0	7[b]	66	0	73
1740		15	52	9	76
1765	8	15	44	3	70
1780	4	28	56	1	89

SOURCE: Comptes; Tabel. Pont-St-Pierre.

[a] Sources for 1506–73 and 1740 do not distinguish between farm income and meadow income.

[b] Estimate based on previous year's revenues.

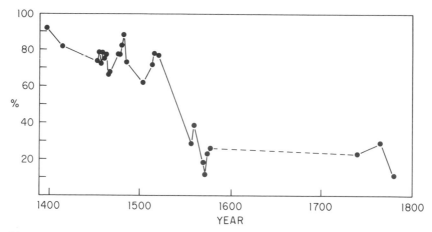

Figure 15. Seigneurial revenues as percentage of total revenue (no data available between 1574 and 1740)

relative to the barony's domain. Pont-St-Pierre's seigneurial sources of income had not altogether vanished, but they had lost their central place within the barony's economy.

Was Pont-St-Pierre typical? Few French estates have been studied in detail, and fewer still have been followed through the Old Regime. Within Normandy, though, Pont-St-Pierre's structure seems to have been characteristic of large estates both in the late Middle Ages and in the eighteenth century. Guy Bois has shown the heavy reliance of upper Norman large estates on seigneurial incomes during the fourteenth century,[10] and the same appears to have been true of the barony of le Neubourg, to the southwest of Pont-St-Pierre; Jacques Bottin has shown the increasing reliance of the convent of Montivilliers on domain revenues over the sixteenth and early seventeenth centuries.[11] For the eighteenth century, fiscal rolls provide clearer statistical evidence. The rolls of the *vingtièmes* in the area around Rouen (as analyzed above, in Chapter 3) suggest that in the eighteenth century Pont-St-Pierre was among the more heavily taxed seigneurial large estates; only a small minority of estates matched even its feeble sei-

10. Guy Bois, *Crise du féodalisme: Economie rurale et démographie en Normandie orientale du début du XIVe siècle au milieu du XVIe siècle* (Paris, 1976), 195–214, 230–34.

11. André Plaisse, *La baronnie du Neubourg: Essai d'histoire agraire, économique, et sociale* (Paris, 1961); Jacques Bottin, *Seigneurs et paysans dans l'ouest du pays de Caux (1540–1650)* (Paris, 1983), 301–11. See also the analyses presented in Jonathan Dewald, *The Formation of a Provincial Nobility: The Magistrates of the Parlement of Rouen, 1499–1610* (Princeton, 1980), 340–42, for other examples of Norman lordships.

gneurial revenues.[12] But examination of the lesser nobles and their holdings around Pont-St-Pierre has suggested also the sharp differences between the large estates and the mass of smaller properties around them. These smaller estates often had trappings of seigneurial authority: seigneurial rents, pigeon houses, rights of low justice. At base, however, they were large farms, pieced together from peasant tenures and royal land sales.[13] Pont-St-Pierre appears to have been representative of the evolution of the large lordships; it was far from typical of nobles' estates considered more generally.

The chronology of Pont-St-Pierre's evolution deserves emphasis. The importance of seigneurial revenues declined only gradually during the fifteenth century. During the first twenty years of the sixteenth century, seigneurial revenues still made up three-fourths of the barony's income; and even fixed rents retained substantial importance, amounting to 43 percent of the estate's value in 1521–22. The stability of Pont-St-Pierre's seigneurial orientation during these years illustrates yet again the feudal system's tenacity during the aftermath of the Hundred Years' War.[14] The Roncherolles survived their personal disasters during these years; their estate likewise survived, with its structure essentially intact.

Structural change came not amid the castastrophes of the fifteenth century but during the prosperity of the sixteenth. By the early 1560s, seigneurial revenues were less than half as important to the estate's total income as they had been in 1521–22; a decade later their importance had declined further still, falling to a low point of

12. For a different view, emphasizing the continuing importance of seigneurial revenues throughout the Old Regime, see Guy Le Marchand, "La féodalité et la Révolution française: Seigneurie et communauté paysanne (1780–1799)," *Annales historiques de la Révolution française* 252 (October–December 1980): 536–58, and James Lowth Goldsmith, *Les Salers et les d'Escorailles: Seigneurs de Haute Auvergne, 1500–1789* (Clermont Ferrand, 1984), 217–27.

13. Cf. the similar situation described in Jean Gallet, *La seigneurie bretonne (1450–1680): L'exemple du Vannetais* (Paris, 1983), 591–93 and passim.

14. This in contrast to the argument presented in Bois, *Crise du féodalisme*, and in his "Noblesse et crise des revenus seigneuriaux en France aux XIVe et XVe siècles: Essai d'interprétation," in Philippe Contamine, ed., *La noblesse au moyen âge, XIe–XVe siècles: Essais à la mémoire de Robert Boutruche* (Paris, 1976), 219–33, that the Hundred Years' War and its aftermath were manifestations of a fundamental crisis of the feudal structure. For emphasis on the continuities of the seigneurie after the war, see, for instance, Guy Fourquin, "Un siècle de calamités," in Michel Mollat, ed., *Histoire de l'Ile de France et de Paris* (Toulouse, 1971), 167, and Pierre Charbonnier, *Une autre France: La seigneurie rurale en Basse Auvergne du XIVe au XVIe siècle*, 2 vols. (Clermont-Ferrand, 1980), 1:487–501, 2:744–74. For a synthesis of these two viewpoints, see Hugues Neveux, "Déclin et reprise: La fluctuation biséculaire, 1330–1550," in Emmanuel Le Roy Ladurie, Neveux, and Jean Jacquart, *Histoire de la France rurale* (Paris, 1975), 2:90ff.

11 percent of total income in 1571–72. In the course of fifty years, the lordship had been transformed.

This happened partly because of the inflation that characterized the sixteenth century, the result of population growth and the arrival of American treasure. Prices of grains in northern France increased four- or fivefold over the sixteenth century. Because they were set primarily in money rather than in kind, the barony's fixed rents failed to keep pace with this inflation. Indeed, during the early sixteenth century there was a slight decline in even the nominal value of these rents: from about 421 l. in 1521–22 to about 406 l. in 1558–59.[15] Fixed rents revived somewhat thereafter, but even in the 1740s their typical yearly value was only 543 l.[16]

But as important as the role of inflation in the collapse of Pont-St-Pierre's fixed rents were choices and habits in the Roncherolles' administration of the estate. The estate's accounts at several points display carelessness in controlling and collecting rents. In 1515–16, the estate's receiver noted of one pair of tenants "that they do not acknowledge owing the said rent and the receiver has no documents that make mention of it." In 1560–61 there was the note "for all these [rents] it is noted 'nothing' because the receiver does not know where the said properties are located on the ancient rolls"; and there were similar complaints in 1572–73.[17] All lordships faced comparable problems during the fifteenth and sixteenth centuries because of the ravages of the Hundred Years' War: documents were lost, lands fell out of cultivation, the turnover of manorial tenants was rapid.[18] Nonetheless, Pont-St-Pierre's administration appears to have been exceptionally lax. Rouen's cathedral canons drew up at least two *terriers* of their manor in la Neuville during the first half of the sixteenth century; but the first surviving *terrier* of the entire barony of Pont-St-Pierre dates from about 1635.[19] The real value of seigneurial rents in Pont-St-Pierre collapsed partly because the Roncherolles failed to make the efforts that would have been necessary for their survival.

Their choice may have been the more economically rational, for the defense of seigneurial rights was expensive. The cathedral canons made the point themselves in 1598, when they sold a fief in Romilly to a Rouennais official. The fief, they claimed, consisted "only in an enfeoffed domain of a few small seigneurial rents, . . .

15. Comptes, 1521–22, 1558–59.
16. Ibid., 1740ff.
17. Ibid., 1560–61, 1570–74.
18. Excellent discussion by Bernard Guenée, *Tribunaux et gens de justice dans le bailliage de Senlis à la fin du moyen âge (vers 1380–vers 1550)* (Paris, 1963), 58–60, 392–95.
19. See Appendix C.

whose collection is nearly impossible both because of distance and because of the poverty of those who owe them, who cannot be pursued without many expenses that eat up and absorb the greater part of what they might pay."[20] As the real value of such rents diminished during the sixteenth century, the costs of litigation to defend them must have seemed less and less worth undertaking.

Similar concerns touched the economics of the barony's judicial rights. Judicial rights retained genuine economic importance in the late fourteenth century: they counted for 15 percent of total revenues, slightly more than the banal mills and four times as much as sales of wood. As late as 1515–16 they brought 12 percent of total income—nearly equal to the 15 percent of the total that came from sales of wood. But by the 1560s they amounted to about 2 percent of the total, and by the 1570s they rarely rose above 1 percent. Part of their decline was relative, a reflection of the rising importance of other sources of income. But its main source was political. Judicial profits were increasingly absorbed by the costs of justice, especially the costs that derived from the monarchy's growing influence. From the early sixteenth century, the Crown insisted on higher standards of education for all judicial officials, seigneurial as well as royal, and this in itself probably increased expenses.[21]

More directly, the growing frequency of appeals to the king's justice meant a heavy drain on judicial profits. A case of 1574 illustrates the expenses to which growing royal influence led. The barony's judge had condemned a woman named Robinette du Bois to be tortured in the course of a homicide case. She appealed the decision to the Parlement of Rouen, and immediately expenses began to mount up: 10 s. to the Parlement's clerk just for accepting the documents in the case, 45 s. to three Rouennais midwives who examined Robinette's claim that she was pregnant (and therefore could not be tortured), 116 s. to the councillor who reported the case to the Parlement, 58 s. to the sergeants who conveyed Robinette to Rouen, 19 l. 10 s. to the lawyers who took part in the initial decision, and 13 l. 18 s. as the costs of Robinette's stay in prison, her travel back to Pont-St-Pierre, and the purchase of a copy of the Parlement's judgment, in this case confirming the original decision. The total cost during the month that this phase of Robinette's case lasted was nearly 45 l., about half of the barony's total judicial receipts in the year 1571–72. (There were no judicial receipts at all in 1573–74, the year in which

20. Caillot, liasse 237, "Droits en général," sale of 26 August 1598 (eighteenth-century copy).
21. Guenée, *Tribunaux et gens de justice*, 185–216.

Robinette was tried.)[22] Even without appeals, the court's normal activities might require the intervention of specialist royal officials. In 1631 the High Justice condemned a resident of la Neuville to be beaten publicly for having stolen two pigs. For this task, it was necessary to call on the Parlement of Rouen's executioner, at a cost of 18 l.[23] The costs of exercising justice did not rob the barony's High Justice of all importance; as we shall see, it remained an important center of local political life into the eighteenth century. But justice had ceased by the mid–sixteenth century to be a source of profits. As a result the barons made fewer efforts to maintain their judicial role, at least in the potentially unprofitable area of criminal prosecutions.[24] With justice as with seigneurial rents, lax administration might be an intelligent economic choice.

Other parts of the lordship, however, were the object of aggressive attention in these same years. The barony's grain mills, to which all residents were obliged to bring their grain for milling, increased rapidly in value after the mid–fifteenth century. At that time there was one grain mill in Pont-St-Pierre; in 1455–56 it was rented for 71 l., and its value remained about constant over the next thirty years. But by 1515–16 its rent had risen to 120 l.; by 1551 a second mill had been constructed in Pont-St-Pierre, and the two mills together were leased for 320 l.; by 1585 there was a third mill, a windmill in la Neuville; and by 1670 the three mills together were leased for 2,500 l.[25]

Ultimately these increases resulted from growth in the barony's population, which created a rising demand for the milling services that the barony monopolized. In the same way, rising population was partly responsible for the prosperity of the barony's market rights, the dues known as *coutumes*. Receipts from the market were 12 l. annually in the later fifteenth century, then rose to about 40 l. in the early sixteenth century, 85 l. in the 1580s, and climbed to over 300 l. in the mid–seventeenth century.[26] The sixteenth and seventeenth centuries had undermined important seigneurial rights in Pont-St-Pierre, but the same years had enhanced the value of other

22. Comptes, 1570–74.
23. Caillot, liasse 245, "Pont-St-Pierre, Haute Justice," 1 February 1631.
24. Cf. for the eighteenth century, Nicole Castan, *Justice et répression en Languedoc à l'époque des lumières* (Paris, 1980), 106–27.
25. Comptes 1454–56, 1515–16; Caillot, liasse 252, "Paroisse de Romilly, Baux"; AD Eure, E 1260, Tabel. Pont-St-Pierre, 21 October 1585.
26. See above, Chapter 1.

aspects of the seigneury. To some extent growth and decline reflected the same basic changes. Population growth was a principal
cause of the inflation that undercut the barony's seigneurial rents;
but it was also a source of profits for other aspects of the lordship.

Links between the lordship's vitality and the social changes at
work around it were most evident in the case of the barony's rights to
the forest of Longbouel. In the fifteenth century the Roncherolles'
cuttings in the forest usually amounted to between 16 and 26 acres
each year, and in some years even less: only 9.4 acres in 1481–82, for
instance. Any single year's cutting took only a small share of the
forest's 850 acres, never more than 3 percent of its area during the
fifteenth century. This practice allowed at least twenty years' growth
between cuttings and assured that its timber remained of high quality. Through much of the fifteenth century, in fact, the timber that the
forest supplied had less financial importance than the seigneurial
rights that the Roncherolles exercised over it: their judicial rights in
the forest and the dues that they received from tenants who grazed
their animals there. In 1398–99 these rights produced 63 l., sales of
wood only 45 l. Like the barony as a whole, the forest was important
above all for its seigneurial aspects, its judicial profits and rents.[27]

As late as 1515–16 these two aspects of the forest remained in
rough equilibrium; sales of wood in that year brought the Roncherolles 140 l., grazing dues and judicial profits 83 l. But already the
Roncherolles' exploitation of the forest had dramatically changed. In
the years 1506–7, 1513–14, and 1515–16 cuttings averaged 64 acres,
three or four times typical cuttings in the fifteenth century; in 1570–
74 they averaged 60 acres. By this point, the financial importance of
the forest's seigneurial elements had virtually disappeared. In 1560–
61 sales of wood brought 1,289 l., the forest jurisdiction 35 l., and
grazing rights nothing at all; in the years 1570–74, judicial rights
apparently produced no profits, but sales of wood produced at least
3,500 l. annually.

Heavier financial reliance on sales of timber meant rapid deterioration in the forest's quality. In the fifteenth century cuttings had
never taken more than 3 percent of its area; in the early years of the
sixteenth century, about 7 percent of the forest's area was cut annually; and in the mid–seventeenth century the annual cutting took 10
percent of the forest.[28] In the early eighteenth century there was

27. Comptes.
28. Comptes; Caillot, liasse 241, "Droits en général," lease of 1656.

apparently an attempt to allow more time between cuttings—twelve years in some parts of the forest, fourteen in others—but by the 1770s ten years of growth was again the norm.[29]

The effects of these policies were visible in the 1570s, when Jean Bodin undertook his abortive reform of the Norman forests. The Roncherolles, Bodin complained, "have burned so much charcoal and cut so much wood in this forest that they have devastated nearly two leagues of the countryside."[30] A decade later one of the baron's own forest sergeants offered a more detailed but fundamentally similar view. The area of the forest that he guarded included one section of trees nine years old, "planted fairly sparsely, with many bushes among them." Three other sections had young trees but were in good condition: 10 acres "nicely planted in young oaks," an adjoining area of six-year-old trees, and a section of six- and seven-year-old trees, "fairly well grown back excepting some empty areas that have not grown back." The remaining three sections that he guarded—about 40 percent of the total—had almost no trees of any value. One of these was "mostly cleared and in bushes"; another had been cut five or six years earlier but "in it no trees have grown back except for thorns and bushes"; the third consisted only "of clearings planted with bushes and holly."[31] The sergeant's report suggests the rapid pace at which the forest declined in the sixteenth century. Areas that had been worth cutting only a few years earlier had failed to grow back and were now covered only with undergrowth. The oldest trees were no more than nine years old. In these circumstances the forest was useful mainly for firewood. Probably the forest received more careful treatment in the seventeenth century.[32] But such concern could not restore the forest to its fifteenth-century quality.

In their growing dependence on the forest over the sixteenth century, the Roncherolles were typical of the Norman nobility. At the time of Colbert it was claimed that there were three thousand owners of woodlands in the province, most of them lay nobles.[33]

29. Pont-St-Pierre, Registre de Fermages, 1738; AD Eure, C 318, *Vingtièmes* of Pont-St-Pierre, 3.

30. Quoted in Michel Devèze, *La vie de la forêt française au XVIe siècle*, 2 vols. (Paris, 1961), 1:242.

31. AD Eure, 86 B 121: Verderie, Forêt de Longbouel, 15 April 1587.

32. For instance, merchants who bought the right to cut the forest were required to leave eighteen trees standing on each arpent that they cut, so as to assure proper regrowth; Caillot, liasse 241, lease of 1656.

33. Devèze, *La vie de la forêt*, 1:202.

TABLE 49. *Forest Cuttings and Revenues*

Years	Area Cut (arpents)	Total Price (l.)	Price per Arpent (l.)
1414–1415	33.06	91	2.75
1466–1467	41.60	70	1.68
1479–1483	23.49[a]	66	2.81
1506–1516	101.73[b]	215	2.11
1560–1561	81.25	1,289	15.86
1570–1574	99.19[a]	5,663	57.09
1738	75.75	8,240	108.78
1770–1774	89.08[c]	11,098	124.58
1775–1778	84.71[b]	12,790	150.99
1780–1784	79.39[a]	10,134	127.65
1785–1790	73.92[b]	12,093	163.60

SOURCE: Comptes; AD Eure, 86 B 126.

[a] Mean of four years.

[b] Mean of three years.

[c] Mean of five years.

What did such reliance on a deteriorating resource mean for these nobles' financial prospects? Decaying forest resources might be thought to have offered only a short-term replacement for declining seigneurial dues. At Pont-St-Pierre and other upper Norman estates, however, the steadily growing demand for wood more than compensated for the forest's declining quality.[34] The combined pressures of population growth, urbanization, and industrial development produced enormous demand for wood of even low quality. Because of its location—near Rouen, with easy transportation along the Andelle and the Seine to both Rouen and Paris—the barony could profit fully from this demand.

Table 49 displays the consequences of this situation: despite the forest's declining quality, cuttings remained extensive and prices high to the end of the Old Regime. The value of each arpent cut

34. Bois, *Crise du féodalisme*, 185, 233, and "Noblesse et crise des revenus seigneuriaux," 226; Suzanne Deck, *Etude sur la forêt d'Eu* (Caen, 1929), 116–18. See also, for the Ile de France, Guy Fourquin, "La part de la forêt dans les ressources d'un grand seigneur d'Ile-de-France à la fin du XIIIe siècle et au XIVe siècle," *Paris et Ile-de-France* 18–19 (1967–68): 7–36; and Hiroyuki Niromiya, "Un cadre de vie rurale au XVIIe et au XVIIIe siècle: La seigneurie de Fleury-en-Bière," ibid. 18–19 (1967–68): 37–97 and 20 (1969): 65–126.

increased about sevenfold over the first two-thirds of the sixteenth century, then trebled again by the 1570s; by 1730 values had doubled again, and they increased about 50 percent by the 1780s. The forest was a fragile natural resource, which Pont-St-Pierre's owners mistreated for nearly three centuries. But demand for wood was sufficiently strong to make up for this exploitation; and Pont-St-Pierre's geographical situation allowed its owners to profit fully from this demand. In this respect, capitalist development allowed the lordship to retain its economic importance to the end of the Old Regime.

In fact the real threat to the barony's forest revenues was political rather than ecological. It derived from the Crown's periodic efforts (traced above, in Chapter 5) to reclaim the forest or, at the least, to restrict the barons' use of it. These efforts produced costly litigation and during at least one period—between 1662 and 1677—a prohibition against any cuttings in the forest, "even for heating and repairs." Given the scale of the revenues that the barons took from the forest, the Crown's efforts at reform were a serious threat, an assault on the barony's central component. The barony's changing structure made the financial stakes of reform enormous.

In contrast to the development of forest revenues, the Roncherolles' dependence on income from arable land and meadows increased slowly and fitfully. This was not for lack of opportunity. Norman law permitted lords to intervene in any sales of land within their lordships; by meeting the buyer's offer and reimbursing any expenses, the lord could acquire the property himself. Even without this effort on the lord's part, a number of properties inevitably came under his control when their owners died without heirs or found themselves unable to pay the rents set on them.[35] The lord who wanted to expand the amount of land under his direct control had few obstacles in his way.

But in Pont-St-Pierre this did not happen before the late seventeenth century, well after the inflation of the sixteenth century ought to have indicated the wisdom of directly controlling the land. Pont-St-Pierre's landed domain scarcely existed in the fourteenth and early fifteenth centuries. Meadows had supplied 4 to 5 percent of the barony's income, arable land nothing at all. These percentages increased significantly in the later fifteenth century. Tenures left

35. For the frequency with which these rights might be exercised, see above, Chapter 2.

vacant in the aftermath of the Hundred Years' War came under the barons' direct administration, and the income that they produced counted in some years for about one-fifth of the barony's total revenue. But this expansion of the barony's domain was only a temporary response to demographic and economic disaster. Unable to find tenants who would take these lands for permanently fixed seigneurial rents, the barons were forced to lease them for short-term rents or administer them directly. They apparently did so unwillingly, for the recovery of the sixteenth century brought with it a decline in the importance of short-term leases and direct administration. When they could, the barons made use of permanently fixed rents.

The Roncherolles retained this habit over a strikingly long period of time. During the sixteenth century they continued to make substantial grants of land to dependents and local nobles in exchange for permanently fixed rents.[36] But this was not only a means of assuring local fidelities. The policy reflected their assumptions about what was important in landownership. Thus in 1585 Pierre de Roncherolles sold "each and every one of the arable lands and meadows belonging to the said lord because of the noble fief, estate, and lordship of Mynières" –but kept the fief's seigneurial rights.[37] In 1613 he arranged with a *laboureur* to take a plot of land in la Neuville "a rente et fieffe seigneurialle a tousiours"; despite a century of price revolution, the rent was set entirely in money. A year later Pierre's son arranged for an agent to "pass a contract of a *rente fonciere & seigneurialle*" of a mill that he owned. In 1625 there were two more grants, these of substantial pieces of land, each for a "rente fonciere et irraquitable" that combined money and payments in kind.[38] By this point the Roncherolles had accumulated ample experience of the corrosive effects of inflation; they had seen their fixed rents lose much of their real value to the rising prices of the sixteenth century. Nonetheless, they continued to grant properties out in exchange for fixed money rents. Direct control of land was simply not a fundamental economic objective, despite the possibility that such control would have offered of flexible short-term rents, responsive to the effects of inflation.

Attitudes changed only during the seventeenth century. Only then, apparently, did the Roncherolles cease to think of their lord-

36. Above, Chapter 2.
37. AD Eure, E 1254, Tabel. Pont-St-Pierre, 29 January 1585.
38. AD S-M, Tabel. Pont-St-Pierre, 23 November 1613, 14 July 1614, 7 January 1625, 21 January 1625.

ship in fundamentally seigneurial terms and begin a sustained effort to expand its domain. By 1715 they had bought two large farms—worth in all about 50,000 l.—and had integrated them into Pont-St-Pierre's domain.[39] In about 1715 they also constructed three large fulling mills on the Andelle, in an effort to profit from the developing cloth industry in Elbeuf.[40] Other nobles found this an attractive investment as well: in 1717 a Rouennais *trésorier de France* joined with two drapers from Elbeuf to buy another fulling mill in Pont-St-Pierre.[41]

Finally, the Roncherolles invested in smaller pieces of land, especially in the meadows that were among the principal resources of the Andelle Valley. In 1600 Pierre de Roncherolles' *aveu* had listed 25 acres of meadow; by 1768, when the barony was sold to the Caillot de Coquéraumont family, meadows included at least 66 acres.[42] The Roncherolles used the law as well as purchases in this effort. In 1759 Michel de Roncherolles announced to the parishioners of St-Nicolas de Pont-St-Pierre "that he intends to bring to an end the liberty that his ancestors had allowed them to pasture their animals in a part of the meadow situated in the valley of the said place; that wishing to convert this meadow to his own use he intends to take back the enjoyment of it; that since the tolerance and goodness of his progenitors had been the sole source of their possession, he claims to forbid it to them from today." The villagers sought legal advice but finally relinquished their claim; Michel de Roncherolles, assuring the villagers that he would "willingly exert himself to give them new proofs of his goodness by according them some assistance (*soulagement*)," offered another pasture nearby.[43] Michel viewed his eco-

39. Les-Maisons-Bernières, purchased for 26,000 l. in 1715: AD S-M, Coignard, notaire à Rouen, 5 January 1715; Douville-Calleville, reference to acquisition in 1610: AD Eure, E 2392, Chartrier de Pont-St-Pierre, 128.

40. Caillot, liasse "Paroisse de Pont-St-Pierre . . . moulins," agreement between Roncherolles and André Le Tourneur and Nicolas Lancelevée, 1748–49: reference to the "moulins . . . que mondict sieur . . . a fait construire depuis trente ans ou environ."

41. Ibid., liasse "Paroisse de Romilly, Matières diverses," 6 April 1717. For discussions of eighteenth-century nobles' involvement in such industrial enterprises, see, for instance, Guy Richard, *Noblesse d'affaires au XVIIIe siècle* (Paris, 1974); Guy Chaussinand-Nogaret, *La noblesse au XVIIIe siècle: De la féodalité aux lumières* (Paris, 1976), 119–61.

42. Caillot, liasse 241, "Matières diverses," act of sale, 24 September 1768.

43. AD Eure, E 1266, Tabel. Pont-St-Pierre, 31 January 1759. Michel de Roncherolles' contrast between his ancestors' acceptance of the community's rights and his own individualism is essentially that of Marc Bloch; see for instance *French Rural History: An Essay on Its Basic Characteristics*, trans. Janet Sondheimer (Berkeley and Los Angeles, 1966), 197ff.

nomic aims as fundamentally unlike those of his ancestors. In his view, they had been bountiful to the villagers and indifferent to their own property rights; he intended to assert his rights despite his ancestors' neglect. What Michel ascribed to tolerance, though, reflected deeper changes in economic orientation. Michel's ancestors had been interested in the seigneurial rents that villagers could pay. He himself sought to control what the land produced.

In fact, by this time the Roncherolles' financial troubles and Parisian interests had slowed down the domain's expansion. But expansion resumed after they sold Pont-St-Pierre in 1765. The estate went first to Anne Pierre de Montesquiou, a soldier from a well-known aristocratic family and a resident of the stylish faubourg St. Honoré in Paris.[44] Montesquiou kept Pont-St-Pierre only three years, then in 1768 he sold the estate in order to purchase a house in the still more stylish place Vendôme.[45] Pont-St-Pierre's purchaser was Anthoine Pierre Thomas Louis Caillot de Coquéraumont, already the owner of several important fiefs and a president in Rouen's Chambre des Comptes, Aides et Finances. Caillot was probably the wealthiest member of Rouen's *noblesse de robe* in the later eighteenth century. In 1774 his assessment for the capitation was the highest in both the city and the rural election of Rouen,[46] and his *hôtel* in Rouen was one of the city's most magificent (fig. 16).

With such resources available, the Caillots undertook an impressive expansion of Pont-St-Pierre's domains. The extent of their efforts can be seen from an inventory of the property in 1792, during its brief confiscation by the revolutionary authorities.[47] The fact that the Caillots had been absentee owners, with other estates to visit, was evident in the dilapidation of the château itself; the buildng had already shown signs of the Roncherolles' neglect in 1765, but by 1792 it was described as "in a state of decrepitude." On the other hand, the estate's productive resources had been carefully attended to. Its meadowland had increased to over 100 acres, about 50 percent more than a generation earlier. There were now six substantial farms, worth in all 130,291 l., the value of a large estate; in 1765 there had been only two. Even in 1792 the forest remained the

---

44. AD S-M, Tabel. Pont-St-Pierre, 1764–73, 12 March 1765. Montesquiou paid the enormous sum of 253,400 l., 41 percent of Pont-St-Pierre's worth, for his new town house.

45. Caillot, liasse 241, "Matières diverses," 24 September 1768.

46. AD S-M, C 358, Intendance de Rouen, Capitation des nobles, 1774.

47. AD S-M, QP 1975, Biens des émigrés.

Figure 16. The urban landowner: The hôtel *of the Caillot de Coquéraumont (Cliché COUCHAUX, RAUFASTE © 1982 Inventaire général/SPADEM)*

barony's most valuable single resource, but the Caillots had dramatically increased their control of the land around it.

The Caillots brought more careful administration to Pont-St-Pierre as well. The Roncherolles had begun the compilation of a *terrier* by the 1740s, but it was during the Caillots' ownership that the effort was completed; by about 1780 seven folio volumes had been drawn up summarizing the seigneurial *aveux* of all the barony's tenants. Much closer attention seems also to have been given to land sales within the barony. This assured the collection of one of the barony's more valuable seigneurial rights, the *treizièmes* that were charged on all sales; more important, it assured the Caillots of the possibility of using their right of *retrait féodal,* their right to purchase any land that was offered for sale within the barony's limits. Likewise, there appears to have been closer accounting of the costs and revenues of the barony's domain.[48] As the Revolution began, Pont-St-Pierre was a more imposing property than ever. During the

48. For Caillot's reputation as a demanding landowner, Pierre Duchemin, *La baronnie de Pont-St-Pierre* (Gisors, 1894), 66–70.

generation before 1789, its seigneurial revenues had received a new degree of careful attention and its domain had expanded vigorously.

THE PROBLEM OF TOTAL REVENUES

Between the late fourteenth century and 1789, Pont-St-Pierre's owners transformed the estate, to the point that the final dismantling of the seigneurial system affected only its marginal revenues. To evaluate the success of their efforts requires systematic analysis of the total income that the barony produced. It is clear that the barony shed its seigneurial character in the course of the sixteenth century, and in the seventeenth and eighteenth centuries it oriented itself increasingly toward the direct control of land and other resources. The price of this transformation remains uncertain, however: were the new revenues that the barony's domains brought sufficient to replace what was lost in seigneurial rights? How costly was the estate's transition to a capitalistic form, in which control of property rather than control of people was the main source of value?

Answering these questions requires a history of the barony's total revenues, but such a history is no simple matter. The inflation of the early modern period limits the usefulness of comparison in terms of nominal values; monetary values must be converted into some measure of real value if comparisons are to be made over the centuries considered here. Table 50 and figure 17 present two views of the barony's changing real income: they convert the barony's nominal income into two measures of real value, wheat and poultry.[49]

Figure 17 and table 50 depict a complex story. They present, first, the nominal revenues that Pont-St-Pierre provided its owners between the late fourteenth and the late eighteenth centuries. These revenues fell off sharply in the fifteenth century, following the most devastating phase of the Hundred Years' War, and recovered only slowly thereafter. Between 1454 and 1483 the barony's revenue stagnated at about 40 percent of its 1398–99 value, and even in 1521–22 nominal revenues amounted to only 86 percent of what they had

---

49. Because no *mercuriales* exist for Rouen between the sixteenth and the late seventeenth centuries, I have used here prices of wheat—*froment*—in Paris; when the two markets can be compared, their evolution is virtually identical; see Guy Bois, "Le prix du froment à Rouen au XVe siècle," *Annales ESC* 23, no. 6 (November–December 1968): 1262–82; Jean-Pierre Bardet, *Rouen aux XVIIe et XVIIIe siècles: Les mutations d'un espace urbain*, 2 vols. (Paris, 1983), 1:220.

TABLE 50. *Total Revenue*

Years	Nominal Revenue (l.)	Index[a]	Setiers of Froment	Index[a]	Poulets	Index[a]
1398–1399	1,149	100	1,270[c]	100	18,388	100
1414–1415	785	68	1,734[c]	137	12,555	68
1454–1455	412	36	496[d]	39	—	—
1455–1456	488	39	521[d]	41	—	—
1458–1459	463	40	487[d]	38	—	—
1459–1460	455	39	468[d]	37	—	—
1460–1461	463	40	538[d]	42	—	—
1461–1462	441	38	565[d]	44	—	—
1465–1466	519	45	824[d]	65	—	—
1466–1467	519	45	895[d]	70	10,388[f]	56
1477–1478	464	40	414[d]	33	9,279[f]	50
1479–1480	493	43	541[d]	43	9,857[f]	54
1480–1481	581	51	641[d]	50	11,611[f]	63
1481–1482	511	44	587[d]	46	10,215[f]	56
1482–1483	449	39	401[d]	32	8,986[f]	49
1506–1507	1,063	93	—	—	14,977[f]	81
1513–1514	989	86	—	—	—	—
1515–1516	926	81	—	—	14,814[f]	81
1521–1522	986	86	347[e]	27	13,146[f]	71
1558–1559	3,009	262	693[e]	55	—	—
1560–1561	2,544	221	547[e]	43	—	—
1570–1571	6,161	536	696[e]	55	27,380[g]	149
1571–1572	12,625	1,099	1,423[e]	112	56,112[g]	305
1572–1573	4,826	420	547[e]	43	21,451[g]	117
1573–1574	5,568	484	619[e]	49	24,746[g]	135
1645–1654	13,000	1,131	827[e]	65	—	—
1656–1666	16,000	1,392	807[e]	64	—	—
1740	15,754	1,371	807[e]	64	31,508[h]	171
1765	22,929	1,996	1,090[d]	86	50,953[h]	277
1780[b]	32,192	2,802	1,467[d]	116	53,653[h]	292

SOURCE: Comptes; Tabel. Pont-St-Pierre; Caillot, liasse 241.

[a] 1398–1399 = 100.

[b] This estimate does not include new farms added to barony by 1792.

[c] Calculated from (1) *appréciation* of the *mine* of *froment*, Comptes; (2) relation to setier of froment in Paris, from Bois, "Le prix de froment," 1279.

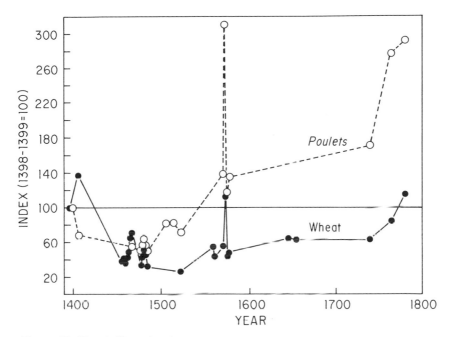

Figure 17. Two indices of real revenue

been in 1398–99. The decline translated directly the destruction and depopulation that the war had caused. In 1466–67, for instance, the barony's receiver noted that most of "the section of la Vente Ponchet in la Neuville is totally worthless" because its tenants had departed and the "*masures* of the said place of Boos are all to be discounted." In all, more than half of the barony's fixed rents were "useless" for one reason or another—at a time when fixed rents counted still for

---

Notes to table 50, continued from page 234

[d] Calculated from nine-year moving averages from Micheline Baulant, "Le prix des grains à Paris de 1431 à 1788," *Annales ESC* 23, no. 3 (May–June 1968): 520–40.

[e] Calculated from nine-year moving averages from Jean Meuvret and Micheline Baulant, *Prix des céréales extraits de la mercuriale de Paris (1520–1698)*, 2 vols. (Paris, 1962).

[f] From *appréciations*, comptes of Pont-St-Pierre.

[g] From *appréciations*, comptes of St-Ouen, Rouen, AD S-M, 14 H 104.

[h] From André Dubuc, "L'appréciation des redevances en nature dans le bailliage principal de Rouen," in *Actes du 87e Congrès National des Sociétés Savantes, Poitiers, 1962, Section d'histoire moderne et contemporaine*, 839–43.

39 percent of total income.[50] Destruction and depopulation had brought uncertainty about the barony's basic rights. In about 1454 the barons paid for an announcement to be read in the parishes around Pont-St-Pierre "to the effect that anyone who had knowledge of any of the rights of my said lord, such as letters, charters, or other alienated things,—that they return them"; and the receiver noted his expenses "for more than forty trips that he has taken from his hotel in Rouen to the lawcourts of both Pont-St-Pierre and Cailly [another of the Roncherolles' fiefs], to deal with the lawsuits of my lord, which arise daily without number: oppositions to judicial seizures, declarations of nonpayment of rents, and otherwise."[51] The immediate destructiveness of the war was compounded by the uncertainties that followed it. These prevented the barons from collecting revenues and required of them constant litigiousness.

By the mid–sixteenth century, however, much of this uncertainty had ended, and population losses had been made good. By this point, nominal revenues had surpassed their late fourteenth-century level. Population growth and the barony's reorientation from seigneurial to domanial revenues allowed revenues to double by the late 1550s; by the 1570s revenues were more than four times what they had been in the late fourteenth century, and by the mid–seventeenth century they were more than thirteen times their initial level.

But the evolution of the barony's real revenue was less straightforward. Seen in terms of the amount of wheat that it could purchase (table 50, above), the barony's revenues stagnated throughout much of the early modern period. Before 1780 there had been only two years among the twenty-two for which total revenue is known in which income reached its late fourteenth-century level. In seven years during the sixteenth century, mean real revenue was only 55 percent of its level in 1398–99; in the mid–seventeenth century total real revenue was two-thirds of what it had been in the late fourteenth century, and it was slightly below that level in 1740. Despite changes in its structure and the exploitation of new sources of revenue, Pont-St-Pierre's transition to modernity was apparently not an easy one. When revenues are set against wheat prices, the seigneurial crisis of the late Middle Ages was an event whose consequences persisted to

---

50. Comptes, 1466–67.
51. Ibid., 1454–56, chapter "autre despence." Cf. Guenée, *Tribunaux et gens de justice*, 58–60, 392–95, on the explosion of litigation after the Hundred Years' War.

the end of the Old Regime; full recovery appears to have come only in the 1780s.

When revenue is measured in terms of the poultry that it could buy, however, a very different picture emerges (table 50). Measured thus, Pont-St-Pierre's revenue had reached three-fourths of its 1398–99 value by the first decades of the sixteenth century; in the 1570s it was about three-fourths higher than in 1398–99, and in the late eighteenth century it approached three times what it had been in 1398–99. By this measure of real value, Pont-St-Pierre had largely recovered from its late medieval crises by the mid–sixteenth century; and recovery was followed by real growth.

The disparity between these two measures of the barony's real income suggests two quite different meanings of the concept itself.[52] Measurement in terms of the poultry that the barony's income could buy is essentially a measure of the barons' own purchasing power; meat was one of the few goods that they purchased in large quantities even in the sixteenth century.[53] An index in terms of manufactured goods, were it possible to construct one, would probably give a still brighter view of the barons' purchasing power, for prices of manufactured goods rose more slowly than those of food.[54] Even these indices understate somewhat the solidity of the barons' purchasing power. Before the eighteenth century, the Roncherolles depended for most of their basic needs on what could be produced by the household and the estate themselves, without recourse to purchases on the market. From the first decades of the sixteenth century to the end of the eighteenth century, Pont-St-Pierre amply supplied its owners' basic needs.

But measures of real income involve more than questions of purchasing power. To measure the quantity of wheat that the barony's revenue could purchase is to measure, in an indirect and approximate way, the barony's hold on agricultural production in the region. Between the mid–fifteenth and the mid–eighteenth centuries, the barony controlled—whether by its seigneurial levies or by its other sources of income—less than two-thirds of the grain that it

52. Such disparity, of course, also suggests the difficulties confronting any effort to base interpretation of seigneurial evolution on conversion of nominal to real values. Cf. the debate between Guy Bois, *Crise du féodalisme*, and John Day, " 'Crise du féodalisme' et conjoncture des prix à la fin du moyen âge," *Annales ESC* 34, no. 2 (February–March 1979): 305–18.

53. See above, Chapter 5.

54. See Harry Miskimin, *The Economy of Later Renaissance Europe, 1460–1600* (Cambridge, 1977), 44, 88.

had controlled in the late Middle Ages. A smaller share of the region's most basic agricultural product flowed to the barony. Instead
of the seigneurial lord, those who profited from the rising grain
prices of the sixteenth and seventeenth centuries were the peasants
and lesser landowners whose changing fortunes were discussed in
Chapter 2. These were the groups that produced and marketed surpluses of grain and that profited from the period's rising prices.
Only in the late eighteenth century, when the barony had been fully
oriented to production for the market, did the share of the region's
grain supply that it controlled surpass the share that it had taken in
1398–99. The conversion of the barony's income into quantities of
grain, thus, says less about the purchasing power that the barony
supplied its owners than about the economic opportunities that they
missed. The barony's place in the regional economy had declined.
Other groups, controlling estates of a different character, produced
food for the booming markets of the sixteenth and seventeenth centuries; they, rather than the barons of Pont-St-Pierre, received the
main profits from the opportunities that these centuries offered. The
owners of Pont-St-Pierre only recovered their domination of the local economy during the last decades of the Old Regime.

ECONOMIC ASSUMPTIONS AND ACTION

Such a perspective suggests the incompleteness of the barony's
adaptation to a market economy and points to ways in which its
presence was a burden to the local economy. To understand the
extent to which this was the case requires that we examine some of
the assumptions that the barons and their agents brought to managing the lordship and some of the effects that these assumptions had
on economic life around Pont-St-Pierre.

A first point is clear: from the late sixteenth century and probably
earlier, the Roncherolles were sensitive to the market for agricultural
products and the profits that it offered. Their assumptions about the
rural economy were not naive or governed by tradition alone. In
1590, for instance, Pierre de Roncherolles arranged the receivership
of the barony of Maineville on behalf of his nephew and ward.
Among the conditions that he set out for the new receiver were that
he produce a careful accounting of both expenses and receipts and
that he "for all [products] await the season to sell at the highest
price of the year"; parts of the property that ordinarily were leased

out were to be auctioned off, "at the courtroom in Maineville, to the highest bidder, for the profit and increase of the said receipt, as has been done in the past."[55] Careful accounting, competitive bids for leases, and seasonal sales of what the estate produced were all normal procedures in 1590. They ensured that the estate's revenues would evolve with changes in the rural economy: with both the economy's demand for food and the rural population's demand for leaseholds.

Such awareness of the market was doubtless encouraged by the long existence (traced above, in Chapter 2) of effective markets in Pont-St-Pierre for both agricultural products and land. There had been a public grain market in Pont-St-Pierre since at least the thirteenth century and a significant land market since at least the fourteenth century. Alertness to the workings of the market was also encouraged by the fact that, from at least the later sixteenth century, urban merchants took a substantial role in the barony's management. In 1574 the Roncherolles leased many of Pont-St-Pierre's revenues to "Pierre Le Maistre, merchant, residing in Heuqueville"; a decade later Le Maistre was described as an *"honorable homme . . . bourgeois, merchant, residing in the city of Rouen,"* and a few months after that there was another lease of the barony's revenues, to *"honorable homme* Pierre Le Maistre, bourgeois of Rouen, residing there."[56] Le Maistre combined with apparent ease commercial activity in the countryside and in Rouen itself. His involvement in the barony's management must have affected the Roncherolles' own attitudes to their property. Bourgeois and estate-owners found themselves in a necessary symbiosis.

Pursuit of gain and sensitivity to market forces did not of themselves, however, constitute a "capitalist mentality."[57] The most visi-

---

55. AD Eure, E 1250, Tabel. Pont-St-Pierre, 23 August 1590. For the frequency of lease auctions in sixteenth-century upper Normandy, see Dewald, *The Formation*, 209–10. For the slow development of these attitudes in the Cambrésis, Hugues Neveux, *Vie et déclin d'une structure économique: Les grains du Cambrésis (fin du XIVe–début du XVIIe siècle)* (Paris, The Hague, and New York, 1980), 319–23.

56. Caillot, liasse "Baux du revenu général, Pont-St-Pierre, 9 October 1574, 31 December 1585; AD Eure, E 1254, Tabel. Pont-St-Pierre, 29 January 1585.

57. Cf. Weber's distinction between greed and capitalism: "The impulse to acquisition, pursuit of gain, of money, of the greatest possible amount of money, has in itself nothing to do with capitalism. . . . This impulse . . . has been common to all sorts and conditions of men at all times and in all countries of the earth. . . . capitalism is identical with the pursuit of profit, and forever *renewed* profit, by means of continuous, rational, capitalistic enterprise" (*The Protestant Ethic and the Spirit of Capitalism*, trans. Talcott Parsons [New York, 1958], 17 [emphasis in original]). See also Neveux, *Vie et déclin*, 323–29, for landowners' limited ability to calculate profit in this period.

ble limitation on the barony's economic modernity concerned investment. The halting progress of the Roncherolles' investments in land
has already been traced; before the seventeenth century, they preferred the acquisition of seigneurial rents and powers to an expansion of the amount of land and other directly productive resources
that they controlled. More striking still was their limited investment
in maintaining and improving those resources that they did control.
The barony's accounts of 1515–16 illustrate the problem. Total expenditures for the year amounted to 2,882 l. Of this total, 61 l.—2.1
percent—was spent on the construction and repair of such basic
capital as mills, barns, bridges, and roads; an additional 15 l. (.5
percent of the total) was spent to clear and plant a new vineyard in
Pont-St-Pierre. In contrast, 460 l. was spent on embellishing the
château itself, and 330 l. was spent on meat for the baron's table.[58]
This was inadequate for even the most basic maintenance. In the
seventeenth and eighteenth centuries, maintaining a mill was commonly supposed to consume at least 20 percent of the gross revenue
that it produced.[59] Such failures of maintenance had immediate consequences in losses of grain that had been stored in poorly maintained barns or milled in inadequate mills.[60]

Levels of investment rose somewhat in the later sixteenth century. The Roncherolles built a second water mill in Pont-St-Pierre
and a windmill in la Neuville; in the seventeenth century they began
to extend their ownership of arable land and meadows and to construct fulling mills along the Andelle. But throughout the eighteenth
century complaints continued about their inadequate maintenance
of their properties; and this failure of investment seriously affected
their revenues. In 1739 the baron himself argued that his market
rights could be of little value "until the road by which one approaches the said market, which is unusable and renders the said
market almost deserted, is repaired (which has not yet been done,
as the attached certificate shows)."[61] By this time the windmill in la
Neuville had disappeared and had not been replaced, and complaints about the dilapidated condition of the baron's remaining
mills in Pont-St-Pierre were widespread. In 1714 these complaints
led to the assassination of the "conservateur des droits de banalité
de monsieur" (above, Chapter 3); a witness to the altercation that

58. Comptes, 1515–16.
59. See above, Chapter 2, pp. 82–83.
60. Comptes, 1570–74, 1571.
61. Caillot, liasse 237, "Droits en général."

began the incident reported that "there were some people who were saying why make us go to your mill, it is not in good condition, there are no weights or benches, which made it clear to the witness that it must have been one of M. de Pont-St-Pierre's men who was arresting some vassal for the *banalité*."[62] Complaints about the state of the barony's mills, it appears, were taken for granted. Experts echoed this popular consensus in the course of a lawsuit about the baron's mills in 1749; they were "of a very ancient construction," and their millraces were filling up with silt.[63]

Farm buildings were in a similar state of disrepair. At the farm of les Maisons, the tenant's father-in-law complained in 1768, "the buildings are in bad shape, most of them lack doors, the flooring is almost in ruins, the apple press has been useless this year"; another statement in the case complained that "the two barns are uncovered (*sont à découvert*), their foundations are falling apart." Part of the harvest had been spoiled as a result, and—after extensive negotiation—the tenant's rent was reduced by 300 l., more than one-third of the farm's yearly value.[64] Comparable neglect was visible throughout the estate. When the barony was sold, later in the same year, it was noted that "it is necessary to make a number of repairs, even to reconstruct the different buildings and walls belonging to the said domains, to enclose and to plant the *masures* and arable lands." Caillot de Coquéraumont counted on spending 10,000 l. on these tasks immediately after buying the estate.[65]

By the 1760s, it appears, virtually every element in the barony reflected the Roncherolles' failure to maintain and improve their property. Roads, mills, barns, even the land itself were all in poor condition, and all occasioned complaints by tenants and seigneurial "vassals." Obviously the uncertainties of the Roncherolles' finances bore some responsibility for this state of affairs. Their debts had grown over the eighteenth century and in 1765 compelled them to sell Pont-St-Pierre and their other principal Norman properties. But their troubles did not prevent extravagant expenditures of other kinds, and it was clear even at the time that inadequate investment was as much

62. Ibid., liasse 236, "Moulins-Banalité."

63. Ibid., liasse "Pont-St-Pierre, . . . moulins," lawsuit 1739–49, marquis de Pont-St-Pierre against André Le Tourneur and Nicolas Lancelevée.

64. Ibid., liasse 241, "Matières diverses," letter of 21 April 1768, Le Mercier to Montesquiou; statement of 9 July 1768; agreement of 29 May 1768; AD S-M, Tabel. Pont-St-Pierre, 12 February 1767, lease of les Maisons for 885 l. and a *cochon à lait* yearly.

65. Caillot, liasse 241, "Matières diverses," act of sale, 1768.

a cause as a consequence of falling revenues. Michel de Roncherolles himself claimed—although with a great deal of exaggeration—that his market was worthless because the road to it was impassable; and the broken-down state of its barns and buildings reduced les Maisons' value by at least one-third. To deal with these problems would have required only modest and obvious expenditures, expenditures on basic maintenance rather than on English innovations. Failure to make these expenditures reflected basic economic values. However concerned the Roncherolles were with profit, they simply did not see investment and improvement as means of increasing their income.[66]

Where the seigneurial market and mills were concerned, a further consideration strengthened this attitude: all residents of the lordship could be compelled to use Pont-St-Pierre's market and mills, however dilapidated or difficult to reach. Such an assumption had both economic and social costs, however. To maintain the barony's banal rights demanded police efforts that were costly to the barons and vexatious to their seigneurial tenants. Evasions of the *banalité* were an ongoing problem and in the early eighteenth century flared into at least one instance of violent resistance.

After 1768, when the barony passed to the Caillot de Coquéraumont, the problem of investment lost some of its urgency. From the outset the Caillots were prepared to spend substantial sums to repair walls, barns, and other buildings, and this willingness apparently endured through the late eighteenth century.[67] Caillot was also willing to experiment with the suppression of fallows on the farm of les Maisons—although the initiative for this experiment came from his tenant, and the experiment itself was ultimately a failure.[68] In these ways the barony's administration had become considerably more alert to needs for investment at the end of the Old Regime. But other tensions between the demands of rational management and extra-economic goals persisted to 1789. The most visible of these was the problem of hunting. Caillot's tenant farmer at les Maisons, whose complaints about the farm's dilapidation have been quoted above, complained more bitterly still about his losses to wildlife. He "sees

66. On the problem of investment as a central obstacle to French agricultural development, see Robert Forster, "Obstacles to Agricultural Growth in Eighteenth-Century France," *American Historical Review* 75, no. 6 (October 1970): 1600–1615; see also above, Chapter 2.

67. For instance, Caillot, liasse 218, "Par. Pîtres, matières diverses," for the Caillot's expenditures on a new house near one of Pont-St-Pierre's banal mills, presumably to make the mill more attractive to tenants.

68. Above, Chapter 2.

himself," he reported, "having lost the whole of his grain harvest, . . . because of the number of rabbits, who eat everything, either right after the sowing or later, before the harvest." Unless the problem were corrected, "his complete ruin would follow. The cause of this difficulty is the excess of game; a number of other lords have dealt with this by the destruction of the game"; and he begged, "Both on [my] own behalf and on that of your other vassals, . . . order the destruction of the game that lays waste your parishes."[69]

The problem was real. An independent inquest at les Maisons confirmed the losses that its farmer complained of and noted that in one field scarcely any grain had grown.[70] A generation later the same complaints were repeated in the *cahiers de doléances* of both Pont-St-Pierre and la Neuville-Chant-d'Oisel. La Neuville's *cahier*, with characteristic concreteness, noted that "several farmers (*laboureurs*) and others with lands near the forest complain that game—rabbits, stags, boars, and others—does considerable damage to their harvests." Equally characteristically, Pont-St-Pierre's *cahier* presented the issue in broader and more abstract terms: game regularly destroyed one-eighth of the harvest and sometimes more, it claimed.[71]

But hunting was a social as well as an economic fact, a symbol of aristocratic privilege and seigneurial authority. In some parts of France, it has been suggested, lords prohibited use of the scythe so as to maintain stubble for wildlife.[72] In Pont-St-Pierre, the lordship was principally concerned with repressing unauthorized hunting. In 1736 the barony's *procureur fiscal* complained that "several persons give themselves the license, without any right, some to carry firearms and to hunt, others to lie in wait for game, others to lead dogs, others to allow [their dogs] to wander about throughout the barony, which causes the total destruction of the wildlife"; at his request, the lordship's court prohibited "all persons *sans qualité*" from hunting.[73] Forty years later the lordship was enforcing the same policy, again at the behest of its *procureur fiscal*; in 1775 he complained that during

69. Caillot, liasse 241, "Matières diverses," undated letter, Pierre Duval to marquis de Montesquiou.

70. AD Eure, 86 B 100: sale of *meubles*, Pierre Duval, 4 July 1768.

71. AD S-M, 4 BP 6012, Bailliage de Rouen, Cahiers de doléances, Sergenterie de Pont-St-Pierre: la Neuville, p. 3; Pont-St-Pierre, art. 9, p. 10. Cf. Deck, *Etude sur la forêt d'Eu*, 41, for the more serious efforts to enforce hunting monopolies there also during the eighteenth century.

72. Jean Meuvret, *Le problème des subsistances à l'époque Louis XIV: La production des céréales dans la France du XVIIe et du XVIIIe siècle*, 2 vols. (Paris and The Hague, 1977), 1:173.

73. AD Eure, 86 B 102, "Police, 1702–1789," 22 February 1736.

the past year unknown individuals had been hunting "with guns throughout the barony of Pont-St-Pierre, in both plain and woods"; and again the court ordered that such poaching be stopped and punished.[74] Such efforts displayed the barons' readiness to confront habits that were deeply rooted in the communities around Pont-St-Pierre. Gunpowder (we have seen) was commonly sold in the shops of the bourg itself, and the more prosperous villagers owned guns and apparently used them.[75] In these circumstances, to create an effective seigneurial monopoly on hunting was a difficult matter, but the barony's eighteenth-century efforts appear to have been relatively successful. When the *procureur fiscal* complained in 1775 about illicit hunting, the problem turned out to be mainly the work of just two poachers; and one of them, in speaking to a barroom companion, described the blood on his coat (the companion had noticed it and inquired) as *"relatif à son métier.* The witness asked whether he still pursued it, and [he] replied that he had given it up for some time but that the guard of M. de Belfbeuf had so often threatened him with prison that he had let himself go and taken up poaching again." Hunting had become a "métier," reserved for such marginal figures as this; the second poacher told a chance acquaintance that he hunted with companions "with whom he'd been together in prison."

Tension between the barons' orientation to profits and their concern with extra-economic goals extended more broadly, to their efforts to regulate the economic life within the estate's boundaries. The range of activities that the barony was expected to regulate was broad. As the principal justice within its boundaries, the barony's High Justice exercised the same *police* functions as any French jurisdiction, royal or seigneurial. It determined the price of alcoholic beverages and the conditions of their sale; it governed the sale of a range of other commodities, requiring that transactions take place in the market of Pont-St-Pierre and supervising the conditions of sale; it attempted to protect consumers against grain merchants by limiting merchants' access to the market and forbidding them to buy grain directly from farmers; it enforced the guild system, receiving the oaths of new masters and punishing violations of guild rules. In these and other ways, the barony remained throughout the Old

74. Ibid., 86 B 110, Procédures criminelles, 19 July 1775.
75. Above, Chapter 1.

Regime the institutional representation within its boundaries of pre-physiocratic modes of economic reasoning; it stood for an economy controlled by moral and political ideals and against the allowance of full freedom to the market.

More than ideals underlay the barony's efforts to regulate economic life. Profit too was an important consideration. The barons of Pont-St-Pierre, we have seen, derived a significant income from their market rights in the seventeenth and eighteenth centuries; in the mid–eighteenth century, these accounted for 5 percent of the barony's total revenue. Many of the barony's economic regulations were intended to preserve this market monopoly and thus to preserve the barony's market revenues—despite the inconveniences that the market's poor condition might create.

Profit was an important concern, but other aims were at least as important. From the early eighteenth century the barony had included two large, grain-producing farms; and after 1768 the Caillot de Coquéraumont family added still more farms to the estate. The eighteenth-century owners of Pont-St-Pierre had at least as much interest in free markets and high grain prices as in maintaining their lordship's market monopoly. Nonetheless, their officials sought to enforce market controls because, first, they shared a set of assumptions about the morality of the grain trade, derived from a long-standing tradition of economic reasoning. Anthoine de Montchrétien, the Norman nobleman who in 1615 surveyed the French economy, denounced the magistrates who permitted free trade in food and the merchants who participated in it, but he concluded that "the most dangerous and prejudicial of all are those large tenant farmers of the principal properties, . . . who have the finest granaries in the kingdom and collect so much grain and wine . . . that the majority of villagers are completely under their power. . . . I would speak here of the millers," he added, "if everyone did not already know how capacious their consciences are."[76] Pont-St-Pierre's seigneurial officials inherited this tradition.

More fundamental, however, were the seigneurial officials' anxieties about public order. Although they were employed by a private landowner who had strong interests in the grain trade, Pont-St-Pierre's officials shared assumptions that most French officials held during the Old Regime, especially in urban settings: public order,

76. Antoyne de Montchrétien, *Traicté de l'oeconomie politique* . . . , ed. Th. Funck-Brentano (Paris, n.d.), 261, 263.

they believed, depended on their ability to assure the food supply. In Pont-St-Pierre, this required controlling local merchants and farmers; only thus could seigneurial officials protect the mass of the population and control its tendency to riot. Pont-St-Pierre's administrators faced essentially urban problems. The bourg was small, but its residents depended mainly on commercial and artisanal activities and virtually all needed to buy their food.

Baronial officials developed these themes at length during times of high prices. In 1735 the *procureur fiscal* announced to the High Justice that he "has received word that several grain merchants (*blatiers*) . . . come to the grain market in this bourg on market days and there buy wheat, so that the people (*le peuple*) cannot have any, which causes emotion and tumult." A merchant from la Neuville-Chant-d'Oisel had been an especially conspicuous buyer. His insulting response to the crowd's complaints that he was driving up prices—"Bugger, I'll make you eat at a still higher price next week"—seemed especially dangerous to the *procureur fiscal*; this was a "violation of the ordinances and a step likely to stir up the people (*propre à mettre le trouble dans le peuple*)." There was also the more general problem that the merchants had arranged with the *laboureurs* to buy their grain elsewhere than at the market. The court shared the anxieties that the *procureur fiscal* expressed and repeated its long-standing regulations of the grain trade: no merchants were to enter the market before 12:30, so that they could not drive up prices or corner supplies before other buyers had filled their needs; and *laboureurs* were not to sell their grain anywhere but in the market.[77] In 1768 the *procureur fiscal* again demanded that the court deal with the problem of grain supplies. There had been insufficient grain at the previous week's market, he told the court, "which is prejudicial to the public good and might occasion riots (*troubles*) if it happened again." The court again heeded his advice and ordered that all *laboureurs* within the barony bring grain to the next week's market, on pain of a 100 l. fine; a sergeant was sent to each of the twenty-two *laboureurs* who resided within the lordship, to ensure that they would hear and obey the court's decision.[78] This was an especially clear statement of the baronial officials' hostility to free trade, for it came during the Crown's efforts to eliminate such controls. In 1764 the Crown had liberalized the grain trade in the physiocratic hope of

---

77. AD Eure, 86 B 102, "Police, 1702–1789," 26 April 1735.
78. Caillot, liasse 237, "Droits en général."

stimulating agricultural production; such efforts as the baronial officials undertook in 1768 directly violated royal declarations.[79]

Sensitivity to popular feeling was justified by the real threat that
grain shortages might produce popular upheaval. In 1699 several
men from Pont-St-Pierre, "with the complicity of their wives, daughters, and several others," stopped two *laboureurs* from la Neuville
who were attempting to ship their grain "to other places than the
ordinary market." The crowd seized and "mistreated" the *laboureurs*
and refused to relinquish their horses. The crowd's language on this
occasion testified to their perception of the barony's role in such
matters and to the Roncherolles' own continuing presence in the
area. For several members of the crowd claimed to be acting on orders
of the baron himself. A young leather-worker from Pont-St-Pierre
testified that he had entered a local tavern "with the intent of drinking a round . . . and to await there the orders of monsieur le comte de
Pont-St-Pierre, who had forbidden them to allow the release of several horses that had been taken." Imagination, rumor, and perhaps
canny self-justification had created the belief that the comte had
ordered the seizure, and it was the comte's own business agent who
sought to return the farmers' horses to them.[80] Although factually
inaccurate, however, the crowd's belief that the comte had directed
their actions accurately reflected the barony's approach to the grain
trade and to those involved in it. Like the crowd, the barony's officials
wanted to prevent the free trade in grain and to control the machinations of the large farmers and merchants. This was yet another way in
which the residents of the bourg shared interests and assumptions
with the barons, and in this instance their common interests united
them against the farmers of the plain.

Both Pont-St-Pierre's inhabitants and the barony's officials retained these attitudes through 1789. In February of that year, a moment of very high grain prices throughout France, there was again
commotion at the market of Pont-St-Pierre, and the *laboureurs* were
again the principal objects of popular anger. The lieutenant and the
procureur fiscal of the High Justice visited the market; "we found,"
they reported, "an infinite number of persons of both sexes, who

79. Steven L. Kaplan, *Bread, Politics, and Political Economy in the Reign of Louis XIV,*
2 vols. (The Hague, 1976), speaks of the "revolt of the local police" (2:478); he notes
the particular hostility of the Parlement of Rouen to the policy of liberalization, and
the prevalence of grain riots in the area near Rouen from 1764 on (1:183–91; 2:413–23,
453–57).

80. AD Eure, 86 B 105, 22 September 1699.

were gathered around five sacks of wheat. . . . The *laboureurs* at first offered it at 36 l., and finally, in view of the tumult and fearing a sedition, they determined to sell it at 30 l. the sack; having seen this, we had the five sacks, along with a sixth from the market's reserves, lifted up and distributed by *boisseau* to everyone, which was accomplished with all the order that one can hope for in such circumstances. . . . all those who were unable to have any went away, some dismayed, the rest determined to go to the *laboureurs'* farms to get grain (*s'en faire livrer*) at the price of the market."[81] The event thus described had all the elements of lawfulness and order that George Rudé, E. P. Thompson, and others have taught us to see in early modern grain riots.[82] The crowd threatened violence but did not attempt to seize the grain by force; it was seeking to restore a just price in the market, and when that had been achieved it was ready to buy. Baronial officials were correspondingly tolerant of the crowd's aims. Although they had some police at their disposal—a *maréchal des logis* and three *cavaliers des maréchaussées* from the town of Ecouis—they did not interfere with the crowd's efforts; and they made no effort to stop the disappointed buyers from visiting nearby *laboureurs* and demanding their grain.

Obviously the officials were not entirely happy with the crowd's behavior, but neither were they shocked by it. Such an attitude to the crowd was encouraged by the fact that suspicion of the grain trade and of those who profited from it was not limited to Pont-St-Pierre's poorest residents. The enlightened and relatively well-off residents who drew up the bourg's *cahier de doléances* in 1789 took the same view. They asked the king to prohibit "the export of grains, whether within the kingdom or outside it," and they denounced "the spirit of greed that has reigned and now reigns more and more in the minds of those men who give themselves over to the commerce in grain."[83] The crowd that gathered at Pont-St-Pierre's market expressed a consensus of the community, a consensus of suspicion toward agrarian capitalism and its principal agents. The barony's officials shared these values.

Comparable suspicion of unrestricted freedom governed the offi-

81. Ibid., 110, 28 February 1789.
82. George Rudé, *The Crowd in the French Revolution* (Oxford, 1959), 114–17, 195–209, 232–39; E. P. Thompson, "The Moral Economy of the English Crowd," *Past and Present* 50 (February 1971): 76–136.
83. AD S-M, 4 BP 6012, Cahiers de doléances, Bailliage de Rouen, Sergenterie de Pont-St-Pierre, art. 13, p. 11.

cials' interventions in other areas of economic life. By the eighteenth century, the most important of these was the manufacture of cotton thread, a crucial economic resource for the residents of Pont-St-Pierre itself and the surrounding villages; in 1788 it was reported of both Pont-St-Pierre and la Neuville-Chant-d'Oisel that the principal occupation was cotton spinning and that for most inhabitants no real alternatives existed.[84] Villagers' dependence on cotton spinning meant that its regulation was nearly as important to them as control of the food supply.

As with regulation of food supplies, the barony had financial as well as political interests in regulation. At the market of Pont-St-Pierre, the barons levied 3 d. on every pound of raw cotton sold and 6 d. on every packet of cotton thread; they charged as well for every use of the market's scales.[85] Baronial officials had to prevent the development of a free market in cotton if these rights were to maintain their value. Early in the eighteenth century, in fact, Michel de Roncherolles sought to extend still further his control of the cotton market. For 150 l. yearly, he leased to three residents of the bourg "the right and power to sell and buy cotton in the said bourg of Pont-St-Pierre, to the exclusion of all others and free of the *coutumes*." The baron hoped to establish a complete monopoly of the cotton business, but the effort had a short life; three months after the initial agreement, the parties abandoned the lease by mutual consent.[86] Monopoly proved impossible, but until the Revolution the barons' agents did their best to assure that all cotton sales took place in Pont-St-Pierre's market, where the barons could collect their dues.

Profit was not the only issue, however. Regulation of the cotton business, like regulation of the trade in foodstuffs, reflected deeply held values. The barony's *procureur fiscal* set forth some of them in 1769 in the course of requesting that the High Justice control the cotton business more carefully. What was necessary, he began, was to establish for both sellers and purchasers "the liberty that is the essential base of any commerce." His language suggests the extent to which liberal economic ideology had penetrated even the milieu of seigneurial officials; but the rhetoric of liberty introduced a demand for closer regulation.[87] To achieve real liberty, it was necessary

84. AD S-M, C 2212, "Etat des pauvres," dossier 7; discussed above, Chapter 1.

85. Caillot, liasse 237, "Pont-St-Pierre, droits en général."

86. Ibid., 12 February, 24 May 1729.

87. Cf. Kaplan, *Bread, Politics, and Political Economy*, 1:62, 83, for other examples of the language of liberty in contexts of close regulation.

that cotton be traded only at Pont-St-Pierre's market. Merchants were not to buy or sell either in the spinners' villages or in their own shops; they were not to force spinners to buy more cotton than they wanted; above all, they were not to exploit their own stronger economic position to gain excessive profits. The *procureur fiscal* asked that the court order merchants "to set the prices of raw and spun cotton at their true value and with regard to the legitimate gain that they ought to make, without being able to set disproportionate prices, on pain of a 50 l. fine." The seigneurial justice agreed, and these regulations were duly passed and registered with the Parlement of Rouen.[88]

Even in the later eighteenth century, these demands suggest, there remained a substantial distance between the seigneurial officials' outlook and that of the cotton merchants. The economic assumptions of the seigneurial officials remained those of a world in which there was a "true value" of such commodities as cotton, in which "disproportionate prices" could be clearly seen and deserved punishment, in which excessive profits were destructive of economic and social health. Unless the seigneury interposed its power between merchants and spinners, the merchants would unjustly increase their profits at the spinners' expense. They would, as the *procureur fiscal* complained of one merchant in about 1776, make themselves "the master of the price."[89]

Baronial officials not only proclaimed these ideals but sought seriously to enforce them. Sergeants were sent to pre-dawn ambushes outside cotton merchants' shops in the hope of catching the merchants buying thread and selling raw cotton. They arrested merchants who loitered at the approaches to the market, planning to buy thread from the spinners who arrived from surrounding villages. They accused merchants of using false measures and of vandalizing packets of thread offered in the market, to discourage spinners from coming to the public market and to force them to come instead to the merchants' shops.[90] These efforts enjoyed little success. The High Justice was forced to repeat its regulations of the cotton trade in 1729, 1738, 1747, and 1769, and the cotton merchants responded with

88. AD Eure, 86 B 102, "Police, 1702–1789," 14 January 1769. For a brief overview of this episode, see André Dubuc, "Un ancien marché du coton à Pont-Saint-Pierre," in *Le textile en Normandie: Etudes diverses* (Rouen, 1975), 161–65.

89. AD Eure, 86 B 102, n.d., probably 1776, case of Pierre Hubert, merchant, Romilly.

90. Ibid., 25 July 1770, 4 November 1775, 18 May 1776; Caillot, liasse 237, "Droits en général," 9 July 1729.

sneering indifference. One merchant told the sergeant who had lain in ambush outside the shop between four and seven o'clock in the morning that what was being done there—selling cotton, he freely admitted—"was none of our business, and that we might enter to pay our respects"; six years later the same merchants were again before the High Justice for evading the barony's market.[91]

To the end of the Old Regime, thus, the barons of Pont-St-Pierre and their officials expressed dislike of the commercial relations developing around them. Baronial officials sought to force producers and merchants to use Pont-St-Pierre's markets partly because of the market dues that they collected on everything sold there. But market regulations derived also from concern with problems of public order and welfare. To allow grain merchants and farmers excessive freedom was to risk popular unrest; cotton merchants too had to be restrained if village impoverishment were to be avoided. Alongside these political concerns, finally, there lay a set of moral assumptions about economic activity. The barons and their officials shared the suspicions of unrestrained commerce that were commonplaces of early modern thought.[92] Trade in foodstuffs had inherent moral dangers. Other forms of commerce might be morally neutral, but only if prices and profits were confined within reasonable bounds. Pont-St-Pierre's owners had both economic and political interests in sustaining this moral vision of the economy, and their efforts to do so continued to the eve of the Revolution.

LORDSHIP, JUSTICE, AND POLITICAL POWER

Political concerns, I have suggested, long continued to permeate the barony's economic life. This fact gives particular importance to a closer examination of the barony's judicial and political powers. Pont-St-Pierre was one of a relatively few lordships in upper Normandy that enjoyed rights of high justice: that is, the right to try all civil and criminal cases arising within its boundaries, including even cases that might lead to capital punishment.[93] Such rights demanded

91. Caillot, liasse 237, "Droits en général," 9 July 1729, 29 July 1747; AD Eure, 86 B 102, 15 March 1738, 14 January 1769, 25 July 1770, 1 June 1776, n.d. (1776 by place in liasse), case of Pierre Hubert.
92. Kaplan, *Bread, Politics, and Political Economy*; Joyce O. Appleby, *Economic Thought and Ideology in Seventeenth-Century England* (Princeton, 1978).
93. See Roland Mousnier, *Les institutions de la France sous la monarchie absolue, 1598–1789*, 2 vols. (Paris, 1974–80), 1:391–98, 401–9; Dewald, *The Formation*, 164–65.

a large judicial personnel. In 1600 Pierre de Roncherolles employed two judges—a *bailli vicontal* and his lieutenant—to decide cases in his High Justice; an *avocat* and a *procureur fiscal*, to prosecute cases and watch over baronial interests in them; two sergeants to enforce decisions and apprehend criminals; and a notary (*tabellion*), "who passes all of the contracts that are needed throughout the extent of the said High Justice." As part owner of the forest of Longbouel, Pierre de Roncherolles also employed a forest judge—the *verdier*—to judge cases of illicit grazing and woodcutting, and four sergeants who patrolled the forest. Defendants could appeal decisions of the forest judge to the High Justice. From there appeals in civil cases went to the royal bailliage of Rouen and thence to the Parlement of Rouen; in criminal cases appeals went directly to the Parlement.[94]

Through the sixteenth century, we have seen, positions in the barony's administration attracted substantial local figures, including members of the local nobility. They were drawn by the hope of gifts from the Roncherolles rather than by what the positions themselves offered, for salaries were low. The *bailli,* for instance, earned a salary of 10 l. in 1560–61, 25 l. in 1572–73.[95] Judges and sergeants might supplement these salaries with the fees that litigants paid, but the modesty of their earnings often required that they take other positions. Many of Pont-St-Pierre's seigneurial judges doubled as lawyers in the Parlement or other Rouennais jurisdictions or served in other seigneurial courts. This fact had important implications. It meant that Pont-St-Pierre's judges had an acquaintance with the litigation, argument, and modes of thinking in the higher courts of the region; they were not merely local practitioners. By the sixteenth century, moreover, all judges in seigneurial high justices were expected to hold university degrees and to have received the Parlement's approval, following an examination of their competence and morals.[96]

Pont-St-Pierre's High Justice met almost every Saturday during the sixteenth and seventeenth centuries in a house that served as both jail and courtroom.[97] These meetings coincided with the bourg's weekly market, and the coincidence helped to make the judicial audi-

94. Pont-St-Pierre, Aveu, 10 July 1600.

95. Comptes, 1560–61, 1570–74.

96. Guenée, *Tribunaux et gens de justice,* 379–430; Marcel Marion, *Dictionnaire des institutions de la France aux XVIIe et XVIIIe siècles* (Paris, 1923; repr. New York, 1968), 319–20. For the similar situation of a nearby High Justice, Marcel Boudet, "La haute justice de Préaux," *Revue des sociétés savantes de Haute Normandie* 38 (1965): 59–67.

97. AD Eure, 86 B 3, 4, 8, 21, 22, Plumitifs; AD S-M, Tabel. Pont-St-Pierre, 17 April 1735, sale of a house "nommé [sic] la maison de laudiance et de la géolle."

ence a focal point of local life. At the audience a wide range of public business was transacted, of which litigation and criminal prosecution formed only a part. Normally it was at these weekly sessions that economic regulations were discussed and announced. The *bailli* also read and registered the regulations that superior authorities—notably the Crown and the Parlement of Rouen—had put out; relatives of orphaned children gathered to select guardians and have their choice approved by the *bailli;* other acts concerning inheritance—the sale of minors' properties, the renunciation of inheritances overburdened by debt, the formal declarations of orphans who had attained their majorities—were made before the *bailli* and received his approval; unmarried women who had become pregnant announced the fact and described its circumstances, in accord with royal legislation aimed at preventing seduction and infanticide; men chosen for such public offices as village field guards or herdsmen received the *bailli*'s approval and took their oaths of office; new members of Pont-St-Pierre's guilds took their oaths; after consultation with leading farmers, the *bailli* set dates for the harvest and for gleaning; and the *procureur fiscal* might demand that the court deal with all manner of public problems, ranging from an individual's dangerous fireplace to violations of the Sabbath, inadequate maintenance of the bourg's roads and ditches, and the machinations of grain and cotton merchants.[98]

From the late sixteenth century (with a long lacuna between 1581 and 1661), it is possible to trace the court's level of activity: to analyze, in effect, the extent to which it touched residents' lives. Such an analysis (table 51) shows a striking contrast between the sixteenth-century High Justice and its eighteenth-century successor. In 1580–81, the court met almost every week, and it dealt with a large number of matters; on average, almost thirty-two cases were taken up at each meeting. Many were continued from one week to the next and others were simple matters of registration. Nonetheless, the High Justice was a crowded center of local life. At least fifty villagers must have been present at typical sessions.

The court remained important through the late seventeenth cen-

98. Examples from AD Eure, 86 B 61, 28 January, 9 July, 15 October 1768; 22 April, 27 May 1769; 86 B 3, 30 January 1580 (inheritance, *déclarations de grossesse*); 86 B 103, "Réceptions de procureurs, greffiers, tabellions . . . ," passim (oaths of office); 86 B 67, 23 July 1785, 25 July 1789 (harvest); 86 B 102, "Police, 1702–1789," 20 November 1700 (Sabbath), 12 August 1737 (dangerous fireplace), 12 December 1693 and 31 March 1696 (roads), 1702 (no month given) (appearance of guild officials), 21 June 1721 (oath and registration of a new guild master); 86 B 49, 16 July 1740 (ditches); above, pp. 246–51 (regulation of grain and cotton trades).

TABLE 51. *Judicial Activity in Pont-St-Pierre, 1580–1790*

Year	Number of Sessions	Average Number of Matters Considered per Session
19 November 1580– 14 October 1581	48	31.9
5 February 1661– 28 January 1662	43	register illegible
1 August 1682– 31 July 1683	37	register illegible
1700	37	10.0
1720	28	7.5
1740	30	6.7
1761–1770 (mean for 10 years)	17	6.7
1781–1790 (mean for 10 years)	15	9.2

SOURCE: AD Eure, 86 B 3, 4, 8, 12, 21, 37, 48, 59–62, 67, Plumitifs, Pont-St-Pierre.

tury; although the state of its registers prohibits the calculation of numbers of cases, the court continued to meet most weeks. By the early eighteenth century, however, important changes were visible. The number of sessions had dropped significantly since the late sixteenth century; in 1720 there were twenty-eight sessions, in 1740 there were thirty. The number of cases taken up had fallen more sharply still, to an average of ten at each session in 1700 and to about seven in 1720 and 1740. After the mid–eighteenth century, the court met more infrequently, just over once each month, and its case load remained low: an average of seven cases per session in the 1760s, nine cases in the 1780s.

Declining numbers reflected a more general decay of the institution. In February 1763 it was noted that "the audience [has been] postponed for a lack of lawyers"; a week later, the only case presented at the court's session "cannot be argued for a lack of judges"; and at the court's next session, two weeks later, there were simply no cases at all.[99] In 1720 the clerk noted that "since the courtroom of this High Justice has been knocked down in order to be rebuilt, its sessions in the future will be held in the house of the sergeant Tierce"; but in 1735 the marquis sold the house that had served as

99. AD Eure, 86 B 60, 5, 12, 26 February 1763.

TABLE 52. *Leases of the "Tabellionage et le greffe de la haute justice de Pont-St-Pierre"*

Dates	Yearly Rent
1515–1516	8 l.
1642–1648	270 l., 24 lbs. sugar
1651–1656	300 l., 24 lbs. sugar
1656–1666	270 l., 24 lbs. sugar
1671–1680	220 l.
1680–1689	130 l.
1690–1696	110 l.
1700–1701	100 l.
1706–1709	100 l.
1709–1712	100 l. (lease canceled after one year)
1710–1713	80 l.
1724–1727	60 l.
1744–1747	50 l.
1747–1753	50 l.
1764–1770	50 l.
1773–1782	50 l.

SOURCE: Comptes, 1515–16; Caillot, liasse 241, "Matières diverses" (1764, 1773); AD Eure, E 2401, Chartier de Pont-St-Pierre (1642–1753).

the jurisdiction's courtroom and jail,[100] so that casual arrangements became a permanent necessity.

The declining worth of the jurisdiction's clerkship offers a final sign of decay. Throughout the early modern period, local notaries and attorneys leased in a single contract both the barony's notarial practice—its *tabellionage*—and the clerkship of its High Justice. Both positions offered profits. Clients paid for the drawing up of notarial acts, and litigants paid for the clerk's labors both during the trial and afterward, when they needed copies of the court's decisions. The rents charged for these rights (table 52) suggest that the barony's public powers reached their greatest importance in the mid–seventeenth century, then declined rapidly. Much of the decline came during the personal reign of Louis XIV; between 1656 and 1700, rents fell by about two-thirds. After a brief period of stability in the early eighteenth century, the decline resumed, and by 1744 the clerkship's value was half what it had been in 1700. In

100. Ibid., 86 B 37; AD S-M, Tabel. Pont-St-Pierre, 17 April 1735.

contrast to nearly all of the barony's other revenues, there was no mid-eighteenth-century revival in the clerkship's value.

A variety of evidence thus points to the shriveling of the barony's public powers after about 1650. No single cause fully explains the change. The barons themselves clearly had scant interest in maintaining their judicial powers. Judicial profits had been high in the fourteenth century, but by the 1560s they had almost disappeared; and judicial costs rose steadily, as the Crown enforced steadily higher standards of judicial expertise and made appeals to its own jurisdictions easier.[101] Under Colbert, the Crown challenged the barony's very right to hold a High Justice; this meant further costs for the maintenance of judicial rights and must have encouraged litigants to seek justice elsewhere.[102] Colbert's forest reform of 1669 weakened Pont-St-Pierre's forest court by encouraging royal judges to intervene in its cases.[103] Villagers apparently took advantage of these possibilities, for in the eighteenth century the *verderie* had only a phantom existence.

The barons' notarial monopoly faced a similar challenge, from the proliferation of royal notaries in nearby towns and even in Pont-St-Pierre itself. The Roncherolles undertook a series of lawsuits in the hope of ending this competition, but with little real success. In 1717 the Conseil d'Etat itself confirmed the barony's monopoly against the pretensions of royal notaries in Rouen, Gisors, Lyons, and Maineville; in 1721 there was another decision maintaining these rights, and in 1729 there was yet another, maintaining the monopoly of the baron's notaries and prohibiting royal notaries from even residing within the lordship.[104] These decisions had little practical import. By the later eighteenth century, royal notaries were an established institution in Pont-St-Pierre, and the barons themselves made use of them. In 1764 Claude de Roncherolles leased the barony's own notarial rights to a royal notary residing in the bourg, and a decade later Anthoine Caillot de Coquéraumont did the same. Of the barony's monopoly on notarial practice, there remained only an abstract distinction between the same notary's acts as royal and seigneurial official: "All the acts [so his lease specified] that the said

101. Above, pp. 223–24.

102. Above, p. 186; see also Goldsmith, *Les Salers et les d'Escorailles*, 153–80, for the impact that the Grands Jours of Auvergne had on seigneurial powers.

103. François Isambert et al., *Recueil général des anciennes lois françaises depuis l'an 420, jusqu'à la Révolution de 1789*, 29 vols. (Paris, 1821–33), 18:222 (title 1, arts. 11, 12, 13).

104. AD Eure, E 2392, Chartrier de Pont-St-Pierre, 45ff.

sieur lessee will receive within the area of the said High Justice between those who are subject to it and for properties held from it are to be passed in his function as *tabellion* [of the High Justice] and not in that of royal notary, with a penalty of 50 l. fine for each violation."[105]

Did the High Justice's decline reflect also the quality of justice that it rendered?[106] Pont-St-Pierre's forest jurisdiction, its *verderie*, was clearly an oppressive institution to villagers of all social levels. Important economic interests were at stake for both lordship and villagers: the forest court defended the barony's single most valuable resource, and the firewood and grazing that the forest illicitly provided was an important supplement to villagers' incomes. As a result, the *verderie*'s fines were heavy, and large numbers of villagers found themselves having to pay them. In the mid–sixteenth century, the court normally fined villagers 5 s. for each of their cows caught grazing in the forest; by 1579 the typical fine for this offense had risen to 10 s., and by 1654 it reached 120 s. In the sixteenth century, fines typically amounted to about one-tenth of the animal's value; by the mid–seventeenth century, fines typically amounted to about one-fourth.[107] Fines for hunting and for cutting wood in the forest were equally severe.[108]

Every year, Pont-St-Pierre's *verdier* assessed hundreds of these fines. There were 359 fines between April 1540 and March 1541; 301 in the year 1568; 954 in 1636; 537 in 1637; 234 in 1654.[109] Of course, many of those brought before the *verdier* were poor; in the 1630s, about one-third of the fines that the forest court assessed were

---

105. Caillot, 241, 17 November 1764, 25 September 1773.

106. Cf. Abel Poitrineau, "Aspects de la crise des justices seigneuriales dans l'Auvergne du XVIIIe siècle," *Revue historique de droit français et étranger*, 4th series, vol. 39, no. 4 (October–December 1961): 552–70; see also the summary of eighteenth-century complaints about the quality of seigneurial justice in John Mackrell, "Criticism of Seigniorial Justice in Eighteenth-Century France," in John Bosher, ed., *French Government and Society, 1500–1850: Essays in Memory of Alfred Cobban* (London, 1973), 123–44. For the contrary view, emphasizing the basic effectiveness of seigneurial justice and its utility as an inexpensive and readily accessible court, see Pierre Goubert, "Le paysan et la terre: Seigneurie, tenure, exploitation," in Fernand Braudel and C. E. Labrousse, eds., *Histoire économique et sociale de la France*, vol. 2, *1660–1789* (Paris, 1970), 119–58, 123–24, and Mousnier, *Les institutions*, 1:409. Forthcoming studies by Steven Reinhardt and Julius Ruff will present further evidence of this effectiveness.

107. For examples, AD Eure, 86 B 114–19, passim; Caillot, liasse 9, "Plés de la verderie de Longbouel." For livestock values, above, Chapter 2.

108. Examples AD Eure, 86 B 114–19; Caillot, liasse 9.

109. AD Eure, 86 B 112, 115; Caillot, liasse 9.

levied on people too poor to pay them, and they had to be given up as "useless" in the court's accounts.[110] But the *verderie* affected local notables as well as the poor. The forest guards occasionally arrested members of the local nobility. They also arrested local merchants and farmers prosperous enough to employ servants.[111] Such arrests must have seemed especially oppressive because of the uncertainties that continued to surround forest rights into the eighteenth century. All the communities around the forest claimed some rights of usage in it, but the baron's forest jurisdiction enforced his version of these rights. It is hardly surprising that villagers took advantage of the possibility of having their cases tried in the royal courts. Only residents of the bourg of Pont-St-Pierre had enjoyed some degree of protection against the vexations of the *verderie*, for the bourg had clear title to pasture animals in 102 arpents of the Crown's share of the forest.[112] In this area as well as many others, the residents benefited from their special relationship with the lordship.

Villagers' interests found a more hospitable response in the barony's High Justice itself, for the barony's financial interests were only slightly engaged in the High Justice's workings. By the mid–eighteenth century, the High Justice was almost entirely in the hands of the small congregation of local lawyers who dominated its proceedings. In 1768, for instance, there were six such lawyers. They divided among themselves the modest number of litigants; although Pont-St-Pierre's jurisdiction typically heard cases involving very small amounts of money, virtually all of the parties sought legal advice. And the six lawyers divided among themselves the court's principal offices, as *procureur fiscal* and principal judge.[113] In the sixteenth and seventeenth centuries these offices had been seigneurial appointments, and the individuals who held them had usually retained them over a long career. But in the eighteenth century the offices tended to pass each year from one lawyer to another, and the lawyers also exchanged them more casually as immediate circumstances demanded. At the court's lone meeting during December 1768, for instance, the judge was absent. The *procureur fiscal* took his place, although at the same session he represented four private cli-

110. Caillot, liasse 9.
111. For examples, AD Eure, 86 B 122, Haute Justice de Pont-St-Pierre, Verderie, 5 March, 9 April, 24 September 1584, 9, 23 February, 9 March, 27 April, 11, 27 May, 8, 22 June, 3 August, 6 October 1587.
112. AN, KK 948, "Arpentage de la forêt de Longbouel, 1565."
113. In the case of the *procureur fiscal*, this shift between private and public duties was legitimate practice; Houard, *Dictionnaire*, 3:680–81.

ents. Yet another lawyer with his own clients present took over the functions of *procureur fiscal:* representing the public interest and that of the barony, and standing ready to prosecute serious crimes.[114]

Such haphazard arrangements were a further sign of the High Justice's dilapidation in the mid–eighteenth century. But they also indicate the closeness that might prevail between villagers and the seigneurial judiciary; in the eighteenth century seigneurial judges and prosecutors depended for their incomes more on their local clientele of litigants than on the profits of office. And in fact this clientele appears to have been eager to come to court. The barony's residents appeared before the High Justice, lawyers in tow, to argue over the most trivial matters: whether, for instance, a workman was to be paid 9 l. or 6 l. (this a case from 1769).[115] Other sources tell a similar tale. In 1764 a cotton spinner in Boos sued a day laborer in Franquevillette for "insults, atrocious and scandalous words against [her] honor"—to the effect that she had once placed a stone in a packet of cotton thread with the intent of defrauding the merchant to whom she sold it. Both parties were illiterate. In 1768 the guardians of the children of a day laborer from Pîtres presented their accounts: the only receipts they listed came from the sale of the laborer's possessions, worth less than 200 l., but the children had been involved in two lawsuits, in each case with legal representation.[116] Even the village poor had recourse to the law and to lawyers.

When they appeared in court, villagers encountered an outlook that was receptive to their own values. Given the weakness of baronial police powers, officials necessarily relied on public rumor as the basis of their inquiries. Rumor provided an acceptable basis for questioning witnesses, and the judges rebuked those whose statements diverged from what they had learned from other sources.[117] *Procureur fiscal* and judge alike deferred to popular views of the grain trade (as has been seen), and they also enforced popular religious assumptions. A dramatic example came in 1690, when the court tried an innkeeper from Franquevillette, near la Neuville, for sorcery and theft. Guillaume Doublet had been widely suspected of sorcery for at least a decade; in 1680 a resident of Pont-

114. AD Eure, 86 B 62, Plumitif, July 1768–July 1771.
115. AD Eure, 86 B 62, 14 January 1769.
116. AD S-M, Tabel. Pont-St-Pierre, 12 June 1764, 29 June 1768.
117. AD Eure, 86 B 104, Procédures criminelles, 23 February 1690; 106, 22 August 1712. Cf. T. J. A. Le Goff and D. M. G. Sutherland, "The Revolution and the Rural Community in Eighteenth-Century Brittany," *Past and Present* 62 (February 1974): 96–119, for the importance of hearsay in criminal investigations.

St-Pierre had informed Doublet's father-in-law that "you've married your daughter to a shepherd who is a sorcerer," and Doublet himself had brought suit for slander.[118] In 1690 Doublet was caught breaking into a shop in la Neuville, and the baronial officials pursued the issue of sorcery with complete seriousness.[119] For them as for Doublet's neighbors, a career of theft and sorcery was the most plausible explanation for his surprising ascent from shepherd to innkeeper.[120] Doublet's wife received especially intense questioning. The judge asked her "whether when her husband was a shepherd, she had not seen him casting spells (*faire des imprécations de sortilleges*) and whether she had not seen him [take] the sacred host, with the intention of using it for evil, exhorting her to tell the truth." When she denied all these accusations, the judge "remonstrated that she is not telling us the truth, that it has been testified that her said husband had been in possession of the sacred host"; further denial was met with further rebuke "that she is not telling us the truth," and Doublet's own denials were similarly treated. To the judge, the economic implications of sorcery had particular importance. His first question to Doublet's wife was "at the time that she was married, what was her husband's status (*condition*) and what properties did he possess at the time of the said marriage."

In the end the court convicted Doublet only of theft and "d'avoir meschamment vecu," but this verdict did not mitigate his punishment: after a ceremonial *amende honorable*, he was tortured to name his accomplices and hanged. The severity of the punishment suggests that the court took seriously his neighbors' view of Doublet as a sorcerer, although they were unwilling to condemn him formally for that crime. Doublet's death testified to the continuing solidarity in the late seventeenth century between popular assumptions and those of the learned lawyers—nearly all of them practitioners before the Parlement—who ran the High Justice of Pont-St-Pierre; the

118. AD Eure, 86 B 105, Procédures criminelles, 15 January 1680.
119. Ibid., 23 February, 11 March 1690.
120. Shepherds had been prominent victims in sorcery prosecutions because of their marginal place in rural society and because of the vulnerability of livestock; see Alfred Soman, "Les procès de sorcellerie au Parlement de Paris (1565–1640)," *Annales ESC* 32, no. 4 (July–August 1977): 790–814. The response both of his neighbors and of the judicial authorities to Doublet's career illustrates anthropologists' stress on peasant views of "limited good" (George M. Foster, "Peasant Society and the Image of Limited Good," repr. in Foster et al., *Peasant Society: A Reader* [Boston, 1967], 300–323).

Parlement of Rouen itself remained anxious about sorcery in these years and resistant to the Crown's efforts to end its prosecution.[121]

The lawyers of the High Justice brought more than simple affirmation of village superstitions. They brought new interpretations of individuals' situations as well, for their courtroom rhetoric described these in powerful and emotional language. In 1712 Jeanne Letellier, adult daughter of a farmer in Pîtres, was accused of undeclared pregnancy, a very dangerous accusation in view of royal legislation to prevent infanticide.[122] One of the barony's sergeants claimed as well "that he had learned by common rumor that Letellier and his wife had given their said daughter potions . . . to abort her alleged pregnancy"; here again the seigneurial justice acted as the agent of village rumor. The result was a series of medical examinations, following which Jeanne's father sought her outright release. His request, drawn up by a local lawyer, suggests the ways in which legal rhetoric might redefine personal situations. "Finally that poor girl," ran the request, "who has never been a rebel against the orders of justice, . . . suffered much when it was necessary that she present herself to be examined even in the most secret parts of her body, since she was accused of having sinned in the most shameful part of her body; she had to expose herself entirely naked to the eyes of three men; nonetheless, to prove her innocence it was necessary for this unfortunate victim to expose herself to that examination. How many times did she blush to see herself in that state that is so opposed to the modesty of her sex."[123] Her lawyer's request for Jeanne's release defined her circumstances in terms of several powerful ideas: about feminine modesty and obedience, about the shameful secrets of the body, about privacy and its violation, about innocence and injustice. The lawyer emphasized Jeanne's dignity and delicacy of feeling, and he placed her sufferings in a large conceptual framework; he linked her troubles to larger notions of rights and injustices. Such rhetorical flourishes, it is important to remember, took place in a public setting, crowded with litigants and petitioners. For all of them, the law offered the rhetorical reinterpreta-

---

121. Robert Mandrou, *Magistrats et sorciers en France au XVIIe siècle: Une analyse de psychologie historique* (Paris, 1968), 444–58, 507–12.

122. See Cissie Fairchilds, "Female Sexual Attitudes and the Rise of Illegitimacy: A Case Study," *Journal of Interdisciplinary History* 8, no. 4 (Spring 1978): 629–30, for the functions and characteristics of judges' investigations of illegitimate pregnancies.

123. AD Eure, 86 B 107, 14 July 1711, 7 July 1712, 23 July 1712.

tion of commonplace situations, their neighbors' as well as their own.[124]

Rhetoric was not the only way in which even in the early eighteenth century the High Justice functioned as a mechanism of cultural change. The demands of justice also worked to encourage, in some instances even to require, literacy and numeracy. The High Justice required that guardians keep track of disbursements and receipts on behalf of their wards; and the threat of litigation when the ward attained adulthood was a powerful incentive for the careful keeping of accounts and supporting documents. The threat of litigation of other kinds likewise encouraged careful attention to words and numbers. Thus extensive collections of such documents appeared in farmers' inventories after death by the later seventeenth century, two or three generations before the appearance of printed books.[125]

At the end of the Old Regime, villagers' readiness to litigate continued to impress contemporaries. Those who drew up the *cahier de doléances* of la Neuville-Chant-d'Oisel—in large measure, members of the village's economic and cultural ruling class—took litigation for granted as a fact of village life. "We ask also," they wrote, "that all the small cases arising in the parish, which after having been in the courts are finally sent back to the *laboureurs* of the parish, who are named arbiters, but to arrive at this goal considerable expenses have been incurred—instead of which, [we ask that] if these little difficulties at their beginnings were given to the sieur curé and the members of the municipal council, who could decide them, this would avoid a great deal of expense; and if the parties did not agree to the decision that the municipal assembly had rendered, they could provide for themselves in whatever royal jurisdiction it pleased His Majesty."[126] The *cahier* took for granted village litigiousness, but it also made clear the villagers' complicated relationship with the formal apparatus of the courts. Formal litigation was seen to be only a stage in the process by which

---

124. For suggestive insights into the intellectual role of the rural lawyer in the eighteenth century, see Robert Forster, *The House of Saulx-Tavanes: Versailles and Burgundy, 1700–1830* (Baltimore, 1971) 162 (for the role of judges and notaries in the development of radical ideas in rural Burgundy); and the forthcoming work of Hilton Root (on lawyers' role in redefining the seigneurial system in eighteenth-century Burgundy). On the issue of villagers' honor, Yves Castan, *Honnêteté et relations sociales en Languedoc, 1715–1780* (Paris, 1974).

125. See the inventories analyzed above, Chapter 1.

126. AD S-M, 4 BP 6012, Bailliage de Rouen, Cahiers de doléances, la Neuville, 2.

settlements were reached. In most instances, so the *cahier* of la Neuville claimed, the village's *laboureurs* arranged final settlements through arbitration.[127] The *cahier* also assumed that residents of la Neuville would turn to royal rather than seigneurial justice; and it makes no mention of the possible roles of seigneur, seigneurial officials, or other large landowners as having a role in mediating disputes. Rather, the *cahier* supposes what has been seen throughout this study—the power of the *laboureurs* in the late eighteenth-century village. By 1789 they, rather than the formal apparatus of seigneurial justice or more informal modes of seigneurial patronage, took the pivotal role in settling village litigation.

La Neuville's *cahier* points to the same conclusion as statistics concerning the High Justice's case load: the lordship had become less significant as an institutional framework in which villagers resolved their conflicts. The informal power of the *laboureurs* and the formal institutions of royal justice had in large degree taken its place. It is unlikely that conflict itself had become less frequent. Elsewhere in France the later eighteenth century witnessed an impressive rise in the number of judicial cases: in Toulouse, the number of criminal decisions issued by the Parlement more than doubled between 1730 and 1786, a change that Nicole Castan has seen as part of an explosion of judicial activity of all kinds.[128] If in the eighteenth century villagers came less often before Pont-St-Pierre's High Justice, it seems, the cause was competition from other judicial institutions, not a decline in judicial needs. In this and many other matters, eighteenth-century villagers moved in a wider world than their ancestors.

THE WEIGHT OF LORDSHIP

A final question remains: how oppressive was the seigneurial structure in Pont-St-Pierre? How much of a real burden did it represent for those over whom it was set? No simple answer is possible. The example of Pont-St-Pierre's economic and judicial functions

127. This procedure has been shown to have been typical of southwestern France, where the hold of the formal judicial system was probably less developed than in Normandy. See Nicole Castan, *Justice et répression*, 15–51; Steven G. Reinhardt, "Royal Justice and Society: The Redress of Grievances in the Sarladais in the Late Eighteenth Century" (Ph.D. dissertation, Northern Illinois University, 1982).

128. *Justice et répression*, 133–34.

shows that the lordship brought benefits as well as vexations to rural society; to the end of the Old Regime, it continued to offer local society a degree of protection from the effects of unrestricted markets in food and labor, and a competent level of judicial service.

Even such benefits, however, were inextricably bound to the lordship's defense of its own interests. Pont-St-Pierre's forest jurisdiction, of course, must have seemed simply oppressive; its fines were heavy, and it brought no benefits. Less directly, most of the barony's regulatory efforts were bound up with an effort to preserve baronial monopolies, and inevitably they meant enforced inefficiencies for residents of an outlying village like la Neuville. As a result they inspired episodic resistance from merchants, farmers, and even the local nobility.

Other seigneurial rights had more uneven histories. In the violence of the late Middle Ages, the barons of Pont-St-Pierre had claimed the right to compel local residents to guard their château. They continued to demand such service after peace had been re-established, but encountered concerted resistance: in 1498 Pierre de Roncherolles had auctioned off the lands of several inhabitants of la Neuville for their refusal to serve in his guard, a move that the *bailli* of Rouen finally overturned.[129] In the late sixteenth century comparable resistance briefly flared over the barony's demands for seigneurial rents; in 1581 most of the residents of la Neuville failed to present themselves to acknowledge their obligations to the barony, and the *procureur fiscal* demanded that their properties be confiscated.[130]

What precisely did such refusals mean? An answer requires measuring the economic impact on tenants of the seigneurial dues that were thus contested. Because la Neuville-Chant-d'Oisel had been cleared and settled over a span of centuries and probably also because its land was of varying fertility, seigneurial rents within its boundaries varied widely: from a minimum of 3 s. an acre in the triage of le Chouquet to a maximum of 12 s. and two hens—in the early sixteenth century, worth about 15 d. each—in the triage of la Londe (table 53).

Only fragmentary comparisons are possible with the other charges that villagers confronted, but they suggest that seigneurial dues remained a major burden well into the sixteenth century for

129. Pont-St-Pierre, sixteenth-century inventory, 28 June 1498; cf. Charbonnier, *Une autre France*, 2:707, 1147–48, for the importance of such rights during the Hundred Years' War and through the sixteenth century.
130. AD Eure, 86 B 3, Plumitif, 8 April 1581.

TABLE 53. *Seigneurial Rents, la Neuville-Chant-d'Oisel, 1515–1516*

Triage	Rent per Acre	Area
Masures de Mautruble	5 s., 2 *poules*	15.12 acres
Les Grandes Masures	4 s., 1.6 *poules*	107.82 acres
Le Chouquoy	3 s.	73.77 acres
Le Boquet	7 s.	135.88 acres
Le Cocheux	10 s., 2 *poules*	20.01 acres
Les Grands Boscz	12 s., 2 *poules*	15.20 acres
La Cousture	12 s.	51.09 acres
La Salle	8 s.	4.39 acres
Le Buisson	4 s.	6.69 acres
La Vente Ponchet	9 s., 2 *poules*	106.00 acres
La Londe	12 s., 2 *poules*	55.69 acres
La Croutclet	12 s., 3 *gelines*	unknown: nothing received from this triage

SOURCE: Comptes, 1515–16.

NOTES: Total area: 588.66 acres. Total rents (*poules* evaluated at 15 d. each): 244.30 l. Mean rent per acre: .415 l. (= 8.3 s.).

those who had to pay them. Dues on each acre of land in la Neuville took the equivalent of three or four days of unskilled labor each year.[131] They represented a considerably heavier burden than royal taxation: in the early sixteenth century in la Neuville, a substantial family might pay only 20 s. for the *taille*.[132] Above all, seigneurial dues in the early sixteenth century remained a substantial percentage of the short-term rents that land in the area might bring: roughly between 10 and 20 percent.[133]

This relationship ceased to prevail as the sixteenth century advanced. While short-term rents increased at about the rate of inflation, seigneurial dues remained essentially fixed. Taxation increased still more dramatically, especially after 1630. Seigneurial dues thus became a relatively small part of families' budgets. But they were not insignificant for that reason. Families whose margins of eco-

131. Bois, *Crise du féodalisme*, 391–92.
132. AD Eure, E 1216, Tabel. Pont-St-Pierre, 7 June 1507.
133. In 1543, thus, the Rouennais magistrate Thomas Maignart leased eighteen small pieces of land at his property of les Maisons all for 100 s. per acre; AD Eure, E 1224, Tabel. Pont-St-Pierre, 21 September 1543ff. See also Goldsmith, *Les Salers et les d'Escorailles*, 222–23, for emphasis on the effective weight of even small seigneurial rents.

nomic maneuver were narrow confronted in seigneurial levies a significant and continuous drain on their resources: in an example from 1649, dues represented 5.8 percent of what one family spent on short-term leases; between 1757 and 1764, the orphaned children of a day laborer paid a total of 126 l. in seigneurial rents,[134] about a year's income for a laborer. Lordship remained a serious economic burden into the late eighteenth century.

In Pont-St-Pierre and elsewhere in France,[135] this burden probably became heavier during the last generation of the Old Regime. For the Caillot de Coquéraumont brought improved administration of seigneurial dues as of much else. Seigneurial dues had lost their primacy both among the lord's revenues and among his subjects' burdens, but they were supervised with increasing exactitude at the end of the Old Regime.

Lordship in Pont-St-Pierre remained significant to the end of the regime. Nonetheless, the principal theme of this chapter has been the lordship's declining centrality over the course of the early modern period. In the late Middle Ages, the large majority of Pont-St-Pierre's income had come from seigneurial sources: fixed rents, judicial rights, milling monopolies, and so on. These sources of income retained much of their relative importance during the period of reconstruction that followed the Hundred Years' War, but in the sixteenth century they declined rapidly: by the later sixteenth century, three-fourths of the barony's income came from domanial sources. The Roncherolles were able to survive this transition because, like many Norman lords, they controlled a large tract of forest. Demand for firewood was enormous throughout the period, and the vitality of this market meant that the Roncherolles could misuse their forest property without serious economic consequences: the forest could be profitable even when in poor condition, since its timber was used for fires rather than for construction.

A second transition came more hesitantly. In the seventeenth and eighteenth centuries, the Roncherolles began to interest themselves in the direct control of land and nonseigneurial mills. Medieval Pont-St-Pierre had included no landed domain of any consequence, and

---

134. AD S-M, Tabel. Pont-St-Pierre, 8 December 1649, 3 June 1764.
135. For recent studies of the eighteenth-century seigneurial reaction, Forster, *The House of Saulx-Tavanes*, 92–104; Jean Bastier, *La féodalité au siècle des lumières dans la région de Toulouse (1730–1790)* (Paris, 1975), 243–57, Jean Nicolas, *La Savoie au XVIIIe siècle: Noblesse et bourgeoisie*, 2 vols. (Paris, 1978), 2:827–37.

into the mid–seventeenth century the Roncherolles continued to grant out domain lands that came into their possession in exchange for permanently fixed rents. This practice receded only in the course of the seventeenth century, and only in the late eighteenth century did the barony take a substantial role in rural production.

Change in the barony's political role came at the same halting pace. Into the eighteenth century, the barony's High Justice remained a vigorous center of local political life. Villagers of all social classes appeared in its courtroom, both as litigants and to make use of its administrative functions. The High Justice was a powerful mechanism through which both the tools of literacy and the attitudes of the city reached local society.

Its eighteenth-century decline is all the more significant in view of this role as a cultural mechanism. Over the eighteenth century, the High Justice met steadily less often and heard a declining number of cases at each meeting. The presence of lawyers and judges became more haphazard; the courtroom itself was sold. Litigiousness itself had not declined. Rather, so it seems, local residents were turning elsewhere to settle their disputes and to carry out the mass of quasi-judicial business that French legislation demanded. These needs increasingly drew villagers away from Pont-St-Pierre to the royal courts in the larger market towns of the region.

To the end of the Old Regime, however, the barony's efforts at economic regulation remained vigorous. Through the eighteenth century, its officials sought to enforce a clearly articulated model of economic behavior: a model in which both profits and prices were regulated, in which economic transactions took place under the eye of political authority, in which the poor had significant claims on the economic system. The barony's defense of this system of values was not disinterested, but the barons' efforts were not the less sincere because real economic interests were at stake. In fact the barons and their officials were choosing among their divergent interests, for they owned farms and mills as well as a market. Efforts to regulate economic life were part of a commitment to a certain form of the large estate, in which production for the marketplace held a subordinate place, in which the estate was a political as well as an economic institution.

It was thus the barony that stood as the local embodiment of the regulated economy, against the efforts of *laboureurs* and village merchants. This orientation did not mean indifference to gain or ignorance of what the free market could offer. Although the quality of

Pont-St-Pierre's administration varied with individual owners, the Roncherolles were alert to the profits that sale of agricultural commodities could bring.

Nonetheless, between 1450 and 1750 the barony captured a smaller share of what the rural economy produced than it had during the late Middle Ages. It lost ground relative to those who directly controlled the land and what it produced: to those urban landowners and lesser nobles who during this period were piecing together substantial farms oriented to grain production. Only as the barony absorbed some of these farms in the seventeenth and especially in the eighteenth century, did it regain its dominance of the rural economy.

Pont-St-Pierre thus illustrates the difficulty with which a large lordship might adapt to the developing free-market economy. Three centuries passed as the barony progressively renounced its seigneurial character and acquired characteristics of a large domain. Even in 1789 adaptation remained incomplete. Seigneurial officials continued to struggle against the free market in such commodities as grain and cotton, and they devoted considerable efforts to assuring the collection of seigneurial dues. The barony was a different kind of property in 1789 from what it had been in the previous three centuries, and its role in local political life was much reduced. But rural capitalism had other, more committed representatives in late eighteenth-century Pont-St-Pierre: not the barony but its most restive subjects—the farmers and merchants whom its regulations sought to control.

VII

THE REVOLUTION IN PONT-ST-PIERRE

Revolution in 1789 brought little violence and only gradual change to Pont-St-Pierre and the villages around it.[1] In February 1789, grain shortages at Pont-St-Pierre's market led to the threat of rioting; but officials intervened to reduce prices, and those in the crowd who were unable to find grain at these prices marched off to visit local *laboureurs* and buy directly from them.[2] The availability of food remained a source of anxiety throughout the Revolution,[3] and so did popular discontent about the food supply. Such fear led to a grandiloquently seigneurial announcement "de par Monsieur" in September 1789: "The love and attention that we have for the well-being and improvement of the inhabitants of our barony and High Justice . . . lead us to do all that we can to engage the farmers (*laboureurs*) of neighboring parishes to provision this market." To encourage farmers to bring their grain to Pont-St-Pierre, Caillot renounced collection of the normal market rights for the following year and promised to limit his taxation to the measurers' fee of 6 s. for each sack of grain.[4]

Popular discontent was a recognizable threat in Pont-St-Pierre, but

1. For brief overviews of the Revolution in Normandy, Michel de Bouard, ed., *Histoire de la Normandie* (Toulouse, 1970), 391–411; Michel Mollat, ed., *Histoire de Rouen* (Toulouse, 1979), 279–305.
2. See above, pp. 247–48.
3. See above, p. 34.
4. AD Eure, 86 B 102, Haute Justice de Pont-St-Pierre, "Police 1702–1789," 12 September 1789.

it had not yet—this a month after the National Assembly had abolished "feudalism"—inhibited seigneurial language or the principle of seigneurial rights; Caillot's declaration insisted that his concession was a temporary measure, meant to solve short-term problems. In fact the Caillots continued to levy some of their most valuable seigneurial rights through the fall of the monarchy. As late as 1793, their receiver continued to record payments of the *treizièmes*, the mutation tax collected on every sale of land within the barony's borders.[5] Apparently other elements of the estate also continued to function normally. Late in October 1791—a moment of explosive tensions in Parisian politics—an agent of the Caillots wrote from Pont-St-Pierre. His letter displayed the tranquil survival of deference: it was addressed to "monsieur le président de Coquéraumont at his *hôtel* in Rouen." Most of the letter was devoted to the normal cares of estate management. It noted the price of cider, described some trees that had been overturned in a storm, noted that "the hay is selling very late this year"; and it described the brief visit of "M. de Penthièvre" to the nearby village of Radepont: "The entire neighborhood (*tous les environs*) heartily wished that his stay had been longer." "There is nothing new," this section of the letter concluded—before going on to describe one troubling problem. "The tenants in Pîtres do not wish to give more than one-fifth of the price of their rent for the value of the tithe, . . . if I cannot draw more from them, I am of the opinion to settle, since we will not get more and perhaps not as much." Here were signs of a challenge to traditional routines. Villagers were apparently refusing to pay the tithe, and their refusal had cut into one of the Caillots' revenues.[6]

Only after 1791 did serious trouble beset the Caillots. By 1793 Anthoine Caillot de Coquéraumont had died and his son André had joined the emigration.[7] All of the Roncherolles had also emigrated, by early 1791. But emigration proved to be only an interruption in these families' histories, for by 1800 both had returned to their positions and properties. The Roncherolles had remained in touch with an agent at Paris, and he had the power to handle their affairs.[8] In

5. Pont-St-Pierre, "Recettes des treizièmes, 1769–93." This document is discussed above, Chapter 2.

6. Pont-St-Pierre, an unmarked and unnumbered liasse, letter of 21 October 1791, Clouet, Pont-St-Pierre, to "le président de coquéromont en son hôtel à Rouen." Clouet had been the Caillots' "agent des affaires" in Pont-St-Pierre since the mid-1770s: AD S-M, E, Tabel. Pont-St-Pierre, 13 March 1775.

7. AD S-M, QP 1975, QP 2033, "Biens des émigrés."

8. AD S-M, 16 J 119 bis, Roncherolles, 8 June, 28 September 1791.

the Year V the Republic lifted its seizure of the properties of Marie Louise Amelot, widow of Claude de Roncherolles. Marie resided in the faubourg St. Germain, and she was rich: her properties were worth more than 1,000,000 l., 360,000 l. in the form of two estates in lower Normandy, the rest in *rentes*. Against this were over 500,000 l. in debts, most of them inherited from her mother and sister. Marie secured the restoration of her properties in exchange for a large payment to the Republic, but she managed to pay most of this levy in the form of worthless obligations on other émigrés.[9] With a landed base thus restored, the family returned to a degree of prominence during the Restoration: one Roncherolles became lieutenant general in the restored Bourbons' army, another *maréchal de camp*.[10] Another branch of the family continued to reside near les Andelys and regularly figured in the Empire's lists of the district's "persons most notable by their birth or their fortune." A cavalry captain before the Revolution, Anne Charles Léonor de Roncherolles now lived from his revenues, variously estimated at 10,000, 16,000 and 20,000 F. The authorities described him as "an honest man and obedient to the laws," and they recommended his older daughter as one of the eligible heiresses of the region: "an interesting and agreeable physiognomy, graceful, . . . useful and pleasing talents, a brilliant education, good judgment and religious principles"—along with a dowry that was expected to amount to 80,000 F.[11] But Anne Charles Léonor had only two daughters and no sons. Like the Parisian Roncherolles, the Roncherolles of Heuqueville came to an end because of a declining birthrate, not because of revolutionary violence.

The Caillots' history was only slightly more complicated. At the death of Anthoine Caillot, the property of Pont-St-Pierre passed to his daughter and her husband, the baron d'Houdemare. Thereafter the d'Houdemares settled tranquilly into the role of local notables, restoring to the château of Pont-St-Pierre a local political significance that it had not held since the early eighteenth century. Three generations of the family were mayors of Pont-St-Pierre, with a fine disregard for changes of regime: they served (although not without opposition) during the Restoration, the July Monarchy, the Second Empire, and

9. Archives de Paris, DQ 10 1363, dossier 1087.
10. Service Historique de l'Armée de Terre, "Répertoire alphabétique des Maréchaux de France, Lieutenants généraux, et maréchaux de camp: Période moderne," 691.
11. AD Eure, 1 M 171, "Statistiques personnelles du département . . . 1809–1812."

briefly during the Third Republic.[12] As a "man of order who has never deviated"—his words of praise for his *adjoint* in 1852—Jean-Aimé d'Houdemare could deal confidently with conservative administrations; he could invite the secretary general of the prefecture to "spend a few days at my home," as preface to threats to decline his nomination as mayor if his choice of *adjoint* were not confirmed.[13]

All through the region there were comparable survivals from the Old Regime. The Asselin des Parts family, leading members of Rouen's Parlement and owners of a large estate in la Neuville, resided there throughout the Revolution; they took an active role in local affairs during the Directory.[14] Just upstream from Pont-St-Pierre, at Radepont, there were the marquis Dubosc and his widowed mother, with incomes that totaled 100,000 F. in 1812; Napoleonic officials described the marquis as an "honest man and devoted to the government."[15] At nearby Belbeuf there was the Godard family, which had supplied the last king's attorney of the Parlement of Rouen. Although the Godards' estate had been briefly seized during the Terror, it had been restored to them by the Year IV.[16] Such survivals reflected a larger pattern. Emigration and executions were less frequent in upper Normandy than in most regions,[17] and even those families that had suffered because of emigration could take advantage of the provisions of Norman law to recover much of their property. A frustrated official complained in 1797 that "the whole of the revenues of the émigrés passed into the hands of their relatives," because of the claims that wives and children were permitted to make on properties that had been seized.[18]

At the popular level, too, the Revolution passed with few dramatic upheavals. In la Neuville-Chant-d'Oisel, political power es-

12. AD Eure, 2 M 626, "Maires, adjoints, et conseillers municipaux," dossier Pont-St-Pierre.

13. Ibid., 16 July 1852.

14. André Plaisse, *L'évolution de la structure agraire dans la campagne du Neubourg,* Cahiers des études rurales (Paris and The Hague, 1964), 2:80; AD S-M, L 3504, "Administration municipale, canton de Franqueville," fol. 30r, 10 Brumaire An VI.

15. AD Eure, 1 M 171, "Statistiques personnelles du département . . . 1809–1812."

16. AD S-M, L 3500, "Adminstration municipale, canton de Franqueville, fol. 46r–v, 6 Ventôse An IV.

17. Lynn Hunt, *Politics, Culture, and Class in the French Revolution* (Berkeley and Los Angeles, 1984), 138–39.

18. Quoted in Marc Bouloiseau, *Etude de l'émigration et de la vente des biens des émigrés (1792–1830)* (Paris, 1963), 124–25; see also Bouloiseau, "A propos du tiers coutumier normand et des biens des émigrés: Consultations pour les héritiers de Philippe-Egalité en 1817," *Annales de Normandie* 9, no. 3 (October 1959): 217–28.

caped the grip of the local *laboureurs* only during the year of the Terror: only during 1793 was the village's mayor an outsider, a mercer from the suburbs of Rouen.[19] The ten other mayors who served between 1790 and 1871 all came from the *laboureur* and merchant families that had dominated the village during the Old Regime. These families, to be sure, confronted difficult episodes. During the Terror, two mayors—brothers of the Bétille family—were incarcerated because of their refusal to assist Rouennais authorities in requisitioning grain; but they were released in July 1794, and thereafter the village elite's hold on political power was unchallenged. Continuity in political office became the rule, continuity of both individuals and families. The *laboureur* Jacques Hardy served as mayor between 1800 and 1808; his cousin Philippe Hardy from 1821 to 1826, and Philippe's son Louis Philippe between 1829 and 1840. Gilbert Mignot, from one of the village's most important families of *laboureurs,* held the office from 1808 to 1821; Louis Charles Bultel—himself from Bourgbaudouin, but also related to a leading la Neuville family—served from 1840 to 1871.[20] Bultel, Mignot, and Louis Philippe Hardy all remained in office despite changes of regime; in la Neuville, continuity of local power was the most visible legacy of the Revolution.

Continuity characterized even la Neuville's experience of religious division, for many regions the most explosive issue of the Revolution.[21] In 1791 the village's curé refused the oath of allegiance to the nation, and eventually the district authorities removed him from office; by May he had been replaced by his former vicar, the abbé Sevestre. The step led to conflicts within the clergy, both locally and within the diocese, and to accusations against the former curé of vandalism. But despite such conflicts the community remained fundamentally unified. The village council was solidly favorable to Sevestre, and in 1793 he was elected to join it. After the suppression of religious practice in 1794, the village continued to employ him, now as municipal clerk, charged among other functions with reading the laws to the assembled villagers on the republican days of leisure, the *décadis;* in effect, he continued to perform

19. Jules Lamy, *La Neuville-Chant-d'Oisel* (Darnétal, 1981), 42–43. La Neuville's experience during the Revolution thus accords with Lynn Hunt's argument that the strongest impetus for revolution came from village outsiders, who were able to link local politics to those of the region and nation (*Politics, Culture, and Class,* 180–212).

20. Lamy, *La Neuville-Chant-d'Oisel,* 43–45.

21. T. J. A. Le Goff and D. M. G. Sutherland, "Religion and Rural Revolt in the French Revolution: An Overview," in Janos M. Bak and Gerhard Benecke, eds., *Religion and Rural Revolt* (Manchester, 1984), 123–45.

one of his clerical functions, interpreting the outside world to the village and offering moral instruction. He served as *agent municipal* during the Directory. The municipality continued to champion Sevestre during the Empire, when the archbishop of Rouen refused to restore him as curé and, as punishment for the village's support of the constitutional clergy, placed la Neuville within the parish of Boos. Only in 1820 was la Neuville's parish church restored—and Sevestre, now seventy years old, was named its priest.[22]

We gain a more intimate sense of how these communities experienced the Revolution from their political deliberations during the Directory.[23] Both la Neuville and Pont-St-Pierre had been frightened by the Terror and responded enthusiastically to the Directory's restoration of order. When the possibility arose that a former Jacobin might be named commissar of the Republic in the region, the municipal assembly of Pont-St-Pierre threatened resignation; "The republican sentiments that have constantly directed its conduct do not permit it to sit next to a Jacobin," argued one member.[24] In the canton of Franqueville, of which la Neuville-Chant-d'Oisel was a part, there were elaborate preparations during the Year V to celebrate 9 Thermidor, "anniversary of the fall of France's cruelest oppressor and of the abolition of the most infamous tyranny"; marchers were to carry banners expressing "implacable hatred for tyranny, inviolable love for just government," "respect for properties," and "submission to the laws."[25] Such sentiments derived some of their force from the brutality with which higher officials had treated municipal governments during the Terror. In the Year II the *agent municipal* of Pont-St-Pierre failed to forward sufficient information about the grain supply in the area and received an impressive warning from his superior: "I will see myself obliged to denounce you to the Commission of Commerce and to the Committee of Public Safety in order to shelter my head from the terrifying responsibility with which it is constantly threatened."[26]

22. Lamy, *La Neuville-Chant-d'Oisel*, 19–33.
23. AD Eure, 220 L 1, "Registre des déliberations et arrêtés de l'Administration Municipale du Canton de Pont-St-Pierre"; AD S-M, L 3500–3509, "Registre des déliberations, administration municipale, canton de Franqueville," An IV–An VIII. No earlier documents of local political life appear to be available. During the Directory, municipal administration was carried out at the cantonal level, in an assembly to which each commune sent representatives.
24. AD Eure, 220 L 1, fol. 29v.
25. AD S-M, L 3503, fol. 59r–v.
26. AD Eure 122 L 3, "District de Louviers, Correspondance d'agent national," 7 Prairial An II–23 Nivose An III, 43, 4 Vendémiaire An II.

Bitterness resulted also from the fact that *sans culottes* clubs had functioned in these towns during the Terror. Echoes of the experience persisted into the Year IV in intermittent demands from the lower classes: for bread, for the preferential hiring of local workers.[27] Other tensions also found expression during the Directory. In Franqueville, a small tumult broke out over conscription in the Year VII, but speeches by the cantonal administrators sufficed to calm the conscripts and send them marching off to Rouen.[28] Tensions about religious observance occasionally flared, and more obscure conflicts produced occasional vandalism and in one case arson; in the same year the *garde champêtre* of la Neuville was shot at and his horse killed, the result (so the cantonal administration believed) of "the wickedness that, kept in check by the guard's zeal, uses the most perfidious means to harm him."[29] Constant demands by regional authorities for taxes, food, and horses posed much more persistent problems. Seemingly endless warfare placed local administrators in an almost impossible situation; they had to maintain harmony within their cantons while satisfying requirements from the central administration.

Despite these burdens and tensions, the main theme in the municipal deliberations was one of success and unity in meeting difficult situations. An outgoing president of the municipality of Franqueville expressed this view in a speech to his fellow administrators in the Year VI: "Numerous tasks that we had persuaded ourselves to be impossible have nevertheless been carried out by our efforts; taxes have been assessed and collected, public order has been rigorously maintained, the wicked have been controlled. . . . their sinister projects have always been uncovered. It is satisfying for us at the end of our service to have no violence by our fellow citizens to complain of. Thanks to the good outlook that animates this canton, the most perfect tranquillity has not ceased to reign."[30] His smug assessment was confirmed by the monthly reports that the municipality was required to send to the Rouennais authorities about the state of the canton. The departmental administration wanted to know "what is the public spirit," whether any crimes had been committed in the canton, whether any émigrés, refractory priests, or royalists resided there, whether laws against vagabondage were enforced, and whether any riots or seditious gatherings had taken place. Month after month, the

27. AD Eure, 220 L 1, fol. 18r; AD S-M, L 3501, fol. 21v.
28. AD S-M, L 3506, fols. 53v–54r, 30 Frimaire An VII.
29. AD S-M, L 3504, fols. 3r, 8r, 44v.
30. AD S-M, L 3505, fol. 17v.

municipality of Franqueville returned satisfying answers. In twenty-five such reports, public spirit was invariably good, and there were no problems with vagabondage or public disorder; only one report mentioned a returned émigré, and only twelve mentioned crimes of any kind, for the most part small thefts or incidents of vandalism. Reports of brigandage, *chouans*, and disorder reached these communities and created fear within them, but they described conditions elsewhere.

The Revolution brought change to the region, but not in the form of cataclysmic events. Most visibly, the Revolution brought an end to Pont-St-Pierre's status as the focus of urban activity within the Andelle Valley. Its long-standing seigneurial functions gave it some importance during the Revolution itself. In 1787 it was declared the capital of an arrondissement of thirty-three parishes, with a population of 3,500 households.[31] In 1790 it remained the center of a canton of fifteen communes, with a market monopoly over nine of them and with a series of important bureaucratic functions: notaries, a judge, a *huissier*, the secretariat of the cantonal administration were all established in the bourg.[32] Already, however, Pont-St-Pierre had lost its jurisdiction over two of the four villages that had formed the core of the lordship, for la Neuville and Pîtres were placed in different cantons. In 1801 the bourg's decline was completed with the transfer of the cantonal administration to another commune.[33] Pont-St-Pierre retained only its notary and its market, now stripped of monopolies. In every other way its role as a local capital had ended. La Neuville's situation in these years made clear the dimensions of Pont-St-Pierre's political decline, for the canton of Franqueville into which it was placed included no such former seigneurial center whatsoever. There were no notaries at all within the canton, and only one of its nineteen communes had a factory;[34] none of them had a market.[35] Like la Neuville, these were purely agricultural villages, villages of the *plat pays*. The Revolution completed their entry into full political life, a political life no longer mediated by such market towns as Pont-St-Pierre.

31. Marc Bouloiseau, "Notables ruraux et élections municipales dans la région rouennaise en 1787," *Commission de recherches et de publication des documents relatifs à la vie économique de la Révolution: Mémoires et documents* (Paris, 1958), 12:9.

32. AD Eure, 220 L 1.

33. Marquis de Blosseville, *Dictionnaire topographique du département de l'Eure . . .* (Paris, 1877), 173.

34. AD S-M, L 3504, fol. 41r.

35. AD S-M, L 3500, fol. 25v.

The Revolution accelerated change in the region's political geography, and it also intensified local political education.[36] For those involved in municipal government—and through 1800 they were very numerous—the Revolution meant above all new political tasks. There was a constant stream of new legislation from the central government; to keep up with it, the canton of Franqueville took nineteen subscriptions to the *Journal officiel*, so that each commune could have a copy.[37] Local record keeping acquired new importance, and local bureaucracies blossomed accordingly. In Franqueville during the Year IV there were seven full-time, paid officials to keep track of the canton's records.[38] From the central administration came also a constant demand for information. Local administrators needed to supply details about taxation, agricultural production, confiscated properties, public opinion and behavior. Dealing with legal documents and numerical calculations became for them a fact of daily life. Literacy and numeracy were central to revolutionary culture. The Revolution gave a new force and practical importance to abilities that had been spreading through the region during the eighteenth century.

Local political leaders also gained a new sense of history. They saw the Revolution as a new historical era, in which they and their fellows had achieved previously impossible successes. "History," so the president of Pont-St-Pierre's cantonal administration told a crowd gathered in the Year IV to celebrate French victories, "told us that it was nearly impossible to cross the Alps and the Pyrenees; those mountains flatten out before the intrepidity of our warriors."[39] When local officials congratulated themselves on the more modest obstacles that they had overcome in assuring the food supply and maintaining public order, they too expressed their sense that a period of new historical possibilities had opened.

In all of these ways, the Revolution brought sharp changes to well-off commoners in both bourg and village. Despite their ability to survive the Revolution, the nobles of the region found their position decisively changed as well. In part this change reflected the very fact of commoners' intensified political role. Aristocratic claims to privilege and power had remained lively and abrasive in 1789. When the nobles of the bailliage of Rouen gathered to draw up the

36. This point is stressed in general terms by Hunt, *Politics, Culture, and Class.*
37. AD S-M, L 3503, fol. 46r.
38. AD S-M, L 3500, fol. 197r.
39. AD Eure, 220 L 1, fol. 28v.

political program that they wished their representatives to defend at the Estates General, their views were vigorously conservative.[40] The first article in their *cahier*, unanimously adopted, instructed the deputies not to "cooperate in any deliberation by head that might be proposed." Article 35 insisted that if new taxes were needed, "then the deputies shall declare that the nobility cannot cede any of its rights, any of its prerogatives"; if taxation of the nobility was needed to meet the current financial crisis, this could only be a temporary measure, to end with the fiscal crisis itself. Later articles called for royal assistance to the nobility, assistance that would sustain the order economically and clarify its privileged position within society: the guards of the Maison du Roi were to be reestablished "as an inexpensive means of offering the nobility new occasions to display its inviolate love for the sacred person of the king and its ardent zeal for the service of the fatherland" (art. 44); "Corps des cadets gentilshommes" were to be established in each province (art. 45); cathedral chapters and schools restricted to the nobility were to be created (art. 46); nonnobles were to be strictly prohibited from carrying swords outside the military, "whatever their profession" (art. 48); ennoblement by office was to be strictly limited and subject to the veto of the provincial estates, and usurpations of nobility were to be strictly punished (arts. 49, 50); and the *franc-fief*, a tax on nonnobles who bought fiefs, was to be maintained (art. 51).

Along with these specific measures to defend their special standing in society, the nobles also called for efforts to limit the impact of economic change. They instructed their deputies to direct "all of their efforts to place on the capitalists (*les capitalistes*) and businessmen (*individus commerçants*) a just share of the state's expenses" (art. 33); and they asked that some of the most flamboyant institutions of late eighteenth-century capitalism be suppressed: "If the current financial situation or the nature of the agreements that have been entered into does not permit the immediate suppression of the privileges of the new Company of the Indies, that of the Waters of Paris, of Fires, and others like these, at the least let the strongest measures be taken to stop the frantic gaming on the so-called public stocks, and thus to destroy even the idea of that shameful stockjobbing that, after having corrupted morals, driven out public faith, and

---

40. *Cahier des pouvoirs et instructions à remettre aux Députés de l'Ordre de la Noblesse du Bailliage de Rouen* (Rouen, 1789) (BM, Nm 856/15); *Procès-verbal de l'assemblée de l'ordre de la noblesse du bailliage de Rouen* (Rouen, 1789) (BM, Nm 856/14).

strangled national feeling, would soon succeed in drying up the two true sources of the state's wealth, agriculture and commerce" (art. 65).[41] Economic as well as political change disturbed these nobles.

The nobles who assembled in Rouen were not unanimously reactionary. Despite unanimity on the question of voting by order, a minority at the meeting of the bailliage had urged that the nobles accept taxation.[42] Such moderation, however, had succumbed to the argument that fiscal privilege was fundamental to the nobility's existence as an order; as one nobleman argued, "the gentleman of small means, who has no vassals and who can have no pretensions to the places and graces of the court, would be degraded and mixed in among the people."[43]

Such expectations, of course, were disappointed by the events of the Revolution. There were also material losses. Feudal dues had little importance for most nobles in the region, and very few of their properties were sold as *biens nationaux*. Families of any importance reappeared in the region once the Terror was over and (as they did in Pont-St-Pierre) assumed an important political role through the nineteenth century. Nevertheless, the Revolution had fundamentally altered their circumstances. Short-term problems arose from confiscations and neglect of their properties. In the Year IV the municipality of Franqueville reduced the tax burden on the nobleman Godard de Belbeuf because "since the Revolution and because of the various events that have followed, the Citizen has been pillaged, robbed, and stripped of his most precious belongings. . . . the serious losses that he has sustained, the spoliations and vexations that he and his family have suffered have singularly diminished his fortune and revenues; . . . the confiscation of his goods has in no small way contributed, since during this time the upkeep of his properties was so neglected that he has had to make enormous expenditures to reestablish them."[44] Godard could count on the sympathy of the revolutionary authorities as he set about repair-

<hr />

41. For the ethical and political problems posed by stock market speculation in the early modern period, see J. G. A. Pocock, *The Machiavellian Moment: Florentine Political Thought and the Atlantic Republican Tradition* (Princeton, 1975), 440–77.

42. *Nouvelle édition de la copie de l'expédition de l'acte de déclaration de partie de la noblesse du bailliage principal de Rouen* (Rouen, n.d.) (BM, Nm 856/7); AD S-M, 4 BP 6009, "Liste par Bailliage de Messieurs de l'ordre de la noblesse. . . ."

43. "Lettre D'un Abonné à l'Auteur du Journal de Normandie, sur la Déclaration d'une partie de la Noblesse du Bailliage" (n.p., n.d.), 7 (BM, Nm 856/5).

44. AD S-M, L 3500, fol. 46r.

ing his fortune, and this was true in other cases,[45] but his losses were severe.

More important than such short-term losses, however, was the fact that the nobles had lost their economic dominance of local society. After the Revolution, their wealth simply failed to keep pace with that of groups around them. Anthoine Caillot de Coquéraumont's landed income from Pont-St-Pierre alone dwarfed that of his rural neighbors during the last decades of the Old Regime. Caillot's heirs, the d'Houdemare family, resided in his château in Pont-St-Pierre throughout the nineteenth century and dominated local politics. To that extent there was continuity with the Old Regime. But by the 1830s the d'Houdemares were no longer even the wealthiest family in Pont-St-Pierre itself. That honor belonged to a local factory owner,[46] and the fact was symbolic of a new social order. The owners of Pont-St-Pierre no longer enjoyed the economic advantages over their neighbors that seigneurial rights conferred, and some of their neighbors had grown rich because of the Revolution itself. Romilly's copper foundry, for instance, profited from the revolutionary wars, and its director used some of his profits to buy one of the few large properties sold in the area as national lands, a domain that had belonged to Fontaine Guérard.[47] After 1815 there was more new wealth in the region, as the industrialization of the Andelle Valley began in earnest. Families such as the d'Houdemares were not impoverished by the Revolution, but they no longer controlled the levers of wealth within even the small society of Pont-St-Pierre.

45. The municipality of Pont-St-Pierre complained that the *agent municipal* of Radepont "est d'un civisme très équivoque & qu'il est plus occupé des intérêts de la maison de Radepont que de ceux de la République" (AD Eure, 220 L 1, fol. 138r).

46. Archives Communales, Pont-St-Pierre, "Délibérations Municipales," 1822ff., fol. 54, 15 June 1839; AD Eure, 2 M 626, letter from the sous-préfet des Andelys to the préfet de l'Eure, 18 May 1839.

47. AD Eure, Q 886, "Décomptes pour acquisition de biens nationaux, arrondissement des Andelys"; see also AD Eure, Q 889, for the same figure's purchase of a mill at Romilly. I have not attempted a systematic investigation of the sales of national properties.

Conclusion

"Rural social structures," wrote Guy Fourquin in 1964, "hardly underwent any transformation from the time of Philip the Fair to the eighteenth century: a fact that would be definitively proven if historians would interest themselves, following Marc Bloch's wish, in the 'vertical' history of a few villages from the Middle Ages to the modern era. During this half millennium, then, the rhythm of rural history consists solely in the alternation of periods of troubles with periods of relative prosperity."[1] Fourquin's remark prefigured what is today a dominant theme in historians' understanding of the Old Regime: the theme of an "histoire immobile" stretching from the Black Death to the mid–eighteenth century, four centuries in which social change involved only cyclical movement within an unyielding framework of Malthusian checks.[2]

This book has attempted to measure change and continuity in one region of rural France during the Old Regime, and it argues for a different assessment of their importance. In important ways, to be sure, the region around Pont-St-Pierre changed little over these four centuries. Most important, agriculture probably remained as inefficient on the eve of the Revolution as it had been four hundred years earlier. Yet the main theme in the histories of Pont-St-Pierre, la Neuville, and the villages around them is change, of fundamental kinds.

The most visible of these changes was the decline of the seigneurial system, a transformation that involved nearly all aspects of rural

1. Guy Fourquin, *Les campagnes de la région parisienne* (Paris, 1964), 530.
2. Emmanuel Le Roy Ladurie, "L'histoire immobile," repr. in *Le territoire de l'historien*, 2 vols. (Paris, 1973–78), 2:7–34.

281

life. In Pont-St-Pierre, seigneurial rents lost most of their importance in the mid–sixteenth century; the barony's formal political powers— its judicial and regulatory functions—survived well into the next century, but they rapidly declined thereafter. Lordship had involved more informal elements as well, and they decayed in the same years. Until the eighteenth century, the barons of Pont-St-Pierre had occupied the center of a web of local friendships and loyalties. Their household had been a center of rural literacy; both friendship and material interests attached local nobles and wealthy *roturiers* to it. Little of this remained in the mid–eighteenth century. By that point the barons of Pont-St-Pierre enjoyed few ties of any kind with local society. Their relations with the local nobility were essentially hostile, and their household no longer employed leading members of the Third Estate; even as consumers they had little impact on local society. The final phase in the disintegration of seigneurial authority in the region of Pont-St-Pierre was the disappearance of the local nobility itself, following the departure of the Roncherolles from the countryside. By 1789 the nobility was not a significant presence in local life.

As seigneurial relations decayed in the Andelle Valley, relations based on monetary transactions, on market exchanges, increased in frequency and importance. Even in the thirteenth and fourteenth centuries, market transactions had been important in the region of Pont-St-Pierre. By the seventeenth century, there remained few remnants in the region of a peasant economy, based on tradition, indifference to profit, and orientation to domestic subsistence. The vast majority of villagers owned little or no land, and only one or two families within the lordship could have fed themselves from their own properties.[3] Nearly all land was held for short-term money rents. The arrival of cotton spinning in the countryside only completed a process that had begun in the sixteenth century: the creation within the countryside of a wage-labor force, bound to the village by monetary rather than traditional ties.

The spread of rural markets and marketplace transactions corresponded to the rise of wage labor. Contemporaries were justifiably impressed with the spread of shops and unlicensed markets in the

---

3. Cf. R. H. Hilton, *Bond Men Made Free: Medieval Peasant Movements and the English Rising of 1381* (London and New York, 1973), 37: had landless laborers been a majority of the rural population, writes Hilton, "this very fact would have implied the end of the peasantry, since the essence of peasant society is that the basic form of productive labour within it is that of the peasant family living on its own holding."

eighteenth-century countryside, but in the Andelle Valley—so the evidence of market tolls in Pont-St-Pierre indicates—the rapid expansion of market transactions began earlier, in the mid–seventeenth century. Important elements of a market economy had been in place in this region during the high Middle Ages; by the age of Louis XIV, there were only scant traces of a peasant economy.

The third group of changes that this study has traced resulted directly from the decline of seigneurial authority and the spread of market relations. This was the rise of a village ruling group, consisting chiefly of farmers and local merchants. Of all the social groups in the region around Pont-St-Pierre, it was the farmers whose behavior most closely approximated historians' models of a peasantry: they were tightly bound to the village and married chiefly among themselves; they had some hope of self-sufficiency, although nearly all had to rent their farms for cash. But such traditional attachments concealed a more fundamental modernity of behavior and outlook. We can trace from the late seventeenth century their increasingly comprehensive collections of business papers; other forms of writing entered their lives in the course of the eighteenth century. In the same period they began to involve themselves in the cotton trade, an economic change with important cultural implications, for it involved them in exchanges throughout northern France. At the village level, farmers and merchants had apparently dominated political life throughout the early modern period. But the nobility's disappearance from the countryside in the eighteenth century removed the only plausible limit on their power. In la Neuville-Chant-d'Oisel, the rise of a middle class in the eighteenth century was a simple and fundamental historical fact. This was not the urban bourgeoisie that has been at the center of so much historical debate, but a middle class of farmers and rural merchants.[4]

Revolution after 1789 consecrated their dominant position. Regions such as the Andelle Valley have perhaps little to tell us about the immediate causes of Revolution. All through the eighteenth century residents might jeer at noblemen and noisily evade seigneurial demands, but there were few signs of deep hatreds or a sense of oppression. Revolution came to the region from outside, as an expression of political events and experiences in settings quite unlike Pont-St-Pierre and la Neuville. This region does help us, however,

---

4. Cf. Jean Nicolas, *La Savoie au XVIIIe siècle: Noblesse et bourgeoisie*, 2 vols. (Paris, 1978), 2:857–901, 1116–20.

to understand how the old order could collapse so quickly and completely after 1789. Seigneurial authority had been decisively weakened in the region long before the Revolution. Events after 1789 simply gave final shape to this process.

Much of this book has been devoted to exploring the complicated and numerous causes of these changes. The success of the state both in controlling violence and in challenging seigneurial powers, the spread of literacy and cultivation among farmers and nobles, the rise of the cotton industry, the price revolution of the sixteenth century and the urban amenities of the seventeenth and eighteenth—each of these powerfully changed rural society. Each operated in some measure independently of the others, often in ways that surprised the actors involved: church and state alike encouraged rural literacy, for instance, but surely not with the intention of advancing villagers' independence from seigneurial authority.

Yet real and important connections linked these particular causes of change. All involved an enlargement of social space and a quickening of exchanges within that space. Until the eighteenth century, Pont-St-Pierre stood at the center of a small solar system of villages, the source of culture, political authority, and commerce. Thereafter, villagers could turn elsewhere to fulfill these needs, to Rouen or the region's smaller cities. Nobles too cut their attachments to local society and pursued careers and pleasures without reference to Pont-St-Pierre.

I have argued here that the seigneurial system was ultimately unable to adapt to this set of changes. I do not mean that nobles lacked the capacity for careful economic reasoning or that they failed to respond to the currents of early modern thought. Even so conservative a family as the Roncherolles enjoyed close connections with leading members of the state, sought to take advantage of the market for agricultural products, and in the eighteenth century read enlightened literature. Although they could adapt to change in these ways, however, they could not adapt and preserve their dominance of the countryside. That dominance had rested on attitudes to the household and the community that could not be sustained in the exchange-oriented society of the eighteenth century. Indeed, adaptation was sufficiently difficult even when the family had relinquished its seigneurial role. In the eighteenth century the Roncherolles lived within a national market, with goods of all kinds available to them; the result was nearly ruinous debt and the enforced sale of their principal estates. With pressures of this order, the preservation of rural power and paternalism was an unaffordable luxury.

Seen from the perspective of these transformations of rural social structure, the problem of French agrarian underdevelopment assumes a paradoxical form. Agriculture in the region of Pont-St-Pierre progressed little over the early modern period, but its poor performance coincided with social changes that might be expected to have revolutionized it. Peasant property virtually disappeared from the region; seigneurial rents lost most of their importance; urban landowners constituted substantial domains; market transactions assumed great importance for villagers and nobles alike, and involved both in exchanges with a large part of northern France; new goods and wants appeared in the countryside. In Pont-St-Pierre, it appears, agrarian capitalism emerged without bringing significant technological development.

Two broad sets of causes, I think, explain this paradoxical situation. First, the rising activity and expanding scale of the market in the seventeenth and eighteenth centuries did not bring only benefits to the agricultural economy. As commercial exchanges more efficiently linked Europe together, for instance, Spanish wool replaced Norman in the manufactures of Elbeuf; sheep raising drastically declined in the eighteenth-century Andelle Valley, and the area's agriculture lost what had been its principal source of fertilizer. The success throughout northern France of goods from the pays de Bray likewise threatened local producers. As superior butter, cheese, and poultry became available over a widening range of markets, local production faced intensified competition and stagnated as a result. A balance between livestock and grain production had been the foundation of French agriculture since the Middle Ages. One effect of the expanding markets of the seventeenth and eighteenth centuries was to upset that balance, to make stock rearing a more competitive, more demanding enterprise. The eighteenth century also changed the directions in which rural capital might flow. Farmers in the eighteenth century could invest in the cotton trade as well as in agriculture; an increasingly efficient market system had enlarged the economic opportunities that wealthy villagers enjoyed and encouraged them to place their money outside agriculture. The eighteenth-century market economy produced new forms of backwardness as well as new areas of expansion.

A second source of agrarian backwardness was the nobility itself. Recent historical writing has often contrasted a dynamic nobility with a tradition-bound peasantry, exemplars of Weber's dictum that "a man does not 'by nature' wish to earn more and more money, but simply to live as he is accustomed to live and to earn as much as is necessary for that purpose."[5] In the Andelle Valley, however, the nobility was far more an obstacle than the peasantry to economic development. Partly this reflected the fact that through much of the early modern period the nobility was largely sheltered from the market economy—far more sheltered than the peasantry. Until about 1700 the Roncherolles lived to a surprising degree from the products of their own household and estates and carefully limited their purchases of even such goods as wine. They derived a substantial income from their service to the government. Investment in agriculture had little significance in this situation; indeed, the main element of their estate in Pont-St-Pierre was the forest rather than farms.

This situation changed dramatically in the eighteenth century. The Roncherolles like their poorer neighbors felt the impact of the eighteenth-century consumer revolution; and government pressures forced them to diminish their dependence on the forest and required them to turn their attention to their property's farms and meadows. Yet through their departure from the countryside in 1765, their investment in agriculture remained very low. Hostility and suspicion toward tenant farmers was one cause. The continuing force of the lordship was another. Feudal dues and monopolies remained a genuine drain on villagers' resources, and the lordship remained committed to an economy of just price and limited competition. In the Andelle Valley, pressure for agricultural innovation came chiefly from tenant farmers, not from large landowners. To the end of the Old Regime, large property remained a burden on the rural economy.

In fact, the advances that the eighteenth century brought to the countryside made these problems more serious. Because village farmers and merchants enjoyed a wider range of economic choices, the seigneurial system and landlords' demands weighed more heavily on the rural economy than they had in the past. Seigneurial vexations that had changed little in absolute terms acquired new economic importance in a setting of increasingly capitalistic calculations, in which farmers could direct their energies and money to alternative enterprises. Village capitalism magnified obstacles to agricultural change.

---

5. *The Protestant Ethic and the Spirit of Capitalism*, trans. Talcott Parsons (New York, 1958), 60.

In these circumstances, the limits on the region's productive capacity were more flexible and more artificial than a Malthusian model suggests.[6] Theoretical limits to production there may have been, but the inadequacies of eighteenth-century agriculture around Pont-St-Pierre resulted from failures to use even the rudimentary technology available to it: from lack of livestock, poorly tended livestock and buildings, resistance to methods of continuous cultivation, careless techniques in producing butter and managing animals. Rustic traditionalism, ignorance, and listlessness do not explain these failures. Rather, they arose from the specific economic choices of farmers and landowners. Farmers responded quickly and competitively to the developing commerce in cotton thread. They failed to make comparable choices in the realm of agriculture because they could not expect similar returns from what they invested in it and because much of the wealth that their investments might create would not go to them.

Reflections of this kind bring us back to the problem from which this book began, the problem of the early modern nobility's character and fate. The example of the Roncherolles accords with much recent scholarship to show that the nobility were no mere "caste of feudal remnants." The Roncherolles had some involvement with many of the most dynamic influences in early modern France: with the absolutist state, with the commercialization of agriculture, with the Enlightenment. When they and their fellow nobles talked about the social order, they rarely used the language of caste; they spoke instead of their calling as military men, separated from other groups not by birth but by social function.

The Roncherolles were certainly not remnants, at least before the nineteenth century, but (so I have argued here) in important ways they were feudal, and this fact shaped much of their history. Few historians today are comfortable with such terms, and I use them with a keen sense of the ways in which they are anachronistic. But even the most rudimentary analysis demands anachronism, demands, that is, that the historian impose modern categories and explanations on the complexities of the past. If we understand feudalism to be the ownership of public political power as private property,

---

6. For a more extended critical examination of Malthusian interpretations from a somewhat different point of view and with a larger comparative perspective, James Lowth Goldsmith, "The Agrarian History of Preindustrial France: Where Do We Go From Here?" *Journal of European Economic History* 13, no. 1 (Spring 1984): 175–99.

feudalism defined much about the Roncherolles' position before the eighteenth century. In a variety of ways, it was this commitment to public power that limited their capacity to adapt to economic change in the seventeenth and eighteenth centuries.

Did feudalism stand in the way of capitalistic economic development? Again, to ask such a question about French rural history is to make many historians uncomfortable. The example of Pont-St-Pierre suggests, however, that such terms are worth using and that the tensions between feudalism and capitalism were real and significant. Although the French nobility was in many ways capable of successful adaptation to the modern economy, feudal values obstructed the nobles' ability to deal with capitalism and, more important, were an economic obstacle to rural society as a whole. In Pont-St-Pierre, the eighteenth-century destruction of feudalism was a necessary stage in the development of a market economy.

Appendix A
Inventories After Death

4 May 1746	Jean Le Boucher	Ibid., 1745–46
14 April 1747	Jacques Gilbert Hardy	Ibid., 1747
14 July 1749	François Boelle	Ibid., 1749
2 April 1751	Charles Bultel	Ibid., 1751
28 July 1751	Pierre Monnoye	Ibid.
19 May 1760	Claude Getz	AD Eure, 86 B 98
1 December 1760	Pierre Louis Alexis	AD S-M, Tabel.
	Le Boucher	Pont-St-Pierre, 1760
15 March 1762	Gilbert Mignot	Ibid., 1762
28 April 1762	Michel Dubosc	Ibid.
7 June 1763	Pierre Le Baube	Ibid., 1763
13 February 1764	Jean Cordonnier	Ibid., 1764
20 October 1766	Jacques Dupasseux	Ibid., 1766
13 January 1768	Charles Bultel	Ibid., 1768
14 October 1768	Jacques Guiffard	Ibid.
27 August 1769	Jean Gilbert Mignot	Ibid., 1769
14 September 1769	Michel Bultel	Ibid.
23 October 1769	Pierre Hardy	Ibid.
12–13 April 1771	Jean Hardy	Ibid., 1771
18 November 1771	Charles Bultel	Ibid.

BOURGEOIS OF PONT-ST-PIERRE

DATE	NAME	SOURCE
25 August 1679	Gérard Hellot	AD Eure, E 1262
7 January 1687	Pierre Chenevièvre	AD S-M, Tabel.
		Pont-St-Pierre, 1679–89
18 July 1693	Martin Leber	Ibid., 1693
12 July 1701	Charles Le Hec	Ibid., 1701
28 February 1729	Jacques Bouffard	Ibid., 1729
18 February 1736	Jean Lefebvre	Ibid., 1735–36
1 June 1746	Noel Du Ponché	Ibid., 1745–46
30 August 1748	Mathieu André	Ibid., 1748
	Du Domaine	
29 October 1750	Martin Lefebvre	Ibid., 1750
3 October 1752	Jean Le Tourneur	Ibid., 1752
11 October 1752	Antoine Le Grain	Ibid.
17 October 1754	Nicolas Nollent	Ibid., 1754
13 February 1761	Pierre Antoine	Ibid., 1761
	Ibid., 1761	
18 September 1764	Jean Baptiste Lambert	AD Eure, 86 B 99
29 December 1764	Pierre Vallet	AD S-M, Tabel.
		Pont-St-Pierre, 1764

9 November 1765	Nicolas Evrecin	Ibid., 1765
24 October 1767	René Louail	Ibid., 1767
29 August 1771	Charles Boromée Leclerc	Ibid., 1771
1 September 1775	Mathieu Aveline	Ibid., 1774–75
25 September 1775	Jacques Le Tellier	Ibid.

Appendix B
Laboureurs'
Marriage Contracts

DATE	SPOUSES	SOURCE
29 January 1603	Laurens Revel Anne Du Tac	AD S-M, Tabel. Pont-St-Pierre, 1601–3
13 January 1619	Estienne Bultel Margueritte Vaast	Ibid., 1619–24
3 January 1621	François Veel Marthe Hardy	Ibid.
19 February 1621	Laurens de Lespine Perrette Desmarests	Ibid.
16 July 1623	Nicolas Bulletel Margueritte Bourdin	Ibid.
15 February 1626	Gerard Perier Marion Poitevin	Ibid., 1625–32
30 April 1626	Charles Thibault Marye Hubert	Ibid.
24 May 1628	Laurens Hubert Margueritte Hacon	Ibid.
30 July 1630	Robert Blanchart Jenevieve Revel	Ibid.
17 October 1642	Jacques Thibault Louize Bulletel	Ibid., 1641–46
5 June 1644	Jacques Gossent Perrette Hacon	Ibid.
26 June 1644	Robert Hacon Marye Hubert	Ibid.

6 August 1650	François Jamelin Marye Perier	Ibid., 1647–52
8 December 1650	Louis Hacon Louise Lambert	Ibid.
19 November 1657	Michel Hardy Marguerite Bessin	Ibid., 1655–59 (inserted 16 August 1658)
30 August 1663	Louis Hardi Marie Vaillant	Ibid., 1693 (inserted 3 August 1693)
14 May 1682	Louis Perier Marguerite Hardy	Ibid., 1682
11 June 1682	Jean de la Mare Marie Bultel	Ibid., 1682–87
18 April 1686	Jacques Bultel Madellaine Guiffard	Ibid., 1679–89
27 December 1686	Isacq Mullot Marie Cavé	AD Eure, E 1262
17 November 1701	Rollin Hacon Catherine Le Bret	AD S-M, Tabel. Pont-St-Pierre, 1701–2
27 December 1704	François Monnois Marie Hardi	Ibid., 1703–5
24 February 1705	Jacque Monnoye Madelaine Hardy	Ibid.
29 December 1722	Nicollas Monnoye Marie Mignot	Ibid., 1703ff.
2 December 1728	Claude Allexis Lebouchei Marie Thereze Hardy	Ibid., 1727–28
4 January 1731	Denis Getz Marguerite Lesage	Ibid., 1730–31
3 May 1733	François Le Rat Cecille Thereze Angelique Daniel	Ibid., 1733–34
30 June 1734	Jacques Cordonnier Anne Mouquet	Ibid.
5 November 1734	Clement Foubert Marie Elizabeth Monnoye	Ibid.
13 June 1737	Jacque Michel Martin Hardy Marie Anne Perier	Ibid., 1737
25 February 1745	Gabriel De Veillant Marie Anne Monnoye	Ibid., 1745–46
19 April 1750	Gilbert Mignot Madelaine Hubert	Ibid., 1750

13 February 1752	Denis Gests Marie Le Roux	AD Eure, E 1265
23 April 1752	Jean Baptiste Perier Catherine Marette	AD S-M, Tabel. Pont-St-Pierre, 1752
20 April 1753	François Guiffard Elizabeth Mignot	Ibid., 1753
12 August 1753	Hylaire Laurents Marie Françoise Duval	Ibid.
20 October 1754	Jacques Dupasseux Marie Anne Cordonnier	Ibid., 1754
1 December 1760	Charles Bultel Marie Briard	Ibid., 1760
11 July 1761	Etienne Guiffard Marie Anne Monnoye	Ibid., 1761
18 April 1762	Michel Bultel Marie Catherine Le Rat	Ibid., 1762
11 July 1765	Estienne Flais Marie Françoise Hardy	Ibid., 1764–73
14 May 1766	François Monnoye Marie Thereze Perier	Ibid.
23 February 1770	François Guiffard Elizabeth Mignot	Ibid.
13 May 1770	Pierre Perier Genevieve Duchesne	Ibid.
13 June 1772	Jacques Emmanuel Gaillard Marie Therese de Pitre	Ibid.
19 January 1773	Nicolas Hellot Marie Thereze de Pitre	Ibid.
3 March 1777	Pierre Hardy Marie Françoise Bultel	AD Eure, E 1267
3 February 1782	Denis François Monnoye Marie Rose Mignot	AD Eure, E 1268

Appendix C
Measuring Landownership

In the absence of cadasters and detailed tax rolls, the historian of northern France must turn to seigneurial sources in order to trace the evolution of landholding. These sources reflect the aims of seigneurial administrators, who compiled them in order to keep track of those who owed seigneurial dues; as a result, they list not all the landowners within a community, but only those who in one way or another held land from the lordship. A number of historians have used these sources and have drawn attention to the distortions that they sometimes contain. Normally these documents present information only about the area of land held and say little about its value or productivity. Village landowners did not arrange their holdings by seigneurial boundaries; some of their holdings may be left out of documents that describe only a single lordship, and this is certainly true in the case of urban nobles or merchants who owned land in the village. The lordship itself was an artificial entity, rarely covering an entire community, its limits subject to fluctuation. Seigneurial documents usually do not include properties held by the Church and may underrepresent properties held by the privileged. All of these problems become especially acute, of course, in a study limited to a single lordship, where the aberrations of an individual case are not evened out by a large sample.

The data that I have presented on landowning in la Neuville-Chant-d'Oisel (Chapter 2) are subject to additional cautions. From the early seventeenth century on, complete *terriers* list tenants and their holdings in nearly all of the lordship.[1] For earlier centuries, however, I have found only partial listings. In the sixteenth century, three *terriers* list landowners and their

---

1. Caillot, unclassified terrier of la Neuville-Chant-d'Oisel (ca. 1635); Pont-St-Pierre, unclassified terrier, 1736; Caillot, liasse 238, "Paroisse de Pont-St-Pierre, Pleds."

TABLE 54. *Two Measures of Landownership, 1776*

Landowners	Imposition territoriale[a] (% of revenue)	Gage-Pleds (% of area)
Top 5 percent	53.7	54.0
Top 10 percent	67.5	72.9
Top 25 percent	83.7	88.3
2d 25 percent	9.4	8.0
3d 25 percent	4.8	2.7
Lowest 25 percent	2.1	1.0

SOURCE: AD S-M, C 582, no. 114.

[a] Excluding lands owned by the Church.

properties in the Haute Justice du Chapitre in la Neuville, a lordship that was merged with the barony of Pont-St-Pierre after the church land sales of the later sixteenth century.[2] (The lands in the Haute Justice du Chapitre are included in the barony's seventeenth- and eighteenth-century *terriers*.) Finally, for the fifteenth century I have turned to the three-volume *Inventaire des aveux* that Pont-St-Pierre's administrators compiled from the lordship's archives late in the eighteenth century.[3] These volumes were drawn up with the self-interested care characteristic of seigneurial researches on the eve of the Revolution; one volume deals with the Haute Justice du Chapitre, the others with the remainder of the lordship's tenants in la Neuville. For purposes of comparison, I also analyzed these volumes for the years 1600–1604.

Obviously such disparate data, spread over nearly four centuries, can be treated as only an approximate view of landowning in la Neuville. Nonetheless, there are several reasons for accepting these sources as a basically accurate picture of landholding patterns. First, I have not attempted here to determine from these documents the amounts of land that specific groups in the village held; from the partial evidence that is available for the fifteenth and sixteenth centuries, such an attempt would indeed be misleading. I have limited my inquiry to what these sources can tell us about the relative shares of land held by specific groups.

Second, two sources from the late eighteenth century allow evaluation of the fundamental usefulness of the *terriers* as documents by comparing their measurements of areas of land with measurements of its value (table 54). In 1776 the residents of la Neuville produced a remarkably accurate tax roll, covering all the land within the village. The congruence between these two measures of landowning, the one based on the revenues that property produced, the other based on its area, is imperfect but striking, especially for

2. AD S-M, G 4020 (1524); Caillot, liasse 1 (1544); Caillot, unclassified (1587).
3. Pont-St-Pierre, Inventaire des aveux.

the wealthiest landowners within the community. The superior value of smaller properties appears to reflect a common situation: large properties needed to devote a larger share of their area to forage crops to feed horses and other livestock, whereas owners of small plots could devote their tiny area entirely to food crops; and competition for leases of small plots was more intense than for large farms, thus increasing their rental value.[4] In this instance, the measurement of areas within the lordship gives a very accurate picture of how land was distributed within the community as a whole.

In the same way, data drawn from the Haute Justice du Chapitre appear to fit well with data from the lordship as a whole. Comparison is possible in both the early fifteenth and the early seventeenth centuries. In both periods the two sources show a basically similar pattern of landowning.

Finally, la Neuville was a very large parish. The *terrier* of 1635 included 292 landowners, 244 of whom owned arable land; the arable included in the register covered 1,089.53 acres. Its size certainly does not make la Neuville a representative village. But it does reduce the distorting effects that aberrant individual cases might have on our statistical picture of village landowning.

4. Cf. Jacques Bottin, *Seigneurs et paysans dans l'ouest du pays de Caux (1540–1650)* (Paris, 1983), 106–11.

Bibliography

MANUSCRIPT SOURCES

Most of the research for this study was carried out at the Archives Départementales of the Seine-Maritime and of the Eure. Because the lands occupied by the barony of Pont-St-Pierre were divided at the Revolution between the two departments, documents concerning the estate are to be found in each archive, divided somewhat haphazardly. Archives are listed below in order of their importance for this study.

Archives Départementales, Seine-Maritime
1 BP 5202: Parlement de Rouen, Tournelle
2 B 440–47: Chambre des Comptes de Rouen, Aveux
4 BP, Bailliage de Rouen
    1 BPxxx, 2: "Rôle du ban et arrière ban, bailliage de Rouen, 1635"
    4 BP 5569: Jean-Baptiste Gaudoit
    4 BP 6009: "Liste par Bailliage de Messieurs de l'ordre de la noblesse . . ."
    4 BP 6012: Cahiers de doléances, Sergenterie de Pont-St-Pierre
C, Intendance de Rouen
    C 53: "Police administrative"
    C 112: Récoltes
    C 311, 343, 358, 390: Capitation des nobles, élections de Gisors et Rouen, 1703, 1757, 1788
    C 410, 411: "Capitation. Requêtes des contribuables"
    C 555, 556, 558: Vingtièmes, cantons de Boos, Buchy, Darnétal
    C 582, no. 114: Imposition territoriale, la Neuville, 1776
    C 1111, 1112: "Subdélégation de Rouen, . . . Assemblées municipales . . ."
    C 1679: "Registre du controlle des ensaissinements"
    C 2212: "Etat des pauvres et des secours . . . ," 1788

E, Baronnie de Pont-St-Pierre (unclassified)
Aveu: 1600
Comptes: 1398–99, 1414–15, 1454–56, 1458–59, 1459–60, 1460–62, 1463–64, 1465–66, 1466–67, 1477–78, 1479–80, 1480–81, 1481–82, 1482–83, 1506–7, 1513–14, 1515–16, 1521–22, 1539–40, 1558–59, 1560–61, 1570–74, 1738–43
Inventaire des aveux: Pont-St-Pierre, la Neuville (additional volumes concerning Romilly and Pîtres were not analyzed)
Sixteenth-century inventory of estate papers and acts (undated)
Recettes des treizièmes: 1769–93
Terrier, Pont-St-Pierre (undated: ca. 1605)
E, Tabellionage de Pont-St-Pierre: Sixty-seven volumes, 1601–1776 (classified by date)
E, Tabellionage et notaires de Rouen (not systematically investigated; occasional references, as noted in text)
E, Fonds Caillot de Coquéraumont (about 260 liasses, unclassified but arranged according to numbers and notes on the spine of each liasse; the Caillot de Coquéraumont series contains mainly papers concerning the family's properties, and appears to contain little material specifically concerning the family itself)
4 E 1900, 1904: Registres paroissiaux, la Neuville-Chant-d'Oisel
G 1457: "Archévêché de Rouen: statuts des confréries et charités"
G 2868: La Neuville-Chant-d'Oisel
G 4020: Chapitre cathédral de Rouen, terrier, Haute Justice de la Neuville
80 H: Abbaye de Fontaine Guérard
80 H 8: Arpentage, ferme de Cardonnay
80 H 10: Baux, ferme de Cardonnay
J, Chartrier de la Rivière Bourdet, no. 2643
10 J 13: Chartrier de Bosmelet, Comptes
16 J 119 bis: Roncherolles
L 475: "Enquête agricole, An VI"
L 3500–3509: "Administration municipale, canton de Franqueville," An IV–An VIII
6 M 1–1,2: Population
QP 1975, 2033: Biens des émigrés, Caillot, d'Houdemare
Plans 178 (la Neuville-Chant-d'Oisel), 322 (Forêt de Longbouel)

Archives Départementales, Eure
2 B 40: Bailliage des Andelys, "Appositions de scellés"
86 B: Haute Justice de Pont-St-Pierre
86 B 2, 3, 4, 8, 12, 21–23, 37, 48–49, 59–62, 67: Plumitifs, 1580–81, 1661–62, 1682–83, 1700, 1720, 1740, 1761–70, 1781–90
86 B 99–100: Ventes des meubles
86 B 102: "Police, 1702–1789"

86 B 103: "Réceptions de procureurs, greffiers, tabellions . . ."
86 B 105–10: Procédures criminelles, 1642–1789
86 B 112–22: Plumitifs, verderie de Longbouel
86 B 126: Adjudications de bois
C 318: "Minute du Rôle [des vingtièmes] de la Paroisse de St-Nicolas du Pont-St-Pierre"
E 1216–68: Tabellionage de Pont-St-Pierre (partially inventoried)
E 2391–94, 2396, 2401: Chartrier de Pont-St-Pierre
H 1266 8, 20: Abbaye de Fontaine Guérard, ferme de Letocqué
122 L 3: "District de Louviers, Correspondance d'agent national," An II–An III
220 L 1: "Registre des délibérations et arrêtés de l'Administration Municipale du Canton de Pont-Saint-Pierre . . ."
1 M 171: "Statistiques personnelles du département . . . 1809–1812"
2 M 626: "Maires, adjoints, et conseillers municipaux"
6 M 35: "Tableau du dénombrement de la population . . ."
Q 883, 886, 889: "Comptabilité des biens nationaux," Pîtres, Pont-St-Pierre, Romilly

Bibliothèque Municipale, Rouen

MS Martainville Y 40: "Mémoire concernant la Généralité de Rouen Dressé par M. de Vaubourg, Me des Requêtes Intendant en lad. Gnalité 1698"
MS m30: Cotton des Houssayes, correspondance autographe
MS m55: "Manuscrits de l'abbé Cotton des Houssayes sur la Botanique"

Bibliothèque Nationale, Paris

Cinq Cents Colbert, 274: Voysin de la Noiraye, "Estat et déscription de la généralité de Rouen"
Mélanges Colbert 322: "Pentions des officiers de la couronne, mareschaux de France, et principaux officiers d'armée"
Mélanges Colbert 324: "Gouverneurs de provinces et places"
Mélanges Colbert 325: "Pensions de gens de qualité et autres personnes qui ont titre"
MS Français 25902, 25911, 25921, 25926: Feux de monnéage
MS Français 3329: Correspondance
MS Français 20478: Correspondance
Carrés d'Hozier, 369 (Landault), 527 (Rassent)
Pièces originales, 874 (Cotton), 1634 (Landault), 2539 (Roncherolles)

Archives Communales, Pont-St-Pierre

Registres paroissiaux
"Déliberations municipales," 1822ff.

Archives Nationales, Paris

   3 AP 17, 20, 50: Fonds Nicolay
   KK 948: Arpentage, forêt de Longbouel, 1565
   KK 1083: Normandie, Lettres et mémoires . . . , 1643–60
   T153/83: Choiseul-Gouffier
   Minutier Central: Specific acts from Etudes LIII, LXVI, LXVII, XCI (no
      systematic exploration)

Bibliothèque de l'Arsenal

   MS 1191: "Livre d'heures de Louis de Roncherolles"

Archives of the Busquet de Caumont family, consulted at the residence of the
   comte de Caumont, Versailles

Service Historique de l'Armée de Terre, Vincennes

   A 1: Correspondance
   "Répertoire alphabétique des Maréchaux de France, Lieutenants généraux
      et maréchaux de camp," 2 vols.

Archives de Paris

   5 AZ 2939
   6 AZ 505
   DC 6 20, 235R
   DQ 10 1363: Domaines, dossier 1087 (Amelot)

PRINTED SOURCES

Bérault, Josias. *La coutume réformée du pays et duché de Normandie.* . . . Rouen,
   1614.
Bernier, P., ed. "Voyage de Antoine-Nicolas Duchesne au Havre et en
   Haute Normandie, 1762." *Mélanges, Société de l'Histoire de Normandie,* 4th
   series (1898): 185–275.
Boutaric, E., ed. *Actes du Parlement de Paris: Première série, de l'an 1254 à l'an
   1328.* 2 vols. Paris, 1863–67.
Brown, Sydney M., and Jeremiah F. O'Sullivan, eds. *The Register of Eudes of
   Rouen.* New York, 1964.
*Cahier des pouvoirs et instructions à remettre aux Députés de l'Ordre de la Noblesse
   du Bailliage de Rouen.* Rouen, 1789. (BM Nm 856/15.)
Clarac, Pierre, ed. *Chateaubriand, Mémoires d'outre-tombe.* 3 vols. Paris, 1973.
Cobbett, William. *Rural Rides.* Ed. George Woodstock. London, 1967.
Coornaert, E., ed. *Vauban, Projet d'une dixme royale.* Paris, 1933.
Cotton des Houssayes, Abbé. *Eloge historique de M. l'abbé Saas, chanoine de
   l'Eglise Métropolitaine de Rouen.* . . . Rouen, 1776.
———. *Eloge historique de monsieur Maillet-Du-Boullaye.* . . . Rouen, 1770.

————, ed. *Oeuvres de M. de Chamousset.* . . . 2 vols. Paris, 1783.

Courronne, M. de. "Notice biographique sur la vie et les ouvrages de M. l'abbé des Houssayes." In *Précis analytique des travaux de l'Académie Royale des Sciences, Belles Lettres et Arts de Rouen.* . . , 5 (1781–93): 294–96. Rouen, 1821.

de la Noue, François. *Discours politiques et militaires.* Ed. F. E. Sutcliffe. Geneva, 1967.

Délibérations et mémoires de la Société Royale d'Agriculture de la Généralité de Rouen. 2 vols. Rouen, 1763–67.

Delisle, Léopold. *Cartulaire normand de Philippe-Auguste, Louis VIII, Saint Louis, et Philippe-le-Hardi.* Caen, 1882; repr. Geneva, 1978.

Esmonin, Edmond, ed. *Voysin de la Noiraye: Mémoire sur la généralité de Rouen (1665).* Paris, 1913.

Estienne, Charles. *La guide des chemins de France.* Ed. Jean Bonnerot. 3d ed. Paris, 1553; repr. Paris, 1936. (Bibliothèque de l'Ecole des Hautes Etudes, fasc. 267.)

Fauroux, Marie. *Recueil des actes des ducs de Normandie (911–1066).* Mémoires de la Société des Antiquaires de Normandie, vol. 36. Caen, 1961.

Houard, David. *Dictionnaire analytique, historique, étymologique, critique, et interprétatif de la coutume de Normandie.* 4 vols. Rouen, 1780.

Isambert, François, et al. *Recueil général des anciennes lois françaises depuis l'an 420, jusqu'à la Révolution de 1789.* 29 vols. Paris, 1821–33.

La Chesnaye-Desbois, François-Alexandre Aubert de. *Dictionnaire de la noblesse.* . . . 15 vols. Paris, 1770–86.

La Rochefoucauld, François, duc de. *Oeuvres complètes.* Bibliothèque de la Pléiade. Paris, 1964.

Le Cacheux, Paul. *Actes de la chancellerie d'Henri VI concernant la Normandie sous la domination anglaise (1422–1435).* 2 vols. Rouen and Paris, 1908.

"Lettre D'un Abonné à l'Auteur du Journal de Normandie, sur la Déclaration d'une partie de la Noblesse du Bailliage." N.p., n.d. (BM Nm 856/5.)

Masseville, le sr. de. *Etat géographique de la province de Normandie.* 2 vols. Rouen, 1722.

———— *Histoire sommaire de Normandie.* . . . 6 vols. Rouen, 1698–1704.

Les mémoires de messire Martin Du Bellay. In Claude-Bernard Petitot, ed., *Collection complète des mémoires relatifs à l'histoire de la France* . . . , vol. 17. Paris, 1821.

Meyer, Jean. "Un témoignage exceptionnel sur la noblesse de province à l'orée du XVIIe siècle: Les 'avis moraux' de René Fleuriot," *Annales de Bretagne* 79, no. 2 (June 1972): 315–47.

Monluc, Blaise de. *Commentaires, 1521–1576.* Ed. Paul Courteault. Paris, 1964.

Montchrétien, Antoyne de. *Traicté de l'oeconomie politique.* . . . Ed. Th. Funck-Brentano. Paris, n.d.

Nemours, duchesse de. *Mémoires.* In Jean-François Michaud and Jean-Joseph-François Poujoulat, eds., *Nouvelle collection des mémoires relatifs à l'histoire de France,* 23:613–60. Paris, 1854.

Nouvelle édition de la copie de l'expédition de l'acte de déclaration de Partie de la Noblesse du Bailliage principal de Rouen. Rouen, n.d. (BM Nm 856/7.)

Pinard. *Chronologie historique militaire.* 8 vols. Paris, 1760–68.

Porée, Chanoine, ed. *Du Buisson-Aubenay: Itinéraire de Normandie.* Rouen and Paris, 1911.

Prévost, G. A. "Documents sur le ban et l'arrière ban, et sur les fiefs de la vicomté de Rouen en 1594 et 1560, et sur la noblesse du bailliage de Gisors en 1703." *Mélanges, Société de l'Histoire de Normandie,* 3d series (1895): 231–423.

———, ed. *Notes du premier président Pellot sur la Normandie: Clergé, gentilshommes et terres principales, officiers de justice (1670–1683).* Rouen and Paris, 1915.

Procès-verbal de l'assemblée de l'ordre de la noblesse du bailliage de Rouen. Rouen, 1789. (BM Nm 856/14.)

Robillard de Beaurepaire, Charles de, ed. *Cahiers des Etats de Normandie sous le règne de Charles IX.* Rouen, 1891.

———, ed. *Cahiers des Etats de Normandie sous le règne de Henri IV.* . . . 2 vols. Rouen, 1880–82.

———, ed. *Cahiers des Etats de Normandie sous les règnes de Louis XIII et de Louis XIV.* 3 vols. Rouen, 1876–78.

"Rôles normands et français. . . ." Mémoires de la Société des Antiquaires de Normandie, vol. 23. 1858.

Roncherolle, Messire Pierre de. *Harangue prononcée en la salle du petit Bourbon, le 27 Octobre 1614, à l'ouverture des Estats tenus à Paris.* . . . Paris, 1615.

Strayer, Joseph R. *The Royal Domain in the Bailliage of Rouen.* Princeton, 1936; rev. ed., London, 1976.

Vallet de Virville, M., ed. *Chronique de la Pucelle, ou Chronique de Cousinot suivie de la chronique normande de P. Cochon.* . . . Paris, n.d.

Young, Arthur. *Travels in France during the Years 1787, 1788, and 1789.* Ed. Constantia Maxwell. Cambridge, 1950.

SECONDARY WORKS

Agulhon, Maurice. *The Republic in the Village: The People of the Var from the French Revolution to the Second Republic.* Trans. Janet Lloyd. Cambridge, 1982.

Appleby, Andrew B. "Diet in Sixteenth-Century England: Sources, Problems, Possibilities." In Charles Webster, ed., *Health, Medicine, and Mortality in the Sixteenth Century.* Cambridge, 1979.

Appleby, Joyce O. *Economic Thought and Ideology in Seventeenth-Century England.* Princeton, 1978.

Arundel de Condé, comte d'. "Les anciennes mesures agraires de Haute-Normandie." *Annales de Normandie* 18, no. 1 (March 1968): 3–60.

―――. *Anoblissements, maintenues, et réhabilitations en Normandie (1598–1790): La noblesse normande sous l'ancien régime.* Paris, 1981.

Bardet, Jean-Pierre. *Rouen aux XVIIe et XVIIIe siècles: Les mutations d'un espace social.* 2 vols. Paris, 1983.

Bastier, Jean. *La féodalité au siècle des lumières dans la région de Toulouse (1730–1790).* Paris, 1975.

Baulant, M. "Le prix des grains à Paris de 1431 à 1788." *Annales ESC* 23, no. 3 (May–June 1968): 520–40.

Beik, William. *Absolutism and Society in Seventeenth-Century France: State Power and Provincial Aristocracy in Languedoc.* Cambridge, 1985.

Benedict, Philip. *Rouen during the Wars of Religion.* Cambridge, 1981.

Bergeron, Louis. *France under Napoleon.* Trans. R. R. Palmer. Princeton, 1981.

Berlanstein, Lennard. *The Barristers of Toulouse in the Eighteenth Century (1740–1793).* Baltimore, 1975.

Bien, David. "The Army in the French Enlightenment: Reform, Reaction, and Revolution." *Past and Present* 85 (November 1979): 68–98.

―――. "La réaction aristocratique avant 1789: L'exemple de l'armée." *Annales ESC* 29, no. 1 (January–February 1974): 23–48; no. 2 (March–April 1974): 505–34.

Bloch, J. R. *L'anoblissement en France au temps de François Ier.* Paris, 1934.

Bloch, Marc. *French Rural History: An Essay on Its Basic Characteristics.* Trans. Janet Sondheimer. Berkeley and Los Angeles, 1966.

Blosseville, marquis de. *Dictionnaire topographique du département de l'Eure* Paris, 1877.

Bluche, François. *Les magistrats du parlement de Paris au XVIIIe siècle (1715–1771).* Paris, 1960.

Blum, Jerome. *The End of the Old Order in Rural Europe.* Princeton, 1978.

Bois, Guy. *Crise du féodalisme: Economie rurale et démographie en Normandie orientale du début du XIVe siècle au milieu du XVIe siècle.* Paris, 1976.

―――. "Le prix du froment à Rouen au XVe siècle." *Annales ESC* 23, no. 6 (November–December 1968): 1262–82.

Bonney, Richard. "The French Civil War, 1649–53." *European Studies Review* 8, no. 1 (1978): 71–100.

―――. *Political Change in France under Richelieu and Mazarin, 1624–1661.* Oxford, 1978.

Bottin, Jacques. *Seigneurs et paysans dans l'ouest du pays de Caux (1540–1650).* Paris, 1983.

Bouard, Michel de, ed. *Histoire de la Normandie.* Toulouse, 1970.

Boudet, Marcel. "La haute justice de Préaux." *Revue des sociétés savantes de Haute Normandie* 38 (1965): 59–67.

Bouloiseau, Marc. "A propos du tiers coutumier normand et des biens des

émigrés: Consultation pour les héritiers de Philippe-Egalité en 1817."
Annales de Normandie 9, no. 3 (October 1959): 217–28.

―――. "Aspects sociaux de la crise cotonnière dans les campagnes rouennaises en 1788–1789." In *Actes du 81e Congrès National des Sociétés Savantes, Rouen-Caen, 1956: Section d'histoire moderne et contemporaine*, 403–28.

―――. "Election de 1789 et communautés rurales en Haute Normandie." *Annales historiques de la Révolution française* 142 (January–March 1956): 29–47.

―――. *Etude de l'émigration et de la vente des biens des émigrés (1792–1830)*. Paris, 1963.

―――. "Notables ruraux et élections municipales dans la région rouennaise en 1787." In *Commission de recherches et de publication des documents relatifs à la vie économique de la Révolution: Mémoires et documents*, 12:7–36. Paris, 1958.

―――. *Le séquestre et la vente des biens des émigrés dans le district de Rouen (1792–An X)*. Paris, 1937.

Bourde, André. "L'agriculture à l'anglaise en Normandie au XVIIIe siècle." *Annales de Normandie* 8, no. 2 (May 1958): 215–33.

Boutelet, B. "Etude par sondage de la criminalité dans le bailliage de Pont-de-l'Arche (XVIIe–XVIIIe siècles)—De la violence au vol: En marche vers l'escroquerie." *Annales de Normandie* 12, no. 4 (1962): 235–62.

Boutruche, Robert. *La crise d'une société: Seigneurs et paysans du Bordelais pendant la Guerre de Cent Ans*. Paris, 1947.

Braudel, Fernand. *Civilisation matérielle, économie, et capitalisme, XVe–XVIIIe siècle*. 3 vols. Paris, 1979.

Brenner, Robert. "Agrarian Class Structure and Economic Development in Pre-Industrial Europe." *Past and Present* 70 (February 1976): 30–75.

―――. "The Agrarian Roots of European Capitalism." *Past and Present* 97 (November 1982): 16–113.

Brunner, Otto. *Neue Wege der Verfassungs- und Sozialgeschichte*. 2d ed. Göttingen, 1968.

Burke, Peter. *Popular Culture in Early Modern Europe*. London, 1978.

Busquet de Caumont, Robert. *Histoire économique et sociale d'une lignée de huit conseillers au parlement de Normandie: Les Busquet de Chandoisel et de Caumont*. Mémoire, D.E.S., Paris, Faculté de Droit, 1961.

Cabourdin, Guy. *Terre et hommes en Lorraine (1550–1635): Toulois et comté de Vaudémont*. 2 vols. Nancy, 1977.

Carabie, Robert. *La propriété foncière dans le très ancien droit normand (XIe–XIIIe siècles): 1. La propriété domaniale*. Caen, 1943.

Castan, Nicole. *Les criminels de Languedoc: Les exigences d'ordre et les voies du ressentiment dans une société pré-révolutionnaire (1750–1790)*. Toulouse, 1980.

―――. *Justice et répression en Languedoc à l'époque des lumières*. Paris, 1980.

Castan, Yves. *Honnêteté et relations sociales en Languedoc (1715–1780)*. Paris, 1974.

Charbonnier, Pierre. *Une autre France: La seigneurie rurale en Basse Auvergne du XIVe au XVIe siècle.* 2 vols. Clermont-Ferrand, 1980.

Chartier, Roger, and Denis Richet, eds. *Représentation et vouloir politiques: Autour des Etats généraux de 1614.* Paris, 1982.

Chartier, Roger, and J. Nagle. "Les cahiers de doléances de 1614—Un échantillon: Châtellenies et paroisses du bailliage de Troyes." *Annales ESC* 28, no. 6 (November–December 1973): 1484–94.

Chaussinand-Nogaret, Guy. *La noblesse au XVIIIe siècle: De la féodalité aux lumières.* Paris, 1976.

Cobban, Alfred. *The Social Interpretation of the French Revolution.* Cambridge, 1968.

Cochet, Abbé. "Note sur les restes d'un palais de Charles-le-Chauve (861–869), retrouvés à Pîtres." Mémoires de la Société des Antiquaires de Normandie, 24:156–65. 1859.

Colombel, Odile de. "La vaine pâture en Normandie." *Normannia* 11, nos. 2–3 (April–September 1938): 91–107.

Constant, Jean-Marie. "Gestion et revenus d'un grand domaine aux XVIe et XVIIe siècles, d'après les comptes de la baronnie d'Auneau." *Revue d'histoire économique et sociale* 50, no. 2 (1972): 165–202.

———. "Les idées politiques paysannes: Étude comparée des cahiers de doléances (1576–1789)." *Annales ESC* 37, no. 4 (July–August 1982): 717–28.

———. "Nobles et paysans en Beauce aux XVIe et XVIIe siècles." Thèse d'Etat, University of Paris IV, 1978.

———. "Les structures sociales et mentales de l'anoblissement: Analyse comparative d'études récentes." Paper presented to the Colloque de Bordeaux, November 1982.

———. "Terre et pouvoir: La noblesse et le sol." *Bulletin de la Société des Historiens Modernistes*, 1983.

Contamine, Philippe. *Guerre, état, et société à la fin du moyen âge: Etudes sur les armées des rois de France, 1337–1494.* Paris and The Hague, 1972.

———, ed. *La noblesse au moyen âge, XIe–XVe siècles: Essais à la mémoire de Robert Boutruche.* Paris, 1976.

Corvisier, André. "L'armée française de la fin du XVIIe siècle au ministère de Choiseul: Le soldat.* 2 vols. Paris, 1964.

———. *Les contrôles de troupes de l'ancien régime.* 4 vols. Paris, 1968–70.

———. "Un officier normand de Louis XV." *Annales de Normandie* 9, no. 3 (October 1959): 191–216.

Dardel, Pierre. *Commerce, industrie, et navigation à Rouen et au Havre au XVIIIe siècle: Rivalité croissante entre ces deux ports—La conjoncture.* Rouen, 1966.

———. "Influence du système de Law sur la situation économique de la Haute Normandie (Rouen-Bolbec-Cany)." In *Actes du 81e Congrès National des Sociétés Savantes, Rouen-Caen, 1956: Section d'histoire moderne et contemporaine*, 121–41.

Day, John. " 'Crise du féodalisme' et conjoncture des prix à la fin du moyen âge." *Annales ESC* 34, no. 2 (February–March 1979): 305–18.

Deck, Suzanne. *Etude sur la forêt d'Eu.* Caen, 1929.

Desmarest, Charles. *Le commerce des grains dans la généralité de Rouen à la fin de l'ancien régime.* Paris, 1926.

Dessert, Daniel. *Argent, pouvoir, et société au Grand Siècle.* Paris, 1984.

Devèze, Michel. *La vie de la forêt française au XVIe siècle.* 2 vols. Paris, 1961.

De Vries, Jan. *European Urbanization, 1500–1800.* Cambridge, Mass., 1984.

Dewald, Jonathan. *The Formation of a Provincial Nobility: The Magistrates of the Parlement of Rouen, 1499–1610.* Princeton, 1980.

Deyon, Pierre. *Amiens, capitale provinciale: Etude sur la société urbaine au XVIIe siècle.* Paris and The Hague, 1967.

Doyle, William. *Origins of the French Revolution.* New York, 1980.

Dubuc, André. "Un ancien marché du coton à Pont-Saint-Pierre." In *Le textile en Normandie: Etudes diverses,* 161–65. Rouen, 1975.

———. "L'appréciation des redevances en nature dans le bailliage principal de Rouen." *Actes du 87e Congrès National des Sociétés Savantes, Poitiers, 1962: Section d'histoire moderne et contemporaine,* 813–47.

———. "Les charités du diocèse de Rouen au XVIIIe siècle." *Actes du 99e Congrès National des Sociétés Savantes, Besançon, 1974: Section d'histoire moderne et contemporaine,* 211–36.

Duchemin, Pierre. *La baronnie de Pont-St-Pierre.* Gisors, 1894.

Dupâquier, Jacques. *Statistiques démographiques du bassin parisien, 1636–1720.* Paris, 1977.

Esmonin, Edmond. *La taille en Normandie au temps de Colbert (1661–1683).* Paris, 1913.

Estaintot, Robert d'. *Recherches sur les hautes justices féodales existantes dans les limites du département de la Seine-Inférieure.* Rouen, 1892.

Fairchilds, Cissie. *Domestic Enemies: Servants and Their Masters in Old Regime France.* Baltimore and London, 1984.

———. "Female Sexual Attitudes and the Rise of Illegitimacy: A Case Study." *Journal of Interdisciplinary History* 8, no. 4 (Spring 1978): 627–67.

Foisil, Madeleine. *Le sire de Gouberville: Un gentilhomme normand au XVIe siècle.* Paris, 1981.

Forster, Robert. *The House of Saulx-Tavanes: Versailles and Burgundy, 1700–1830.* Baltimore, 1971.

———. *Merchants, Landlords, Magistrates: The Depont Family in Eighteenth-Century France.* Baltimore and London, 1980.

———. *The Nobility of Toulouse in the Eighteenth Century.* Baltimore, 1960.

———. "Obstacles to Agricultural Growth in Eighteenth-Century France." *American Historical Review* 75, no. 6 (October 1970): 1600–1615.

———. "The Survival of the Nobility during the French Revolution." *Past and Present* 37 (July 1967): 71–86.

Foster, George M. "Peasant Society and the Image of Limited Good." Repr. in Foster et al., *Peasant Society: A Reader*, 300–323. Boston, 1967.

Fourquin, Guy. *Les campagnes de la région parisienne*. Paris, 1964.

———. "La part de la forêt dans les ressources d'un grand seigneur de l'Ile de France à la fin du XIIIe siècle et au XIVe siècle." *Paris et Ile de France* 18–19 (1967–68): 7–36.

Frêche, Georges. *Toulouse et la région Midi-Pyrénées au siècle des lumières (vers 1670–1789)*. Paris, 1974.

Frémont, Armand. *Atlas géographique de la Normandie*. Paris, 1977.

Frère, Edouard. *Manuel de bibliographie normande. . . .* 2 vols. Rouen, 1858.

Frondeville, Henri de. *Les conseillers du Parlement de Normandie au seizième siècle (1499–1594)*. Paris and Rouen, 1960.

Fruit, Jean-Pierre. *Vexin normand ou vexin parisien? Contribution à l'étude géographique de l'espace rural*. Paris, 1974.

Furet, François. *Interpreting the French Revolution*. Trans. Elborg Forster. Cambridge, 1981.

Furet, François, and Jacques Ozouf. *Lire et écrire: L'alphabétisation des Français de Calvin à Jules Ferry*. 2 vols. Paris, 1977.

Gallet, Jean. *La seigneurie bretonne (1450–1680): L'exemple du Vannetais*. Paris, 1983.

Galpern, A. N. *The Religions of the People in Sixteenth-Century Champagne*. Cambridge, Mass., 1976.

Gauthier, Florence, and Guy-Robert Ikni. "Le mouvement paysan en Picardie: Meneurs, pratiques, maturation, et signification historique d'un programme (1775–1794)." In Jean Nicolas, ed., *Mouvements populaires et conscience sociale, XVIe–XIXe siècles*, 435–48. Paris, 1985.

Gay, Peter. *The Enlightenment: An Interpretation—The Rise of Modern Paganism*. New York, 1966.

Given, James B. *Homicide and Society in Thirteenth-Century England*. Stanford, 1977.

Goldsmith, James Lowth. "The Agrarian History of Preindustrial France: Where Do We Go from Here?" *Journal of European Economic History* 13, no. 1 (Spring 1984): 175–99.

———. *Les Salers et les d'Escorailles: Seigneurs de Haute Auvergne, 1500–1789*. Clermont-Ferrand, 1984.

Goody, Jack. *The Domestication of the Savage Mind*. Cambridge, 1977.

Goubert, Pierre. *The Ancien Régime: French Society 1600–1750*. Trans. Steve Cox. New York, 1974.

———. *Beauvais et le Beauvaisis de 1600 à 1730: Contribution à l'histoire économique et sociale de la France du XVIIe siècle*. 2 vols. Paris, 1960.

———. *Clio parmi les hommes*. Paris, 1976.

———. "The French Peasantry in the Seventeenth Century: A Regional Example." *Past and Present* 10 (November 1956): 55–77.

————. *La vie quotidienne des paysans français au XVIIe siècle.* Paris, 1982.

Goujard, Philippe. *L'abolition de la féodalité dans le pays de Bray.* Paris, 1978.

————. " 'Féodalité' et lumières au XVIIIe siècle: L'exemple de la noblesse." *Annales historiques de la Révolution française* 227 (January–March 1977): 103–18.

Guenée, Bernard. *Tribunaux et gens de justice dans le bailliage de Senlis à la fin du moyen âge (vers 1380–vers 1550).* Paris, 1963.

Gutton, Jean-Pierre. *Domestiques et serviteurs dans la France de l'ancien régime.* Paris, 1981.

————. *La sociabilité villageoise dans l'ancienne France: Solidarités et voisinages du XVIe au XVIIIe siècle.* Paris, 1979.

Harding, Robert. *Anatomy of a Power Elite: The Provincial Governors of Early Modern France.* New Haven, 1978.

Hellot, René. *La bibliothèque bleue en Normandie.* Rouen, 1928.

Henry, Louis. "Ducs et pairs sous l'ancien régime: Caractéristiques démographiques d'une caste." *Population* 5 (1960): 807–30.

Héron, A. *Académie des Sciences, Belles-Lettres, et Arts de Rouen: Liste générale des membres. . . .* Rouen, 1903.

Higonnet, Patrice. *Class, Ideology, and the Rights of Nobles during the French Revolution.* Oxford, 1981.

Hilton, R. H. *Bond Men Made Free: Medieval Peasant Movements and the English Rising of 1381.* London and New York, 1973.

————. *The English Peasantry in the Later Middle Ages.* Oxford, 1975.

Hoffman, Philip T. *Church and Community in the Diocese of Lyon, 1500–1789.* New Haven, 1984.

————. "Taxes and Agrarian Lands in Early Modern France: Land Sales, 1550–1730." *Journal of Economic History* 46, no. 1 (March 1986): 37–56.

Hoskins, W. G. *The Midland Peasant: The Economic and Social History of a Leicester Village.* London, 1957.

Hufton, Olwen. "Attitudes Towards Authority in Eighteenth-Century Languedoc." *Social History* 3, no. 3 (October 1978): 281–302.

Hunt, Lynn. *Politics, Culture, and Class in the French Revolution.* Berkeley and Los Angeles, 1984.

Jacquart, Jean. *La crise rurale en Ile de France, 1550–1670.* Paris, 1974.

Jouanna, Arlette. *Ordre social: Mythes et hiérarchies dans la France du XVIe siècle.* Paris, 1977.

Kaplan, Steven L. *Bread, Politics, and Political Economy in the Reign of Louis XV.* 2 vols. The Hague, 1976.

Kaplow, Jeffry. *Elbeuf During the Revolutionary Period: History and Social Structure.* Baltimore, 1964.

Labrousse, C. E., and Fernand Braudel, eds. *Histoire économique et sociale de la France.* Vol. 2, *1660–1789.* Paris, 1970.

Lamy, Jules. *Histoire de la Neuville-Champ-d'Oisel.* Rouen, 1950.

————. *La Neuville-Chant-d'Oisel.* Darnétal, 1981.

Landes, David. *Revolution in Time: Clocks and the Making of the Modern World.* Cambridge, Mass., 1983.

Lassaigne, Jean-Dominique. *Les assemblées de la noblesse de France aux XVIIe et XVIIIe siècles.* Paris, n.d.

Le Bras, Hervé, and Emmanuel Todd. *L'invention de la France: Atlas anthropologique et politique.* Paris, 1981.

Le Goff, T. J. A., and D. M. G. Sutherland. "Religion and Rural Revolt in the French Revolution: An Overview." In Janos M. Bak and Gerhard Benecke, eds., *Religion and Rural Revolt,* 123–45. Manchester, 1984.

———. "The Revolution and the Rural Community in Eighteenth-Century Brittany." *Past and Present* 62 (February 1974): 96–119.

Legrelle, Arsène. "Les assemblées de la noblesse en Normandie (1658–1659)." *Mélanges, Société de l'Histoire de Normandie,* 4th series (1898): 305–46.

Le Marchand, Guy. "La féodalité et la Révolution française: Seigneurie et communauté paysanne (1780–1799)." *Annales historiques de la Révolution française* 252 (October–December 1980): 536–58.

Léonard, Emile G. *L'armée et ses problèmes au XVIIIe siècle.* Paris, 1958.

Le Roy Ladurie, Emmanuel. *Les paysans de Languedoc.* 2 vols. Paris, 1966.

———. *Le territoire de l'historien.* 2 vols. Paris, 1973–78

Le Roy Ladurie, Emmanuel, and Joseph Goy. *Les fluctuations du produit de la dîme.* Paris, 1972.

Le Roy Ladurie, Emmanuel, Hugues Neveux, and Jean Jacquart. *Histoire de la France rurale,* vol. 2. Paris, 1975.

Logié, Paul. *La Fronde en Normandie.* 3 vols. Amiens, 1951.

Louandre, F.-C. *Histoire ancienne et moderne d'Abbeville et de son arrondissement.* 2 vols. Abbeville, 1834–35.

MacFarlane, Alan. *The Origins of English Individualism: The Family, Property, and Social Transition.* London, 1978.

Mackrell, John. "Criticism of Seigniorial Justice in Eighteenth-Century France." In John Bosher, ed., *French Government and Society, 1500–1850: Essays in Memory of Alfred Cobban,* 123–44. London, 1973.

Magny, E. de. *Nobiliaire de Normandie.* Paris, Rouen, and Caen, n.d.

Major, J. Russell. "Noble Income, Inflation, and the Wars of Religion in France." *American Historical Review* 86, no. 1 (February 1981): 21–48.

———. *Representative Government in Early Modern France.* New Haven and London, 1980.

Mandrou, Robert. *Magistrats et sorciers en France au XVIIe siècle: Une analyse de psychologie historique.* Paris, 1968.

Marion, Marcel. *Dictionnaire des institutions de la France aux XVIIe et XVIIIe siècles.* Paris, 1923; repr. New York, 1968.

Martin, Henri-Jean. *Livre, pouvoirs, et société à Paris au XVIIe siècle.* 2 vols. Geneva, 1969.

Maza, Sarah C. *Servants and Masters in Eighteenth-Century France.* Princeton, 1983.

Meuvret, Jean. *Le problème des subsistances à l'époque Louis XIV: La production des céréales dans la France du XVIIe et du XVIIIe siècle.* 2 vols. Paris and The Hague, 1977.

Meuvret, Jean, and Micheline Baulant. *Prix des céréales extraits de la mercuriale de Paris (1520–1698).* 2 vols. Paris, 1962.

Meyer, Jean. *La noblesse bretonne au XVIIIe siècle.* Abr. ed., Paris, 1972.

———. "Un problème mal posé: La noblesse pauvre—L'exemple breton au XVIIIe siècle." *Revue d'histoire moderne et contemporaine* 18 (April–June 1971): 161–88.

———. *La vie quotidienne en France au temps de la Régence.* Paris, 1979.

Miskimin, Harry. *The Economy of Later Renaissance Europe, 1460–1600.* Cambridge, 1977.

Mollat, Michel, ed. *Histoire de l'Ile de France et de Paris.* Toulouse, 1971.

———, ed. *Histoire de Rouen.* Toulouse, 1979.

Morineau, Michel. *Les faux-semblants d'un démarrage économique: Agriculture et démographie en France au XVIIIe siècle.* Paris, 1971.

Mousnier, Roland. *Les institutions de la France sous la monarchie absolue.* 2 vols. Paris, 1974–80.

———. "Les survivances médiévales dans la France du XVIIe siècle." *XVIIe siècle* 106–7 (1975): 59–79.

———. "Trevor-Roper's 'General Crisis': Symposium." Repr. in Trevor Aston, ed., *Crisis in Europe, 1550–1660,* 97–104. Garden City, N.Y., 1967.

———. *La vénalité des offices sous Henri IV et Louis XIII.* 2d ed. Paris, 1971.

Muchembled, Robert. *Culture populaire et culture des élites dans la France moderne (XVe–XVIIIe siècles): Essai.* Paris, 1978.

Musset, L. "La mise en valeur de la forêt de Gouffern au moyen âge et le bourg rural de Saint-Nicolas de Vignats." *Bulletin, Société des Antiquaires de Normandie* 52 (1952–54): 223–48.

———. "Une transformation du régime seigneurial: L'essor des bourgs ruraux normands (XIe–XIIe siècles)." *Revue historique de droit français et étranger* 26 (1948): 169–70.

Neveux, Hugues. *Vie et déclin d'une structure économique: Les grains du Cambrésis (fin du XIVe–début du XVIIe siècle).* Paris, The Hague, and New York, 1980.

Neveux, Hugues, and Bernard Garnier. "Valeur de la terre, production agricole, et marché urbain au milieu du XVIIIe siècle." *Problèmes agraires et société rurale: Normandie et Europe du nord-ouest (XIVe–XIXe siècles).* Cahier des Annales de Normandie, 11:44–99. Caen, 1979.

Nicolas, Jean. *La Savoie au XVIIIe siècle: Noblesse et bourgeoisie.* 2 vols. Paris, 1978.

Niromiya, Hiroyuki. "Un cadre de vie rurale au XVIIe et au XVIIIe siècle: La seigneurie de Fleury-en-Bière." *Paris et Ile de France* 18–19 (1967–68): 37–97; 20 (1969): 65–126.

Ong, Walter J. *Interfaces of the Word: Studies in the Evolution of Consciousness and Culture.* Ithaca, 1977.

Orlea, Manfred. *La noblesse aux Etats généraux de 1576 et de 1588*. Paris, 1980.

Plaisse, André. *La baronnie du Neubourg: Essai d'histoire agraire, économique, et sociale*. Paris, 1961.

———. *L'évolution de la structure agraire dans la campagne du Neubourg*. Cahiers des études rurales, vol. 2. Paris and The Hague, 1964.

Pocock, J. G. A. *The Machiavellian Moment: Florentine Political Thought and the Atlantic Republican Tradition*. Princeton, 1975.

Poitrineau, Abel. "Aspects de la crise des justices seigneuriales dans l'Auvergne du dix-huitième siècle." *Revue historique de droit français et étranger*, 4th series, vol. 39, no. 4 (October–December 1961): 552–70.

———. *La vie rurale en Basse Auvergne au XVIIIe siècle (1726–1789)*. 2 vols. Paris, 1965.

Powicke, F. M. *The Loss of Normandy*. 2d ed. Manchester, 1960.

Quéniart, Jean. *Culture et société urbaines dans la France de l'ouest au XVIIIe siècle*. Paris, 1978.

———. *L'imprimerie et la librairie à Rouen au XVIIIe siècle*. Paris, 1969.

Reddy, William N. *The Rise of Market Culture: The Textile Trade and French Society, 1750–1900*. Cambridge, 1984.

Reinhardt, Steven G. "Crime and Royal Justice in *Ancien Régime* France: Modes of Analysis." *Journal of Interdisciplinary History* 13, no. 3 (Winter 1983): 437–60.

———. "Royal Justice and Society: The Redress of Grievances in the Sarladais in the Late Eighteenth Century." Ph.D. dissertation, Northern Illinois University, 1982.

Richard, Guy. "Les fonderies de Romilly-sur-Seine et les débuts de la metallurgie non ferreuse en Haute Normandie." *Actes du 88e Congrès National des Sociétés Savantes: Section d'histoire moderne et contemporaine, 1963*, 451–67.

———. "La metallurgie normande en 1845." *Revue d'histoire de la sidérurgie* 5, no. 1 (January–March 1964): 1–54.

———. "Les nobles metallurgistes dans le département de l'Eure de 1789 à 1850." *Actes du 87e Congrès National des Sociétés Savantes: Section d'histoire moderne et contemporaine, 1962*, 741–52.

———. *Noblesse d'affaires au XVIIIe siècle*. Paris, 1974.

Ritter, Georges, and Jean Lafond. *Manuscrits à peintures de l'école de Rouen: Livres d'heures normands*. Rouen and Paris, 1913.

Roche, Daniel. *Le peuple de Paris: Essai sur la culture populaire au XVIIIe siècle*. Paris, 1981.

———. *Le siècle des lumières en province: Académies et académiciens provinciaux, 1680–1789*. 2 vols. Paris, 1978.

Root, Hilton. "Challenging the Seigneurie: Community and Contention on the Eve of the French Revolution." *Journal of Modern History* 57, no. 4 (December 1985): 652–81.

Roupnel, Gaston. *La ville et la campagne au XVIIe siècle: Etude sur les populations du pays dijonnais*. 2d ed. Paris, 1955.

Rudé, George. *The Crowd in the French Revolution.* Oxford, 1959.

Schalk, Ellery. "Ennoblement in France from 1350 to 1650." *Journal of Social History* 16, no. 2 (December 1982): 101–10.

Sion, Jules. *Les paysans de la Normandie orientale: Pays de Caux, Bray, Vexin normand, Vallée de la Seine.* Paris, 1909; repr. Brionne, 1981.

Skinner, G. William. "Marketing and Social Structure in Rural China (Part 1)." Repr. in George M. Foster et al., eds., *Peasant Society: A Reader,* 63–98. Boston, 1967.

Soboul, Albert. *Problèmes paysans de la Révolution, 1789–1848.* Paris, 1983.

Soman, Alfred. "Les procès de sorcellerie au Parlement de Paris (1565–1640)." *Annales ESC* 32, no. 4 (July–August 1977): 790–814.

Spufford, Margaret. *Contrasting Communities: English Villagers in the Sixteenth and Seventeenth Centuries.* Cambridge, 1974.

Stone, Lawrence. *The Crisis of the Aristocracy, 1558–1641.* Oxford, 1965.

———. *The Family, Sex, and Marriage in England, 1500–1800.* New York, 1977.

Tackett, Timothy. *Priest and Parish in Eighteenth-Century France: A Social and Political Study of the Curés in a Diocese in Dauphiné, 1750–1791.* Princeton, 1977.

Taylor, George V. "Revolutionary and Nonrevolutionary Content in the *Cahiers* of 1789: An Interim Report." *French Historical Studies* 7, no. 4 (Fall 1972): 479–502.

Thompson, E. P. "The Moral Economy of the English Crowd." *Past and Present* 50 (February 1971): 76–136.

———. *Whigs and Hunters: The Origin of the Black Act.* New York, 1975.

Tilly, Charles. *The Vendée.* Cambridge, Mass., 1964.

Tocqueville, Alexis de. *The Old Regime and the French Revolution.* Trans. Stuart Gilbert. Garden City, N.Y., 1955.

Tuetey, Louis. *Les officiers sous l'ancien régime: Nobles et roturiers.* Paris, 1908.

Vale, M. G. A. *Charles VII.* Berkeley and Los Angeles, 1974.

Van Kley, Dale K. *The Damiens Affair and the Unraveling of the Ancien Régime, 1750–1770.* Princeton, 1984.

Veuclin, E. *Documents concernant les confréries de charité normandes.* Evreux, 1892.

Vidalenc, Jean. "L'agriculture dans les départements de Normandie à la fin du Premier Empire." *Annales de Normandie* 7, no. 2 (May 1957): 179–201.

Vovelle, Michel. "L'élite ou le mensonge des mots." *Annales ESC* 29, no. 1 (January–February 1974): 49–72.

———. *Piété baroque et déchristianisation en Provence au XVIIIe siècle.* Paris, 1973.

———. *Ville et campagne au XVIIIe siècle (Chartres et la Beauce).* Paris, 1980.

Weber, Eugen. *Peasants into Frenchmen: The Modernization of Rural France, 1870–1914.* Stanford, 1976.

Weber, Max. *The Protestant Ethic and the Spirit of Capitalism.* Trans. Talcott Parsons. New York, 1958.

Wood, James B. *The Nobility of the Election of Bayeux, 1463–1666: Continuity Through Change.* Princeton, 1980.

Yver, Jean. "Les châteaux forts en Normandie jusqu'au milieu du XIIe siècle: Contribution à l'étude du pouvoir ducal." *Bulletin, Société des Antiquaires de Normandie* 53 (1955–56): 28–115.

Index

317